LIVING WITH HITLER

LIVING WITH
HITLER
LIBERAL DEMOCRATS
IN THE THIRD REICH

ERIC KURLANDER

YALE UNIVERSITY PRESS
NEW HAVEN AND LONDON

Copyright © 2009 Eric Kurlander

All rights reserved. This book may not be reproduced in whole or in part, in any form (beyond that copying permitted by Sections 107 and 108 of the U.S. Copyright Law and except by reviewers for the public press) without written permission from the publishers.

For information about this and other Yale University Press publications, please contact:
U.S. Office: sales.press@yale.edu   www.yalebooks.com
Europe Office: sales@yaleup.co.uk   www.yaleup.co.uk

Set in Adobe Caslon by IDSUK (DataConnection) Ltd
Printed in Great Britain by TJ International Ltd, Padstow, Cornwall

Library of Congress Control Number 2009927549

A catalogue record for this book is available from the British Library.

10 9 8 7 6 5 4 3 2 1

To Monika

Contents

Illustrations

Acknowledgements

It is a distinct pleasure to thank the many institutions and individuals who made this book possible. Without the expert assistance of the archivists and staff at the German Federal Archives I could never have assembled the archival research for this volume. I want to extend special thanks to Peter Franz, Antje Märke, and Eva Lanko at the Bundesarchiv Koblenz, who made available thousands of personal papers and party documents, sometimes at few days' notice, and provided numerous copies in less time. I owe an enormous professional and intellectual debt to the wonderful libraries of Harvard University, the University of Chicago, the University of Freiburg, the University of Cologne, and the Prussian Cultural Foundation (Staatsbibliothek zu Berlin, Stiftung Preussischer Kulturbesitz), where I spent many months over the past six years obtaining the published primary and secondary works on which this study is based. Equal thanks go out to the Stetson University library, Susan Derryberry and Susan Ryan in particular, who located scores of hard to find books, microfiche, and articles during the early stages of this project. I would like to express my gratitude also to our departmental secretaries Jennifer Certo and Jen Snyder, as well as to four student research assistants, Jonathan Ballenger, Alexandria Braswell, Richard Plavnieks and Vera Kuntz. I am also indebted to Anne Dorte Krause of the Photo Archive of the German Historical Museum (Berlin), Norbert Ludwig of the *Bildagentur für Kunst, Kultur und Geschichte* (Berlin), and Silka Quintero of the Granger Collection (New York) for helping me to obtain suitable photographs in timely fashion.

The research for this book was made possible by four Stetson University Summer Research grants, the Stetson College of Arts and Sciences Advisory

Board Fund for Faculty Development and the munificence of the Alexander von Humboldt Foundation (Humboldt-Stiftung). I am grateful to Mercedes Barbon and Cäcilia Nauderer of the Humboldt-Stiftung for their continuous support and advice. Above all I am indebted to the Thyssen-Heideking Fellowship Committee of the German Historical Institute, Washington, DC, Christof Mauch in particular, for providing a generous residential fellowship at the Anglo-American Institute of the University of Cologne, where I completed the bulk of the writing. I would specifically like to thank the Director of the Anglo-American Institute, Norbert Finzsch, a brilliant scholar, fantastic host, and true *Mensch*, and his incomparable assistant Sigrid Schneider. Finally, I would like to express my enduring gratitude to David Blackbourn, Geoff Eley, Kevin O'Keefe, Charles Maier, Joachim Scholtyseck, and Margaret Venzke for their unwavering support of the project, whether in helping me obtain funding or in backing my application for tenure and full-year sabbatical leave in 2007–2008, without which I could not have completed the research and writing of the manuscript.

A cursory glance at the bibliography reveals the extent to which this book is a collaborative intellectual effort. Even so, there are a few individuals who deserve special appreciation. First, my thanks go out to friends and colleagues who perused various iterations of one or more chapters. These include Joel Davis, Michael Denner, Jost Dülffer, Geoff Eley, Jürgen Froelich, Jay H. Geller, Heide Marie Lauterer, David Meskill, Emily Mieras, A. Dirk Moses, Bradley Naranch, and Angelika Schaser. Notable among these is Heather McCallum of Yale University Press, who read multiple drafts of early chapters with great enthusiasm and a keen eye for narrative. I cannot imagine a more supportive, professional, or engaged editor. I am likewise grateful to the four "blind reviewers" whose feedback proved invaluable at every stage of this project. Although it goes without saying that all errors are my own, this is surely a better book for their input. I would also like to express my gratitude to a number of scholars who invited me to present papers and publish articles culled from the project or provided important references to unpublished materials. These include Manuel Borutta, Kathleen Canning, Robert J. Culp, Catherine Epstein, Elke Froelich, Maura Henry, Peter Longerich, Patricia Mazon, Guido Mueller, Kevin Passmore, Raffael Scheck, Joachim Scholtyseck, Dennis Sweeney, Richard Wetzell, and Andreas Wirsching.

Finally, I would like to thank my family, especially my two beautiful children, Amelie and Kolya. They were born while I was writing this book and have spent the better part of their young lives accompanying me to Germany to see it through. No one deserves greater thanks than my wife Monika, whose love, patience, and painstaking editorial assistance made this whole endeavor possible. I dedicate this book to her.

Note on Translations and Abbreviations

Wherever possible I have tried to refer to previously translated versions of German-language sources. All other translations are my own.

In the text, notes, and index abbreviations appear for the first time alongside the term to which they refer: e.g. *Die Frau* (*DF*); Deutsche Demokratische Partei (DDP); Reichsverband der deutschen Presse (RVDP). Thereafter the abbreviations are generally employed.

Finally, in the interest of simplicity, I have chosen to dispense with "University Press" in the notes and bibliography. Books published, for example, by Harvard University Press or University of California Press appear with the citation "Cambridge, Mass.: Harvard" or "Berkeley: California" respectively.

Introduction

I

In November 1933, ten months after the Nazi seizure of power, the Nobel Prize-winning dramatist Gerhart Hauptmann wrote a poignant Christmas greeting to the Jewish Democrat and liberal newspaper editor Theodor Wolff, already in exile in Lugano:

> Before this fateful year . . . comes to an end, may these salutations . . . reach you and your dear and honorable wife. I am 70 and you are, I believe, not far off. We have therefore endured nearly the same portion of German and World history, each in his own way, with the intention of doing good to the best of our ability . . . I don't know how you think of your work, but mine lies for most part behind me . . . I do not want to say that I'm tired, or even that I lack courage. But more than that, namely that great courage belongs to the active life: that I no longer have.

Wolff acknowledged Hauptmann's melancholy state of mind, but hoped the once revolutionary author of *The Weavers* might rouse himself to provide the "new [German] youth" with an alternative vision to Hitler.[1] Wolff would be disappointed. Except for publishing a few lesser-known plays and attending the occasional award ceremony, Hauptmann chose to live out the Third Reich in silence and obscurity. A notable minority of liberal democrats followed his lead, retreating into what some contemporaries called "inner emigration."[2] Others, like Wolff, emigrated outright, as did Albert Einstein, the novelist Heinrich Mann, and the Nobel Peace Prize winner Ludwig Quidde.[3]

Because of these and similar stories, the impression remains that nearly all German Democrats fled their country or retreated to their homes at the first glimpse of jackboots. Yet foreign exile and "inner emigration" were not the only choices facing liberals in the Third Reich. In contrast to their Communist and Socialist counterparts, most Democrats escaped arrest and persecution. Some even thrived under National Socialism. Although deprived of political office, the future President of the Federal Republic, Theodor Heuss, and Germany's leading feminist, Gertrud Bäumer, continued to edit prominent journals and to publish numerous books and articles. Several Weimar Democrats, like Hitler's Economics Minister Hjalmar Schacht, Joseph Goebbels's press attaché Werner Stephan, and Rudolf Diels, Reinhard Heydrich's predecessor as Chief of the Gestapo, experienced a career renaissance under Hitler.[4]

These liberals represent just a fraction of those bourgeois republicans whose diverse paths reveal so much about the nature of social, political, and intellectual life in the Third Reich. Little attention has been paid to the last chairman of the German Democratic Party, Hermann Dietrich, or to the eminent feminist and social reformer, Marie Elisabeth Lüders. What of that powerful core of cosmopolitan liberals – some Jewish – who nonetheless chose to weather the Nazi storm? Did all such men and women seek isolation over action, obscurity over accommodation? What happened to individuals like Eugen Schiffer, Weimar's Minister of Justice and also a Jew, or the last chairman of the Defense League against Anti-Semitism, Georg Gothein? Some liberals endorsed the regime; others clearly opposed it.[5] What were their motivations? How significant was their influence? In short, did German liberalism represent "an intellectual force that made it . . . in some part impossible for the National Socialists to carry out their totalitarian designs"?[6]

This is an intriguing question, posed by one of Germany's greatest historians; strangely, few have chosen to address it.[7] Initially, perhaps this lack of interest owed something to the postwar sensitivities of the liberals themselves, who preferred not to revisit their uneven record of resistance.[8] Another explanation is the long academic tradition of blaming the German bourgeoisie, liberal and conservative alike, for the rise of National Socialism.[9] Whatever the reason, the story of German liberalism in the Third Reich has yet to be told and there is no better time to tell it.[10] The public is more preoccupied than ever by the question of how "ordinary" Germans could be taken in by Nazism. A plethora of recent books has touched on women and workers, artists and musicians, Catholics, Protestants, youth groups, gypsies, Jews, and homosexuals in the Third

Reich; even anti-Semitic beach resorts, tourism, and the fashion industry have had their day.[11] This burgeoning interest in "everyday life" under National Socialism has persisted in overlooking the liberals, however, the one group that has come to define both the successes and the failures of German democracy better than any other.[12]

Certainly liberals do not fit neatly into the categories of victims, perpetrators, or bystanders. Despite their republican pedigree, liberal democrats never suffered as profoundly as the Jews, Communists, and gypsies. Nor were they generally complicit in the worst Nazi transgressions. But our unflagging curiosity about the everyday lives of Germans in the Third Reich is not based solely on the degree of their collaboration or victimhood. It has more to do with a widespread awareness that the Third Reich was the product of a liberal democracy not unlike the French Third Republic or contemporary United States. National Socialism was a mass political movement that employed modern techniques of campaigning, recruiting, and fund-raising. It took full advantage of a liberal civil society and constitution that guaranteed free speech and assembly. Most importantly, Hitler's National Socialist German Worker's Party (NSDAP) won open, fair, and democratic elections against myriad other parties, which virtually necessitated an invitation to form a government. It is the vulnerability, not the absence, of liberal democracy in Germany that makes the rise of National Socialism so disconcerting.

For this reason, nearly every new book on Hitler or the Holocaust presumes one basic question: how could the heirs to Kant, Beethoven, and Einstein support a party like the NSDAP? How could so many educated "liberal"-minded Germans be complicit in the twentieth century's most terrible crimes? Or, as the historians Konrad Jarausch and Larry Jones have put it, "the interest of American and British intellectuals" in the collapse of German liberalism as well as in the rise of National Socialism "reflects their own anxiety about the implications of the Nazi experience for the viability of the liberal humanistic values at the heart of their own political culture."[13] Although it may be reassuring to dismiss National Socialism as some peculiar outgrowth of the German national character, our extraordinary fascination with the Third Reich betrays an underlying presumption that something similar could happen to "us."

To appreciate the full gamut of liberal experience in the Third Reich we must explore both continuities and disjunctures; resistance as well as collaboration; coercion but also consent. German liberalism was not only the opponent and victim of National Socialism. It was in some ways Nazism's ideological and sociological antecedent. The fact that liberalism could be both has significant implications for understanding the genesis of authoritarian regimes everywhere. By plumbing liberal motivations, by tracing their preoccupations, hopes, and fears, we might begin to glean how modern, liberal, democratic individuals, Germans who best exemplified the middle-class progressivism of the Weimar Republic, negotiated, resisted, and in some cases embraced elements of what is widely regarded as the most illiberal regime in modern history. In so doing, we might come to understand better the character, complexity, and perhaps even the contemporary allure of National Socialism.

II

The very range of challenges confronting Democrats in the Third Reich compels us to move beyond traditional categories like resistance (*Widerstand*) and collaboration (*Kollaboration*).[14] More useful in this regard are concepts such as "passive resistance" (*Resistenz*), "non-conformity" (*Verweigerung*), and "accommodation" (*Anpassung*). *Resistenz* refers to those individuals or groups who passively "withstood" rather than actively combated the social and political "disease" that was National Socialism.[15] Some have also used the term *Verweigerung*, which literally means "refusal," to distinguish passive resistance – for example, factory workers expending minimal effort due to inflationary pressures on wages – from more conscious and systematic but equally non-violent acts of non-conformity, such as employing a Jewish secretary or publishing articles critical of Nazi economic policy.[16]

 Here we need simply apply the same broad definitions of non-conformity that have been used to reconstruct the lives of Jews, Catholics, and workers over the last twenty-five years. For, as the Gestapo itself noted in 1935, "in [liberal] bourgeois circles . . . a discernible lack of engagement if not even veiled opposition has taken root, which expresses itself in the refusal to answer with a German greeting [Hitler salute] and further in the efforts to differentiate oneself and keep 'amongst themselves.' "[17] Taking up arms or plotting to assassinate Hitler was not the only means of undermining the Third Reich.[18] There were countless other ways, less dramatic but more common, of resisting National Socialism. By extending the lens of everyday history, of resistance with a lower case "r," to liberal democrats we might locate the real limits of free speech and action, coercion and consent.[19]

 At the same time we need to recognize that voluntary accommodation played at least as great a role as terror and coercion in perpetuating Hitler's rule. From Gestapo surveillance to the coordination of the Churches to the persecution of the Jews, the success of Nazi policies was almost always dependent on ordinary Germans' willing participation. Nazi authorities garnered much of their information, not from enthusiastic party members, but from disgruntled clients, spurned lovers, and snooping neighbors.[20] The Third Reich, in the words of Martin Broszat, was never a "monolithic system of total power." Rather, it is because norms and measures that were supposed to be followed could also be broken that "many liberals had a choice of whether and to what degree to collaborate with the regime."[21]

Still, as incomplete as Nazi totalitarianism may have been, when evaluating liberal non-conformity it is crucial to keep in mind Detlev Peukert's pregnant assertion that "each criticism related only to a clearly defined individual case and did not vitiate a person's assent to other policies of the regime." "Even an uncompromising political resister had to make compromises in daily life," Peukert continues, "if only to camouflage his illegal work. But each confrontation . . . not only raised the tactical problem of whether to accede or hold out, but posed the fundamental dilemma that consent to the regime in toto consisted in any case precisely in taking a large number of similar small steps of compliance."[22] Collaboration and resistance; accommodation and non-conformity, were two sides of the same coin. Even though liberal democrats disagreed with National Socialism on some levels, they exhibited indifference, even enthusiasm for the regime on others.[23]

III

So who are the liberal democrats? This question is more difficult to answer than one might think. Germany has a long and indelible liberal tradition, extending back to the eighteenth century. But unlike the British Liberals or French Radical Socialists, German liberals experienced multiple national and regional permutations in the six decades between the foundation of the German Empire in 1871 and the collapse of the Weimar Republic in 1933. In the period leading up to German unification there was one major liberal party, the National Liberals (Nationalliberalen or NLP), which garnered the most seats in the first Imperial Reichstag. It was flanked by a smaller but not insignificant left liberal Progressive Party (Deutsche Fortschrittspartei or DFP).

Over the course of the 1870s many National Liberals became disenchanted with Chancellor Otto von Bismarck's imperialist foreign and protectionist economic policies, seceding from the NLP to form the Liberal Union (Liberale Vereinigung or LibVg). In 1884 the LibVg merged with the DFP to create the German "Freethinking" or Radical Party (Deutsche Freisinnige

Partei). The new party was devoutly liberal, promoting free trade, civil rights, and the separation of church and state. But long-simmering differences over military and social spending divided the Radicals in 1893, with one wing forming the free-trading Radical People's Party (Freisinnige Volkspartei or FrVp) and another the more imperialist Radical Union (Freisinnige Vereinigung or FrVg), which incorporated Friedrich Naumann's National Social Union (NSV) in 1903. Only in 1910, due to Naumann's exhaustive efforts, did the two factions coalesce to form the Progressive People's Party (Fortschrittliche Volkspartei or FVP).[24]

After the collapse of the German Empire and foundation of the Weimar Republic in November 1918, Naumann and the FVP leadership invited all democratically inclined National Liberals to join them, creating the German Democratic Party (Deutsche Demokratische Partei or DDP). Given the FVP's heterogeneous history, not to mention the influx of National Liberals, the DDP represented a diverse constellation of rival liberal traditions. The party was dominated by a welfare-oriented left wing in the Naumannite tradition, which was frequently at odds with a smaller but influential low-tax, free trading "right wing." The DDP was further divided between aggressive nationalists, who wanted a rapid revision of the Versailles Treaty, and moderate internationalists who counseled patience and understanding in restoring Germany's proper place in the world.[25]

Despite these ideological permutations, the DDP was *the* party of liberal democracy. Its leaders played a decisive role in writing the Weimar constitution,[26] restoring the German economy,[27] stabilizing the Weimar justice system,[28] reorganizing the police,[29] rebuilding the military,[30] and developing a foreign policy of peaceful revision.[31] The DDP also included many of Germany's most influential publicists,[32] intellectuals,[33] feminists,[34] and a Nobel Peace Prize winner.[35] To be sure, the DDP's very diversity pulled the party in many directions. By 1930 it had hemorrhaged millions of votes and lost a few of its most prominent leaders to the left,[36] right,[37] and to early retirement.[38] Still, the Democrats expressed the strongest and most uncompromising traditions of German liberalism and invariably upheld the republican constitution.

Liberal Democrats were more than party colleagues. They practiced similar professions, belonged to kindred social networks, and emerged from the same generational cohort.[39] They held degrees and teaching appointments from common universities and contributed books and articles to the same publishers. They were friends, relatives, husbands and wives, even lovers. Many Democrats would later remark on the exceptional intimacy among party members, rare in Weimar's turbulent

political landscape.[40] This rich web of personal and professional relationships, extending back two or three decades before 1933, makes the idea of
collective biography all the more attractive.[41]

Nevertheless, while this book concentrates on individuals who were
explicitly affiliated with the left liberal German Democratic Party, it
makes sense occasionally to introduce a "catholic definition of liberalism"
that takes into account the liberal "cultural attitudes, social practices, and
economic principles that resonated throughout German life."[42] This
sometimes means including members of Gustav Stresemann's right liberal
German People's Party (Deutsche Volkspartei or DVP). Most of the DVP
preferred a monarchy to a republic, and some were privately uncomfortable with equal rights for Jews and other minorities. But the DVP generally agreed with the DDP on many aspects of domestic and foreign policy.
There were also moderate DVP leaders, like Stresemann himself, Werner
von Rheinbaben, and Siegfried and Katharina von Kardorff, who would
have felt perfectly at home in the DDP under different circumstances.
Conversely, there were a number of bourgeois Progressives with close ties
to Naumann, including Rudolf Breitscheid and Anton Erkelenz, who
eventually joined the Socialists (Sozialdemokratische Partei Deutschlands
or SPD) because they disapproved of the ethnic nationalism that pervaded
the left liberal ranks.[43]

Finally, insofar as they corresponded with or visited Reich colleagues,
liberals in exile are likewise relevant. But to concentrate attention on them
would unduly complicate and dilute our endeavor. Liberal émigrés were
often Jews, pacifists, or clearly specified "enemies of the Reich" (e.g.
Theodor Wolff, Georg Bernhard, or Hellmut von Gerlach) who risked
arrest or even murder if they remained. Nor did self-imposed exiles (e.g.
Heinrich Mann, Wilhelm Abegg) face the same choices, circumstances, or
constraints as liberals within the Reich. Since there were few opportunities
for liberal émigrés to resist, much less accommodate, the regime, their
stories tell us little about the nature of everyday life in the Third Reich.

IV

On the eve of the First World War, the Wilhelmine liberal, later Socialist
and eventually Weimar-era Nazi Max Maurenbrecher wrote to his friend
Friedrich Naumann that the "preconditions for . . . creating a left Bloc in
the real sense of the word . . . are still not present." "Whether one joins the
National Liberals, the other the Social Democrats and the third the
Progressives," Maurenbrecher complained, "it could well take at least

another two decades until one can attempt successfully to go before the masses with a national-social slogan. Perhaps a foreign war . . . would essentially hasten this development."[44] Given that Hitler seized power behind a "national-social" slogan exactly two decades later, after a so-called "foreign war," and drew his support primarily from erstwhile liberal voters, Maurenbrecher's observation appears prescient.

One might be tempted to write off such predictions as the wishful thinking of a particularly idiosyncratic liberal if not for the fact that Maurenbrecher's former colleagues and future political opponents, Rudolf Breitscheid and Hellmut von Gerlach, agreed. The "right overwhelmed the left in the Progressive camp," they adduced shortly before the First World War, as left liberals came to accept a "Chauvinistic militarism [that] endangers the peace and security of peoples." True progressives would have to fight not only against the "Conservatives, Anti-Semites, and the [Catholic] Center, but also against a liberalism which does not deserve its name."[45] Maurenbrecher, Breitscheid, and Gerlach ended up on very different sides of the Weimar political spectrum. Yet their like-minded observations, as early as two decades before the Nazi seizure of power, remind us that Naumannite left liberalism and National Socialism were not as ideationally distinct as one might suppose.[46] Indeed, in the early 1930s individuals as disparate as Adolf Hitler, Theodor Heuss, and Gertrud Bäumer would comment on the NSDAP's intellectual debt to Naumann's National-Social movement.[47]

The ideological affinities between German left liberalism and National Socialism do not presuppose the political immaturity or inherent conservatism of the German bourgeoisie.[48] There was no "special path" (*Sonderweg*) from the alleged failure of the (liberal) middle classes to carry out a successful "bourgeois revolution" in the nineteenth century to their support for National Socialism in the 1930s.[49] My point of departure has more in common with those who argue that German liberalism declined because of the sheer number of crises suffered by the Weimar Republic after 1918. The very social and cultural extremes of German modernity, from escalating class conflict and demographic explosion to rapid industrialization and the urban–rural divide, played a decisive role in undermining the viability of laissez-faire liberalism even before the First World War. The ensuing polarization and militarization of German politics and society, not to mention the negative impact of the Versailles Treaty, Socialist and Communist revolutions, hyperinflation, and the Great Depression, were at least as important in undermining German democracy as any latent continuities between liberalism and Nazism.[50]

At the same time, however, some historians have normalized German history to the point where such continuities, to the extent they are acknowledged, are deemed "no more distinctive than the routes [liberal] reformers in other industrializing countries took past the same landmarks."[51] One cannot have it both ways. No matter how severe the effect of the First World War and Weimar's ensuing crises, the more we insist upon Germany's social, political, and economic similarities with Great Britain or France, the more we have to look to differences in ideology and political culture to explain the disparity in outcomes. The most obvious distinction in this regard is the profoundly racialist (*völkisch*) "National-Social" discourse running through Germany's left liberal circles: what I call "*völkisch* liberalism."[52]

If liberals propagated an increasingly racist vision of national identity after 1890, one which they shared with Germans across the political spectrum,[53] they nevertheless retained an overarching belief in bourgeois individualism, the sanctity of the "constitutional state" (*Rechtsstaat*), and a "social market" economy that included substantial investments in health care, education, and unemployment insurance. Nazism, moreover, was never merely a radically conservative movement backed by middle-class reactionaries. It contained socially progressive elements not so different in practice from the program of the left liberals. The NSDAP made a strategic alliance with right-wing German Nationalists (DNVP) after 1928 for largely the same reasons that the left liberals joined the Conservatives in 1907 or 1924: a nationalist foreign policy combined with a shared antipathy to revolutionary Marxism. Conversely, in their social reformism and antipathy to agrarian and industrial elites, the Nazis had more in common with left liberal Democrats than with right-wing conservatives. That is why, for many Democrats in 1933, National Socialism appeared not as the terrifying behemoth it would later become, but as an admittedly demagogic, authoritarian perversion of Naumannite left liberalism.[54]

V

This book makes four main claims. First, that there were certain ideological continuities between German left liberalism and National Socialism that made political accommodation – and in some cases collaboration – with the regime more attractive than one might expect. Second, and related, is the fact that these affinities were not necessarily reactionary, but often "progressive" in nature. Whether one is discussing the Nazi attitude towards science and technology, the separation of church and state, social welfare, industrial organization, even women and the family, there were more than passing similarities between liberal and Nazi programs. Even in those areas where one might contend that Nazism was the most *illiberal* – for example, in terms of racial and foreign policy – there were broad parallels between Nazism and Naumannite left liberalism.

Third, this book shows the ample space for liberal criticism and everyday opposition in the Third Reich, especially before the outbreak of the Second World War. When liberals failed to resist, at least intellectually, it had less to do with fear of arrest or persecution and more to do with a tacit desire to accommodate specific policies. In many cases liberals did encounter pressures to conform in terms of pursuing a career or maintaining a personal or professional relationship. Yet these kinds of pressure – including the necessity of joining Reich organizations, avoiding "minority" hires and clients, or toeing a politically palatable line – were not qualitatively different from those imposed, for example, on Wall Street or in the American South in the interwar period. That is not to exaggerate the Democrats' ability to carry out open resistance, or to downplay the escalating persecution experienced by individuals on the margins of the national or "people's community" (*Volksgemeinschaft*). With several notable exceptions, bourgeois liberals simply enjoyed greater freedom of maneuver and encountered fewer intrusions into their daily existence than Communists and Socialists, the disabled, or the putatively racially inferior.

Fourth and finally, most liberal democrats who at first acquiesced in aspects of the Nazi "revolution" eventually rejected it because of their individual experience of National Socialism. Here again historical context and contingency are paramount. There were various points at which liberals re-evaluated their position and gradually turned away from even a tentative endorsement of Nazi policies. It is indeed remarkable that many Weimar Democrats rationalized and even defended elements of German foreign and domestic policy after 1933. But rather than dismiss their ambivalence as a sign of German peculiarity *vis-à-vis* the "West," we should take it as a warning of the susceptibility of liberal democracy to Fascism, particularly in times of economic distress and political chaos.

CHAPTER ONE

"A Gift to Germany's Future?"
The Liberal Resistance to Hitler

I

Various milestones punctuate the emergence of a Nazi dictatorship. None is more significant than the infamous Enabling Law of 23 March 1933. Granting Hitler the power to enact legislation without the consent of parliament (Reichstag), the Enabling Law required a daunting two-thirds majority, far more than the 52 percent the Nazis and their German Nationalist (DNVP) allies could muster. Yet every bourgeois party voted for the legislation, rendering a stunning 441 votes to the Reich Chancellor. With the Communists already outlawed, only the Social Democrats were left to oppose it.[1] That the German Nationalists or Catholic Center Party endorsed a virtual Nazi dictatorship is hardly surprising. By this time both parties were openly hostile to democracy, desperate for order, and enthusiastic about the NSDAP's suppression of the proletarian left. More troubling for future generations of German liberals is the fact that all five Democrats approved the law as well. Although their opposition would have had little effect on the outcome, the Democrats might have abstained. Why countenance Hitler's ability to rule without constraint, in effect signing the Republic's death warrant?

The conventional explanation is fear: the liberals risked their lives, or at least their livelihoods, if they sided with the Socialists. To be sure, Communists and Socialists faced escalating persecution and arrest in the wake of the Enabling Law. Some members of other parties, especially Jews, also suffered. Still, liberal support for the Enabling Law cannot be explained by coercion alone. Germany was far from a "police state" in March 1933. It would take months, in some cases years, until the Third

Reich was firmly established. As late as August 1934, three million Germans voted against Hitler's assumption of the office of Reich President. Even if one takes into account the most naked form of Nazi domination – the unprecedented expansion of policing, incarceration, and repression in the middle years of the Reich – Nazi Germany was never totalitarian in a Stalinist sense.[2] Democrats enjoyed substantial, if variable, social, political, and intellectual independence. The question is what they chose to do with these liberties, circumscribed though they were.

This chapter divides the question of liberal political resistance into three discrete phases: the Nazi "seizure of power"; the gradual consolidation of the Nazi dictatorship from 1933 to 1938; and the Second World War, including the preceding twelve months of escalating tensions. The first phase lasted less than two months, from Hitler's accession as Reich Chancellor to the Enabling Law. Although liberals, Socialists, and other representatives of the hated Weimar Republic were subject to persistent aggravation and occasional threats, conventional political opposition in parliament and the press was still possible. The *relative* freedom of maneuver makes an analysis of liberal decision-making in this period especially interesting. Did some liberals view Hitler as the lesser of two evils, fearing Communist revolution more than National Socialism? Perhaps they truly believed, as many later claimed, that approving the Enabling Law might help preserve the legitimacy of parliament. Whatever the reasons, one cannot hope to comprehend liberal attitudes to the Third Reich without first understanding this initial, seemingly abject capitulation to National Socialism.

After the Enabling Law the Third Reich entered a period of political, cultural, and socioeconomic consolidation lasting roughly five years, from 23 March 1933, when the new government gained "permanent" emergency powers, to March 1938, when Hitler finished "coordinating" the economy, reorganized the army, and concluded a national union with Austria. The first act in this ongoing process of consolidation is the classical period of "coordination" (*Gleichschaltung*), which sought the formal amalgamation of party and state institutions. It ends roughly when Hitler combined the offices of Reich Chancellor and Reich President following Hindenburg's death on 19 August 1934. This first phase advanced considerably the NSDAP's penetration of German politics, culture, and society. Before March 1933 one could speak of a reasonably open public sphere in which alternative political discourse was not only possible but legal. After the coordination of government, police, press, education, and the arts, the limits of free speech and assembly become much more pronounced; the penalties for crossing them palpably more severe.

The second act of consolidation lasted more or less from August 1934 to March 1938 and involves the Nazi Party's piecemeal "coordination" of the more powerful and enduring Reich institutions: industry, finance, the army, the police, the civil and foreign service. Many Nazi opponents were arrested or interrogated in these middle years of the Third Reich. But liberal democrats experienced only modest persecution. Is this because they constituted less of a threat to the regime, retreating into a private existence of so-called "inner emigration"? Or were they more likely to accommodate Nazi ideology than their colleagues on the left? To what extent did the expansion of the Nazi police state impinge on the everyday existence of bourgeois republicans? How did the Democrats, the very framers of the Weimar constitution, respond to this widespread abrogation of civil liberties?

Finally, we have a third period, extending from spring 1938, when Hitler gained supreme command of the armed forces and disposed of the last remnants of a civilian opposition in the Foreign and Economic Ministries, to spring 1945, when the Third Reich came closest to achieving a totalitarian, police state. Despite – or perhaps because of – increasing repression, this is also the period during which most acts of open political and military resistance occurred, from General Ludwig Beck's tentative plans for a coup in summer 1938 to the student-led White Rose in winter 1942–43 and the Stauffenberg assassination attempt of 20 July 1944. Remarkably, few liberal democrats stood at the center of these actions. Why were the liberals underrepresented, not only in comparison to the proletarian left but also to the nationalist, aristocratic right? Did they simply lack the institutional presence and numerical strength to make an impact? Or are there more profound ideological reasons that help to explain why many Weimar Democrats felt less compelled than their Socialist or Conservative colleagues to risk their lives in overthrowing Hitler? Although individual motivations differ, liberal views and actions throw open a unique window onto the emerging political landscape and provide us with a context in which to evaluate their capacity for non-conformity in other aspects of social, cultural, and intellectual life.

II

Liberal Democrats and the Enabling Law

In 1946, in the interest of "denazification," the Allied occupation authorities circulated a questionnaire requesting German liberals to explain "the circumstances concerning the acceptance of the Enabling Law in the year 1933." There were three questions:

1. Did their position regarding the Enabling Law transgress against the mandate given them by their constitutency?
2. Did approving the Enabling Law secure or hinder Hitler's rule?
3. According to what subjective principles were the law's supporters motivated?[3]

The second question now appears moot. No one would deny the importance of the Enabling Law in securing Hitler's power. It would however be useful to organize our analysis of liberal democratic support for the Enabling Law around the two other queries. First of all, did Democratic endorsement of this law suggest a conflict of interest? That is, did the five remaining Democrats – Hermann Dietrich, Theodor Heuss, Ernst Lemmer, Reinhold Maier, and Heinrich Landahl – serve their constitutents by giving legislative *carte blanche* to Hitler's government of "national renewal"?[4] Where clear popular support was lacking, we might turn to question three and ask why the Democrats might choose to vote yes despite their mandate (i.e., what were their "subjective" motivations). Was there something more than internal political pressure and/or external fear of reprisal motivating Democrats to support the Enabling Law?

During the final three years of the Weimar Republic some liberals sought to build a stronger democratic coalition with the Socialist left. A few abandoned the German Democrats altogether, joining the short-lived Radical Democratic Party (Radikaldemokratischen Partei) or entering the ranks of Social Democracy.[5] Most liberals, however, followed the DDP's decade-long procession down the path of ethnic nationalism and creeping authoritarianism.[6] Telling in this regard was the Democrats' decision to merge with members of the *völkisch* Young German Order (Jungdeutsche Orden) in September 1930 to form the German State Party (DStP). Both the DStP co-chairman, Hermann Dietrich, and the Democratic mayor of Berlin, Fritz Elsas, subsequently recommended "a moderate dictatorship" to make up for the "inadequacy of parliament." At the same time Willy Hellpach, the DDP's candidate for Reich President in 1925, praised the Nazis' dedication to "true [racial] democracy" while the Democratic Vice-Chairwoman Gertrud Bäumer endorsed the NSDAP's "substantive goals" as well.[7] Even Heuss, an outspoken critic of Hitler, would compare National Socialism to Naumann's liberal National-Social movement and wonder whether there were not as many commonalities as differences.[8]

Of course most Democrats were merely hedging their bets, not capitulating to Fascism. After the NSDAP forfeited two million votes and thirty-four Reichstag seats in November 1932, both Hermann Dietrich and

Reinhold Maier were eager to attract erstwhile Nazi voters to a liberal ticket. Changing his tune from a few months earlier, Dietrich insisted that "democracy is inherent across the entire [German] population."[9] In February, only a few days after Hitler's accession as Reich Chancellor, the longtime Prussian Finance Minister Hermann Höpker-Aschoff demanded in the *Vossische Zeitung* that the Nazis elucidate the particulars of their economic program. What good were Hitler's promises that "the German farmer will be rescued from despair" or "unemployment will be overcome," when no one was able to explain how to fulfill them?[10] Otto Nuschke, the DStP General Secretary, and Karl Brammer, one of its leading press functionaries, attacked the NSDAP repeatedly, with Nuschke proclaiming in the Prussian Parliament on 4 February that "violent and race-baiting National Socialism will soon be merely an irritating memory."[11] The Rhineland Democrat W.E. Böckling agreed that the DDP/DStP ought to take a stand against the exclusion of Jews from public life and accused the Nazis of deliberately setting fire to the Reichstag in order to pass the 28 February Emergency Decree banning Communist political activity.[12] In the run-up to the 5 March elections, the German State Party also renewed its electoral understanding with the Socialists to conserve any possible votes in favor of the Republic.[13]

Due largely to this alliance with the SPD, the Democrats won five seats in the 5 March 1933 elections, two more than they received four months earlier. The Nazis, however, exploited a peculiar cocktail of genuine popular enthusiasm and calculated subjugation of political opponents to leap from 33 percent of the vote in November 1932 to 44 percent in March 1933. With the 8 percent garnered by the German Nationalists, Hitler was able to achieve a right-wing majority.[14] This unexpected surge in Nazi support played a significant role in the liberals' decision to back the Enabling Law.

The beleaguered Dietrich spent much of the next two weeks responding to requests from regional party leaders to soften the DStP's position on National Socialism.[15] Georg Borkmann, a ranking Democrat from the liberal mecca of Hamburg, wrote Dietrich to defend the DStP's regional coalition with the Nazis. According to Borkmann, the Nazis were not "conservatives", but radical patriots and social reformers who merely needed guidance: "Even seen from the Jewish perspective, for example, a brutal and open struggle against the National Socialists is in the end not as effective . . . as a slow taming of these . . . exceptionally vocal race researchers."[16] Theodor Heuss and Wilhelm Külz, the Democratic mayor of Dresden, also recommended negotiating with Nazi moderates in order to stave off the DStP's political obsolescence.[17] To be sure, some party members admonished Dietrich "to represent the fundamental rights of the German people ... without [making] any infringements [on liberty] and concessions to now hegemonic fascist ideals." But a clear majority believed it would be more prudent to work out a deal with Hitler than drown alongside the Jews or Communists.[18] After all, the victory of National Socialism, wrote the Democrat Wilhelm Wilms in April 1933, indicated not the triumph of conservatism, but the obsolescence of "right-wing" economic doctrines.[19] After three years of virtual dictatorship and conservative fiscal policy by reactionary notables, it was the NSDAP's youthful dynamism and progressive social program that drew many liberal voters to National Socialism.[20]

A few days before the decisive vote, Höpker-Aschoff published an article titled "The Enabling Law," which epitomized the DStP's change in attitude. Tempering his earlier criticisms of the NSDAP's "socialist" tendencies, Höpker justified the Enabling Law in the name of political and economic stability. He reminded his readers of the first Weimar President Friedrich Ebert's use of emergency decrees to quell the early crises of the Weimar Republic and Hindenburg's similar invocation of Article 48 to support a series of minority governments since 1930. Were rising unemployment, the threat of Communism, and rampant political divisiveness not enough reason to support Hitler's government? At least an Enabling Law would add some parliamentary legitimacy and democratic oversight to the process.[21] Four days later, in the name of the DStP Reichstag delegation, the Württemberg Democrat Reinhold Maier echoed Höpker: "We feel bound by the conviction that the Reich Chancellor put forth today with regard to great national goals. We understand that the present Reich government desires extensive powers in order to work [towards these goals] without hindrance ... In the interest of the people and the fatherland and in the expectation of legality, we withdraw our serious concerns and approve the law."[22] "There can be no doubt regarding our honorable readiness to cooperate in rebuilding a new national community," read Dietrich's simultaneous communiqué to all regional party offices: "these goals of the new government are also ours."[23]

With the notable exception of Gertrud Bäumer, the majority of leading Democrats supported the Reichstag delegation in ceding dictatorial powers to Hitler's government.[24] Some went further, joining the NSDAP outright. These included Ernst Lemmer, one of five remaining Democrats in the Reichstag, Paul Rohrbach, Josef Winschuh, Werner Stephan, and Rudolf Diels. Although Hjalmar Schacht never became a member of the NSDAP, he did step in as Hitler's Reichsbank President and Finance Minister.[25]

How can we explain this about-face in liberal attitudes toward National Socialism at the precise moment when their concerted opposition might have had the greatest impact? One factor is the degree to which all Germans had become accustomed to extra-parliamentary rule since Heinrich Brüning took over the Chancellor's office by presidential decree in spring 1930.[26] After three years of this barely constitutional arrangement, tenuously maintained as the only possible course between the Scylla of Communism and Charybdis of Fascism, many Democrats had become disillusioned with democracy. Founded in defeat and revolution, riddled by economic divisions, on the verge of political stalemate for much of its history, the Weimar Republic was already disintegrating *before* Hitler entered the government. Nothing in the liberal experience suggested that a prolongation of rule by emergency decree to the exclusion of the NSDAP would change matters for the better. Most Democrats were plainly unwilling to stake their political future on the pointless defense of a bankrupt system.[27]

A second reason, no less emphatic than the first, was the growing influence of Friedrich Naumann's National-Social views on the liberal democratic rank and file. The economic interventions and social leveling of the war years, punctuated by revolution and hyperinflation, had pushed the entire German political spectrum to the left. For all its hysterical anti-Communism, Hitler's National Socialism represented a sincere attempt to recast right-wing politics by attracting proletarian and lower middle-class voters through left-leaning economic policies.[28] Former Naumannites and liberal trade union leaders like Anton Erkelenz and Ernst Lemmer were equally passionate about reopening left liberalism to the working classes.[29] Certainly, laissez-faire liberals such as Schacht, Dietrich, Höpker-Aschoff, August Weber, Eduard Hamm, and Hermann Fischer were none too pleased with the DDP's support for increased welfare outlays and a renewed coalition with the Social Democrats in 1928.[30] But while these more devoutly capitalist Democrats enjoyed a disproportionate amount of ministerial influence in the center-right governments of the mid-1920s and waning years of the Republic, they were increasingly outnumbered in the DDP/DStP leadership by social progressives like Koch-Weser, Bäumer, Lüders, Nuschke, Heuss, Lemmer, Landahl, Walter Goetz, Erich Obst, and Alfred Weber. That Dietrich, Höpker, and company would eventually come to support the Keynesian economic policies of the Third Reich – policies spearheaded by their erstwhile laissez-faire colleague, Hjalmar Schacht – reflects the convergence in left liberal and Nazi political economy in the wake of the Great Depression.[31]

A third and related ground for liberal ambivalence in 1933 was the DDP/DStP's legacy of *völkisch* nationalism. Although the Democrats were far from monolithic in this regard, German liberals had inculcated many of the ethnic nationalist dogmas later expounded by the Nazis. Few Democrats were explicitly racist, of course, and some economically "right-leaning" liberals like Gothein and Schiffer were still quite moderate, even pacifistic, in foreign policy terms. Nevertheless, many economically "left-wing" Democrats – especially former Naumannites like Bäumer, Heuss, and Rohrbach – were ethnic nationalists and imperialists. This underlying combination of *völkisch* and social liberalism goes a long way toward explaining the DDP's merger with the anti-Semitic, "anti-plutocratic" Young German Order in 1930. In short, the aspects of Nazi ideology that most offend modern liberals – its virulent, expansionist *völkisch* nationalism and racial anti-Semitism – were the least problematic components of National Socialism for a great number of Democrats during the last years of the Weimar Republic.[32]

A fourth reason for democratic accommodation was the Nazi success in the 5 March elections. Despite the senescent President Paul von Hindenburg's attempt to lend some legitimacy to the Reich government by naming Hitler Chancellor, liberals were keenly aware that the NSDAP had lost thirty-four seats in the November 1932 elections. If a similar drop were to occur in March 1933, many Democrats believed it would be possible to reestablish the old Weimar coalition of Catholics, Liberals, and Socialists or at the very least cobble together a strong minority government of the center-right. When the NSDAP garnered 44 percent of the popular vote and 288 seats, it became clear that these hopes would never materialize. Joined by the German Nationalist People's Party (DNVP), the Nazis now boasted a majority in parliament. Combined with Hitler's quick response to a renegade Communist setting fire to the Reichstag, culminating in a 28 February ban on the Communist Party and hundreds of arrests of left-wing agitators, the Democrats realized that open political opposition was unlikely to succeed.[33]

Which leads us to a fifth and final rationale for supporting the Enabling Law: the threat of persecution. Weimar politics had already become violent and polarized before the Nazi "seizure of power," but few Democrats had to fear for their lives or livelihoods. Despite frequent street battles between Nazis and Communists; despite the *de facto* suspension of parliamentary democracy; despite the rising unemployment; despite Franz von Papen's Prussian coup (which ended in the forcible dismissal of a legitimately elected government in Germany's largest state); despite even Hitler's accession as

Reich Chancellor, the Democrats entered February feeling fairly confident that the center could reassert itself and stem the Fascist tide. Seven weeks later, in the wake of the Reichstag fire and 5 March elections, Democratic opposition seemed futile as well as dangerous. As Dietrich explained it:

> Some colleagues have attacked our Reichstag representatives for having approved the Enabling Law, a position that has certain parallels to the situation in Hamburg. This is nonetheless a different case, because our votes had no influence on the decision, and after it was certain that all bourgeois parties would vote for the Enabling Law, it became difficult for our representatives to do otherwise if they did not want to stand alone in opposition with the Social Democrats. That would have had the consequence that we would have been placed in the same camp as the Marxists, *and it would have made it easier for the government to take measures against us. It was also necessary, moreover, to take into consideration democratic officials, who have a difficult enough struggle already. Here again we had to support measures that we privately opposed.* This can no longer be avoided under the present circumstances. With few exceptions our friends across the Reich feel the same way. *For these reasons I might request . . . that you do not turn your back on the party, since it is more necessary than ever before that all who share our views stand together.* [emphasis mine][34]

Dietrich and his Reichstag colleagues had no illusions about the prospects of open political opposition (*Widerstand*). Democratic support for the Enabling Law, selective participation in regional Nazi coalitions, a general lack of protest: much of this was a pragmatic attempt to buy time and protect Democrats from the wave of persecution being visited on the left. This "accommodationist" attitude may have been abetted by the fact that the affinities between National-Social left liberalism and National Socialism were no mere accident of nomenclature. Either way, Dietrich suggested, such short-term concessions to reality might liberate Democrats from the narrow bounds of party politics and open the door to alternative modes of non-conformity.

III

The Limits of Political Resistance

As Hitler tightened his grip on Germany in summer 1933, employing the government's new emergency powers to ban rival parties, arrest political opponents and curtail individual freedoms, many liberals conveyed a mounting sense of indigation and betrayal. None more so than the last chairman of the German People's Party (DVP), Eduard Dingeldey. Unlike his predecessor Gustav Stresemann, Dingeldey harbored no youthful sympathies for Naumann's National-Social brand of liberalism. To the contrary, as a right-leaning National Liberal, Dingeldey disliked the Republic and did little to prevent the collapse of Weimar democracy. He formed an electoral bloc with the right-wing German Nationalists (DNVP) in 1932, voted for the Enabling Law, and even welcomed the "national government under its Reich chancellor Hitler."[35] Dingeldey would nonetheless respond more fervently and articulately than many liberal democrats to the NSDAP's successive encroachments on civil liberties, suggesting the way in which the everyday experience of National Socialism might galvanize even the most jaded of liberals.

One of the more revealing examples in this regard stems from an exchange between Dingeldey and the DVP leader Albert Zapf that occurred three weeks after the Enabling Law. Zapf conceded that the law had seemed reasonable in the wake of the Reichstag fire, when Germany needed a stronger central government "in order to solve the domestic problems that the [Weimar] party state had failed to solve." Everything that had happened since, however, "contradicts the fundamental principles of the DVP. The loss of the right to political participation and the significant restriction of the inalienable rights of the individual are also changes that one cannot easily and always ignore." Zapf was, like Dingeldey, a vocal critic of the Republic before 1933. But the first weeks of unbridled Nazi rule exercised a profound effect on his conscience. Dissatisfied with his party's failure to combat National Socialism, Zapf resigned in protest. Dingeldey was visibly chastened.[36] Just days after Zapf's emotional departure, the People's Party chairman came out publicly against the decision of both liberal parties, Democrats as well as Populists, to join the local Nazi coalition in Hamburg. He condemned in particular the local DVP's assertion that "following liberal ideas would indicate joining the Nazi Party," characterizing his colleagues as "rats leaving the sinking ship."[37]

As Dietrich and Maier worked feverishly to justify the DStP's decision to support the Enabling Law, some disaffected left liberals turned to Dingeldey. The Hamburg Democrat Ludwig Uthoff wrote to the DVP chairman to "say how joyful it had made [him]" to read Dingeldey's public declaration that one must place "greater worth in the *liberal* national idea."[38] How could any liberal join the NSDAP, Uthoff wondered, a party that wanted to "rename the *Stresemannstrasse* when this man's great liberal policies freed the

Rhineland . . . Though the names of streets may be historically unimportant, such superficial matters can move men to a great degree."[39] The Democrat Wilhelm Wilms thanked Dingeldey for defending liberalism:

> As a liberal who supports the State Party [DStP], I am urged to express my joy and recognition that you have endorsed so energetically in the central committee of the DVP the maintenance of the People's Party as the defender of the liberal world-view, of freedom of conscience and intellectual life. Your vigorous words were certainly no surprise to us liberals, but they are an emancipatory and inspiring deed in the face of the lack of principles and weakness of character that currently prevails. It is a great error if it is widely believed that liberalism has fulfilled its task. Precisely this moment proves how necessary is liberalism. *The struggle of National Socialism against liberalism, whose achievements they made good use of in the election campaign and in all of public life*, shows how little enormous circles of the population have understood the essence of liberalism. Whoever seeks to maintain the liberal worldview must seek to overcome the impediments that stand against these efforts [emphasis mine].[40]

For all its dangers, Wilms observed, the rise of National Socialism had provided an opportunity for liberals to recommit to the Naumannite ideal "that economics is not only a private but a public matter; indeed, that it serves people's necessities in the first place and profit motives in the second; and that seeking profit may not come into conflict with popular morality. Today only *social* liberalism can persist in the economic realm [emphasis in original]."[41] After fifteen years of infighting and useless political posturing, Wilms hoped the experience of the Third Reich would bring both liberal parties together in the defense of national regeneration, social welfare, and civil liberty. At the 14 May meeting of the DStP, the liberal historian Walter Goetz agreed. Naumann's close compatriot before the First World War and co-editor (with Heuss and Bäumer) of *Die Hilfe*, Goetz implored his Democratic colleagues not to disband the party: "we should discuss [rather] . . . in what forms we will continue the party's work and how we will be able to have political effectiveness." The majority of those attending supported the idea.[42]

Still, the harshest criticisms of liberal attempts to sustain their political viability came from the liberals' own rank and file. On 15 May, the day after the Democrats voted not to dissolve their party organization, Dingeldey's Hessian colleague Walter Schnell sent a scathing missive denouncing the DVP's decision to follow suit.[43] Schnell enclosed an article he had written that was rejected by the Nazi mouthpiece, the *Völkischer Beobachter*, ostensibly because of Dingeldey's intransigence. Titled "Nationales Bürgertum und Nationalsozialismus" ("National Citizens and National Socialism"), Schnell's article praised the "better methods, more correct psychology, and more powerful inner strength of National Socialism," concluding:

> After we have recognized as unhealthy the culturally and intellectually destructive effect of the hostile organization of our public life and after we have experienced the destructive role of the Jewish boulevard press, do we have the right and cause to complain if in individual cases the necessity for purifying, clarity, and self-awareness occasionally froths over into excess? . . . Whoever wants to join in because he feels compelled to do so, because he is not too old to be rejuvenated, cannot do this half way, from the outside, but only from within the *Volksgemeinschaft* that National Socialism has created . . . What we have experienced from the end of the nineteenth century until today, in ever starker and more exaggerated fashion . . . was the decline, in an intellectual, artistic, and moral sense, of a great historical epoch, the bourgeois modern. I see in today's events the kernel of something new . . . the express preconditions for achieving a new spirituality and ideology, which will wipe out the cultural foundations of disintegration and leveling inherent in the previous period of materialism.[44]

Without any intervention from Nazi authorities – again, the *Beobachter* had rejected the sycophantic article – Schnell expressed outrage at Dingeldey's resistance to National Socialism. The era of bourgeois liberalism was over. Why could Dingeldey not recognize the "destructive role of the Jewish boulevard press" and embrace National Socialist revolution? Indeed, by the time the NSDAP officially banned the DStP from any further political activity in Prussia in June 1933 most liberals had already determined that the situation was no longer conducive to organized political resistance. Facing pressure from Nazi officials as well as "liberal" colleagues like Schnell, Dingeldey dissolved the DVP in July.[45]

Like their colleagues in the other bourgeois parties, DVP members were permitted to retain their Reichstag mandates as "guests [*Hospitanten*]" of the NSDAP. But a few weeks' caucusing with the Nazi Reichstag delegation merely reinforced Dingeldey's conviction that ideological accommodation was untenable. As he wrote to a DVP colleague shortly before relinquishing his Reichstag seat in November 1933:

The same thing that so painfully moves you and which I feel as a heavy inner burden affects all [our colleagues] as well: we stand at the cross-roads, the stream rushes by us, we are observers who do not however wish to participate in this fluid community . . . to the friend who told you that one must simply transform oneself, closing the door on the past and discarding one's old person, this friend is incorrect on the grounds that we will be held fast . . . by the will of others . . . How has it gone for those who sprang quickly into the rushing waters and in most cases have drowned with this feeling of security? Today there are few cases . . . where these people could consider this leap an act of salva-tion . . . They have been robbed of their personal, essential nature, of their own free will and can in truth no longer regain a new, honest char-acter that originates in good conscience and convictions, that commands and offers respect. If one wanted to answer your question superficially . . . one could point to the Führer's increasingly draconian regulations restricting the acceptance of outsiders into the National Socialist movement . . . But this naturally does not address the intellec-tual problem from which we suffer spiritually. Today there are infinitely many people – and I believe it's reasonable to say that these are often the most worthy and best Germans . . . who cannot find their way to inner accommodation [of National Socialism].[46]

Dingeldey acknowledged that joining the NSDAP might help one's career, but it was the duty of all free-thinking Germans to defend liber-alism, "the essence of which most of those [Nazis] who talk about it do not understand."[47] Liberalism had entered "a struggle with those who, in our opinion, deny the German people their honor and inalienable equal rights in the perfidious exploitation of power."[48]

Furthermore, as Dingeldey admonished another colleague, it was impossible to justify the erosion of individual freedoms and civil rights that accompanied the Nazi revolution:

You know yourself that, even in this serious time, conversations . . . merely touch on the superficial and the anecdotal . . . behind the pretty façade of patriotic unity, do not infinitely many people operate only out of ambition, greed, class hostilities, and a desire for advancement to a degree that endangers the personal trust between ordinary Germans in the worst way? There is still a whole list of very serious problems that I cannot write down here, but which daily oppress every earnest German in the most profound manner. There are moreover the everyday human tragedies that occur precisely to the most worthy and highly esteemed individuals . . . For us we can do no more than appear loyal to others but also to persist in the awareness of our earlier work and our inner convictions . . . In this regard the growing wave of mass approval may not deceive us. We must be ready to lend a helping hand if a return of freedom and equality (that we demand abroad but still need to create domestically) is to take effect in a dignified manner. Until then I regret that I am unable to accept your standpoint.[49]

Far from extinguishing his liberal spirit, Dingeldey's experience of "coordination" in 1933 turned this tepid republican into an outspoken defender of civil liberties and intellectual non-conformity. The former jurist would even write to Hitler's Chancellery to defend liberal colleagues from political persecution and demand due process for Jewish Germans.[50] Still, Dingeldey never managed to build a wider network of resistance among his former right liberal (DVP) colleagues. It remains to be seen whether a close-knit group of left liberal Democrats, working in concert, might have a greater impact.

The Bosch Circle

Like many Weimar Democrats, the liberal industrialist Robert Bosch was a product of Friedrich Naumann's National Social movement. Years later, and despite his multimillion-dollar empire, Bosch still referred to himself as a nationally minded "socialist."[51] Given these ideological underpinnings, it comes as little surprise that Bosch initially feared the agrarian and heavy industrial conservatism of Hitler's German Nationalist (DNVP) coalition partner more than the seemingly "progressive" socioeconomic platform of the NSDAP.[52] Insofar as the Nazi government promised to restore political authority, eliminate the burden of Versailles, and revive the economy through "Keynesian" fiscal and monetary polices, Bosch viewed Hitler's accession with cautious optimism.[53] And to the extent that he and his closest associates – his director Hans Walz; his private secretary Willy Schloßstein; his chief engineer Albrecht Fischer – opposed the initial wave of "coordination," it was primarily a matter of preserving the company's independence.

At first Bosch shared the liberal conviction that no matter how radical its propaganda, National Socialism could never usurp the rights guaranteed by the German *Rechtsstaat*. Hitler could be tamed, or at least bargained with. In January 1934 Bosch wrote that Hitler had "done a good job until now; he will also continue to do a good job. We have a leader that we trust." The left-wing industrialist rationalized the violence of this early period as the "end of the National Socialist 'revolution,'" opining that "National Socialization would eventually succumb to a thoroughgoing political stabilization."[54] He was not alone in ignoring the Nazis' worst excesses. Within the Bosch circle there existed a widespread measure of support for the alternating mix of organized capitalism, public works, and social welfare, of corporatism and competition which defined Schacht's tenure as Finance Minister.[55]

Though Bosch remained cautiously optimistic about the Third Reich, his nearly limitless wealth and impeccable liberal credentials caused evident consternation on the part of the regime. In November 1933 the Gestapo was already reporting that the Württemberg bourgeoisie, of which Bosch was the *éminence grise*, appeared particularly resistant to Nazi "coordination": "These elements are remarkable . . . precisely because of their *financial strength*. From their side there are numerous indications that undertakings are being *financed* that can in fact be defined without question as hostile to the state." Particularly worrying to the authorities was Bosch's financial support for "newspapers . . . certain associations, institutes and large publishers . . . whose sympathies are frequently obscure." "And one must point finally," the secret police observed, "to the widespread network of *foreign relationships* that reach into the great private firms . . . As has been the case in the past a greater than usual attention will be particularly necessary with regard to these circles" (emphasis in original).[56]

The Gestapo's fears turned out to be remarkably prescient. During the first three years of the regime, Bosch insisted on subsidizing the liberal press, most notably the *Frankfurter Zeitung* and Theodor Heuss's weekly journal *Die Hilfe*. He also refused to allow the Nazi Labor Front (Deutsche Arbeitsfront or DAF) to "coordinate" his firm's generous unemployment insurance, health care and workers' compensation programs.[57]

In 1936, as Nazi interventions in the economy became more strident, Bosch started to express open antipathy to the regime. Most problematic was Hermann Goering's Four Year Plan for accelerated rearmament, which, in the words of Bosch's economic advisor Carl Goerdeler, envisioned "war not only as last resort but as a goal [in itself]." The resulting trend toward economic autarchy and the favoring of capital over consumer goods, Bosch observed, would reduce overall levels of productivity, encourage runaway inflation and stagnating wages, and eventually lead to financial collapse. Hence Bosch's tentative commitment to "social liberal accommodation in the sense of Friedrich Naumann" broke down in the wake of the Four Year Plan, whose totalitarian designs could benefit neither labor nor capital.[58]

Given the risks of denigrating a program so near to Hitler's heart, one cannot dismiss this budding opposition as a pragmatic response to Nazi meddling.[59] Yet the Bosch Circle never possessed the political will or ideological coherence to provide real opposition. Bosch's own biographer notes that its members were recruited from the right liberal DVP and conservative DNVP as well as the liberal democratic ranks.[60] One of Bosch's leading engineers for instance, Albrecht Fischer, was a "moderate economic liberal" and "decisive opponent of democracy."[61] Hans Walz was a member of the SS and occasional guest of Heinrich Himmler.[62] Bosch's financial advisor after 1937 and greatest ally in the resistance, the former Lord Mayor of Leipzig Carl Goerdeler, was an anti-republican conservative.[63] The group's eclecticism and lack of concrete goals also helps to explain the fact that members of the firm had few ties to other liberal democratic opponents of the regime.[64] While Bosch and his managers repudiated anti-Semitism and Gestapo repression on a consistent basis, what held the group together was less a common liberal democratic vision of the future than a shared interest in political and economic independence.[65] For this reason they chose their battles carefully, negotiating a space for social, economic, and political non-conformity that fell somewhere between outright resistance and collaboration.[66]

The Marianne Weber Circle

The Bosch Circle confronted National Socialism primarily from a socioeconomic perspective, a combination of practical reservations about Nazi plans for economic autarchy and a deep-seated distrust of totalizing politics. In contrast, Marianne Weber and her academic colleagues rejected the Third Reich on largely ideological grounds. Marianne Weber (née Schnitger) was a second cousin of the brothers Max and Alfred Weber, who were close colleagues of Friedrich Naumann and two of Germany's most distinguished sociologists. In 1893 Marianne married Max, further strengthening the familial and intellectual ties to her famous cousins. Like many of her associates in the National-Social Union, Marianne was a leading feminist and joined Naumann in co-founding the German Democratic Party.[67]

Although not as confrontational as her brother-in-law Alfred, who carried out one of the few acts of open liberal resistance in the first weeks of Hitler's dictatorship (see Chapter Two), Marianne remained skeptical in her attitude toward the regime. In a series of articles from spring 1933 published in Gertrud Bäumer's *Die Frau*, Weber discussed both the positive and negative consequences of the "national revolution." She conceded that patriotic Germans could find much to admire in the new national community (*Volksgemeinschaft*) presided over by Hitler. Nevertheless, Weber added, "belonging to a nation is not the only and not, from my perspective, the most significant aspect . . . of our private existence." Individual freedom was less dispensable than national unanimity, and "it is a sin against humanity to inspire unholy fanaticism that searches for guilty parties."[68]

In order to provide a haven for the aforementioned "guilty parties," namely marginalized Jewish and liberal academics, Weber continued to host a weekly discussion group of Heidelberg faculty members who had met at her house during the Weimar Republic. Members included her cousin Alfred (Max had died of pneumonia in 1920) as well as the left-leaning historian Hans von Eckardt and the philosopher Karl Jaspers, both of whom were loosely affiliated with the Weimar Democrats.[69] During the Republic the circle had always been eclectic, involving future Nazis as well as Jewish liberals. It became monolithic after 1933, "since meeting together with Jewish friends . . . was not permitted for [Nazi] party comrades." The Weber circle also attracted new members, like the progressive theologian Otto Dibelius.[70] According to Steven Remy, in fact, "Marianne Weber's salon remained the only forum where such scholars could discuss their research without fearing denunciation from jealous Nazi colleagues or Nazi students."[71]

Certainly no one was naïve enough to discuss contemporary politics. As the Third Reich progressed, "contemporary issues had to be avoided . . . Members who thought that their academic posts were endangered and who felt under pressure to join the stormtroopers [SA] in order to give evidence of their devotion to the new state ceased to participate." Themes were often historical, theological, or philosophical in nature in order to avoid the fraught terrain of contemporary German politics. As Weber recalls in her memoirs, "Eschewing topical questions introduced depth rather than superficiality."[72] How did the German Republic's decline compare to that of the Romans'; how would Plato describe the Third Reich; was Hitler the next Charlemagne or a charlatan? Politics was not the primary topic, but "meanings of the political sort were allowed to leak out" nonetheless.[73]

Ultimately the group "represented a form of resistance and indirect criticism common to intellectuals under dictatorship." Like the *Boschkreis*, the Marianne Weber Circle was an amalgam of disillusioned bourgeois notables, some from the moderate left, some from the right, none of whom articulated a coherent program of resistance. Indeed, the Gestapo never considered it the least bit dangerous and generally ignored its activities.[74] Weber and her colleagues are worth examining, not because they represented a potential threat to the regime, but because they embody the space for liberal cultural and intellectual life that managed to persist until the final years of the Third Reich.

The "Wednesday Society"

Neither a real "society" nor particularly fond of Wednesdays this inaptly named discussion group convened informally for breakfast on Monday mornings. Composed almost exclusively of Weimar Democrats, the weekly gathering was patterned on the famous Wednesday Society of Berlin academics which the historian Hans Delbrück presided over for decades before his death in 1929. The Democrat Wilhelm Külz's interest in organizing a liberal discussion group stemmed from his earlier involvement in Delbrück's Circle, whose members, while by no means exclusively liberal, would supply a notable reservoir of passive intellectual resistance (*Resistenz*) to National Socialism.[75] As a Democratic Reichstag representative and mayor of Dresden until 1933, Külz was one of the few liberals consistently to resist National Socialist demagoguery and anti-Semitism in the final years of the Weimar Republic. After the Reichstag fire, he urged Germans to repudiate the Nazis' despotic response, which was to ban the Communist Party (KPD) and expand the German police presence. On 7 March he registered an official protest against flying swastika flags from the Dresden City Hall. Not surprisingly, Külz was relieved of his mayoral post a week later. Arrested for a night in December 1934, Külz decided to relocate to Berlin, where he became a financial consultant and reestablished ties to the liberal intelligentsia.[76]

Thereafter Külz's "society" grew organically, drawing primarily on Berlin Democrats with natural personal and political affinities. Close friends and fellow "Southerners," Theodor Heuss and Hermann Dietrich had already organized a Saturday evening circle of democrats that met in Berlin-Dahlem. Heuss had access to foreign radio programs, which he would relate to Dietrich and other members of the circle during walks in the Berlin Tiergarten (where Gestapo surveillance was necessarily thin). In turn, Heuss and Dietrich had for some time visited an informal "Wednesday Society" organized by August Weber, Eugen Schiffer, Otto Gessler, Siegfried and Katharina von Kardorff.[77] Alongside Külz, Heuss, Schiffer, Dietrich, and Weber, the new circle included the erstwhile Minister

President of Lower Saxony and Democratic Reichstag deputy, Theodor Tantzen. It was Tantzen who suggested the Coburger Hof, where he stayed during visits to Berlin, as the Wednesday Society's regular venue.[78]

Unlike the Bosch or Weber Circles, the Wednesday Society was composed exclusively of liberal democrats who held leading positions in the Weimar administration. Five of the society's half-dozen regular participants – everyone save Hermann Dietrich – were arrested or detained at various times during the Third Reich. All six had close contacts to leading members of traditional non-party institutions like the army, church, and civil service, not to mention the press and higher education. As friends and party colleagues, they could communicate subtly and trust one another implicitly, factors which were crucial in planning resistance under more or less constant surveillance.[79] Theoretically at least, one might expect the Wednesday Society to have been particularly well suited to political opposition.

Nevertheless, the Wednesday Society had almost no practical impact on the political or intellectual terrain of the Third Reich. It was neither as well organized and attended as the *Weber-Kreis*, nor financially supported and politically influential as the Bosch Circle. A week after the 20 July plot against Hitler, which led to Tantzen's arrest, the Chief of the Reich Security Service Ernst Kaltenbrunner would write that the liberal "Wednesday Circle" was politically harmless.[80] In stark contrast, many individuals involved in Ludwig Beck and Ulrich von Hassell's more conservative "Wednesday Club," spearheaded by members of the civilian and military resistance, were executed. For all its political and intellectual coherence, the Wednesday Society was typical of liberal "resistance" groups in failing to offer serious opposition to the regime. Perhaps the only exception was the Robinsohn–Strassmann group.

The Robinsohn–Strassmann (RS) Group

Hans Robinsohn and Ernst Strassmann were young left liberals active in the German Democratic Party during the Weimar Republic. Robinsohn was born in 1897 to a comfortable Jewish family. Although his siblings were salesmen, Robinsohn chose politics, becoming an active member of the German Democratic Party in the early 1920s. Ernst Strassmann was nominally "Aryan," although his stepfather Arnold Strassmann was Jewish. A veteran of the First World War, Strassmann began practicing law shortly thereafter. Both men joined the DDP's youth organization, the Young Democrats (Reichsbund der Deutschen Demokratischen Jugendvereine), in 1919 and co-founded the left-leaning 3 October Club in 1924, whose members included Tantzen, Landahl, Erich Lüth, Fritz

Elsas, and Thomas Dehler. As radical republicans bent on defending the cosmopolitan moorings of the Democratic Party, none of the 3 October group was pleased with the DDP's decision to merge with the paramilitary Young Germans to form the German State Party (DStP) in 1930. Although Landahl and Elsas eventually supported the merger on national and social grounds, Tantzen resigned his party posts and Robinsohn abandoned the State Party altogether. Robinsohn and Strassmann were equally appalled at the DStP Reichstag fraction's support for the Enabling Law.[81]

Even as the Nazis began to coordinate German politics and society in 1933, the two young Democrats started planning for the collapse of the Third Reich.[82] In June 1933 Robinsohn composed a fifty-page program articulating his views on the inherent weaknesses of National Socialism. The three main chapters of the *Denkschrift* focused on the NSDAP's obsession with the "Jewish Question," the contradictory *mélange* of progressive and reactionary elements in Nazi ideology, and the Third Reich's unfavorable long-term political prospects. These were controversial subjects in an era when liberals were confining their criticisms to less provocative, "apolitical" areas like economic policy or the loss of certain freedoms. No doubt the two liberals' Jewish background contributed to their wholesale repudiation (and ultimately underestimation) of National Socialism. To Robinsohn and Strassman the Third Reich appeared a temporary phenomenon, a mass psychosis from which the population would soon awake.[83]

Unlike Heuss, Bäumer and many other Naumannites, Robinsohn perceived few similarities between Hitler's National Socialism and German left liberalism. To the contrary, "in its restriction of personal freedom, in its anti-parliamentary attitude, in the corporatist form of economic life," National Socialism constituted the utter rejection of liberal and democratic principles. Robinsohn attacked the totalitarian and racist pretensions of National Socialism, which, he remonstrated, would doom it to failure in a diverse, well-educated society like Germany. Only a truly democratic liberalism, verging on socialism in its cosmopolitanism and proletarian sympathies, was suited to the highly civilized German people.[84]

Inspired by Robinsohn's political program, which he carefully distributed to like-minded colleagues, the group began to coalesce in 1934 around a shared moral and intellectual antipathy to National Socialism. Although its membership was politically and demographically diverse, the organization was headed by younger Democrats who had resisted the DDP's rightward drift during the second half of the Weimar Republic:

Strassmann and Fritz Elsas in Berlin; Robinsohn in Hamburg; Thomas Dehler in Munich. Elected mayor of Berlin in 1931, Elsas was the only member to be directly implicated in the 20 July 1944 plot against Hitler. Dehler was also an eminent Young Democrat and Freemason, who became chairman of the Free Democratic Party (FDP) and West German Minister of Justice after the Second World War. In fact the group's brains trust was composed primarily of civil servants, with only Robinsohn and Dehler working chiefly in the private sector. Whether the dismissal of both men from government positions influenced the group's hostility toward National Socialism is hard to say. But these professional difficulties, combined with the group's Jewishness, youth, and radicalism, did much to create a mutual sense of purpose.[85]

Whilst the group's activities centered on Berlin and Hamburg, its members also built relationships with liberals in smaller cities like Bamberg (Bavaria) and Kiel (Schleswig-Holstein). The conspirators fostered ties to liberal democrats and socialists outside Germany as well, traveling widely in spite of the dangers. The RS group was by no means foolhardy, favoring pragmatic and feasible goals over utopian ideals. But, unlike the liberal "resistance groups" outlined above, Robinsohn and Strassmann were equally dismissive of organizing "fruitless discussion circle(s)" which, for lack of a public forum, must inevitably dissolve into insignificance. Robinsohn believed that the opposition must "help the wagon roll off the tracks as quickly as possible," before Hitler could "garner any political success." The very production and distribution of Robinsohn's program in the mid-1930s constituted an act of undeniable courage, and the group was fortunate either to destroy or export copies of the manifesto before the Gestapo could obtain them. The RS group was also far better organized, widespread, and united in its democratic goals than the Bosch, Weber, or Külz Circles.[86]

It would nonetheless be inaccurate to overemphasize the group's political and intellectual impact. Many "members" actually belonged to very different circles. More importantly, the group's radical democratic principles and doctrinaire antipathy to conservative ideas clearly dissipated over time. National Socialism "corresponded in many points to the German mentality," Robinsohn conceded in 1933. The main reason for lack of opposition was a "desire for unity that is very poignant to the Germans for historically and psychologically explicable reasons." Certain restrictions on civil liberties would have to be preserved, Robinsohn reasoned, while nationalists and military leaders were cultivated to provide the necessary postwar stability. Even Elsas, the group's most distinguished Jewish member, suggested that a temporary dictatorship might be necessary to steer Germany away from National Socialism after the war. The RS group was not as organizationally interwoven with the conservative resistance as the Bosch Circle. But Robinsohn and Strassman did establish connections with traditional elites like Admiral Wilhelm Canaris and Hans Oster of the German Foreign Service (Abwehr), with members of the Kreisau Circle like Adam von Trott zu Solz, Carl Goerdeler, and Fabian von Schlabrendorff, and even with anti-Semitic monarchists frustrated by the direction of the German economy.[87]

Though more politically engaged than other liberal "resistance" groups, Robinsohn and Strassmann's organization was ultimately less coherent and effective than its socialist and right-wing counterparts. Robinsohn himself acknowledged that "no one was in the position to be informed of all the details and contacts" that the RS group had assembled. The dilettant nature of these affiliations, which extended from the Protestant Confessing Church and Kreisau Circle to the Socialist trade unions, only made the participants more vulnerable to Gestapo surveillance. The police nevertheless spent more time monitoring conservative resistance groups. Even the discussion-oriented Wilhelm Solf Circle – which was composed primarily of high-ranking diplomats – was deemed more dangerous by the regime.[88] Indeed, Robinsohn and Strassmann spent the bulk of their time on "long-range planning for a post-Hitlerian Germany rather than on immediate subversive action." As ideologically committed as the members were, the RS group's activities could only ever offer passive resistance to the Third Reich.[89]

IV

Non-Conformity in Everyday Life

In 1936 the SS commander Werner Best outlined the goals of Gestapo (secret state police or Geheime Staatspolizei) surveillance: "The totalizing political foundation of National Socialism, which corresponds to the ideological principle of organic and indivisible unity of the people, tolerates no political will formation [*Willensbildung*] in its sphere, which does not fit in to the will formation of the whole." In response to these tactics many Democrats, largely Jews and/or pacifists, fled the country during the first few months of the regime. As the Nazi Party tightened its grasp on Germany's most important political and legal insititutions in the mid-1930s, mainstream liberals also began to experience the intermittent persecution and professional slights common to those who "were not inclined to celebrate the victory of the *Führer*-state due to political, ethical or religious grounds or who were excluded as pariahs due to 'racial' and multiple other reasons."[90]

Heuss quickly noticed that the Gestapo was tracking his mail. He also canceled his phone service in July 1933, largely to avoid surveillance.[91] After one harrowing Gestapo interrogation Wilhelm Heile chose self-imposed exile in the countryside. Some of Robert Bosch's lower ranking personnel faced harassment and arrest as well.[92] August Weber – who had delivered a particularly inflammatory anti-Nazi speech in 1932 and whose wife was Jewish – was questioned or detained half a dozen times before emigrating in 1938.[93] Democratic mayors Wilhelm Külz and Fritz Elsas were forced to retire from their posts.[94] And liberal women like Marie Baum, Gertrud Bäumer, and Marie Elisabeth Lüders lost their civil service positions; all three were subsequently monitored by the Gestapo. Such "open persecution" only accelerated as time went on.[95]

We should nonetheless be careful not to exaggerate the pressures liberals faced in the middle years of the Third Reich. As the historians Reinhard Mann and Robert Gellately have demonstrated, in 1939 the entire secret state police force (Gestapo) numbered approximately 20,000, or half the number of police currently patrolling New York City. There was simply no way to surveil a population of eighty million, inclusive of Austria and Bohemia, without being selective. Nor was the Gestapo especially motivated in pursuing Weimar Democrats. Rudolf Diels, the first head of the Gestapo, refused to replace liberal civil servants with Nazi party members.[96] Conversely, Diels's direct superior, Reinhard Heydrich, banned the NSDAP's own conservative coalition partner, the German National People's Party (DNVP), and outlawed members of the radically nationalist Pan-German League.[97]

Theodor Tantzen's encounters with the Gestapo provide an excellent case study for this uneven pattern of surveillance and persecution. Like Heuss and other high-profile liberals, Tantzen noticed that some of his mail was taking longer to arrive than it had a few months earlier. Still, there is little evidence that the police opened or delayed more than a small proportion of his correspondence. If he really were the "most dangerous [anti-Nazi] in Northern Germany," as one of Tantzen's colleagues later maintained, the Gestapo was strangely unresponsive. While many conservatives and some Nazi Party members had been closely observed as early as 1933 – and despite a flood of articles by Tantzen criticizing Nazi economic policies – it took at least three years for Heydrich's Security

Service (SD) to open a file on Tantzen. Some Oldenburg locals even speculated after the war that Tantzen had worked out a "secret agreement" with the regional Nazi leader Carl Ostendorf, who promised to apprise the Democrat of any forthcoming investigations or arrests.[98]

For only in September 1939, with the invasion of Poland, did Tantzen begin to experience a regular violation of his rights. He was detained on the day the Second World War began, 1 September, and not released from "protective custody" for three weeks. The grounds for his arrest seem fairly arbitary. Tantzen's name had appeared on one of Heydrich's note cards at the same time that Himmler ordered a few thousand "warning" arrests to discourage "expressions unfriendly to the state during this momentarily stressful situation." For this reason Tantzen was soon released. But the twenty-three days of incarceration in the small detention camp of Nordenham – though hardly comparable to Dachau or Buchenwald – had a profound effect on Tantzen's temperament. According to Enno Stephan, the son of the former DDP General Secretary Werner Stephan, Tantzen returned from Gestapo custody visibly shaken. When the topic of his oppositional activity arose a few weeks later, Tantzen's girlfriend noted his terse response, "I am no martyr." Tantzen's profound distress is confirmed by his aunt, who claimed that he was "psychologically and economically devastated." Fully six years after the Nazi seizure of power, this brief encounter with the naked force of the regime was enough to push a Democratic firebrand into a private realm of "inner emigration."[99] Hence, while there is little doubt as to Tantzen's repugnance toward the Third Reich, his ideological antipathy signifies little more than a passive rejection of Nazi values.

Hermann Dietrich and the Art of "Refusal"

According to most historians, Hermann Dietrich never made a serious effort to resist the Third Reich. Even his close friend Theodor Heuss had little to say about his colleague's activities during the 1930s, recalling that Dietrich withdrew from "political" life after the collapse of the Republic. A practicing attorney with ample real estate investments in Baden and Berlin – his wife was independently wealthy – Dietrich had much at stake in resisting the Nazi regime.[100] Dietrich also had difficulty avoiding controversy. A pugnacious leader during his tenure as DStP co-chairman, Weimar Vice-Chancellor and Finance Minister under Bruening, he had lost none of his edge a decade later.[101] Upon hearing of his rival Hermann Fischer's death in 1941, for example, Dietrich acknowledged that Fischer had been a good and generous colleague. But he then launched into a diatribe about the "appalling difficulties" he had with Fischer's free-trade lobby, the Hansabund, "because he, together with his idiot cronies, made assertions regarding the budget and finances to which one could not possibly respond."[102]

Notwithstanding such fits of pique, Dietrich engendered immense loyalty in friends and associates, including those with whom he disagreed. Theodor Tantzen's long-running antagonism to Dietrich's protectionist agricultural policy would cause Tantzen to leave the Democratic Party in 1930. A decade later the Oldenburg Democrat was still a frequent correspondent and one of Dietrich's regular callers in Berlin.[103] Erich Koch-Weser, with whom Dietrich fought intensely at the end of the Weimar Republic, determined to meet his former colleague and friend upon return trips to Germany (Koch had emigrated to Brazil in November 1933). Indeed, Dietrich preserved close relations with liberals such as August Weber, Eugen Schiffer, and Georg Gothein, whose "philosemitic" reputation caused some consternation even in many liberal circles. Upon visiting the capital, Democrats from all over Germany made a point of meeting Dietrich to discuss contemporary political issues, party matters, or to wax nostalgic in a walk through the Berlin Tiergarten. Ernst Lemmer, Wilhelm Külz, Elisabeth Brönner-Hoepfner, Gertrud Bäumer, and Hermann Höpker-Aschoff are just a few of the leading Democrats who seemed to view Dietrich as a liberal paterfamilias presiding over a vast network of colleagues situated in Berlin.[104]

Given his stable professional situation and considerable investments, Dietrich was often called upon to provide financial assistance to less fortunate colleagues. Rarely did he disappoint. When Tantzen alerted Dietrich to the arrest of the Democrats' erstwhile stenographer in October 1936, Dietrich instantly sent money to provide "a small [defense] fund."[105] When Külz lost his government job in 1933 Dietrich immediately loaned him 2,000 Reichsmarks, nearly twice the average annual worker's salary. After Külz found new employment in March 1935, Dietrich used the capital Külz gradually repaid him to aid other Democrats who had fallen on hard times.[106] Politely ignoring Otto Nuschke's sycophantic attempts to gain his favor by "illustrating [Dietrich's] political accomplishments in a book," Dietrich sent the former DDP General Secretary 300 RM regardless. Two years later he hired Nuschke's wife as his personal secretary and employed Otto to handle some of his rental properties.[107] Dietrich even contributed a monthly pension to the elderly wife of Eugen Richter's private secretary, Reinhold Ißberner, despite the fact that Dietrich had belonged to the rival National Liberal Party at the time of Richter's death thirty-five-years earlier.[108]

Dietrich's generosity extended beyond financial matters. Though retaining no official capacity, he made an enormous effort to maintain a network of liberal friends and associates. He rarely missed an opportunity to congratulate colleagues on their successes, no matter how modest, or to console them on the death of a loved one. He also expended an immense amount of time using his connections to find employment for destitute colleagues or help Jewish Democrats to emigrate.[109] In 1935 Dietrich found a job for Hermann Rönneberg on the preparations committee for the Berlin Olympic Games. He then urged a colleague to invite Rönneberg along on a hunting trip because the latter had no money to afford a vacation.[110] Dietrich likewise subsidized Elisabeth Brönner-Hoepfner's publishing company, which took on the liberal journal *Die Hilfe* when no one else wanted to pick it up.[111] At the same time we find him collaborating with Brönner-Hoepfner to store additional boxes full of books and liberal party documents in his cousin's attic, far away from the prying eyes of the secret police.[112] Given how much he stood to lose, Dietrich's effort to preserve this material displays abundant courage and dedication.

Like many former Democrats, Dietrich's political maneuverability was all the more precarious because his livelihood was contingent on the largesse of the Nazi authorities. Dietrich had to join the National Socialist Legal Association (NSRB), a precondition for practicing law in the Third Reich, and he continued to receive a state pension in return for his years of service as a Weimar minister and Vice-Chancellor. In fact Dietrich's commercial success and political visibility during the last years of the Weimar Republic made him a prominent target. In 1938, for example, one of Heydrich's minions published an article in the SS paper *Der Schwarze Korps* (*SK*) accusing Dietrich of "squandering his pension abroad. In this regard we still don't know whether and to what degree Dietrich is transferring a portion of his pension, which the National Socialist state pays him, as an honorarium to the erstwhile General Secretary of the party." The SS may have been alluding (inaccurately) to Otto Nuschke, or perhaps (equally inaccurately) to Koch-Weser, the former DDP chairman who emigrated in 1933. Regardless of the reason for the accusation, Dietrich's brother-in-law offered to write the *SK* to point out its absurdity: Hermann Goering's Four-Year Plan placed restrictions on the transfer of German currency abroad and Dietrich could not possibly have paid out the sums mentioned in the article. The sober-minded Dietrich insisted that the Gestapo's bark was worse than its bite: "I would like to impress upon you that no intervention is necessary."[113]

Whether it was the Gestapo, the SS, or the NSRB, Dietrich evinced little respect for Nazi authority. He also developed a rare ability to dissemble to political, moral, and economic advantage. In August 1936 Dietrich received the application and by-laws for the NSRB. After an interview a few months later, an official from the NSRB wrote back: "it has been related to me [no doubt by the Gestapo] that you employ a Jewess as a secretary. I ask you to confirm whether or not this is true." Dietrich's wonderfully legalistic response initiated a six-year game of dissimulation, which reflects the porous nature of Nazi racial policy as well as many other aspects of institutional surveillance and repression. Affirming that his "regular" employees were "fully Aryan [*vollarisch*]," Dietrich admitted that he employed "as a private secretary a young woman, Ms Käthe Zolki, who is racially a Jewess." Ms Zolki was formerly employed by a deceased client, Dietrich explained, one Dr Richard Bahr, who requested that Dietrich retain her services in administering his size-able 250,000 RM estate on his widow's behalf. Dietrich confessed that he paid some portion of Ms Zolki's salary from a "personal account." From "his attorney's office she received nothing." Despite the fact that the Nuremberg Laws explicitly forbade Reich-sanctioned professionals employing Jews, Dietrich's response somehow satisfied the NSRB, which sent him his membership card four weeks later.[114]

It would be another two years before the NSRB resumed interest in Frau Zolki's employment status: on 22 June 1939 they wrote that "According to a report in our possession you supposedly still employ a Jew." Dietrich responded in typical fashion by forwarding the same letter he had sent in February 1937, noting that he had hired two additional "full Aryans" in the intervening two years. Of course, he *had* finally "dismissed" Ms Zolki in January 1939, when her duties for Mrs Bahr were completed. But since the regime announced "in February or March that Jewish personnel might continue to be employed in industrial and commercial endeavors, I have retained her." Amazingly, given Dietrich's elusiveness, not to mention the "non-essential" nature of his law practice – something the authorities would use to threaten Dietrich eighteen months later – the NSRB wrote back on 5 July that "the whole issue is considered resolved."[115]

Dietrich's temporizing extended well beyond the Nuremberg Laws. From the moment he obtained his NSRB card, Dietrich received a barrage of invitations to "mandatory" NSRB assemblies and conferences. He managed to avoid nearly every obligation. In March 1937 Dietrich simply ignored the request for his presence at the annual NSRB meeting. In

March 1938 his secretary wrote the NSRB that Dietrich was on vacation. Finally, in March 1939, Dietrich received an inquiry from an exasperated NSRB official explaining that the "NSRB has been assigned the task of writing a report on you . . . In response I ask you to answer the following questions" including "your political inclination before the seizure of power" and current "Party affiliation." Dietrich answered in pithy fashion. He had been a liberal for thirty years before 1933, chairman of the Democratic Party, and had never joined the NSDAP. Not entirely satisfied, the NSRB decided to schedule an interview.[116]

Dietrich now initiated a series of prevarications that reflect an inspired disdain for Nazi protocol. On 27 April 1939 Ms Zolki wrote to inform the NSRB that Dietrich had become "seriously ill" on a trip to southern Germany and would not be able to return for an interview for another two weeks. Exactly two weeks later, Dietrich's office dispatched a note indicating that he would only "be able to resume again his activities in Berlin on 25 June," but that he would then "establish contact immediately, Heil Hitler!" After a few days the local NSRB leader, Eisen, sent a letter urging Dietrich to show up at the May "Conference on German Law" and to consider donating money to poor "comrades." Dietrich's office again forwarded his regrets, citing protracted illness. Arriving back in Berlin on 5 June, Dietrich ignored his new "case worker" Eisen and wrote to the NSRB regarding his interview. He had indeed returned, "but needed to stay in bed" until he was fully recovered. He would contact them to reschedule.[117] Undeterred by Dietrich's repeated tergiversations and exaggerated claims of illness, on 17 June the NSRB sent Dietrich an invitation to a district meeting, which stated: "Absence is only permitted on truly pressing grounds and only after prior legal excusal in writing." Apparently Dietrich recovered quickly from his maladies; his office wrote back only a few days later that Dietrich "can unfortunately not take part on the KAV on 21 June since he is traveling on vital business matters."[118]

As war approached and the proverbial noose of surveillance tightened, Dietrich became even less proactive. He ignored letters in July "requiring" NSRB attendance at the Reich party convention in Berlin. On 9 September, a week into the war, the NSRB requested that all its members take on *pro bono* cases for colleagues who had been called away on military service. After nearly a month's delay, Dietrich's office finally responded "that Herr Attorney Dietrich suffers from a serious heart condition, is under medical care and is therefore unfortunately not in condition to take over representation for colleagues who have been called to military service." Dietrich had suffered a mild heart attack in 1930, but that had obviously not stopped him from chairing the German State Party, running a busy law practice, or managing multiple properties in south-west Germany. Dietrich would in fact live another fifteen years, passing away of natural causes in 1954. From his letters to the NSRB, one gets the impression that the vigorous fifty-nine-year-old was at death's door.[119]

Dietrich was actually working from home, assisted by the indispensable – and still Jewish – Ms Käthe Zolki. Receiving no answer to their repeated inquiries from Dietrich's downtown office, the NSRB leader Helmer finally wrote in March 1940 to confirm Dietrich's current professional address. No doubt instructed not to indicate that Dietrich was working at home with a non-Aryan, his secretary never answered the question; Dietrich was away on business and would contact Helmer upon his return. Twelve weeks later Dietrich finally responded, explaining the necessity of operating from home as "a consequence of my long illness, to which the lack of heat last winter contributed" (a jab at wartime energy shortages). Neither Dietrich nor the NSRB made mention of the fact that Dietrich was now working exclusively with a Jewish secretary. To a subsequent NSRB letter requesting Dietrich's annual dues his office responded belatedly, "[Dietrich] finds himself on a rehabilitation trip of many weeks. We ask you to please wait another four weeks or so for the payment of the contribution."[120] Dietrich was no miser. Over the twelve years of the Third Reich he distributed thousands of marks to aid numerous (Jewish) Democratic colleagues and to finance *Die Hilfe*. His delay in paying dues or making charitable donations to the NSRB can only be understood as a form of conscious protest.

The NSRB was especially frustrated that Dietrich avoided the "mandatory" *pro bono* work central to the Nazi conception of a selfless *Volksgemeinschaft*. Only in February 1941 did Walter Wagner, a by this point apoplectic NSRB functionary, pin him down with a phone call. Dietrich reported the telephone conversation to Ms Zolki: "I could no longer deceive him and had to render some response. I called his attention to the fact that I lack knowledge in many areas and that my specialty lies in the field of corporate law and finance. If I have correctly understood him, I must pay 10 RM a case for a replacement." Shortly thereafter Dietrich received a list of lawyers willing to do *pro bono* work for 10 RM and his first designated court date, should he decide to attend. *Still* intent on avoiding even this minuscule financial imposition – he cleared nearly 11,000 RM (!) in income in 1940 – Dietrich followed up with a long letter to Wagner in which he repeated that his expertise in corporate law was hardly suitable for a position "in which one must deal with all the insignificant legal affairs of daily life." The war had also ruined his "international legal practice," which compelled Dietrich to take up "management of investment properties that are located in South Germany. As a consequence I am frequently absent from Berlin, often for weeks at a time." In short, Dietrich would need a permanent replacement on the list of available attorneys since he was neither competent nor available to perform the duties requested.[121] Indicating the NSRB's mounting exasperation at Dietrich's intransigence, Wagner replied that Dietrich was doubtless *more* capable of helping than attorneys directly involved in handling industrial matters crucial to the war effort. "However, the transfer of those seeking counsel to your office will not occur, since you have refused to take an interest in matters of the poor." Refusing to dignify Wagner's accusation with a reply, Dietrich paid his annual NSRB fee of 54 RM three months late.[122]

On 20 May Dietrich received another request to appear as counsel, on 1 July and 16 September 1941. Doubtless chastened by the repressive atmosphere following Germany's invasion of the Soviet Union (22 June 1941), Dietrich reported to court for the first time on 1 July. Just a few weeks later, however, he was at it again, citing his inability to make the 16 September date due to "significant matters" in south Germany; without asking permission he submitted 20 RM instead. After showing up for a scheduled court date on 11 November 1941, Dietrich then begged off for the duration of 1942, studiously avoiding "mandatory" appearances in February, April, August, and November.[123] The last important correspondence we have between Dietrich and the NSRB is his convoluted explanation for why he would be unable to attend a 15 December 1942 speech by the Reich Minister of Justice Otto Thierack: "The invitation . . . only reached me on the 25th of this month [November] . . . Unfortunately I am not in a position to attend . . . At the moment the focus of my work lies in Baden, where I own considerable property. I had intended to be in Berlin for the whole winter. Nevertheless, my wife has become so ill that she can only return to Berlin in January in the best case scenario. It is therefore necessary for me to leave for Baden as soon as possible in order to look after my wife. It is impossible for me to remain here until 15 December."[124]

Alongside illness, it seems, Nazi authorities were susceptible to claims of financial necessity. Facing an audit of his 1940 income in 1942, including the money he earned from Jewish clients (which was taxed at 40 percent as opposed to the standard rate of 20 percent), Dietrich wrote the Treasury that only 1,500 RM of his legal income of 4,493.73 RM in 1940 came from Jewish clients. He also argued that the majority of his total income of

10,507 RM was from investments and not from his law practice, which the Depression and the war had impacted adversely, forcing his patronage of Jewish clients. These were dubious assertions by any measure, but the Berlin Treasury accepted his reasoning (and numbers) without question.[125] Citing pressing business matters, between 1938 and 1941 Dietrich also requested and received permission to travel to Basel in Switzerland. Given the wartime restrictions on travel and on expending German currency abroad, the former Democratic chairman's easy mobility is surprising. It appears all the more noteworthy when one considers the opportunities these trips to Basel afforded him in consulting with liberal émigrés and gathering uncensored information.[126]

Yet Dietrich would successfully employ the same rhetoric of financial pragmatism in the wake of the 20 July plot against Hitler. Under investigation by the Gestapo for his ties to the plotters, Dietrich wrote the administration on 22 July that he needed to move permanently to Baden since his Berlin-Steglitz office had been "mostly destroyed" and his property in south Germany needed closer management: "My main estate in Wildgutach has lost most of its workers as a result of the war, so that I must now try to hold the business together with a number of women, 5 Poles, a Ukrainian and a young person from Cologne."[127] Evidently convinced by this explanation, the regime made no effort to prevent Dietrich's relocation and the Gestapo called off the investigation. In this fashion Dietrich managed to elude, short-change, and confound an army of Nazi functionaries for nearly eight years.

Like most of his colleagues, Dietrich retreated from active politics in 1933. This move away from public life provided the perfect opportunity to resist the oppressive social, economic, and legal atmosphere of the Third Reich. It was Dietrich's spirited defense of the private sphere, where he could move relatively freely while circumventing the public pressures faced by liberal government employees, which made possible his long-term non-conformity.[128] Whereas the Democrats described above resisted National Socialism in a passive, almost unconscious sense (*Resistenz*) – the way a healthy person might fight off a disease – Dietrich's deliberate efforts to refuse (*verweigern*) Nazi intervention into his personal and professional life verged on active *Widerstand*. Dietrich managed to reject nearly all "mandatory" participation in the Nazi Legal Association; to heavily subsidize the liberal press throughout the Third Reich; to distribute money and favors to Democratic colleagues; and to repudiate Nazi Jewish policy both by representing Jewish associates and by employing a "non-Aryan" secretary long after it was safe or practical.

Though never constituting overt political resistance, Dietrich's extraordinary example demonstrates the capacity for sustained social, cultural, and intellectual non-conformity in the Third Reich.

V

The 20th of July 1944

The story is well known. On 20 July 1944 a leader of the conservative resistance movement known as the Kreisau Circle, Colonel Klaus von Stauffenberg, managed to smuggle two bombs into a conference room in Hitler's "Wolf's Lair," his East Prussian headquarters. One of the bombs went off, killing four people and wounding half a dozen more. Hitler emerged with minor injuries. Rumors of Hitler's survival spread quickly and threw the military and civilian leaders of the coup into disarray. Within hours of the assassination attempt, the Nazis had regained control of the military and begun to round up suspects. Many of the central conspirators were executed immediately, sometimes in grisly fashion (involving piano wire and meat hooks). Inside weeks, most members of the Kreisau and Goerdeler Circles had either committed suicide or been killed, including Stauffenberg, Count Helmuth von Moltke, Ulrich von Hassell, Goerdeler, and General Ludwig Beck. In all, 110 individuals would be tried and executed during the next eight months. Because of these conspirators' extraordinary sacrifice in defense of freedom and morality, Heuss has referred to the 20 July coup, despite its failure, as the wartime generation's greatest "gift to Germany's future." But almost all the victims were conservatives or socialists.[129] Where were the liberals?

Many Democrats had personal and professional ties to the network of bourgeois resistance groups that helped plan and carry out the failed assassination. Tantzen, Elsas, Nuschke, Strassmann, Eduard Hamm, Otto Gessler, and the liberal diplomat Albrecht von Bernstorff were probably aware of the coup. Indeed, Tantzen, Gessler, and Nuschke were designated as ministers in Chancellor Goerdeler's shadow government, while Elsas, named to head the Reich Chancellery, was the first person Goerdeler visited after the coup went awry.[130] By the late 1930s Ernst Strassmann's network also included members of the Kreisau Circle like Adam von Trott zu Solz and the renegade socialist Julius Leber.[131] Meanwhile Robert Bosch and Hans Walz built an extremely close working relationship with Goerdeler and General Ludwig Beck. After 1937, Goerdeler was Bosch's firm consultant and confidant. Walz was the one who informed the

American Office of Strategic Services in Zürich of Goerdeler and Beck's emerging conspiracy in December 1942. All the more remarkable that neither Walz nor Bosch was arrested.[132]

Bosch and his colleagues were not alone in escaping serious punishment for their ties to the plotters. During a Gestapo interrogation in November 1943 Goerdeler revealed Theodor Tantzen's knowledge of plans to undermine the regime. Remarkably, no one followed this up. When Tantzen's name turned up once again on a list of potential ministers in August 1944, his fate appeared sealed. Yet Tantzen emerged unharmed. Despite personal ties both to the Kreisau Circle and to the Beck–Goerdeler group, Thomas Dehler also evaded persecution. Even the openly critical Hjalmar Schacht, a friend of many of the plotters, and Gessler, who was designated as Goerdeler's Munich liaison officer in the event of a coup, survived internment.[133] Other outspoken Democrats whose contacts with members of the resistance are well known – men like Hermann Dietrich, Alfred Weber, Otto Nuschke, Wolfgang Jaenicke, and Theodor Heuss – were never detained.[134] Only a few members of the Robinsohn–Strassmann group's five dozen participants were arrested, most notably Fritz Elsas and Ernst Strassmann. While Elsas, who was Jewish, was later executed for sheltering Goerdeler, Strassmann survived his thirty-two months of incarceration unscathed. In fact Elsas and Eduard Hamm were the only prominent Democrats to pay the ultimate price for their involvement in the 20 July plot.[135]

How do we explain their colleagues' good fortune? Historians who wish to stress the extent of liberal participation in the resistance have come up with various reasons for why they survived. Horst Sassin points to Ernst Strassmann's arrest two years before the conspiracy came to fruition, which prevented his further involvement, while noting that Thomas Dehler was called up for military service before the coup got under way.[136] Jürgen Heß stresses Heuss's auspicious timing in relocating to Heidelberg prior to the coup; had he stayed in Berlin, Heß suggests, Heuss would have been arrested and perhaps even executed.[137] Other historians cite fortuitous personal or professional ties. Martina Neumann alludes to Tantzen's providential friendships with the local Nazi Gauleiter Paul Wegener and high-ranking press functionary Werner Stephan. Sassin reasons that Strassmann may have been protected by the same SS-*Obergruppenführer*, Franz Breithaupt, who ostensibly helped to shield Theodor Tantzen from the worst abuses of the Gestapo as well.[138]

Taken individually, these explanations are plausible. But so many close calls and chance interventions beg the question: Why didn't the liberals' conservative co-conspirators enjoy the same run of good fortune and happy accidents as former Weimar Democrats? We must remember that the vast majority of plotters were right-wing aristocrats or members of military elites with far greater wealth, status, and political capital than bourgeois democrats. Nevertheless, most conservative conspirators perished. Where were their "protectors"?

The simple truth is that most Democrats were only marginally connected to the conspirators and, perhaps more surprising, that Nazis generally did not murder ("Aryan") individuals on personal or political grounds alone. Some evidence of deliberate conspiracy was required. In light of our preconceived notions of Nazi justice, it is astonishing that so many Democrats with ties to the plotters, some of whose names turned up on a list of potential post-Nazi Germany ministers, survived. Yet only two Democrats were "active" conspirators: Goerdeler's "lieutenant" Fritz Elsas and Eduard Hamm, a Bavarian Democrat with close ties to the Kreisau Circle.[139] Albrecht von Bernstorff was eventually killed as well. But his eleventh-hour April 1945 execution by SS guards was only tangentially related to his tenuous affiliation to the 20 July plotters.[140] In almost every case of liberal resistance, the Democrats were deemed "too harmless to be dispatched to concentration or death camps."[141]

That is not to confuse the Nazi state with a liberal *Rechtsstaat*, particularly after the 20 July coup. Many individuals "were executed for insignificant reasons and without sufficient evidence," and putative conspirators were often tortured during their interrogation. Himmler also stepped up Gestapo terror arbitrarily, which explains why some individuals who had been arrested before 20 July 1944 and avoided sentencing were executed thereafter.[142] Heuss would recall the atmosphere of fear and oppressiveness, when he and his family could only refer obliquely to the status of colleagues in detention. In describing the fate of his friend, the 20 July plotter Ernst von Harnack, Heuss's son Ernst Ludwig wrote: "according to the doctor's diagnosis [the judgment of the people's tribunal] he has no more hope. He only has a few more days to live." Discussing the former Democratic Defense Minister Otto Gessler, who suffered multiple injuries during interrogation, Ernst Ludwig wrote that "Otto has been sent home from the hospital [prison]. The illness had certainly struck him hard. In falling he lost all his teeth, and even broken a few bones."[143]

The fact is that even after 20 July 1944 the Third Reich was something less than a totalitarian "police state." When the notorious Roland Freisler, presiding judge in the 1944 trials, unduly favored the prosecution, the Nazi Justice Minister Otto von Thierack intervened. Of the many hundreds of notables who were executed or committed suicide in the wake of 20 July, most *had* played a meaningful role in the plot or had at least known about it and done nothing to prevent it.[144] Given the scale and context of the conspiracy – which sought to murder a legitimate head of state in the midst of war – the Nazi justice system appears less arbitrary and liberal involvement more tangential than one might at first assume. Though it might be reassuring to know that the liberal democrats who contributed so much to both German Republics played a central role in the conspiracy, we must recognize that their "gift to Germany's future" lies elsewhere.[145]

VI

Liberal "resistance" to the Third Reich was as passive as it was pervasive. "After the elimination of the liberal parties and organizations," Horst Sassin correctly observes, "there was a bourgeois-liberal milieu on which the founders of a liberal democratic opposition group could depend. The resonance of liberalism that had sunk almost to nothing in the final phase of the Weimar Republic renewed itself in the face of the thoroughly illiberal and anti-liberal politics of the Hitler regime." Nevertheless, as a member of Reinhard Heydrich's Security Service (SD) reported in 1938, "the impact of liberalism lies not in the forms of organization, but in the private attitude of individual representatives of the liberal way of thinking."[146] That is, for all their "resistance" to Nazi attempts to coordinate German social, cultural, and intellectual life, few liberals demonstrated a willingness to carry out the explicitly political and military opposition exemplified by the conservative elites who plotted Hitler's assassination.

Still, liberal opposition constitutes something more interesting and complex than the sociologically grounded non-conformity of Catholic mothers protesting about the removal of crucifixes from confessional schools, or of working-class teenagers boycotting the "bourgeois" Hitler Youth. It resulted from a combination of sociological and ideological objections embedded in a wide array of shared political experience, democratic sociability, and progressive cultural and intellectual institutions. The persistence of liberal influence out of all proportion to the Democrats' electoral strength had a substantial impact on their potential for non-conformity after 1933. For, just as the Third Reich could never successfully eradicate Catholic religious institutions or working-class social milieu, the Gestapo could do little to prevent a liberal civil society from reproducing itself well into the Second World War.[147]

To the extent that liberals accommodated the Third Reich, we might likewise trace the ideological affinities between German liberalism and

National Socialism. National Socialism was a diverse movement that borrowed numerous ideas and practices from the bourgeois parties it displaced. If German liberalism was not necessarily the strongest of those antecedents, it was prominent among them. By exploring liberal engagement in the everyday social, political, cultural and intellectual life of the Third Reich, the next four chapters help to flesh out the enduring tension between Fascist coercion and popular consent, as well as the fraught relationship between Naumannite left liberalism and National Socialism after 1933.[148]

CHAPTER TWO

"Writing between the Lines":
The Struggle for Liberal Ideals in Cultural and Intellectual Life

I

Nazi Germany "is not like other countries," wrote Hans Robinsohn in October 1937, "where only some news is falsified." In the Third Reich nearly everything is propaganda. The press, the radio, even films work to "eliminate any contradiction, every tiny undesirable deviation" from the party line. German culture deceives foreigners by its outward appearance of "overwhelming unity and national solidarity," Robinsohn asserted, which betrays a false sense of "spontaneous spiritual jubilation." Outside observers were convinced "that the German situation will never improve" because no one can "deal with this crazy fanatic Hitler and his fully submissive people." Such impressions were completely erroneous, Robinsohn suggested, comparing this contemporary perception of a supine, jackbooted Germany "to the view of a doctor who, after very superficial examination, rejects any treatment as hopeless and for the most obvious case recommends only the bloody operation."[1]

Keenly attuned to the pulse of the German population, Robinsohn realized what few non-Germans and fewer historians have subsequently understood: that the Nazi seizure of power did not immediately obliterate cultural or intellectual freedom.[2] Rather, save for a small fraction of openly propagandistic work, the lion's share of art, film, and literature produced in the Third Reich was still determined by the exigencies of a profit-oriented mass market.[3] Or, as Michael Kater reminds us: "On close examination we can find in the Third Reich elements we would not expect in the dictionary definition of a totalitarian regime: a lack of controlling mechanisms, creative movements expressive of freedom such as jazz and swing, and extended influence of Jewish culture and its champions, even avant-garde attempts at modernism." With respect to most artists, writers, and musicians, "These endeavors were motivated and frequently accompanied by various political convictions on the part of their creators; more often than not, and understandably in a time of party and governmental strictures, political opportunism and careerist considerations prevailed over moral ones." "As ordinary Germans under stress who often wished to avoid oppressive political obligations," Kater observes, "they tried to circumvent them as best they could; others played the new game more deftly and ended up on top."[4]

Liberals were no different to other artists and intellectuals. In fact they were probably more eager in their opposition, more skilled in their dissembling, and more informed in their dissent. As the Gestapo reported, "the importance of liberalism lies not in its forms of organization, but in the inner mentality of individual representatives of the liberal way of thinking." This "way of thinking," according to the Nazi Security Service (SD), was embedded in the cultural and intellectual landscape throughout the Third Reich.[5] Though circumscribed in their activities, liberals were surprisingly prolific after 1933. Liberal papers continued to exist. Liberal writers published books and articles. Liberal intellectuals expressed views that departed from the party line. And nearly everything produced by Democrats in this period preserved an essential kernel of criticism and dissent. Without the preoccupations of everyday politics, a number of liberal writers, journalists, and academics were more productive than ever.[6]

This is not to deny the uphill battle facing Democrats who wished to resist the Nazification of cultural and intellectual life. Many who refused to step down or presented an alternative worldview experienced frequent harassment; some liberal writers and intellectuals were banned outright. Yet it is not entirely clear whether the post-1933 inclination towards a less vibrant public sphere, race-inflected Christianity, or anti-Semitic academy was more the product of Nazi repression or a quotidian combination of preexisting ideological proclivities and market pressures. Some liberal writers and academics worked actively to tie their agenda to the National Socialist *Zeitgeist.*[7] Others refused to countenance the Third Reich's attempts to "coordinate" intellectual life, often without retribution. Either way, the liberal experience should cause us to revise our understanding of the risks and resonance of cultural non-conformity.

II

Liberalism and the Press

Liberal writers encountered several challenges after 1933. Not least was a shrinking market in the wake of the Great Depression. The Nazi seizure of power exacerbated lagging demand for republican-era newspapers, art, and literature.[8] Non-Nazi papers verging on bankruptcy finally went out of business. Left-wing and liberal journalists whose columns were already losing readers were fired outright. Others, hamstrung by the need to "write between the lines," chose to serve as German correspondents for foreign papers.[9] Many liberal papers were harassed into changing their content, sometimes to the point of obsolescence. As Gustav Stolper wrote of his liberal economic journal *Der Volkswirt*, which was proscribed briefly then reconstituted under different editors, "The *Volkswirt* has essentially changed its face, no longer contains a critical word and may not speak of important matters. That makes a publication not only intellectually unsustainable and morally ineffective, but also financially impossible in the long term, for I don't believe that people in Germany or certainly abroad will pay . . . for a journal that can satisfy neither the supporters nor the opponents of the regime."[10]

Most bans were temporary, however, usually the reaction of Goebbels's Reich Press Chamber (Reichspressekammer or RPK) to a flagrant "abuse" of "free speech." Government authorities only intervened in the openly satirical *Querschnitt* (Crossfire) in 1936, when the paper published a searing critique of the regime in the guise of a fictive Foreign Language Dictionary.[11] Sponsored by Robert Bosch, the liberal *Stuttgarter Neue Tageblatt* maintained its independence for three years, until the exasperated Reich Press Chief Max Amann invoked an obscure April 1935 law prohibiting anyone with connections to the judiciary – the paper's publisher was also a jurist – from distributing a Reich paper. In light of the fact that the local NSDAP had once called to have Württemberg's entire "democratic clique" shot, Amann's backhanded attempt to cut off funding appears rather civilized.[12]

The Press Chamber's preferred method for "coordinating" the press was to apply financial pressure. Using state subsidies Amann worked to transfer as many local papers into Nazi hands as possible, while pressuring independent-minded industrialists and entrepreneurs like Bosch to withdraw their media investments. When Bosch proved unwilling to give up his minority stake in the local liberal press, he encountered repeated inquiries from Amann and even Goering, who called personally in 1936 to ask why Bosch was reluctant to sell his shares for what was ostensibly a generous price.[13] Hence, despite these annoying, sometimes threatening interventions by the regime, market forces played the largest role in determining whether a particular liberal paper persevered. As one Democrat wrote to Hermann Dietrich in 1934, "There are still rumors here and there that the 'Führer' wants to take over the *Badische Presse* . . . [But] whoever wants to take over the *BP* must naturally bring a sizeable amount of money to the table and the 'Führer' has as little of that as we do."[14]

Finally, we should be careful about confusing the initial wave of anti-Semitic persecution, which resulted indirectly in the purge of many liberal editors and journalists, with premeditated government censorship. Due to their deep pockets and impressive international reputations, the traditional liberal dailies – the *Berliner Tageblatt*, *Vossische Zeitung* and *Frankfurter Zeitung* – were well positioned to resist Nazi interference. Yet all three were owned and edited by Jewish Democrats, including Hans Lachmann-Mosse (*BTB*), Heinrich Simon (*FrZtg*), Theodor Wolff (*BTB*), Louis Ullstein (*VossZtg*) and Georg Bernhard (*VossZtg*). Forced to sell their press empire, the Ullstein family decided to discontinue the *Vossische Zeitung* in March 1934. The *BTB* fared somewhat better. To be sure, under pressure from Goebbels the Mosse family turned over everyday affairs to an "Aryan" consortium in 1933, while the *BTB*'s Jewish editor Theodor Wolff was forced out of his job. But Goebbels subsequently allowed the paper's long-time American correspondent Paul Scheffer to succeed Wolff, assemble a new team of ("Aryan") liberal journalists, and even promised not to intervene in the *BTB*'s content. Although Scheffer himself left the editorial staff in 1936 over conflicts with the RPK, the *Tageblatt* continued to sell 50,000 to 100,000 copies daily and to exercise some measure of intellectual independence until finally closing down in 1939.[15]

All the more noteworthy is the perseverance of the *Frankfurter Zeitung*. Like the *BTB*, the *FrZtg* was compelled to purge itself of "non-Aryan" elements in 1933, especially Jewish-Marxist intellectuals like Theodor Adorno, Siegfried Kracauer, and Walter Benjamin. But afterward the paper was tolerated – even "protected" – by Goebbels, who realized the propaganda benefit of permitting Germany's most widely respected liberal paper to carry on relatively unmolested. Backed by Bosch's financial generosity and guided by a brilliant chief editor, Benno Reifenberg, the *FrZtg* repeatedly tested Goebbels's patience with its none too subtle criticisms of Nazi social, political, and intellectual life and loyal patronage of liberal writers in search of work. Hitler would in fact demand that the paper be shut down at least twice before it was finally suspended in August 1943, ostensibly for publishing an unflattering article about Hitler's mentor, Dietrich Eckart.[16] The survival of these great liberal papers provides abundant evidence of the space for liberal non-conformity after 1933. And no liberal paper explored this space more confidently than Theodor Heuss's *Die Hilfe*.

Theodor Heuss and the Remarkable Persistence of Die Hilfe

Although numerous books and articles attest to Theodor Heuss's role in rebuilding German democracy after 1945, few scholars have examined his twelve tumultuous years under Hitler. Even less consideration has been paid to Heuss's voluminous literary and journalistic activity in the Third Reich. The bulk of scholarly work has focused instead on Heuss's ill-fated support for the Enabling Law and his alleged involvement with the 20 July plot to assassinate Hitler.[17] This preoccupation with exploring Heuss's "active" resistance or collaboration is understandable, given his integral role in shaping the Federal Republic. It is nonetheless regrettable in diverting attention from Heuss's rich cultural and intellectual biography, including the thousands of pages that he published on the Third Reich, in favor of speculations on what arcane connections the literary-minded Democrat might have had to the 20 July plotters.[18]

For Heuss was never merely a politician. "As a publicist and speaker," writes Karl Dietrich Bracher, "Heuss never tired of building a bridge between intellect and power; as a professor at the Berlin College of Politics in the Weimar epoch he sought to lead his students to understand democracy."[19] The cultural historian and Heuss biographer Modris Eksteins agrees, insisting that Heuss was always "more intellectual than politician."[20] Heuss's fellow Democrat and friend Reinhold Maier described him as a true Renaissance man, a classical humanist for whom "God and the world, faith and knowledge, common sense and feeling [were] still a unity."[21] Given these credentials, it is little wonder that Heuss remained critically engaged during the Third Reich.

Born in Brackheim, Württemberg in 1884, Heuss spent his early years developing relationships with working-class liberals, Socialists, and Evangelical progressives in Friedrich Naumann's National-Social Association. After graduating with a degree in political science from the University of Munich, the precocious twenty-one-year-old became a co-editor of *Die Hilfe* in 1905, took over the *Neckarzeitung* in 1912, and began publishing *The German Nation (Die Deutsche Nation)* in 1923. After the First World War Heuss accepted a teaching position at Ernst Jäckh's College of Politics

(Hochschule für Politik), a "liberal" university, conceived by Naumann, which was aimed at educating Germans in democracy. In 1924 Heuss won a Reichstag seat and subsequently took a greater role within the leadership of the Democratic Party. In spite of this headlong leap into Weimar's overheated parliamentary arena, Heuss built a national reputation for extraordinary civility, unparalleled erudition, and a rare liberality of mind even among his right-wing opponents. Consequently Heuss, unlike many Democratic colleagues, found no shortage of publishers after 1933. Indeed, he would become one of the Third Reich's most prolific authors.[22]

Notwithstanding the need to assume a cautious tone, there is an element of resignation, even accommodation, in Heuss's political analysis during the first weeks of the Third Reich.[23] In a long article from April 1933, Heuss credited the National Socialist revolution with completing the centralizing and rationalizing tendencies left unfinished in the revolutions of 1918–19. Perhaps, Heuss remarked, the Nazis might be able to accomplish what the Republic could not, namely "a breakthrough to coherent political leadership of the Reich." " 'Coordination [*Gleichschaltung*]' is not a very attractive word," Heuss went on, but "creating one political will for all public institu-tions . . . possesses epochal meaning . . . that is what the leading men know best, and the Prussian Minister President Goering recognizes most power-fully that unrest in the civil service and uncertainty in the sphere of economic organization could be dangerous for the state and communal life."[24] Indeed, in May 1933 Heuss expressed pity for colleagues who "perceived only the barbarous aspects of this time." This modest enthusiasm for the early political and economic measures of the regime casts doubt on Heuss's later claims that he privately opposed the Enabling Law.[25]

According to Rabbi Leo Baeck, however, the initial experience of National Socialism awoke in Heuss a "spiritual purpose" that made it inconceivable for him to hold his peace.[26] Toni Stolper also recalls how "Heuss did not remain silent . . . many reported to us [in exile] that it was impossible to overestimate what the mere existence of a man like Heuss in the Hitlerian epoch meant for the empowerment of their moral and intellectual character." Heuss was the only leading Democrat, for example, to publish a detailed critique of the National Socialist movement, a scalding 200-page analysis titled *Hitlers Weg* (1932). And two of Heuss's works were selected for immolation during the infamous Reich book-burning of May 1933 – "the best legitimation," in Toni Stolper's words, "of their and his quality."[27]

Heuss may have conceded the political sphere to Hitler when he voted for the Enabling Law, but he was unwilling to follow suit in terms of culture or civil society. Only ten days after the fateful vote, Heuss published an article posing a number of bold questions regarding the future of free expression in Germany:

> Perhaps it is a sign of the "authenticity" of this "revolution" that it wants to interfere in these [cultural and intellectual] fields, and impose its style upon them . . . [But] this is where the greatest intellectual contradictions lie – will the Church be "coordinated?" Will there be a standardization of science? Does the state, in its institutions, have the competence to say what is art? Whoever yields decisions in this sphere to political power spoils the laws of free development.[28]

A few months later Heuss appeared to answer his own questions, characterizing the intellectual mindset of the nascent Third Reich as a "regression into the Middle Ages."[29] Then, in January 1934 he printed an article by Höpker-Aschoff in *Die Hilfe* declaring: "religion, science and art are not means to be employed by the state; for the intellect blows wherever it wishes." It was this early disillusion with Nazi attacks on cultural and intellectual freedom, and not necessarily the end of democratic government, that caused Heuss and his colleagues to open a critical dialogue with the regime in the pages of *Die Hilfe*.[30]

Founded by Friedrich Naumann in 1895, *Die Hilfe* chronicles better than any other periodical the complex trajectories of German liberalism in the first third of the twentieth century. Unlike the *Frankfurter Zeitung* or *Berliner Tageblatt*, *Die Hilfe* was first and foremost a political journal, which admitted no obligation to render an "objective" appraisal of everyday events. At some point in its fifty years of existence nearly every important left liberal contributed an article or letter to its pages.[31] Of course *Die Hilfe* never reached the same number of people as the major liberal newspapers, whose daily readership approached 200,000 even in the early years of the Third Reich. But Naumann's journal fulfilled two important purposes. It furnished Heuss and other Democrats with an opportunity to make a living and, for a time at least, provided a more distinctly liberal message than its larger rivals.[32]

Heuss's three-year tenure as chief editor is best characterized as tumultuous. This was due in part to the underlying hostility of the regime, but also to the economic instability of the early to mid-1930s. Even at its height *Die Hilfe* never turned much of a profit. In the wake of the Great Depression Heuss's predecessors Walter Goetz and Gertrud Bäumer found it necessary to reduce the number of editions from weekly to bi-monthly, and also to switch publishing houses.[33] Heuss lost the active participation of his co-editors Goetz and Bäumer for financial reasons as well. Goetz, a renowned Professor of Renaissance History at the University of Leipzig, was pushed into unpaid retirement, retreating from his editing duties in order to sue the government for wrongful termination. Facing the same challenges as Heuss, Bäumer chose to devote more time to her feminist monthly, *Die Frau*, officially resigning from *Die Hilfe*'s editorial board in early 1935. Although both Democrats would continue to supply articles and advice, the responsibility for keeping *Die Hilfe* afloat fell squarely on Heuss's shoulders.[34]

Left alone at the helm, Heuss acknowledged "that a free-thinking journal can only fulfill its task under restrictions" and that "there could be no security for the journal, authors and publisher" without changing the content measurably.[35] But he still fought tooth and nail to defend *Die Hilfe*'s independence. Accused of publishing anti-Nazi propaganda in July 1934, Heuss replied with a long letter to the Reich Propaganda Ministry defending his right to express political opinions in *Die Hilfe*. Improbably, he received a letter from the ministry agreeing that "one cannot prevent any German from conscientious, concerned participation in political development." Only four weeks later, Heuss received another warning.[36] Because this unpredictable pattern of Nazi criticism and conciliation made it difficult to determine what was permissible from one day to the next, Heuss pushed the envelope more often than not.[37]

He also understood that there was greater room for free expression in the sphere of culture and intellectual life than in politics or economics.[38] A retrospective on the work of Karl Marx or of the Jewish historian Hans Rosenberg, for example, might defy Nazi propaganda without discussing contemporary politics.[39] Putatively literary-minded editorials could also have far-reaching implications. Published only weeks after Hitler and Himmler murdered hundreds of political opponents on 30 June 1934 ("The Night of the Long Knives"), Bäumer's daring "What is Truth" attacked the regime's ubiquitous use of propaganda. It was unfortunate, Bäumer observed, that the German people could no longer trust what they were told. The only thing they knew for certain was that the message they were hearing undoubtedly failed to correspond to reality. "For the English people," Bäumer concluded, "the word 'propaganda' is identical with the word 'lie'." Provocative articles such as these spurred *Die Hilfe*'s small but loyal readership into proclaiming the periodical "an indispensable phenomenon so long as the repression of intellectual freedom continues."[40]

This editorial practice got Heuss into trouble. He was reprimanded for everything, from Bäumer's "Anglophilia" to an anonymous editorial regretting the wave of Jewish emigration. The Propaganda Ministry responded with special vitriol to an article questioning the feasibility of a union with Austria: "This kind of reporting is no longer tenable. I warn you therefore and advise that I will ban the journal and hold the editor accountable for any further indiscretions."[41] Some longtime subscribers canceled their subscriptions for fear of being associated with such controversial content.[42]

Despite these controversies, *Die Hilfe*'s audience grew during the first eighteen months of Heuss's tenure, approaching a thousand subscriptions and four thousand readers. Due in no small part to Heuss's willingness to challenge the Nazi party line, the financial situation also improved.[43] As one subscriber wrote Heuss in August 1934, *Die Hilfe* was crucial "in proclaiming [liberal] convictions loudly in the public sphere."[44] The Karlsruhe historian Franz Schnabel likewise encouraged Heuss in his "tireless and selfless effort to keep [*Die Hilfe*] alive in these times."[45] Otto Dibelius, the progressive theologian whose own journal was proscribed in 1934, marveled at how expertly Heuss "squared the circle," astonished, "given the restrictions that are placed upon the editor today, that the journal isn't banned – and indeed that you lend it simultaneously its own tone and even encourage independent judgements . . . [its] survival is a necessity for as long as the suppression of intellectual freedom lasts."[46] Writing Dietrich in January 1936, Heuss made a similar argument:

> I know that one might consider it proper to let the "*Hilfe*", which no longer has a "political" function, go under. But I will strive against that as long as I can. Never before in my long publicistic activity have I heard so frequent and so intense an echo over the work that we are currently achieving. The continuing existence of the "*Hilfe*" is, if I may say so, felt in moral terms. The unbiased objectivity and the will to a clear historical analysis appears, if I understand the voices that reach me, very much as a good deed and the number of readers is without a doubt many times the number of subscribers. From a publisher's perspective, the unfortunate reality of the shared subscription has become characteristic of many cities since this is one of the first areas in which [Depression-era] frugality takes control.[47]

It is interesting that Heuss cited market forces as a greater challenge than the vast Nazi apparatus of repression.[48] Fortunately Heuss's party colleagues rose to the task, in particular Robert Bosch and Hermann

Dietrich, who contributed thousands of marks to keep "a piece of Naumannian tradition happily alive."[49]

Whilst *Die Hilfe* would survive the Depression, Heuss's tenure as editor would not.[50] From January 1934 all writers and editors needed to renew their annual membership in the Reich Association of the German Press [Reichsvervand der deutschen Presse, or RVDP].[51] Heuss reapplied successfully in 1934 and 1935, but his name did not appear on the official RVDP list for 1936. To Heuss's worried inquiry, the RVDP responded that they could not approve his identification card because he had not filed the proper documentation of his Aryan background – something Heuss had refused to fill out in 1933 to protest against Nazi anti-Semitism.[52] Because the Reich Literary Chamber was notoriously inconsistent in its application of Nazi regulations, it is unclear whether this sudden "racial" scrutiny was a function of the recently ratified Nuremberg Laws or whether the authorities had simply become frustrated with Heuss's mounting literary engagement. Whatever the reason, Heuss was unwilling to relinquish his license, filing multiple requests with the Office of Racial Research for a "hereditary pass" in the winter of 1936–37. After submitting the pass to the RVDP in February 1937, Heuss was asked to reprise his entire literary career as well. Eventually accepted under the rubric of "art critic," Heuss was no longer permitted to helm *Die Hilfe*.[53]

Under its new editor Werner Ziegenfuss, Naumann's journal would persist until September 1944, shifting between accommodation and a measured course of literary non-conformity. By Ziegenfuss's own admission, it was hardly the same. Heuss would never claim that he "steer[ed] his] journal ... without making any concessions" to the times, as his colleague Bäumer characterized her tenure at *Die Frau*. But he never wavered in his conviction that *Die Hilfe* served a higher purpose, a testament to the durability of liberal thought and expression in an otherwise illiberal epoch.[54] This success reflects both the porous nature of Nazi censorship and the remarkable skill with which Heuss negotiated the Third Reich's rocky cultural terrain.[55]

III

"Writing between the Lines"[56]

Like Heuss a former co-editor of *Die Hilfe*, Wilhelm Heile was released from his teaching position at the College of Politics in spring 1933. Detained by the Gestapo shortly thereafter and convinced that the cycle

of persecution was just beginning, Heile moved his family to a farm in
Tzscheeren, Brandenburg. After three years of poor harvests and escalating debts – typical of many farmers' experiences during the Third Reich
– Heile returned to Berlin and found work as a translator of foreign papers
and journals in the Economic and Statistical Division of the Reichstag.[57]

One of the ways Heile supplemented his income was as a literary,
theater, and film critic.[58] In the liberal dailies like the *Berliner Volkszeitung*
and *Morgenpost*, Heile's reviews are notable for their biting appraisals of the
consumerist tripe favored by Goebbels. Anticipating the modern American
movie critic, he became well known for a terse " 'Ja' oder 'Nein' " (thumbs
up or thumbs down), followed by correspondingly acclamatory or
disparaging reviews. At times he took a populist line, praising a book that
highlighted the corruption and speculation which resulted from striking oil
in a rural small town.[59] In other cases, he seemed to risk the ire of the
authorities by mocking the "blood and soil [*Blut und Boden*]" ethos gone
kitsch. Of a *Bildungsroman* titled *Die heimatliche Brücke* (The Hometown
Bridge), Heile wrote: "All in all a sometimes virtuoso and not completely
impossible work, but lacking charm and often flat to the point of
banality."[60] He took a tradition-bound, *Blut und Boden* oriented book to
task for wasting an immense effort on reproducing a sensibility reminiscent
of the "generation of our grandmothers."[61] "Whoever likes a Shirley
Temple film," Heile wrote of another bestselling novel, "would . . . also
have a taste for this book. Shirley Temple may work in [Hollywood] but
. . . not in a good German book."[62] In mocking popular literature as deriv-
ative of American schlock, Heile put the censors in a difficult situation.
Apolitical pulp fiction and film was precisely the kind that Hitler enjoyed
and Goebbels tacitly promoted. By noting this seemingly popular author's
failure to produce a "good German book," Heile's review puts in stark relief
the contradiction between Goebbels's high-minded propaganda and the
typically consumer-oriented, entertainment-driven culture industry.

The 1937 German film *The Man Who Was Sherlock Holmes* received a
decisive 'Nein' as well. A farce about two incompetent detectives who pass
themselves off as Holmes and Watson, the film followed a typically
American pattern of pointless "exaggeration" and "fantasy." Its puerile plot
lacked any semblance of "truthfulness [*Wahrhaftigkeit*]," Heile opined,
invoking a typical Nazi trope used to dismiss politically ambiguous or allegorical work. Yet *Holmes* did very well at the box office and was one of two
films found in Hitler's bunker in 1945, alongside the German version of
The Hound of the Baskervilles (1937).[63] More controversial was Heile's
critique of a "propagandistic novel" which had trouble balancing "harsh

reality" with "believability." The otherwise sympathetic protagonist "brings unfortunately – and unwisely – his emotional Jew hatred forth in so immoderate a tone that the reader has no real trust in him."[64] Taking a pro-Nazi novel to task for its exaggerated anti-Semitism was certainly a departure from the party line.

Ultimately Heile was never a member of the "resistance," as one biographer has contended.[65] But the chief reason for Heile's uneven record of literary non-conformity – which never approached the depth and duration of that of Heuss or Bäumer – was professional, not political. Heile had more difficulty finding reliable income than Heuss, whose wife Elly made considerable money in marketing. And, unlike Bäumer, Heile had a young family to support. His economic desperation is evident in the time spent protesting his "professional ban [*Berufsverbot*]" from the civil service and the partial loss of his pension.[66] It is no coincidence that Heile's most productive period occurred between 1937 and 1939, after Schacht pulled some strings to obtain him a position in the Reichsbank. When Heile was dismissed in 1939, his literary output declined sharply.[67] Notwithstanding these qualifications, Heile's reviews exemplify the way a liberal with sufficient income and a modicum of discretion might produce a critical body of work in the Third Reich.[68]

Siegfried von Kardorff's Nazi-era publishing career was not only non-conformist, but also reasonably successful. Kardorff spent most of the 1930s working on two political histories, *Wilhelm von Kardorff: ein nationaler Parlamentarier im Zeitalter Bismarcks und Wilhelms II, 1828–1907* (1936), and *Bismarck im Kampf um sein Werk* (1943). A biography of the younger Kardorff's father, a powerful conservative politician and close friend of Bismarck, the former work elicited little controversy. Although critics complimented Kardorff on writing a better history than most "in recent years," those who read and appreciated the book tended to be retired politicians and bureaucrats from the imperial era.[69]

The Bismarck biography, to the contrary, offered ample fodder for contemporary political commentary. It appeared at a particularly sensitive time in the war, in 1943, when Nazi cultural institutions were at their most arbitrary and repressive. Before it was published Kardorff's research effort had spurred a voluminous private correspondence regarding Bismarck's life and work, which had already drawn substantial attention to the book. Some correspondents clearly saw Kardorff's ongoing project, which began with a series of lectures two decades earlier, as an opportunity to revise the historical record and counter the exploitation of Bismarck's legacy in the Third Reich. The son of Karl Heinrich von Boetticher, Bismarck's Interior

Minister, wrote Kardorff in April 1942 to complain about the hagiographic portrayal of Bismarck in a new film (*Die Entlassung*), produced by Goebbels, about the Iron Chancellor's dismissal in 1890.[70] Meanwhile Marguerite von Bismarck, Bismarck's daughter-in-law, urged Kardorff to rescue the historical Bismarck from the Nazi propaganda machine.[71] Many leading scholars and politicians lauded Kardorff's assessment, including the Democratic historian Friedrich Meinecke and DVP party leader Paul Moldenhauer.[72] Axel von Bülow thanked Kardorff for countering the prevailing trend toward superficiality and sensation. Instead of appreciating the complexity and humanity of history, Bülow observed, Germans had become "unaccustomed to good taste in the sphere of historical representation in recent years." Popular history eschewed "all nuance on the one side and all illumination on the other, and, in unnatural fashion, sought to simplify and reduce everything to the most basic level by painting an equally desolate black and white picture."[73] One can hardly imagine a greater indictment of cultural and intellectual life in the Third Reich or a better endorsement of Kardorff's renunciation of such trends.

Still Kardorff, whom Goebbels disdainfully referred to as "Kathinka IV" (an allusion to his wife Katharina's three previous marriages), encountered little of the controversy that would surround Heuss's great biographies.[74] This may have had something to do with Bismarck's impeccable nationalist credentials. That Kardorff came from a high-ranking aristocratic family with right-wing proclivities might have shielded him from the censors as well. A great mystery of the 20 July plot is how hundreds of members of the army and civil service could become privy to a plan to assassinate Hitler without Gestapo intervention. One explanation is that Hitler and the Gestapo – accustomed to military and aristocratic grumbling and lacking sufficient evidence of a conspiracy – feared alienating these powerful elites at such a sensitive time in the war. This natural deference to the German aristocracy may have insulated Kardorff. For despite his ardent support for the Republic and the League of Nations, and in spite of his membership of the Committee for a Jewish Palestine and his close friendship with many Jews and Socialists, Kardorff confronted fewer obstacles than more patently accommodationist Democrats.

A case in point is the former DStP co-chair and Prussian Finance Minister, Hermann Höpker-Aschoff. His 1935 book, *Our Way through the Epoch*, published by Hans Bott, received mixed reviews. Karl Jarres, a former liberal (DVP) presidential candidate, commended the book in the *Kölnische Zeitung*. Höpker, Jarres wrote, had great courage in proclaiming the need to work for the sake of Germany even if one did not embrace

National Socialism in all respects. One could pursue liberal goals, improve
social welfare, and defend what was left of the German Rechtsstaat,
Höpker reasoned, and nonetheless work within the framework of
National Socialism.[75] The Nazi-sympathizing journal *Hochland* had rather
less understanding for the Weimar Democrat and Finance Minister's
attempt to reconcile liberalism and Nazism.[76] The book was not well
received by Nazi censors either: "The tendencies represented by the
author, who claims his book is compatible with National Socialism, are to
a great extent unacceptable from a National Socialist standpoint. Also, the
portrayal that Höpker-Aschoff gives of the Weimar Republic is inconsistent with the National Socialist [point of view]."[77] Liberal sympathies
might be tolerated if they appeared in alternative venues like *Die Hilfe* or
the *Frankfurter Zeitung*. But the Reich Culture Chamber did not take
kindly to Höpker trying to capitalize on Hitler's successes three years after
denigrating National Socialism in print.

Marie Lüders's work received a more mixed response. The RSK made no
attempt to prevent publication of her 1935 book *Das unbekannte Heer:
Frauen kämpften für Deutschland 1914–1918* (The Unknown Army: Women
Fought for Germany, 1914–1918), a history of women and the home
front during the First World War. Instead, three widely circulated (and
Nazi-affiliated) women's journals did the RSK's job for them, immediately
attacking the book as "reminiscent of the same spirit that [Erich Maria]
Remarque recalls" in his "pacifist" novel, *All Quiet on the Western Front*.[78]
More combative than Höpker, Lüders responded to what she saw as a slan-
derous derogation of her patriotism, especially the Nazi press's refusal to
print the book's illustrative subtitle (without which the book might sound
like an attack on an absent military). Did the reviewers fail to notice, Lüders
responded angrily, that the Nazi War Minister General Blomberg had
composed the foreword?[79] She implored the editors to soften their critical
tone and recognize, as the equally right-wing journal *Das deutsche Mädel*
seemingly had, that one had to "do justice to millions of German women
who suffered in those years." Like Heile, Höpker-Aschoff, and many other
liberal authors, Lüders had trouble finding an audience. Hans Bott Verlag,
a firm that took chances in publishing the writing of many liberal figures
during the Third Reich, was willing to take on Lüders as an author so long
as she accepted an honorarium based on sales alone.[80] This proved to be an
unprofitable course for her and for many other Democrats who wished to
publish "political" works.[81] By the middle of the war Lüders found herself
researching an innocuous book tracing recent "transformations in the
fishing economy," a topic in which she had little background or interest.[82]

That Höpker and Lüders produced less critical work than some of their colleagues does not mean they feared arrest or persecution. To some extent they genuinely agreed with aspects of Nazi ideology. More importantly, they needed money. But even where concessions were made to market forces, the liberals continued to provide a nearly limitless reservoir of critical public opinion. The Gestapo remarked with some consternation on the dynamism and viability of liberal cultural and intellectual life after 1933. Because art, literature, and history are so open to interpretation, the police noted, such disciplines could not be regulated as easily as politics, biology, or economics. Contemporary history and biography therefore provided a fertile ground for propagating alternative perspectives of politics and society in a "totalitarian" context.[83] No liberal intellectual combined these two disciplines better than Theodor Heuss.

Reclaiming Naumann's Legacy

Born in 1860, Friedrich Naumann was a Protestant pastor whose eclectic political trajectory, from right-wing "anti-Semite" to left-wing Democrat, reflects almost perfectly the ideological and organizational complexity of German liberalism in the first half of the twentieth century. After spending nearly a decade in Adolf Stöcker's virulently anti-Semitic Christian–Social Party, Naumann began to distance himself from the race-baiting pastor. Beginning in 1895 he transformed the relatively conservative, Evangelical weekly *Die Hilfe* into a more progressive, secular-minded journal. A year later Naumann formed his own political "working group," the National Social Association (NSV). In comparison with Germany's existing liberal parties, the NSV was both friendlier to labor, supporting extensive social welfare policies and collective bargaining, and more actively imperialist, seeking the economic exploitation of overseas colonies in order to subsidize sociopolitical consensus at home. The NSV never drew significant votes at the polls – most workers distrusted its imperialism; most middle-class professionals, intellectuals, and small businessmen worried about its utopian and "socialist" tendencies. But the charismatic Naumann, supported by a few dozen renowned intellectuals like Max Weber and devoted protégés like Heuss, helped foment the intellectual transformation and political reorientation of the bourgeois left.[84]

Joining the Progressives in 1903, Naumann and his NSV associates became the most vocal champions of a unified liberal party, one that could work together with the proletarian left in the name of social and democratic reform. By embracing both nationalism and social justice, charismatic leadership as well as political democratization, the National

Socials hoped to renew liberalism's once dominant hold on the German electorate. During the First World War, Naumann toned down his imperialism, which he increasingly viewed as the handmaiden of reaction, and was elected chairman of the newly minted German Democratic Party in 1919.[85] He died months later, depriving the Weimar Republic of one of its staunchest and most widely respected leaders. In time, Naumann became an almost mythic figure to many liberals, coming to embody all the contradictory ideals – imperialism and internationalism; economic freedom and social justice; nationalism and civil rights; authority and democracy – that both defined and divided Weimar left liberalism.

As Hitler's National Socialist movement displaced traditional conservatism over the course of the 1920s, Naumann's rich legacy evoked claims from the *völkisch* right as well.[86] Wilhelm Stapel, a Wilhelmine Progressive who joined the conservative nationalists (DNVP) after 1918, carried on a lively debate with Heuss for much of the interwar period. Though he would later compliment Heuss's biography of Naumann, Stapel accused Heuss of downplaying the *völkisch*-social aspects of Naumann's politics in an effort to rehabilitate him for the liberal cause.[87] Gerhard Schultze-Pfaelzer, another Nazi fellow traveler, published an article in 1937 noting the ideological continuities between Naumann's National-Social views and Hitler's National Socialism. Heuss refuted Schultze-Pfaelzer's claims, insisting that he was much better positioned to assess Naumann's life's work.[88] Ironically, at the same time that Heuss defended Naumann's legacy against appropriation by the Third Reich, he had to intervene to prevent (unsuccessfully) Naumann's monument from being removed from his birthplace outside Leipzig.[89]

Indeed, Heuss's decision to write a biography of Naumann was largely a consequence of the Nazi seizure of power. First, the end of parliamentary politics and of his teaching career afforded Heuss unexpected free time to pursue his literary interests, including his long-gestating Naumann project. It didn't hurt matters that, just before Heuss's dismissal, the liberal publicist and Naumannite Ernst Jäckh, President of the College of Politics, secured for him a $1,000 grant from Columbia University to work on the book.[90] Unfortunately, just as Naumann's controversial reputation guaranteed an audience, it also left his life's work open to misuse and abuse. Intent on protecting Naumann's legacy from the ideological vortex of National Socialism, Heuss approached the biography as a vehicle with which to counter "respectable" thinkers like Stapel, Oswald Spengler, and Gustav Schmoller, who had taken up Naumann's ideas only to make them more palatable to National Socialism.[91] With the Third Reich in the ascendant, there was no better time to produce a definitive biography articulating the differences between Nazism and Naumannite liberalism.[92]

Heuss himself considered the book one of his greatest accomplishments. For, as Werner Stephan recalls, Heuss gave the censors myriad reasons to forbid its publication.[93] Predictably, the Propaganda Ministry initially took the position "that the life and work of Naumann reaches too far into the present to be seen merely historically." The Reich Literary Chamber (RSK) only approved the biography after Heuss insisted that the "book would in no way draw parallels between Naumann's National Social Association and the NSDAP." Of course, as Heuss told his colleagues, he was more than "happy to affirm that no intellectual or political connection exists or ever existed between Naumann and Adolf Hitler!"[94]

The book is replete with instances of Naumann's liberal democratic sympathies. Conversely, the conservative nationalist political ideology of "Wilhelminism" that Naumann fought against, which is subtly characterized as a precursor to Nazism, does not come off well.[95] The biography is equally striking in its manifest rejection of anti-Semitism and of racial pseudo-science of any kind.[96] Heuss wanted to reflect Naumann's "entire character," work, and times, but also to provide an "alternative model to the National Socialist present." Rather than focus attention on the contradictions of Naumann's National-Social project, Heuss tried to articulate the "historical power" of Naumann's "intellectual and moral nature."[97] Reminding his readers of the favorable attention Naumann paid to social democracy, Heuss suggested a "national socialism" that was more moderate, left-leaning, and cosmopolitan than its Nazi instantiation.[98]

Heuss's recounting of *fin-de-siècle* left liberalism was no less controversial. *Die Hilfe*, Heuss recalled, was about the proletariat's need for "self-help, their struggle for justice, their freedom."[99] In contrast to the Manchesterite liberalism of the "night-watchman state," Naumann represented a "German liberalism" that united "church and proletariat, state responsibility and social order." At the same time Naumann renounced the "emotionally charged anti-capitalism of the period," which manifested itself as "unreflective anti-liberalism" – a veiled criticism of Nazi attitudes to individual freedom and civil society that could not have been lost on readers (or government censors). For Naumann liberalism was not a "catalogue of individual natural laws, but [an] element of positive state mentality [*Staatsgesinnung*] and social health."[100]

To print Naumann's 1901 speech to the National-Social convention in Frankfurt was a provocation, particularly in late 1937, at the moment when Hitler was attempting to remove the last financial, diplomatic, and military barriers to his dictatorship: "Germany thirsts for real liberalism; the English elementary liberalism, this liberal groundwater that should underlie all political tendencies is not present in Germany . . . We need true liberalism; not merely in turn of phrase, but popular and pervasive liberal mentality . . . that we call national social."[101] As we will recall, the RVDP had already interrogated Heuss in 1934 for allowing Bäumer to compare National Socialism unfavorably to British liberalism ("What is Truth?"). Citing these lines from Naumann's 1901 speech could only have been more inflammatory. A concluding defense of Naumann's support for cultural and intellectual pluralism was equally provocative.[102] In short, while Heuss acknowledged the intellectual roots of Hitler's National Socialism in *fin-de-siècle*, National-Social liberalism, he articulated a clear preference for the Wilhelmine version.[103]

Naumann's book is noteworthy for the interest it aroused among the liberal intelligentsia at large.[104] Having supplied source materials or interviews prior to the book's publication, many liberals were ecstatic to see the result of Heuss's efforts.[105] The humanitarian Albert Schweitzer complimented Heuss on the book's accuracy and honesty. In portraying the civility and sense of possibility that characterized Wilhelmine political culture, it recalled a "time that the coming [Nazi] generation could hardly understand."[106] After reading the manuscript others regretted only that the scholarly depth and breadth of Heuss's book (751 pages!) might mean it would not be read widely, especially given that "Naumann truly deserves to be recognized and respected . . . precisely now, in the widest circles . . . He has much to say to the present generation." Perhaps, suggested one publisher, Heuss could produce a more popular book, aimed at younger readers, to appear on the twentieth anniversary of Naumann's death.[107]

Despite its daunting length and "liberal" subject matter, initial sales were respectable. Within a year of its release, Heuss received letters from all over Europe and the United States admiring his portrayal of Naumann and his epoch. Liberal émigrés in particular took the opportunity to congratulate Heuss for showing that there were still Germans who thought freely and differently from the Nazi Party.[108] Numerous National-Social colleagues, including Bosch, Heile, Goetz, Jäckh, and Naumann's brother Johannes, thanked Heuss for redeeming Friedrich Naumann's National-Social ideas for future generations.[109]

No one was more grateful than Gertrud Bäumer, who devoted a long, laudatory review to the book in the March 1938 issue of *Die Frau*. In "The Legacy of an Incomplete Life," Bäumer applauded Heuss's underlying argument that Hitler's National Socialism was not what Naumann intended. He was a dedicated "social" Democrat, Bäumer recalled, motivated by progressive, reform-minded Christianity. Naumann's groundbreaking work, *Democracy and Empire*, hardly predicted the Third Reich. It was intended as an antidote to the Wilhelmine conservatives' (read: Nazis) appropriation of liberal nationalism and imperialism as a means to reach the masses. Echoing her colleague Maurenbrecher from a quarter-century earlier, Bäumer agreed that Wilhelmine Germany was not yet ready for Naumann's "national-social idea." But the massive dislocations of the First World War paved the way, as even "Social Democracy placed itself within the national front." Thus "German politics," she continued, "has [finally] embraced an idea of the state that, through its binding together of the words Nation and Socialism, reflects a close relationship – despite all fundamental differences – with the ideas of Naumann." Unfortunately, this "National Socialist" revolution would remain incomplete until it honestly incorporated the Christian-Social aspects of Naumann's legacy. His National-Social idea, Bäumer concluded, "cannot be wished away from German history . . . the legacy of such incomplete revolutions . . . streams forward into the future."[110]

Thus two of Naumann's most loyal acolytes proclaimed, publicly and without ambiguity, that Hitler failed to comprehend true "National Socialism." Coming at the height of Hitler's power, and buttressed by so much eyewitness testimony, it is hard to imagine a more provocative claim. Yet neither Goebbels, who was frequently agitated by Bäumer's acid commentaries on Nazi propaganda, nor Hitler, who became furious whenever he saw Heuss's name in print, took action.[111] And while the book's second printing was delayed, this seems to have had less to do with censorship than with its modest sales prospects and rampant paper shortages in the midst of the Second World War. The regime never invoked an official ban.[112] Whatever the reasons for the government's restraint, Heuss and Bäumer's public reclamation of Naumann's legacy exemplifies the opportunities for propagating a liberal vision of politics, culture, and society in the eye of the Nazi storm.

IV

Liberalism and the Church Struggle

In April 1935 the Democrat Joseph Williger wrote his friend Georg Gothein regarding the latest Nazi "revisions" to the Weimar constitution. After "translating" various passages in predictably sardonic fashion ("Paragraph 2: The people and individuals have no rights"), Williger concluded by "interpreting" the new laws on religious practice: "Paragraph 5: Prayer will be eradicated and all clergy will be hanged. Then we will have a clear path [to salvation]."[113] At the time Williger was writing, the so-called "German Christians," Evangelical Protestants who renounced the Old Testament because of its "Jewish" provenance, were extending their control of the Lutheran Church. The Vatican had already signed away its moral authority in a Concordat with Hitler two years before.[114] Thus recent histories have tended to stress the high degree of political and ideological collaboration between both German Churches and the Third Reich.[115] Thus yet here we have two liberal democrats, neither particularly well disposed to conservative Christianity, accusing the Nazi regime of the harshest kind of paganism and implying that Christianity was both a victim of and bulwark against National Socialism.[116]

To be sure, many liberal Christians were at first optimistic about Nazi church policy. When Marianne Weber wondered whether it was possible to render blind devotion to Hitler without denying those "things that were owed to God," Bäumer countered that Christianity dealt with matters of individual conscience and National Socialism would take care of everything else.[117] Future members of the oppositional "Confessing Church" (*Bekennende Kirche*), which formed in 1934 to defend the traditional Evangelical liturgy against the German Church, were likewise taken in by the Nazi promise of "strong national leadership and moral renewal." Some, like Otto Dibelius, shared the Nazis' ethnic nationalism and anti-Semitism, while rejecting the theological implications of such views.[118] Liberal Protestants in the Naumannite tradition had always distrusted political Catholicism as well, which they viewed as the purveyor of cultural obscurantism, internationalism, and particularism. Most had little problem with the Third Reich depriving the Vatican of influence.[119]

These accomodationist attitudes began to dissipate, however, in the wake of the Barmen Declaration. Composed in May 1934 by the progressive Swiss theologian Karl Barth, its six brief theses represented an overt declaration of war against Nazi incursions into Christian theology. Signed by hundreds of pastors, it also provided the theoretical basis for the Confessing Church, founded simultaneously by Barth, Dietrich Bonhoeffer, and Martin Niemöller.[120] Barth's unadulterated defense of civil liberties and opposition to Nazi race laws was rare even among his "Confessing" colleagues. Not only did the Bonn theology professor underscore Christ's Semitic origins, but he ignored his rector's demand to employ the Nazi salute at the beginning and end of every lecture. After refusing to take the oath to Hitler required of all state employees, Barth was suspended from his professorship and forced to return to Basel in 1935.[121]

Barth's commitment to freedom, civil rights, and humanist values provided inspiration for liberal Christians who wished to salvage Evangelical Christianity from the clutches of the German Church.[122] Emblematic in this regard is Gertrud Bäumer. Bäumer's attitude to National Socialism had never been uncritical. While she privately disagreed with Weber as to the incompatibility of Nazism with Christianity, Bäumer was willing to have a public debate on the matter in the pages of *Die Frau*.[123] But even this cautious optimism receded in the wake of the church struggle, a conflict Bäumer discussed frequently over the course of the 1930s. The Führer's rabidly anti-Christian Party Secretary Martin Bormann became so infuriated by Bäumer's increasingly critical articles and speaking engagements on behalf of the Confessing Church that he advocated banning her publications (apparently to no avail).[124] Himmler's Gestapo was equally distressed. When Bäumer changed the title of an invited lecture from "Goethe and Marianne" to "Goethe's Piety in Old Age" at a 1943 conference in Leipzig, the State Security Service (SD) inquired immediately. "They had the suspicion," Bäumer wrote Emmy Beckmann, "that religion would be smuggled in [to the speech]." Bäumer managed to reassure the authorities and proceed, but the regime monitored her articles and speeches more closely thereafter.[125]

It is hardly surprising that a Lutheran pastor's daughter like Bäumer should come to resist Himmler and Bormann's new *Kulturkampf* against the Churches.[126] But many secular-minded liberals, whose underlying distrust of political Christianity was palpable, became passionate "defenders of the faith" as well. Early on, Heuss was skeptical about the ability of the Churches to stave off National Socialism, admonishing his friend Otto Dibelius "that a piety founded on party politics is worth little." Unconvinced by her "render unto Caesar" approach to the intrusions of the German Church, Heuss wrote Bäumer that the Protestants had done little to inspire confidence.[127] Gothein and Williger agreed that "the upper echelons of the [Evangelical] Church accept their fate without a whimper."[128] And Tantzen ascribed the moral opposition among the Protestant clergy to a negligible minority.[129]

This skepticism among secular liberals rapidly dissipated in the wake of the Barmen Declaration.[130] Gothein and Williger were ecstatic about the Confessing Church's public challenges to Nazi authority and outraged that Bormann might accuse Catholic priests of moral indecency, while the Nazis permitted Hitler Youth to impregnate fourteen-year-old girls.[131] In a famous 1935 speech at Königsberg, Schacht came to the defense of the Confessing Church as well, accusing the regime of "failing to differentiate" sufficiently between politics and the free practice of religion.[132] A declared agnostic before 1933, Robert Bosch joined the more pious Hans Walz in calling Nazi persecution of the Protestant, Catholic, and Jewish confessions "the greatest danger for culture and humanity."[133] And Hans Robinsohn, a secular-minded Jew, wrote enthusiastically in 1937 that the "oppositional position of church circles, whether Catholic or Protestant," was widespread and that "only a small minority is not expressly in the opposition." Any liberal resistance movement, Robinsohn and Strassmann concurred, would have to tap into Christian antipathy to National Socialism.[134]

Thus, for all their historical mistrust of Roman Catholicism, many Protestant liberals acknowledged the importance of Catholic non-conformity. Bosch and Walz lauded the Catholics for their grassroots resistance to Nazi ideology, while Eduard Dingeldey praised Cardinal Faulhauber and Bishop Galen for salvaging Christian morality.[135] Katharina von Kardorff, an iconoclastic divorcée, made extensive efforts to defend the ecclesiastical independence of the Catholic Church and obtained copies of private letters Galen sent to Hitler protesting the Gestapo's use of violence. A practicing Lutheran of ethnic Jewish background, Marie Baum became a Galen devotee as well.[136]

Current scholarship might stress the ideological symbiosis between National Socialism and the Christian Churches, but contemporary liberals clearly viewed Christianity as an ally against Fascism.[137] Perhaps Weimar Democrats perceived something of themselves in the Evangelical Church's initially ambivalent, intermittently hopeful attitude toward National Socialism. As soon as these pretensions were shattered in the 1930s, liberal Christians came to identify with the arguments of the Confessing Church. More pragmatically, secular liberals realized that the Protestant and Catholic Churches, with their deep institutional roots, profound moral authority, and vast constituencies, constituted an important vehicle for non-conformity and the defense of civil liberties.[138] When pressed to recall the extent of German resistance to National Socialism, Marie Baum would eulogize primarily "the courageous opposition of Niemöller, Bodelschwinghs and the Evangelical Bishop Wurm, the Catholic Bishops Faulhaber and von Galen, whose sermons, multiplied in typescript, found their way into all hands."[139] If anything improved the traditionally fraught relationship between liberalism and Christianity, Catholicism in particular, it was the persecution and (certainly uneven) resistance of the Churches during the Third Reich. This experience, more than German liberalism's innate "conservatism," helps elucidate the decision of many Weimar Democrats to join the Christian Democrats (CDU/CSU) after 1945.[140]

V

Liberalism and the Academy

In spring 1936 Hans Robinsohn composed a report looking back on the first three years of the Third Reich. While the general population remained uncritical of Nazi intrusions into cultural and intellectual life, there was "a small minority" of liberals who were "not truly resigned." These liberal academics, Robinsohn reasoned, might still provide the "intellectual and political leadership . . . for the reconstruction" of German culture and society.[141] Scholars paint a less rosy picture. The historian Ingo Haar argues that *völkisch* ideologues quickly displaced "liberals like Friedrich Meinecke, Hermann Oncken, and Eckart Kehr" across the social sciences.[142] The subsequent "participation of the [liberal] academic elite at Heidelberg and other universities," writes Steven Remy, "was of vital importance to the regime's project of 'racial' purification at home, the concomitant war of expansion, and its imperialist economic and cultural offensives in occupied Europe."[143] These " 'antiliberal democrats' . . . advocated authoritarianism to address the nation's chronic political instability and to create a true 'democracy' based on a unified 'people's community.' "[144] Even ostensibly liberal academics either embraced or accommodated the Third Reich.[145]

Such blanket accusations fail to distinguish sufficiently between individuals like Alfred Weber or Walter Goetz, who opposed National Socialism in virtually all respects, and Democratic academics like Erich Obst and Willy Hellpach, who were more enthusiastic about the disciplines of "research on the east [*Ostforschung*]" and "racial anthropology [*Rassekunde*]" propounded by Nazi research institutes. These claims also fail to distinguish between the myriad areas of potential non-conformity and accommodation.[146] All members of university faculties were ultimately required to join the National Socialist Association of University Lecturers (Nationalsozialistische Dozentenbund). Still, relatively few non-Jewish academics were among the 25 to 30 percent of the professoriate who were discharged by 1939. Nor do such statistics differentiate adequately between academics who were already near retirement age and/or chose voluntary retirement and those who were forced out against their will.[147] Liberal intellectuals were neither victims nor collaborators, but free-thinking individuals motivated by the same range of factors we have encountered elsewhere: age, pragmatism, economic wherewithal, and, of course, ideology.

The Exceptional Case of Alfred Weber

The particulars of Alfred Weber's resistance and retirement highlight both the challenges and the opportunities confronting many liberal academics in 1933. Though never as well known as his famous brother Max, the younger Weber lived four decades longer, enjoying a growing international reputation as a geographer, political scientist, sociologist, and historian.[148] He was also head of Heidelberg's famous Institut für Sozial- und Staatswissenschaft (Institute for Social and Political Science, or Insosta), an international center of social scientific research, whose alumni included Weber himself, Erich Fromm, Karl Mannheim, Richard Thoma, Karl Jaspers, and Norbert Elias.[149] The University of Heidelberg had a long and indelible liberal tradition well before Alfred took over the Insosta in the early 1920s. But this reputation was enhanced as Weber attracted a new generation of socially and politically engaged intellectuals eager to transform Germany in the wake of the First World War.[150] A co-founder of the DDP, Weber was also a devoted Naumannite who supported the more national, social, and authoritarian direction of the party in the 1920s.[151]

Weber's latent pessimism regarding the viability of the Republic, however, never dampened his distaste for National Socialism and he protested against inviting Hitler to form a government.[152] In the wake of the 5 March elections Weber went further, denouncing the flood of young stormtroopers who were posting Nazi placards and swastika flags on prominent campus buildings. Not only was this a clear affront to the principles of academic freedom; it was a violation of Article 3 of the Weimar constitution, which permitted only the state flag of red, black, and gold to be raised in an official capacity.[153] On 6 March Weber wrote an angry letter to the mayor of Heidelberg demanding that the administration prevent this kind of "anti-constitutional" activity on the part of the National Socialists. Next day Weber insisted that the local police tear down a swastika banner that had been attached to the Insosta. The police chief complied, but was subsequently put on leave by the new Nazi Reich Commissar, Robert Wagner. On 9 March the swastikas were restored. Undaunted, Weber decided to close his institute outright.

Weber had no legal basis for this protest action. In a radio address a few days after Weber closed the institute, Hitler announced a decree of the Reich President Hindenburg mandating the use of the Nazi swastika on public buildings. Weber's subsequent refusal to permit such displays constituted an illegal act. He also had no official institutional support. Heidelberg's pusillanimous president, the liberal historian Willy Andreas, ordered all Heidelberg faculties to attach swastika flags to their buildings. Andreas also refused Weber's request to protect the left-liberal historian Hans von Eckardt from being terminated according to the new Law for the Protection of the Civil Service. These sycophantic attempts to palliate the Nazi regime, in contrast to Weber's defiance, would cause Heuss to demur in supporting Andreas's bid to retain the university presidency after 1945.[154]

In any event, on 7 March the Nazi paper *Volksgemeinschaft* (*VG*) began to run derisive articles undermining Weber's credibility. Some of his students responded with indignant letters, justifying their professor's stand, and they were soon followed by Weber himself.[155] So began a heated dialogue between Weber and the *VG* that lasted for the better part of a month. On 11 March there appeared an interesting article, worth quoting at length:

> . . . We would see no reason to concern ourselves with this citizen further, if Mr Weber himself did not give us cause to! [in taking down the swastika] . . . We do not want to discuss here the "measureless international importance" of the "great professor Weber". We leave that to the trained specialists. We want to touch on Weber "the politician" here. As a sociologist, Mr Weber should have at least enough insight into political reality to foresee the futility of his protests. In his demonstrative actions Mr Weber appears not to have considered that, through his protest against the government of the new Germany, he might draw colleagues into his own plight who hold perhaps a different political viewpoint. In other words: if we therefore attack the "Insosta" . . . that means an attack on Herr Professor Weber alone! If you close your institute as a sign of protest, you do not hurt us, but German students, and probably a great many Jews as well, whom you have tested and have ostensibly found "sociologically worthy" . . . One last remark: our assertion [in previous articles] of your inadequate mastery of the German language has created the impression in some circles that we want to "belittle" you arbitrarily! Should you consider it necessary, we will happily publish samples without any commentary . . . and we are convinced that these samples will show how mild our judgement has been with regard to your "global relevance".[156]

While sarcastic to the core, this diatribe has an inherent reserve and civility notably absent in Nazi attacks on left-wing political opponents.

Another crucial premise of these exchanges is that no one questioned Weber's right to intellectual freedom. According to the *VG*, it was Weber, the elitist academic mandarin, and not the Nazi government who had shut down an entire academic institute to make a political point. Facing similar protests from colleagues and students who wished to continue their teaching and research, Weber gave up the fight in late March.[157]

It is clear that Weber's failure to insulate the Insosta from National Socialism as well as the careerist preoccupations of his colleagues had a profound effect on his outlook. During a March meeting at his cousin Marianne's, for example, Karl Jaspers observed that Nazism was a cloud that would soon pass. Weber begged to differ: Nazism was a "cloud that will soon douse us with poison and acid rain."[158] A few days later Weber announced his retirement from teaching, effective from 1 August 1933. On 27 April the new Nazi Gauleiter, Robert Wagner, issued Weber's official "documents of dismissal."[159] Interestingly, he was permitted to continue teaching when he wished, to administer the Rockefeller Fellowship Program, and to travel to international conferences at will. There is absolutely no archival evidence of physical threats or of a government request for his resignation. Weber's retirement appears voluntary.[160]

Certainly Weber's decision had something to do with preserving his personal reputation and privileged academic lifestyle. Over the course of March, Weber had become painfully sensitive to attacks on his "German national" character. He insisted, for example, that the Insosta was guided "on the basis of free market principles and a national spirit."[161] When the *Volksgemeinschaft* questioned Weber's patriotism, citing his supposed indifference to the proletarian revolutions of 1918–19, Weber again responded defensively: "In November 1918 I had better things to do than to protest against the waving of particular banners. At that time in Berlin I took part from the first day of revolution onwards in forming Freikorps against the [Communist] Spartacus Bund."[162] The Freikorps, it should be remembered, was a hyper-nationalist, largely right-wing paramilitary unit, formed to combat the revolutionary left.

Still, whatever personal slights Weber experienced in the Nazi press, his early retirement was *not* coerced.[163] He could have protested longer and risked more. He chose not to. The odds of effecting real change through the brazen repudiation of Nazi coordination policies were simply too overwhelming. Rather than accommodate himself to the new state of affairs, Weber decided to pursue his "non-conformist" intellectual agenda in comfortable semi-retirement. He fought harder against the Nazi takeover of Heidelberg than many Democratic colleagues, including

Walter Goetz in Leipzig.[164] But Weber's abrupt change of heart indicates how daunting it must have been for even the most principled and influential academics to sustain their opposition in the face of goose-stepping students, cowardly administrators, and career-minded colleagues.[165] Weber's two-week refusal to coordinate the Insosta is the exception; his passive intellectual non-conformity over the ensuing twelve years the rule.

Academic Non-Conformity

For many liberals the most offensive aspect of the Third Reich was its disdain for intellectual freedom. As Eduard Dingeldey lamented to a friend in November 1937, "If I think back to my student days, not only to the total freedom from material cares ... but more than anything else the related drive toward freedom [*Freiheitsdrang*] ... what a world has since drowned."[166] Writing Gothein in March 1934, Joseph Williger contended that the Nazis had lowered academic standards on purpose. Since the Third Reich was founded on "stupidity and brutality [*Dummheit und Brutalität*]," ignorant students meant more support for the regime. Unfortunately, Williger concluded, this also meant that the average university graduate could not use the German language properly.[167] Or, as Heuss put it, in the Nazi educational system "knowledge was inconsequential, while the will, or in any case that which one understands as the expression of will, was valued highly." In making supposedly minor concessions to the philistine spirit of National Socialism, an academic colleague wrote to Heuss, scholars forget "what indispensable intellectual values ... hang in the balance."[168]

Thus, just as many intellectuals retreated into their ivory towers, a number of liberal academics took up the cause of intellectual freedom. Marie Baum, herself a "non-Aryan", publicly denounced the racial "cleansing of the university" and defended Jewish colleagues against dismissal. She also risked arrest by teaching long after the Nazi brownshirts had demanded her termination.[169] The liberal poet Ricarda Huch, whose august reputation, indisputable patriotism, and unambiguous racial status made her less vulnerable, advocated intellectual opposition at every turn.[170] Moving from Freiburg to Jena in 1935, Huch made a point of collecting literature critical of the Nazis, including Heuss's banned diatribe against National Socialism, *Hitlers Weg*. She defended Jewish colleagues at both universities and published books and articles suggesting the moral and political corruption of the regime.[171] As a state employee the Democratic law professor Heinrich Gerland fulfilled government requests to organize welfare contributions, but made few concessions to Nazi political or legal theory.[172] Alfred Weber and Walter Goetz took their premature hiatus from full-time teaching as an opportunity to write harsh appraisals of racist trends in sociology, history, and anthropology.[173]

Goetz's case is illustrative of the potential for academic non-conformity. After acquiescing to forced retirement in spring 1933, the Leipzig historian grew indignant when he realized the terms of his *Emeritierung*. Unlike Weber's university, which granted him full rights as an emeritus professor – including the opportunity for part-time teaching – the University of Leipzig prohibited Goetz from any official contact with students. The university likewise refused to pay him the part-time salary that "active" retirement normally entailed. No doubt Goetz's inauspicious treatment had something to do with Nazism's deeper roots in Saxony as well as the fact that Goetz never enjoyed Weber's international reputation.[174]

Frustrated at the repeated denials of the Saxon administration to explain his prejudicial treatment, Goetz enlisted the legal services of his Democratic colleague Eduard Hamm, the former Weimar Economics Minister and future 20 July conspirator, in order to request reinstatement. In building his case, Goetz did make some ideological concessions. He noted for example the many similarities between Naumann's National-Social and Hitler's National Socialist movements and downplayed his involvement in the republican paramilitary (Reichsbanner) before 1933. Nevertheless, in July 1935, nearly two years after his dismissal, the Saxon government reversed its decision. It restored Goetz's emeritus status and paid him twenty-two months of lost salary; this despite the open hostility of the Nazi student union and of many Nazi professors.[175] All the while Goetz upheld his arguments against Nazi racial theories and published articles insisting on the need to respect "fundamental [human and civil] liberties."[176]

In the end, it is easy to exaggerate both the overt repression exercised by the Nazi regime and the "totalitarian temptation" that supposedly prevented liberal academics from resisting a Nazi worldview.[177] Many liberals rejected the most offensive aspects of Nazi cultural and intellectual policy, such as the subordination of the Churches, the coordination of the universities, and the suppression of intellectual freedom. Those who did endorse Nazi-influenced ethnopolitical or sociobiological research, as we shall see in the next chapters, generally did so because they apprehended continuities between Weimar liberalism and National Socialism, not because they supported Fascism, war, or genocide. After losing her teaching position in 1933, the "non-Aryan" Democrat Marie Baum, who would go on to write the preface to the first German edition of *The Diary of Anne Frank*, acknowledged that her liberal colleagues could have done more to counter the Nazi tide. But she never believed they were peculiarly susceptible to Nazism.[178]

VI

The War for Intellectual Freedom

Even in democracies, military conflict is rarely conducive to fostering civil liberties. From the French Revolution to the Cold War, liberal democracies have deprived writers, artists, and academics of some measure of intellectual freedom, physical liberty and, occasionally, of their lives. For liberal intelligentsia living in a Fascist regime in the midst of the bloodiest war in history, the climate could hardly be hospitable. We nevertheless need to be careful about writing off liberal cultural and intellectual life after September 1939. Though repressive by the standards of the western democracies, wartime Nazi Germany afforded many individuals the space to produce and disseminate liberal ideas. As it did in Allied countries, the war brought greater restrictions on speech, mobility, even on paper. So long as one did not fly too close to the Nazi sun, however, it was possible to sustain liberal discourse into the last years of the war. A perfect example is Theodor Heuss.

As we will recall, Heuss dutifully joined the Reichsverband der Deutschen Presse (RVDP) in 1933, and for another seven years was *relatively* free to pursue his literary interests.[179] The gradual erosion of Heuss's intellectual freedom, like that of many liberals, was closely linked to the radicalization of Nazi domestic and foreign policy. Heuss lost his position as editor of *Die Hilfe* at the end of 1936, just as Goering took over the German economy and Hitler determined to accelerate rearmament. With the economy, army, and civil service subordinated to Hitler, and war on the horizon in autumn 1938, Heuss received a message from the RVDP containing new regulations on the "free exchange of ideas."[180] Matters got worse after Hitler called off the Battle of Britain in October 1940. A few weeks later, the Reich Literary Chamber (RSK) wrote Heuss and his publisher regarding a recent biography, *Anton Dohrn in Naples*. Dohrn was an internationally renowned zoologist whose work had fascinated Heuss ever since he befriended Dohrn's son Boguslav at university.[181] Despite approving the more controversial Naumann and Poelzig biographies (see below) just a couple of years earlier, the RSK now demanded a copy of the Dohrn book and proof that the author (Heuss) was a member of the requisite organizations. Heuss secured permission to continue writing, but the literary noose had tightened noticeably.[182] As Heuss would relate in early February 1941, "one [no longer] sends political or historical reflections over the border, only privately."[183]

Little did Heuss know that he had incurred Hitler's personal wrath. In 1939 Heuss had published a biography of the Expressionist architect, artist, and filmmaker Hans Poelzig. Heuss was close to the left-leaning Poelzig, Vice-President of the Prussian Academy of Art and a leading Weimar set designer. Already before the war Heuss, Naumann, and Poelzig had helped found the German Craft Federation (Deutsche Werkbund), which later sponsored proponents of the Bauhaus movement like Walter Gropius and Mies van der Rohe.[184] When Poelzig was fired from the Prussian Academy in February 1933, Heuss came to his defense, writing an article deploring the "illiberalism and impoverishment in intellectual matters" following the Nazi seizure of power. After Poelzig's death in 1936, Heuss began working on the architect's biography, which he published with relatively little fanfare three years later.[185] At the same time someone in the Führer's entourage (probably Bormann) brought to Hitler's attention Heuss's openly critical 1932 attack on National Socialism, *Hitlers Weg*. When the architect-turned-Munitions Minister Albert Speer followed up by forwarding the Poelzig book – Hitler already detested the socialist architect's "degenerate" aesthetic – the Führer flew into a rage and insisted the biography be confiscated.[186]

As a result of Hitler's intervention, Heuss was fined 50 marks for breaking a 1937 law requiring all authors to be members of the RSK. Heuss had been allowed to bypass this law twice in the previous three years, first with his Naumann biography (1937) and later with the Dohrn book (1940). Further reflecting the inconsistent nature of Reich repression, upon Heuss's protestation that he lacked the funds to pay the fine – which, he pointed out, had never been levied in the past – the RSK repealed it with a warning. In March 1941, at the same time as he was ordered to pay the fine, Heuss was required to submit his original Poelzig manuscript to the RSK's Oversight Commission for the Protection of National Socialist Publications (Prüfungskommission zum Schutz des Nationalsozialistischen Schrifttum). In April 1941, due evidently to Hitler's involvement, the commission decided that Heuss's "work could no longer be allowed to appear as a matter of principle."[187] Upon noticing Heuss's byline in the liberal *Frankfurter Zeitung* a few months later, Hitler angrily demanded never to see Heuss's name in print again.[188]

Heuss was bewildered at this sudden reversal of fortune, remarking that he had "once again become *persona non grata* without being given any reason why."[189] Undaunted, he consulted his former Democratic colleague, Werner Stephan. Stephan was an erstwhile DDP party secretary and journalist whom Goebbels had retained in the Reichspropaganda Ministry after 1933. In 1938 Stephan joined the NSDAP, advancing to personal consultant of the Reich Press Chief Otto Dietrich.[190] Ignoring the Führer's transparent intention to ban Heuss's work outright, Stephan followed the letter of Hitler's request by facilitating Heuss's adoption of a pseudonym ("Thomas Brackheim"), which was registered with the RSK in July 1942.[191] The RSK and RVDP would continue to raise questions about Thomas Brackheim's racial background and political reliability, but the pen-name, an open secret at best, alleviated much of the pressure. Afterward Heuss hardly troubled himself about the ban, speaking openly of his reasons for a pseudonym. Publishers seemed unconcerned as well, coming to Heuss with multiple projects, including a proposal for a massive biography of Robert Bosch.[192]

Heuss had contemplated a Bosch biography for some time before the industrialist's death. He had already written a biography of Bosch's colleague, the liberal industrialist Georg von Siemens, and edited a collection of essays in honor of Bosch's seventieth birthday in September 1931. Still, Heuss had reservations regarding the difficulty of composing a "life picture of the democratic businessman in the time of dictatorship." That another liberal writer, Theodor Bäuerle, had since undertaken a semi-independent Bosch biography of his own did nothing to facilitate the project. Circumstances changed in 1942, when Bosch determined that Bäuerle's draft was too anecdotal, schematic, and "apolitical" for his tastes. As the historian Joachim Scholtyseck puts it, Bosch "was far too proud to have to read between the lines that his political principles corresponded to precisely the opposite of that which was pursued by the National Socialist worldview." In spring 1942, just before his death, Bosch had a chance to read Heuss's earlier biography of the nineteenth-century chemist Justus von Liebig. Convinced that Heuss could explain complex scientific matters to a lay audience – Bosch was an engineer and inventor, after all – he offered his life story and extensive archives to Heuss. The final impetus for Heuss's decision to undertake the biography may have been Goebbels's attempt to turn Bosch's 1942 funeral into a glorification of Nazi industry, a vulgar display that misrepresented the progressive Democrat's life and work.[193]

This book was potentially more controversial than the Naumann biography. By the time the latter appeared in 1937 Naumman had been dead for nearly two decades and so had written nothing directly endorsing or condemning the Third Reich. Bosch, on the other hand, had expressed his criticism throughout the 1930s, actively opposing the regime in some cases and disregarding it in others. Heuss nevertheless hoped to publish the book sooner rather than later. Fritz Seitz, one of Bosch's more sympathetic Nazi associates, was realistic. "Perhaps," wrote Seitz, "the biography can have some effect in quite another historical context than we see before us today." One "chapter will prove especially difficult to write: what was Robert Bosch's perspective on National Socialism . . . Here perhaps the incorruptible love of truth of the history writer will indeed have to take into account the tactical requirements and interest of the [Bosch] firm in choice of material and formulation."[194] Such qualms did little to dampen Heuss's enthusiasm for the project. Nor did his wife's recurring illness, the destruction of his Berlin apartment in August 1943, or the fact that thousands of additional documents were lost during the 1944 bombing of Stuttgart. Indeed, Heuss's subsequent move to Heidelberg offered him and Elly a safer environment, free of the omnipresent tumult (and surveillance) of Berlin, where he could concentrate on the momentous task at hand.[195]

In the meantime Heuss submitted articles to his favorite venues, including the still extant *Frankfurter Zeitung*. The liberal paper's content had changed noticeably since 1933, but Goebbels remained loath to attack the *FrZtg* too vigorously.[196] The editor Benno Reifenberg even made a special effort to obtain permission from the RSK to publish Heuss's articles under his new pseudonym.[197] Although Heuss chose to focus on less controversial "historical" topics, these included articles on the "liberal" revolutions of 1789 and 1848 as well as on famous liberals like Georg von Siemens and Ricarda Huch.[198] Unfortunately the days of the *Frankfurter Zeitung* – and with it Heuss's days as a working journalist – were numbered. With the escalation of hostilities, scarcity of paper, and heightened police presence – not to mention the enduring hostility of Hitler – the *FrZtg* was officially discontinued in early summer 1943. Heuss was given final notice a few weeks later.[199]

Over the next few months Heuss faced mounting pressures to conform. In April 1944 he was ordered to submit new documents to the RVDP proving his Aryan origins and literary merits (!).[200] Like many liberals with superficial ties to the 20 July plotters, Heuss became more furtive after the failed coup. He stopped speaking openly of his pseudonym, writing the culture editor of the *Neue Wiener Tageblatt* "confidentially" that he had changed his name when a "ranking political figure raised objections to my publicistic activity." This ban had "nothing to do with the content of my work," Heuss added reassuringly, "but my earlier political activity."

He signed the letter "Heil Hitler!", a mode of address he had religiously avoided in the past.[201]

After the June 1944 Normandy landing, and after 20 July in particular, the situation deteriorated. Democrats experienced additional travel restrictions and liberal publishers found it difficult to publish a critical word. Many magazines encountered outright bans or regulations that made turning a profit nearly impossible: for example in the government not permitting sales outside German-occupied Europe (a rapidly shrinking market).[202] Now even the semblance of conspiracy, such as the periodic walks that Heuss and Dietrich took in the Berliner Tiergarten, became too dangerous. As Heuss's successor at *Die Hilfe*, Werner Ziegenfuss, wrote Wilhelm Heile in December 1944, it was no longer feasible to stay vital and profitable.[203] Or, as Heuss explained to Sissi Brentano in November, "it's not necessary for you to send me your long essay. Its 'value' today would never be appreciated."[204] "The 20 July was a really hard blow," the liberal publisher Max Wiessner noted in late 1944, "and has cost us much blood." Though intended to liberate Germany from Hitler's increasingly repressive rule, Wiessner concluded ironically, it was the failure of the plot that had forced liberals to relinquish "our last planks of [intellectual] independence."[205]

VII

For those who cared to explore it, there was sufficient room for liberal thought and expression after 1933. As late as 1938, the Gestapo would bemoan the powerful liberal undercurrent that continued to "oppose the spirit of the times" in "the administration, the economy, the free professions, publishing, the universities, the schools and other educational institutions, the theater and liberal theology."[206] At least initially, the Democrats' greatest challenge was not government repression, but a changing marketplace of culture and ideas. In facing the erosion of free speech, wrote the Democrat Margaret Schecker in 1933, one might presume "the entire population would become outraged and not simply lay the news to one side and go about their daily work." But after fifteen years of cultural experimentation and intellectual polarization, most Germans preferred simplistic headlines, pulp fiction, and broad comedies. Public apathy, indeed popular approbation, Heuss observed, was at least as decisive as government repression in explaining the change in cultural and intellectual content.[207]

This indifference dissipated as Nazi censorship began to exercise a more profound effect on cultural or intellectual content. The subtle change in consumer tastes, combined with Goebbels's obsession with accommodating public opinion, paved the way for a minor renaissance in liberal cultural and intellectual life. According to Gertrud Bäumer, "the reader displays a growing antipathy toward 'exaggeration', toward large-print headlines 'thundering pompously' in sensationalist fashion, behind which often lies nothing. This no longer has an effect on the reader. He wants moderation. He desires more civilized material and worthwhile reporting."[208] While the "difficulties of freely exchanging [critical] ideas . . . are obvious," added the Badenese liberal Gustav Wittig, many Germans "spoke very openly" on a variety of topics. In return for political acquiescence and economic complacency, the Nazis appeared to make notable concessions to bourgeois cultural and intellectual life.[209]

The liberal experience also confirms that cultural and intellectual "coordination," unlike its political or economic variant, was hardly a linear process defined by a relatively systematic repression of alternative points of view.[210] In the opening flurry of *Gleichschaltung*, to be sure, a great many liberals modified their discourse to mollify the censors, turning their attention from politics and economics to biography and history.[211] Nevertheless, such works still expressed a liberal, often critical engagement with the Nazi present. There were liberal (if no longer Jewish-owned) presses that profited from publishing books and newspapers by prominent Democrats.[212] Finally, we cannot ignore the influence of economic recovery and of the liberals' own clever negotiation of changing political circumstances in maintaining a cultural and intellectual space in which to propagate liberal ideas.[213] Hardly radical enough to warrant extirpation, Democratic writers, journalists, and academics were successful in preserving elements of a liberal civil society and democratic public sphere that outlived the Third Reich, helping to provide the intellectual foundation for both postwar German republics.[214]

CHAPTER THREE

"The Woman" in the Third Reich:
Gertrud Bäumer, Social Policy, and the Liberal Women's Movement

I

For many years women were deemed to be Nazism's first victims. According to the conventional wisdom, from the moment Hitler took power women were pushed out of politics, relegated to the home, and subjected to a regime of reproductive totalitarianism.[1] In the 1980s new research on women in the Third Reich began to complicate matters. Some historians now suggested that National Socialism harnessed women's collaboration, not by exercising fear and oppression, but through generous welfare programs, nationalist propaganda, and the clever manipulation of prevailing conceptions of motherhood.[2] Questions of perpetration and victimhood receded, replaced by growing interest in the affinities between the Weimar and Nazi-era women's movement.[3] After all, women had also faced significant barriers to inclusion in German politics, culture, and society during the Weimar Republic. Not least of these hurdles was the movement's own conflicted relationship with *völkisch* nationalism.[4] While liberal women's interest in eugenics to some extent reflected a "progressive" devotion to health care and education, it also revealed a sociobiological commitment to "improve" the race not dissimilar to that of National Socialism.[5] Given these ambivalences, it is hardly surprising to find continuities as well as breaks after 1933.[6] The question is: what kinds of continuity?

No Democrat sheds more light on the problem of women's collaboration and victimhood, on liberal continuity or discontinuity, than Gertrud Bäumer.[7] A DDP vice-chairwoman, professor at the College of Politics, and longtime editor of the feminist monthly *Die Frau*, Bäumer was also a

German nationalist and imperialist.[8] During the Weimar Republic the Lutheran pastor's daughter opposed legalizing abortion (except in cases of rape or incest) and attacked left-wing feminists for their lack of patriotism.[9] Several historians have intimated that Bäumer, despite her liberal pedigree, was at least partially responsible for the proto-fascistic tendencies within the German women's movement after 1914.[10] Others contend that, regardless of Bäumer's nationalist proclivities, her broad defense of women's rights and prerogatives reflected a progressive, forward-looking way of thinking.[11] Most recently Kevin Repp and Angelika Schaser have proposed a more complex picture of Bäumer's activities after 1933, which Schaser characterizes as a vacillation between "accommodation and resistance."[12] Notwithstanding these contradictory claims, historians have paid little attention to Bäumer and her colleagues after 1933. Neither Nazism's worst victims nor its most enthusiastic collaborators, liberal women ostensibly retreated into private life, declining to engage in the vital social and political questions of the day.[13]

Yet Democratic women, like their male counterparts, enjoyed considerable freedom of action and followed a number of paths after 1933. Where concessions were made, they had little to do with slavish emulation of Nazi policies or, even primarily, with a fear of persecution. Liberal women could never abide Nazi conservatives who endorsed traditional women's roles of "Kinder, Kirche, Küche."[14] At the same time, many contributors to *Die Frau* were cautiously optimistic about the NSDAP's national and social dynamism, which they loosely associated with Naumann's antebellum National-Social movement. By encouraging women's commitment to biological health, motherhood, and social service, they reasoned, Nazi rhetoric drew on "biomaternalist" traditions inherent to Wilhelmine liberal feminism.[15]

Still, Bäumer and her colleagues demanded something more than the "mechanistic" political and legal equality they attributed to the British or French women's movement. By attempting to construct a more inclusive, "feminized" vision of the German *Volksgemeinschaft*, the contributors to *Die Frau* adumbrated an early model of "second wave" or "difference" feminism hardly seen elsewhere in Europe at this time.[16] Thus *Die Frau* provided a real liberal alternative somewhere between active collaboration and passive victimhood, between right-wing conservatism and western feminism, a progressive space in which "female actors could exercise agency within a system that had stripped women of most parameters of power."[17] If Bäumer and her colleagues occasionally seemed to coopt Nazi ideas or took care to disguise their critiques, they also promoted a liberal, even "feminist" agenda that contrasts starkly with the masculinist discourse prevalent under the Third Reich.

II

Gertrud Bäumer and *Die Frau* after 1933

No historian has made an extensive study of Gertrud Bäumer's feminist monthly *Die Frau*. This is due largely to the erroneous assumption, formulated in the wake of Bäumer's denazification proceedings and maintained ever since, that *Die Frau* was an apolitical mouthpiece: "for the most part refraining from commenting on the position of women and discussing laws affecting them under the Third Reich . . . it withdrew from the political scene . . . Instead, the magazine devoted itself to the propagation of a vague Christian mysticism."[18] Even the most superficial survey of *Die Frau* after 1933 indicates otherwise.[19] For the duration of the Third Reich high-profile Democrats like Bäumer, Marie Baum, Emmy Beckmann, Marie Lüders, and Marianne Weber produced articles on major issues of the day.[20] Bäumer also avoided most of the conflicts faced by Heuss's *Die Hilfe* or Reifenberg's *Frankfurter Zeitung* without losing as much content.[21] Perhaps it was the journal's relative obscurity or the Nazis' dismissive attitude toward women in politics; perhaps it was a result of Bäumer's more expert negotiation of the often capricious but nonetheless porous intellectual terrain of the Third Reich; perhaps it was due in part to Bäumer's innate National-Social sympathies or even to the intermittent intervention of her party colleague Werner Stephan.[22] Whatever the reason, Bäumer's *Die Frau* furnishes a rich and variegated source for tracing the evolution of liberal opinion after 1933.

Born near Hamburg in 1873, *Die Frau*'s longtime publisher was the daughter of a liberal Evangelical pastor. Bäumer cultivated a strong Christian faith and dedication to social issues throughout her life. Her interest in politics emerged later, when she came into contact, as a young high school teacher, with Friedrich Naumann's National Social Association, the first liberal party to endorse female suffrage.[23] Encouraged by Naumann, Bäumer took a Ph.D. in German literature in 1904 and was elected head of the German Women's Association (Bund deutscher Frauen, or BDF) in 1910. Bäumer also moved in with her mentor in the women's movement, Helene Lange, maintaining what they likened to a "Boston marriage" after the novels of Henry James. Late-Victorian discretion has left few sources with which to gauge the depth of their relationship, except to say that it was profoundly intimate.[24] Bäumer subsequently took over the editing chores for Lange's groundbreaking feminist journal, *Die Frau*.[25]

As both a progressive social reformer and an imperialist preoccupied by nationalism and eugenics, Bäumer embodied German liberalism's fraught relationship with modernity.[26] She sympathized with the working classes and vaguely accepted Naumann's conception of "German socialism." But Bäumer flatly rejected the Marxist demand for social revolution. Unlike her National-Social colleagues Anton Erkelenz or Rudolf Breitscheid, she had little appreciation of the class struggle or the plight of the so-called "proletariat."[27] Her approach to social problems was more communitarian, recalling the corporatist arrangements of the pre-industrial era.[28] Like many feminists before and since, Bäumer viewed the world more through the lens of gender difference than of ethnic or class distinctions. For Bäumer a "focus on women's biological functions, rights, and duties helped to forge bonds across the boundaries of class" and paralleled her "conviction that modernity's current ills could be transcended without sacrificing its genuine promise."[29] Thus, despite her lack of revolutionary fervor, Bäumer forcefully articulated the demands of the Wilhelmine women's movement. She spearheaded women's suffrage reform and proposed a "feminization" of society that presaged second wave feminism in advocating a workplace and public sphere that both invited and reinforced women's unique contributions.[30]

Bäumer defended the Weimar republican order even though she was increasingly pessimistic about its prospects for national and social unity. In her 1924 work, *The Crisis of the Soul*, Bäumer quoted Hermann Hesse in blaming Europe's decline on the "Asiatic ideal" embodied in *The Brothers Karamazov*. Dostoevsky's work expressed the "repudiation of every firmly rooted ethic or morality in favor of understanding everything, tolerating everything, a new, dangerous gruesome piety . . . a wholly amoral way of thinking and feeling." In order to reintroduce "a holistic, healthy consciousness" into German social and political life, Bäumer countered, one must nurture "the creative power, the creative will" of German culture.[31] Pursuing her analogy between postwar Germany and the novels of Dostoevksy, Bäumer argued that Weimar, like Raskolnikov, could only be "relieved of moral confusion" by privileging emotion over sober rationality and empathy over class-obsessed materialism.[32] Much of this neo-romantic, vaguely racist, and subtly anti-republican rhetoric is reminiscent of National Socialism. Still, Bäumer's skepticism regarding democracy's long-term prospects always had less to do with the republican state form than with the German people's seeming inability to master it.

Indeed, unlike some "graduates" of Naumann's *fin-de-siècle* National Social movement, Bäumer never entertained thoughts of joining the Nazi ranks.[33] Germany required a Führer who could unite all Germans behind a common national, social, and democratic mission: a liberal Naumann, not a fascist Hitler.[34] Bäumer was certainly reticent about employing the term "liberal" or "democrat" to describe the new state party and lauded the Young German merger as a way out of the "asphalt-democratic Jew atmosphere of the DDP." But she continued to support the Republic, individual rights, and free expression, publishing a series of articles attacking Nazi Judeophobia and urging voters not to abandon the erstwhile liberal parties.[35] Hitler's cynical exploitation of the Weimar constitution troubled Bäumer, and she was one of the few leading Democrats to protest the Reichstag delegation's decision to endorse the Enabling Law.[36] National Socialism, Bäumer wrote in March 1933, constituted "a passionate and ... unjustified struggle" against republican principles in which "popular democratic ideas and convictions are noticeably mixed with fascist authoritarian ones."[37] Bäumer also worked to dispel the conventional wisdom that women were more attracted to Hitler than men.[38] She reserved special vitriol for the other bourgeois parties, whose sycophantic attempts to accommodate Hitler made it impossible for the few who wished to oppose him.[39]

Having warned against the Nazis' "primitive instinct of violence and fear," however, Bäumer nonetheless believed that "the inhuman elements of the regime" might be ameliorated over time. For "Bäumer, despite her vehement critique of and bellicose attitude toward National Socialism, nevertheless did not entirely recognize the danger of this movement and especially the demonic talent of Hitler – like so many of her contemporaries."[40] She perceived several similarities between Naumann's National-Social and Hitler's National Socialist worldviews, particularly their mutual belief in social welfare, imperialism, and the necessity of building a Greater Germany inclusive of all ethnic Germans. Like the Nazis, she hated the politicization of class conflict endemic within the Weimar party system and bemoaned the inability of parliament to defend the rights and interests of society in an "organic" sense.[41]

This combination of distrust and fascination, resistance and accommodation, makes Bäumer's journal especially interesting as a case study for investigating the continuites and disjunctures between liberalism, feminism, and National Socialism in the Third Reich. *Die Frau* is also a wonderful resource because liberal women had few other outlets for public engagement in the period. Countless Weimar Democrats, including Bäumer, lost their civil service positions in spring 1933.[42] Within weeks the

German State Party and the Bund Deutscher Frauen were also dissolved.[43] Inauspicious as they were, these events reduced *Die Frau*'s competition for authors as well as readers. In this regard we should remember that, for Bäumer and many liberal women, their political marginalization commenced a decade earlier, with plummeting support for the German Democratic Party and a diminishing role of female politicians in general.[44] In 1930 only two liberal women – Bäumer and Marie Lüders, who was nominated to fill Naumann's seat upon her mentor's passing in 1919 – remained in the Reichstag, and they possessed little voice in parliament or on the relevant committees.[45] Even before 1933 numerous female Democrats had begun to turn their attention away from party politics and toward the kind of publicistic activity we find in the pages of *Die Frau*.[46]

Die Frau's critical tone *vis-à-vis* the Third Reich emerged early on. Many Weimar organizations faced "coordination," as *Die Frau* acknowledged in March 1933, but women's groups seemed to be suffering disproportionately in the new "political division of labor."[47] *Die Frau* also criticized the fact that feminine interests were relegated more to women's clubs after 1933, while the Nazi Party, which claimed to value women highly, included virtually no women's issues in its platform. Here, borrowing from the nineteenth-century feminist Louise Otto-Peters, Bäumer employed words like "borders [*Grenzen*]" and "restrictions [*Hemmungen*]" to describe the barriers to women's engagement in the public sphere. The concerted attempt to "privatize" women's activities in the home would lead to disaffection, Bäumer warned, not mobilization.[48]

In order to prevent this division of spheres and labor, *Die Frau* insisted that "women must mutually support each other more than they currently do wherever a party promotes political, ideological, or associational alienation based on illiberal pedantry."[49] In the same March 1933 issue, Bäumer published an editorial asking what the new regime would do for women, "for them, the last 'class,' who worked themselves into full civic responsibility and did not have much time to become familiar with it, everything is once again open to question? All campaign positions that play any role today are simultaneously directed against them."[50] Those who considered everything in the Weimar constitution an "error of baseless liberalism" and viewed "the man as the single carrier of all decisive state power" were seriously misguided.[51]

Bäumer was not without hope that more progressive forces within National Socialism might win out.[52] As she reassured Emmy Beckmann in April 1933, "A new, spiritually different phase of the women's movement has arrived, and I personally have the desire to join it."[53] Within the

Nazi Party, she wrote another colleague, "[y]ou can see that even here there exists a women's movement in a real sense and that it begins to fight."[54] A "kernel" of Friedrich Naumann's National-Social tradition was preserved in National Socialism, Bäumer contended.[55] There were likewise "signs that the dilettantish, unreflective phrases of the National Socialist program could no longer hold up against the more intelligent portion of its followers" who wanted to work positively towards the "solution of Germany's most fateful questions." "I am convinced," she concluded, "that Naumann's National-Social world of ideas provides an especially suitable point of departure" for the inevitable debate between progressive and conservative forces within National Socialism.[56]

Such statements cannot be easily dismissed, whether as a sign of cynical accommodation or of naïve ideological complicity. These sentiments were expressed in private letters to like-minded colleagues. Given the Gestapo's relatively restrained presence in early 1933, there is little reason to presume that Bäumer was filtering her ideas. She would publish more censorious views in Die Frau years later, when police repression was much more overt. The historian can take Bäumer at her word: she truly believed that the "progressive" elements of National Socialism might be coopted by the liberal women's movement. Many Nazis echoed Naumann in emphasizing the need to moderate capitalism through national unity, economic redistribution, and social intervention. The movement's only real limitation, wrote Annemarie Doherr in the November 1933 issue of Die Frau, lay "in the limits that the National Socialist state idea sets out for the cooperation of women in administration, policy making, and occupational organization." For National Socialism to fulfill its promise, Doherr reasoned, "the regime must expand to give room for the active participation of women in the new state."[57]

One of the best ways for Bäumer and her colleagues to carve out a space in a chauvinist Reich was to indicate how liberal women had always participated in solving the national and social questions that preoccupied the Nazis. By regularly commemorating, quoting, and endorsing the views of Helene Lange, Gertrud Le Fort, Emma Enders, and other prewar feminists, Die Frau hoped to (re)inscribe the language of liberalism into the biomaternalist discourse of the Third Reich.[58] Rather than assert women's absolute equality with men, Bäumer appealed to the Nazis' own obsession with history. In one particularly pointed article, Bäumer took a government official to task for extolling the "masculinization" of German life in the Third Reich. Were not a few goals of National Socialism, from improving health care to promoting engenics, first articulated by the

German women's movement? Were not many of Germany's health professions and social institutions inherently "feminine"?[59]

Bäumer was not ashamed of German feminism's liberal pedigree. After
the 1937 Nuremberg party rally, which praised the role of German women
in typically vague fashion, Bäumer asked why there were no more (left
liberal) individuals like Henriette Schrader and Helene Lange in the
Third Reich: "Who will inherit their mantle? Not only in terms of the
issues, but more than anything else with regard to their uncompromising
and fearless attitude."[60] In "Women Make History" Bäumer attacked the
cliché, only slightly more pervasive in the Third Reich than the Weimar
Republic, that "men make history." She praised a December 1939 exhibition, "Woman and Mother – Lifeblood of the People," for acknowledging
women's roles in politics, culture, and society. The young guide, Bäumer
noted, had stopped in front of pictures of Helene Lange, Henriette
Schrader, and Louise Otto-Peters – all Wilhelmine Progressives – in order
to highlight their impact on the German women's movement. If this was
a government-sponsored exhibition, Bäumer concluded wryly, then why
didn't the regime's policies match its values?[61]

To be sure, Bäumer's reproving tone sometimes dissipated when
confronted with criticism from abroad. The German women's movement
was still German, after all. In a detailed 1937 article "On the 'Status' of the
German Woman," Bäumer remarked that the League of Nations' recent
study of women's roles in politics would no doubt fail to mention Germany.
And, were the Germans included, "there could be little doubt that the situation . . . would not be judged favorably."[62] This prejudice, Bäumer added,
reflected less the adverse situation of the German woman and more the
"mechanistic" conception of feminism in western democracies. Granting
women political and legal equality was undoubtedly a step forward, though
it had little meaning if unaccompanied by policies that recognized gender
differences as well.[63] Quoting Gertrud Scholtz-Klink, head of the Nazi
Women's Service, Bäumer argued that drawing natural distinctions
between male and female politics was very different from subordinating the
latter to the former: "the guiding principle of German women today is not
to campaign against men but to campaign alongside men."[64] Women
received special treatment with regard to marriage loans, maternity leave,
and in obtaining certain civil service positions: "the women's share in
everyday life is not only essentially different from the man's . . . but therefore must also be specially nurtured and administered." Women might have
lost the ability to practice law in some areas or to serve in the upper
echelons of the administration, which they never had to a great extent

before 1933 either. But the Third Reich offered exciting new opportunities to women in the fields of "social policy, state and youth welfare."[65]

Nevertheless what began as qualified support quietly evolved into implicit criticism. Chauvinism was not to blame for the fact that women were under-represented in high political office, Bäumer noted, because women had belonged disproportionately to liberal and socialist parties (which were of course outlawed in 1933). She then damned the regime with faint praise. While women still held posts in typically "feminine" arenas like education and welfare administration (this was Bäumer's "defense" of the Nazi regime), in all other spheres "German women had experienced a step backwards in their professional and public opportunities for action." The only areas where women were publicly engaged in large numbers were party organizations with restricted prerogatives. Her conclusion was more admonition than apologia: "To help develop these broad beginnings one will require armies of women who must receive the best conceivable education (not merely 'schooling') and greatest conceivable responsibility, without losing additional time making [erroneous] observations regarding the limits of women's capability."[66] Resentful though she was of western condescension, this article could not be clearer in delineating the areas in which women had lost ground. While Nazi Germany had made strides in accommodating women's needs in juggling aspects of work and family life, it had turned back the clock on women's political and legal equality.

Defending the Third Reich was easier where Germany's Gallic neighbor was concerned. On the eve of the French Revolution's 150th anniversary, Bäumer devoted a sardonic lead article to "Women and Human Rights: 'A Propos of an Anniversary.' " In honor of the occasion French women had inquired whether the government was prepared to give women full citizenship, in particular the vote. And as it had for one hundred and fifty years, the republican government ignored them. Bäumer could have used this opportunity to indict French republicanism and western liberalism *tout court*, without mentioning any of Nazi Germany's own egregious human rights violations. Yet she chose a different tactic. While "the fate of women in the French Revolution [was] nothing but a tragedy," 1789 *had* paved the way for a number of positive changes in European politics and society.[67] Bäumer praised the moderate liberals (Girondins), who promoted equal rights for all. She reserved special approbation for Condorcet, the Enlightenment writer who, along with Girondin feminists such as Madame Roland and Olympe de Gouges, defended women's rights and the abolition of slavery. Instead of indicting the revolution *per se*, Bäumer directed her anger at chauvinist radicals (Montagnards) like Robespierre, who murdered female revolutionaries while proclaiming the "Rights of Man." Napoleon – who was after all a Montagnard officer – then consolidated this revolutionary chauvinism in his Civil Code, which affirmed women's political and legal inequality.[68]

Here one sees parallels between *Die Frau*'s repeated emphasis on the failure of the Nazi "revolution" to involve women in politics and society and the insistence of French "democracy" on preserving the Napoleonic Code. When Bäumer mocks Napoleon's assertion that "A woman who does whatever she wants is not French," she attacks Nazi "Montagnards" as well. Bäumer likewise made sure to cite the greatest *exception* to French chauvinism: "In one respect France has certainly been more generous than, for example, Germany: in allowing women into all types of higher education . . . a more just appreciation of their abilities than elsewhere. In the republic of the intellect one can therefore speak of a real victory of human rights."[69] This was a transparent condemnation of Nazi attempts to reduce the number of women in higher education. Her desire to highlight the contradictions of the Nazi "social revolution" becomes even clearer when she takes the left-center Popular Front to task for opposing female suffrage because women might vote disproportionately for the conservative parties. Whatever the reasoning, French republicans had once again repudiated "the great, clear, historically powerful ideology of human rights . . . for the rather unpleasant exigencies of everyday politics."[70] Thus, rather than dismiss French Revolutionary principles of liberty and equality as inherently Judeophilic, outdated, or "un-German," as the Nazis were wont to do, Bäumer stressed France's inability to live up to them. Her readers could not have missed the embedded critique of National Socialism.

Liberal Women at War

It should come as no surprise that Bäumer and her colleagues took up the cause of rearmament after 1933. The German women's movement, liberal as well as conservative, had never been pacifistic.[71] But it is worth highlighting the degree to which liberal feminists insisted – as they had before the First World War – that women be allowed a greater role in military affairs. In her 1936 book, *The Unknown Army*, Marie Lüders carried forward a long-term campaign to promote peacetime military service for women. Lüders then urged Hitler's General Staff to modify the new Army Law (*Wehrgesetz*), which permitted a women's draft only in wartime. Failure to enlist women in peacetime, Lüders wrote, had led to economic bottlenecks and unnecessary "improvisation" during the First World War.[72] For Lüders the crucial issue was not whether Germany should have a larger military – all other great powers had hundreds of thousands of men at arms – but whether women would be afforded the same opportunities to serve. Like many of her colleagues, Lüders accepted that women were biologically different; all the more reason that their military mobilization and employment become more than an *ad hoc* technical matter. Realizing women's full participation in time of war was both a pressing social issue and a matter of Germany's survival.[73] Lüders's book echoed beyond the women's movement. The Nazi Education Ministry considered promoting her work "as objective and psychologically preparatory material" for the military as well as the general population. Hitler's War Minister General Blomberg composed the foreword.[74]

Bäumer accorded *The Unknown Army* a glowing review in the pages of *Die Frau*: "it must be read. Must – in every sense: as a piece of German history; in order to do justice to a generation of women who took great part in a fateful time; and in the name of historical accuracy. A mature people will neither sublimate the past, because it only wishes to see heroic glory; nor however will they degrade it by criticizing without understanding the failure of overburdened forces." Not only did Lüders's book make the case for women's participation in the military, Bäumer argued, but it dispelled once and for all the "myth of the stab-in-the-back [*Dolchstoßlegende*]" propagated by the Nazis. Had women been more integrated into the war economy and better utilized at the front, Lüders's book suggested, perhaps the war's outcome would have been different. Germany lost because her chauvinist government made insufficient use of her resources, not because she was betrayed by Jews or Communists.[75]

In anticipation of *The Unknown Army*, Bäumer dedicated an entire 1935 issue of *Die Frau* to women and the military. She began by extolling German foreign policy. Given Hitler's early successes – exiting the League of Nations' sponsored Disarmament Conference, signing the Polish-German Non-Aggression Pact and Anglo-German Naval Agreement, and regaining the Saarland – she had little reason to do otherwise. She also commended Reich Interior Minister Wilhelm Frick's decision to retain women's suffrage, no small matter given the chauvinist attitudes of other Fascist countries, not to mention the western democracies (such as France). Bäumer cited the regime's decision to conscript women into national service as another step forward.[76] Her support for women's engagement in military matters might seem to denote collaboration. Yet, as she later pointed out to her Allied interlocutors, the idea of women's participation in defense of the country had originated with liberals like Helene Lange and Marie Lüders (also a Naumann protégée) before the First World War.[77]

Bäumer was especially frustrated by what she viewed as "pro-Allied" bias in the international women's movement. In January 1939, the British chairwoman of the International Alliance for Women's Suffrage, Margery Corbett-Ashby, gave a speech proposing that the principles of morality and democracy must supersede international women's solidarity. In a world divided between "tyranny or democracy," the women's movement had to condemn any "repression of belief, race, and class." The "total state" made everyone inferior: women, minorities, and the poor. For the time being, Corbett-Ashby argued, women's issues belonged on the back burner. One must first secure "the survival of the principles which are the basis of their [women's] own movement" in "defense of a system that will allow humanity the path to greater freedom, a true peace, a general prosperity, a free justice."[78]

Bäumer translated and printed the speech in full, along with its unqualified defense of liberal democracy. More remarkable is the way she interprets it: "t[he] sense is clear. The international Women's Suffrage Alliance wants to leave the politically neutral ground" it has held for centuries in the name of "the ideals of democracy, and indeed a specific kind of democracy." These ideals were not "the only nor the most sufficient ones . . . to serve the woman as a basis for the full expression of her powers in every worthy facet of life." This was particularly true with regard to a "doctrinaire liberalism" that had proved so inadequate in the wake of "the economic and political developments of the century." How just were the reparations imposed by "liberal" France and Great Britain after the First World War, or was American economic liberalism that allowed millions to suffer in poverty? Never, Bäumer observes, does Mrs Corbett-Ashby mention "the people." How can she speak of individual rights when the world's greatest democracies deprived whole nations – namely Germany and Austria – of those same rights? Bäumer concludes historically, noting that the western democracies also practiced racism as well as chauvinism. Was it not arrogant to sacrifice the international solidarity of the women's movement in the name of liberal democracy, "an ideology which – in this ever so summary form – has failed to solve a whole complex of economic, social and political matters and, if it remains so blind and abstract, will fail in the future as well"?[79] Bäumer's subtext is not that liberal democracy was inherently wrong, only that it had lost much of its philosophical potency in the wake of western imperialism, Versailles, and the Great Depression.

Her critique of women's "false emancipation" in the Soviet Union also promotes liberal views under the guise of attacking Allied hypocrisy. Bäumer begins by offering a fairly positive appraisal of egalitarian tendencies in the Soviet Union. Women in the Soviet Union "have the same rights and duties as the man, with the exception of military service." Even in military matters, Bäumer adds, women volunteers had been known to distinguish themselves in battle. After describing Russia's famous women fighter aces, army engineers, and political leaders, Bäumer relates that 227 women sit in the upper council of the Soviet Union as well, including in the presidency. The lower levels of the Soviet bureaucracy employed nearly half a million women. Eight women belonged to the highest court. Still more compelling, in "holding party and state offices women are employed not as women but as compatriots and specialists." "In contrast to some forms of petty bourgeois restriction of women to their proper place," Bäumer reasons acidly, "this could appear rather attractive."[80]

None sat on the Politburo, Bäumer admitted, and only one quarter of all elected officials since 1937 were women (this last observation being more indicative of growing chauvinism under Stalin than of traditional Soviet bias). Women were likewise under-represented in the Communist Party apparatus of the Islamic republics: only 16 percent in Kazakhstan and 12 percent in Kyrgyzstan, in contrast to 34 percent and 33 percent respectively in Russia and the Ukraine. Bäumer knew that her audience would hardly be impressed by the uneven percentage of women's participation across the Soviet Republics. Her readers would focus instead on the fact that women (and Jews) made up far fewer than 12 percent of any meaningful political or economic institutions in Nazi Germany, much less the 33 percent they comprised in ethnic Russian territory.[81] Bäumer's intention to reflect a critical mirror back on Germany becomes even clearer when this article is viewed in the context of *Die Frau*'s frequent publication of statistics on the marginalization of women in Nazi Germany. Her putative attack on women's rights in the Soviet Union was nothing but a Trojan Horse in which she might smuggle in a stronger indictment of the Third Reich.

Of course Bäumer was no Communist. She was genuinely put off by the lack of any special laws for the "protection [of women] in fulfilling their family tasks," such as marriage loans, as well as the Communists' refusal to acknowledge "that it could possibly bring joy to a woman to work for her husband and her children."[82] Bäumer betrayed no hidden agenda when she denounced "anarchist" repression of women in the Spanish Civil War or deplored the situation of Finns, whose Nordic *Volkstumskampf* (struggle for ethnic self-determination) was threatened by the Soviet Union.[83] Her outrage at Soviet atheism was honest as well. This criticism takes on a special resonance in the context of the Nazis' own attacks on Christianity, which, in contrast to those of the Soviet Union, actually picked up during the war.[84] Bäumer made it her business to discuss the "adverse" situation of women in the Allied countries, not primarily to discard liberal (British, French) or socialist (Russian) conceptions of equality, but to point out their failure to live up to them. By "defending" Germany, Bäumer shone a spotlight on the Third Reich's own delinquency.

III

Liberal Women at Work

German conservatives had always been vocal about restricting women's access to employment and education, even during the boom years of the Weimar Republic. The economic crisis of the 1930s made the question of women's competition in the labor market a pressing issue for liberals and socialists as well. With as much as 30 percent of the labor force unemployed, few male workers, regardless of party affiliation, welcomed additional competition from millions of newly emancipated women. The NSDAP exploited these resentments, instituting legal barriers to women's employment, quotas in higher education, and generous marriage loans to help push women back into the home. This assault on women's employment was reinforced by a powerful chauvinist strain that coursed through Nazi ideology. Nevertheless, within five years German wives and mothers were being reintegrated into the economy in unprecedented numbers. And by the end of the war there were more women studying at university than at any time in German history, including the Weimar Republic.[85]

This dynamic social reality makes it difficult to gauge whether economics or ideology played the larger role in dictating both liberal and Nazi attitudes to female labor in the Third Reich.[86] Like Hitler, Gertrud Bäumer realized that promoting women's employment in the wake of the Great Depression was politically unwise and economically impractical. A few years later she found herself demanding, alongside leading members of the NSDAP, that the government do more to ensure women's unfettered access to higher education, full integration into the professions, and equal pay in all sectors.[87] There is consequently little doubt of the convergence in liberal and Nazi attitudes toward women's employment and education. The question is whether these similarities signified a pragmatic response to economic circumstances or whether there were aspects of real ideological congruence between liberal feminism and National Socialism.

Painfully aware of the lack of jobs for men *and* women in 1933, Bäumer employed *Die Frau* at first to illustrate the economic necessity of – not the egalitarian argument for – women's participation in the workforce. She focused on the existing tendency to channel women into lower-paying occupations. In the civil service, for example, women made up the vast majority of postal workers. Yet post office workers made less money than male employees with shorter tenures and less impressive careers in other areas of the civil service.[88] Bäumer also questioned government pressures on women to return to the home. Given the high unemployment rate, it was natural (if hardly admirable) that men should view positively the return of women to the home. Nevertheless, women now outnumbered men by the millions, due to the horrific casualty rates of the First World War. This demographic trend, Bäumer suggested, meant that many women *could not expect* to become wives or mothers, because there were not enough men to marry them.[89] In 1925 the German economy employed nearly five million women younger than twenty-five. Could all such women be permanently replaced?[90] What of families that depended on dual incomes for their survival? Did the state have the right to deprive such families of their economic well-being? Denying women the right to work had nothing to with building a healthy "people's community [*Volksgemeinschaft*]," Bäumer averred, and everything to do with bourgeois chauvinism.[91]

Although the Nazis were correct to claim that women were biologically different from men, Bäumer granted, sexual difference did not mean that women should be relegated to the home. Too many Germans, Bäumer reasoned, accepted a simplistic view of history that looked at everything before 1918 in a positive light. The Depression made Germans yearn for the "good old days," when women could neither vote nor work in the same occupations as men. Such preconceptions belonged "in the rubbish bin of 'national kitsch.'"[92] Among the ancient Germanic tribes of pre-Christian Europe, women were the priests, the teachers, and the medical assistants. Why couldn't they fulfill "the sense and essence of National Socialism" as teachers, doctors, or academics in the Third Reich?[93] Promoting female participation in fields like education, medicine, and social services, Bäumer maintained, was a matter of utilizing women's natural proclivity for nurturing.[94] Nazi leaders who called for the removal of female doctors or professors to make room for male ones neglected the lessons of both history and biology.[95]

Bäumer looked back on the first two years of National Socialist economic policy with skepticism. The Nazis were correct to repudiate the outmoded tenets of laissez-faire and the polarizing class warfare of Marxism. Neither ideology could account for the "complex web of economic interconnections" that defined any modern industrial state. Whether one was a Socialist or a

National Socialist, however, the need to manage a "monstrously oversatu-
rated labor market" did not justify the fact that, at least for women, "all the
achievements of the last decades" had been rolled back. Bäumer was especially distressed by the rhetoric which described women's reentry into the
domestic sphere as a "Return to Nature [*Rückkehr zur Natur*]." There was
nothing natural about depriving perfectly competent women of equal
employment opportunities, fair pay, occupational training or education.
Bäumer insisted that work should be given to those who want it most or are
the most talented, not to those who are most socially "acceptable" – namely,
unemployed men. In the Weimar Republic it was the free market, which
had shown how indispensable women's participation in the economy actually was. Favoring men regardless of qualifications contradicted every free
market principle, undermined the economy, and left women with access
only to the worst-paid, least-skilled jobs.[96]

Hence, while Bäumer argued that women had "natural" proclivities for
some occupations, she conveniently rejected the idea that "biology was
destiny" in others. In primary teaching for example, to which women were
thought to be most suited, they were twice as likely to leave due to dis-
satisfaction or incompetence as men; yet men found it twice as hard to
obtain a job. Conversely, despite excellent performance, women administrators had been dismissed in extraordinary numbers since 1933.
Chauvinism, according to Bäumer, not biology, explained this contradictory trend. How could women ever fulfill their "natural" role as mothers
without access to well-paid jobs?[97]

Borrowing liberally from the Nazi women's leader Gertrud Scholtz-
Klink, Bäumer declared, "In the more complicated social body of the
present we need a female elite who can 'think along [*mitdenken*]' with the
men due to their disciplinary training."[98] She admonished the Third Reich
to make greater use of women in health and education, where they had
proved so useful since the First World War. Though women professionals
took the same initiative as their male colleagues, their interests were consistently ignored in terms of "determining work hours, vacation, pay, promotion in a profession, the division of the work day, health, [etc.]."[99] Their pay
remained poorer than that of their male colleagues as well, especially for
those who lived in cities like Berlin. Many received fewer than two weeks'
vacation.[100] Though no one would deny the decline in unemployment,
women had played too meager a role in the resurgence.[101]

By 1936, however, economic realities began to collide with the more
chauvinist elements in National Socialism. Indeed, as "the unemployment
situation eased and the shortage of skilled personnel became apparent and

then acute, the idea which had found currency in earlier Nazi theory – that high intelligence and womanliness were incompatible – was categorically denied."[102] Even despite the growing demand for skilled female labor, previously instituted economic (e.g. lower wages for women), social (marriage loans), and cultural ("cult of motherhood") policies persisted after 1936, tending to encourage middle-class women – those women whose training was best and whose participation in the economy was lowest – to stay at home.[103] Although restricting women's employment was no longer explicitly intended, comments one historian, a typical Nazi "confusion and disagreement in the upper echelons of the Party and Government" prevented women's full and equal participation in the economy.[104]

Bäumer essentially arrived at the same conclusion. While women were being hired in greater numbers, she observed, they received the worst-paying, most amateurish work. Well-trained, university-educated women still found it difficult to obtain an interview, much less a job offer.[105] Marie Lüders perceived only slight increases in women's factory work as well, believing, like Bäumer, that factories were doing very little in terms of competitive pay, hours, or benefits to facilitate or ensure the productivity of female work.[106] Women had yet to exploit their improved negotiating position.[107] When it came to white-collar opportunities there was even more room for improvement, as the regime continued to suggest that women professionals would be remiss if they relinquished their natural roles as mothers.[108] Instead of being deemed a stopgap measure to make up for temporary bottlenecks in the Four Year Plan, Bäumer argued, women's professionalization had to be seen as the culmination of a decades-long trend, interrupted only at the height of the Great Depression.[109]

Another persistent bone of contention, hardly unique to Nazi Germany, was the assumption that women's work invariably constituted a second income. In this regard Bäumer made no effort to conceal the similarities between a supposedly outdated Manchesterite liberalism and National Socialism. The problem began in the nineteenth-century British textile industry, Bäumer explained, which tended to pay per family and not per head, meaning that women and children often worked as unpaid labor alongside their husbands. The presumption that women could work for little or nothing became embedded in the culture of industrialization and in the language of European capitalism. One hundred and fifty years later, women were still not as well trained as men and the Nazi regime had made no effort to remedy this problem. Poor training, Bäumer added, was never the primary reason why they received lower pay. It was the outmoded argument – no longer honestly accepted by anyone – that "the man is the lone breadwinner." For everyone could see that unmarried women, not their absent paramours, carried the brunt of family responsibilities, both in raising children and in taking care of elderly relatives.[110]

When it came to married women whose husbands made an excellent living, one might privilege the "racial-biological necessities" of building a healthy *Volksgemeinschaft* over the need to integrate women into the national economy.[111] Of course this rare dilemma did nothing to justify male hypocrisy about women's employment in the higher professions: "For decades the German women's movement could not dispel its astonishment that no one raised an objection if women engaged in difficult, monotonous, strenuous, motherhood-endangering factory work." There was nonetheless immediate outrage whenever "it concerned any more comfortable, reputable, intellectual or even merely better paying employment." Due to the sheer greed of men who coveted the best jobs for themselves, women had been thrust into the hardest and lowest-paying work, not because of any real male respect for women's femininity or familial role. The Third Reich exploited women's work in direct contradiction of the regime's maternalist rhetoric, employing it selectively in order to keep unskilled women's wages down and women professionals out of the workforce altogether. Anticipating later arguments for affirmative action, Bäumer urged that the state step in and regulate the labor market in order to ensure that women who had previously been discriminated against be employed in greater numbers.[112]

In the wake of the rearmament drive spearheaded by the Four Year Plan, some of these recommendations seemed to bear fruit. *Die Frau* and the German Women's Bureau (Deutsche Frauen Werk or DFW) no doubt played a role. Mounting labor shortages in crucial armament industries, as Lüders predicted two years earlier, also enhanced women's negotiating position within the German Labor Front (DAF). As Bäumer happily related in *Die Frau*, the DAF's *Frauenamt* (Women's Office) reported 3.834 million active women members in 1938. The report also asserted that wherever women were employed in work "that required a special physical effort, and therefore generally could be performed by men, they received the men's pay of the appropriate age level." Where women were as "productive" as men they likewise enjoyed the same salary or wages. Most remarkable, laws that had previously permitted employers to pay women 40 percent less than men had been revised in favor of women.[113] These numbers proved that women – at least those who were employed in the armaments industry – had become something more than "mothers of the next generation" whose entry into the economy was a temporary, if necessary, evil.[114]

Bäumer was still quick to point out the inefficiency of Goering's Four Year Plan.[115] The government's own publications indicated that many of the 6.5 to 8 million potential female workers were not being employed in crucial industries like steel or armaments. Citing an article in Robert Bosch's factory newsletter, Bäumer urged the state to rectify this situation through improved training, greater rights, and better pay. Because women were physically weaker than men and more responsible for family life, their training and participation ought to be valued *more*, not less.[116]

This increased involvement would only be feasible, Bäumer wrote in 1941, if industries became more accommodating toward women's special needs. Employers should offer the possibility of half- and part-time jobs, for example, so women who needed extra income might still balance their work and family life.[117] Utterly insensitive to the challenges facing working women, whether in Germany or America, Allied authorities would later claim that this article – titled "Women's Reserves" – advocated total war. Bäumer found this interpretation laughable. Instead, "Women's Reserves" was part of an ongoing critique of Goering's Four Year Plan, which ignored the millions of potential women workers whose familial or financial situation made it impossible for them to work full time.[118] Bäumer was frustrated by an ostensibly "pro-family" Nazi regime which insisted on employing women without the considerations necessary to ensure a safe workplace and stable home life. If she remained coy about her patriotism, which she obviously shared with female counterparts in America and Great Britain, her defense of women's economic opportunity was undoubtedly sincere.

Education

Liberal women were among the first to note an unpleasant change in the culture of higher education which threatened to delay the gains in the professions experienced during the Wilhelmine era and the Weimar Republic.[119] Quite a lot of women who attended university after January 1933 received a chillier reception from their professors than in the Weimar Republic. No matter how much more competent she might be than her male counterparts, a woman who pursued an academic career was labelled *lebensfern*, or "denatured." The culture of the Third Reich, according to even the conservative feminist Lenore Kühn, had begun to reduce "the woman to a simple object of man's 'use.' "[120] In the same January 1934 issue of *Die Frau*, Maria Schlüter-Hermkes reasoned more pragmatically that closing the universities and academic careers to women would severely dilute the next generation of German scientists and scholars.[121]

Taking a long-term perspective, Bäumer pointed out that Nazi attitudes
to women in higher education had deep roots in the German soil.[122] Only
a handful of women obtained Ph.D.s under the Empire. And while the
Weimar constitution guaranteed equal rights *de jure*, women were still *de
facto* discriminated against in terms of access to education and the professions.[123] The Third Reich's emphasis on women's "distinctive" role was
more explicit than Weimar's. One could hardly say it was original: "Already
before the [Nazi] political revolution in Germany there were negotiations
in regard to restricting women's study . . . due to the really immense over-
crowding of the academic professions."[124] The coordination of the universities since the Nazi seizure of power reconfirmed "how difficult it has been
for women to find a place within this closed bastion of what has until
now been a purely male science."[125] For ideological as well as pragmatic
reasons – in order to allay competition in the professions – Hitler made a
special effort to discourage women from studying medicine, law, and
theology. Thus women faced the "double pressure of an overburdened labor
market and a fundamental exclusion of women." As Bäumer intoned
repeatedly, it was not Germanic tradition that placed women in a domestic
role, but "the Anglo-Saxon model" imported into Germany with the
Industrial Revolution.[126]

Bäumer's complaint about the Victorian origins of Hitler's "cult of
domesticity" was not confined to liberals. According to Alfred Rosenberg,
Hitler's deputy for educational matters:

> The age of Victorianism and the "dreamy romantic girl's life" are natu-
> rally finished once and for all. The woman belongs deeply to the total
> life of the people. All educational opportunities must be open to her.
> Through rhythmic gymnastics and sport the same care must be given
> to her physical training as is the case with men. Nor should any diffi-
> culties be created for her in the vocational world under present-day
> social conditions (whereby the Law for the Protection of Mothers
> should be more strongly implemented). Hence all possibilities for the
> development of a woman's energies should remain open to her.[127]

Here we see a powerful "feminist" conviction within the Nazis' own biomaternalist discourse. Women should be afforded the same opportunities as
men in the name of racial and social harmony, not because of any outmoded
adherence to Marxist egalitarianism. Statements like Rosenberg's caused
Bäumer to complain that the regime expected women to do too much: to be
well educated, economically viable, and physically fit while at the same time

fulfilling the role of wife and mother. Perhaps the kind of "New Woman" described by Rosenberg was possible with greater economic and educational opportunities. But the Third Reich's haphazard and contradictory policies toward women did not match the regime's exaggerated expectations.[128]

Though Nazi leaders complimented women's contributions to the fields of health care and social work, the regime provided little support to enhance professional training. How could women become effective professionals when they remained mostly untrained, uncompensated volunteers? In order to remedy this Bäumer demanded a complete "reform of the meaning and content of mandatory civil service," which focused primarily on male military contributions.[129] More attention to non-military, female service and training, especially in the realm of welfare and social work, would yield more professional options for women. According to the 26 June 1935 law, all Germans regardless of sex were required to enlist in the Reich Labor Service. Why not create a service year directly after high school during which young women and men could gain valuable professional training in order to compete for a relatively meager number of jobs? At the very least, Bäumer opined, one could institute a ninth year of secondary school to prepare women practically for obtaining jobs. Despite women's disproportionate interest and engagement in social work, they were still outnumbered by men three to one in terms of paid civil service positions.[130]

Liberal women were especially troubled by the regime's lack of consideration for the future generation of German women. In October 1935 the prominent educator Emmy Beckmann commented on recent changes in the state of girls' education, which dictated that female students would have less time for math and the natural sciences than their male counterparts. The new curriculum also privileged "racial" pedagogy over scientific training in preparing primary school teachers, still largely a female profession.[131] The stereotype that women were somehow discouraged intellectually by competing with men was completely undermined by the thousands of female university students engaged daily in "free intellectual exchange and competition with the opposite sex" in seminars across Germany. It was by separating women from men and offering them a less demanding curriculum that the regime risked creating a sense of intellectual inferiority.[132] Beckmann also criticized a 1937 law that reduced the length of secondary school, where women were already getting a second-class education.[133]

In May 1937 Bäumer followed up Beckmann's frosty reception of "curricular reform" with a critical appraisal of her own. Overall, girls performed better than boys in 1932–33 – the year before the Nazis took power – with 70.4 percent passing their final exams compared to only 58.2 percent of the men. Well aware of the accusation that girls' schools were less rigorous – a circular argument since the Nazis had *made* them that way – Bäumer sought to buttress her claims by "a comparison of boys' schools that admitted girls: the number of those who didn't pass in the 1932 school year included 10% of boys and 5% of girls."[134] In fact, the average exam scores of female students were higher than those of males across the board. Yet the Nazi regime's changes in women's education would make their high school diplomas obsolete. The new curriculum was utterly useless "as preparation for the study of mathematics, and in the field of the natural sciences . . . hardly sufficient for [the study of] physics or chemistry." Condemning women to a watered-down education and fewer job prospects was not the only consequence of the "reforms." For a woman educated solely in "domestic (*hauswirtschaftlich*)" matters could never be a true intellectual partner to her husband or model for her children.[135]

Bäumer had monitored for some time the sharp reduction in women gaining higher degrees during the Third Reich.[136] In August 1937 she analysed women's participation in the fields of law, economics, and other social sciences because they counted as the most "masculine" disciplines. Acknowledging that women did not have complete freedom to choose their dissertation topics, which accounted in part for the overwhelming focus on women's and social issues, Bäumer noted that there had been no shortage of dissertations in the "harder" social sciences. This trend in rising numbers of female Ph.D.s suddenly reversed in 1933. Though related to the "overfilling of the university" as a result of the poor job market, there was absolutely no empirical evidence, Bäumer contended, in support of Nazi claims that women were unsuited to certain professions. The only explanation for the lack of qualified women after 1933 was the regime's antipathy toward women pursuing advanced degrees.[137] As part of the solution, Bäumer advocated a formal organization to sponsor women college students; if not women's colleges along Anglo-Saxon lines, then at least women's intellectual associations. It was neither "unnatural" nor "masculine" that women desire their own form of academic organizations to counter the exclusionary, militaristic "fraternities [*Burschenschaften*]." On the contrary, women should be provided access to the same social and professional networks as men.[138]

As in the sphere of employment, the economic resurgence of the late 1930s opened the door to a fundamental reassessment of Nazi attitudes to women in higher education. No longer threatened by female competition for jobs and flush with higher wages, men seemed to forget, in Bäumer's words, about "the panic that had broken out over women's education" a few years earlier.[139] In 1933 or 1934, at the height of the Great Depression, there were still too many trained professionals – women as well as men – to match the meager number of positions. But a lack of opportunities could not account for the dearth of women professionals in the wake of full employment. Young men with little experience were gaining prestigious positions in law, medicine, and the academy, while the most talented young women were wasting away in secondary schools that focused on the boring repetition of simple skills and on preparation for life as a housewife.[140] The numbers of well-trained and well-educated women had not kept pace with the demands of the economy.[141]

In this ongoing struggle to counter successive generations of chauvinist critics there was one concrete argument that trumped all others: women's consistent academic achievement.[142] There was an exponential increase in female students between 1902, when 70 women pursued university study, and 1931, when there were 22,084. This number plummeted to 15,501 in 1934. Just as compelling, women had completed 10,595 dissertations in the previous twenty-five years. More than 40 percent were in medical fields, with 1,800 each in math, the natural sciences, and law. Only 2,300 were in the humanities, thereby dispelling "widespread preconceptions regarding the scientific aptitude of women." Lastly, there was clear evidence that women performed better than men in their civil service, philological, and legal exams. Despite numerous studies "prov[ing] women's aptitude and talent," no one has "articulated this reality in the sphere of public opinion."[143]

Bäumer then damned the regime with faint praise. Of the fifty-two women professors employed in 1932 many retired in 1933 for obvious reasons, while a "rather significant number . . . departed, in part due to racial-political grounds, so that today there are still 32 women who practice their profession at German universities – in any case a number that is sufficient to correct certain ideas abroad regarding the complete disappearance of the woman from the academic profession."[144] By linking the plummeting number of women professors to racism and political prejudice instead of chauvinism, Bäumer dismissed the idea that women were *intellectually* inferior while at the same time attacking Nazi illiberalism in higher education.

In devoting so much attention to women professionals, Bäumer and her colleagues might seem maddeningly oblivious to the needs of working-class women. But liberal women had good reasons to downplay socioeconomic

distinctions. First, they shared the Nazis' virulent anti-Communism as well
as the conviction that national unity was more important than class-
consciousness in resolving the ills of modern society. Secondly, working-
class solidarity was undermined in all respects during the 1930s. This was
due in part to the Third Reich's success in privileging a sense of national or
racial community (*Volksgemeinschaft*) over traditional class distinctions. To
the extent that Nazi propaganda fell short in this regard, the Gestapo's
massive system of surveillance and denunciation *did* break down proletarian
social networks, creating a more atomized, privatized, and henceforth less
class-conscious society. Third, the erosion of class-consciousness was a function of the narrowing gap in living standards between proletariat and lower
middle class (*Mittelstand*) due to industrial workers reaping the benefits of
full employment.[145] Finally, we should not forget the fact that Bäumer and
company were, like many modern feminists, primarily interested in issues of
gender. Although they may have elided socioeconomic distinctions between
bourgeois and working-class women, Bäumer and her colleagues articulated
several of the demands of "second wave" feminism at least thirty years
before the movement's efflorescence in most of Europe and the United
States.[146]

IV

Biology, Sexuality, and Social Policy

Notwithstanding their skepticism toward Nazi economic and educational
policies, some Liberals still hoped that Nazism might somehow fulfill the
collectivist and biomaternalist social promise of *fin-de-siècle* German feminism. Particularly attractive to liberal women was the malleable concept of
"national community" so often bandied about in Nazi circles. It was through
the ideal of (racial) community, centered on the family and reproduction,
that women might reenter and reform society.[147] As Dagmar Herzog shows
in her recent study of sexuality in post-1945 Germany, the Nazis embraced
a peculiar combination of liberal and conservative attitudes to women and
sexuality. According to Herzog, Nazi views had more in common with the
sexual reform movements of the 1920s and 1960s than with the Christian
conservatism of the 1950s.[148] In surveying liberal women's responses to Nazi
social and sexual policy, we ought to keep in mind that racism and genocide
were not the only natural consequences of the new "biopolitical orthodoxy."
Welfarism, sexual liberation, and state support for non-nuclear family
arrangements were among the possible outcomes.[149]

Biology and the Welfare State

Like her mentor and life partner Helene Lange, Bäumer believed that recognizing men and women's inherent sexual difference was essential to ameliorating the social crises arising within modern society. Or, as Lange put it, "the 'biological fact' of motherhood as a natural 'calling' elicited a 'physical and psychological singularity' in women that could substantially improve public life precisely because it eluded male norms . . . in social and health services, education, and municipal welfare administration." Both women emphasized that these public activities were the sites in which "women who never became mothers in a physical sense could perform vital functions." Because of their innate maternal instinct, even unmarried, childless women like Bäumer or Lange might contribute to a strong German national community through social work.[150]

Despite her optimistic belief in the power of eugenics, one widely shared by turn-of-the-century liberals, Bäumer always worked to distance her progressive biomaternalism from the explicit racism and illiberalism of the Pan-Germans and anti-Semites.[151] She agreed, for example, that the Weimar welfare state was too preoccupied by "physically and mentally sick elements" to the detriment of "the people as a whole."[152] But anyone who looked honestly at the development of liberalism since the 1890s would appreciate its efforts to revise the traditionally "liberalistic view of the lack of responsibility of the individual toward the whole and the whole toward the individual." The strength of the Weimar welfare state was its concern for the sick or defenseless individual; it did not discard human beings who failed to enhance the health of the *Volksgemeinschaft*. Should one ignore the "difficult cases," the children and the elderly, because they could not work as hard or reproduce as successfully as healthy adults? In our skepticism toward classical liberalism, Bäumer warned, we cannot "fall back into administrative methods, in which the individual again becomes a mere number" subordinate to the goals of the state. Here Bäumer salvages the legacy of Wilhelmine progressivism, which she hoped to differentiate from anachronistic classical liberalism on the one hand and racist collectivism on the other.[153]

This social liberal tone becomes clearer when Bäumer turns to the issue of youth welfare. She was deeply troubled by the Third Reich's "sharp separation of youth care [*Jugendfürsorge*] and youth welfare [*Jugendpflege*]" which prevented "the dangerous elements amongst young people . . . from being brought along with the healthy." Bäumer disliked the fact that supposedly "asocial" youths were institutionalized while "healthy" ones received an education.[154] She also opposed the use of the term "asocial" to separate out those who did not submit to authority or had some kind of developmental disability as biologically unsalvageable. After initially agreeing that the Weimar Republic had paid perhaps too much attention to the mentally and physically ill, Bäumer countered: "Nevertheless there remains . . . a sphere for compassion [*Nächstenliebe*] . . . precisely toward such human beings, for whom, from the material perspective of pure racial values any efforts must be wasted." No German could repudiate fellow citizens whose physical bodies or minds were weak, but whose human worth was as valuable as any.[155]

Here Bäumer dismisses the Nazis' artificial division between socially and biologically determined disease, from the supposedly lazy or "workshy" to the dubious category of "imbecile." In creating biologically and psychologically healthy children, mothers bestowed more than their genes. Bäumer therefore published a letter in *Die Frau* from a reader who questioned the Law on Hereditary Health (*Erbgesundheitsgesetz*). Why should women who would do everything to keep their children healthy be barred from motherhood because of a higher *potential* of hereditary illness, when so many racially "healthy" women end up with poorly raised or neglected children? Although circumspect in her answer, Bäumer obviously disagreed with the regime's exclusive emphasis on nature over nurture in constructing a "people's community [*Volksgemeinschaft*]."[156] Instead of seeking to exclude citizens on the social margins, the state was obliged to provide more programs to address the adverse consequences of industrialization: namely dangerous or insanitary workplaces, higher infant mortality among the poor, the proliferation of working mothers, and the lack of safe and affordable housing.[157]

In later articles Bäumer acknowledged that some Nazi welfare programs did an excellent job of taking care of disavantaged social strata, but rejected the putative racial criteria on which this aid was based.[158] It would take a combination of "compassion toward those close to you and those who are farther [*Nächstenliebe und Fernstenliebe*]" to counter a faceless, state bureaucracy that neglected the individual: "Is it inconceivable that both streams of brotherhood flow together in a will to help that encompasses human beings in their dual form as historical carriers of their ethnicity and the individual soul whose character is not perfected here on earth?"[159] Quoting Martin Luther, Bäumer reminded the regime: "wherever it is harmful (to men), the law should bend and give . . . The wise ruler must leave a space for love."[160]

Bäumer was never afraid to point out the "gaping contradiction" between the regime's family-friendly claims and German social reality.[161] In a 1934 obituary honoring the children's activist Hedwig Heyl, Bäumer praised her struggle "against the calcifications and blind spots in the social order, which the masses today oppose in National Socialism."[162] Six years later Bäumer complimented a leading Reich official for perceiving, in contrast to his biology-obsessed colleagues, that "Motherhood . . . is more than a biological concept, but an intellectual-spiritual attitude."[163] Even as the regime pursued a genocidal war, Bäumer flouted the idea "that 'biological' goal-setting" may only be understood in terms of " 'physical strength' " or racial character. One must take into account social reality. "The 'living belief [*Lebensglaube*]' of a nation is not only physical. Nothing proves this better than the fact that a great upswing was carried out ten years ago by a people that had experienced the physical effects of unprecedented economic crises."[164] What separated the "biologically" healthy from the unhealthy was a consequence of the Darwinistic essence of capitalism, not something reducible to biological character.[165] By tempering the Nazis' race-obsessed eugenicism with the universalist conviction that the state owes every individual an equal degree of care and compassion, Bäumer worked to preserve the national and social, but also *liberal*, paradigm of "people's community" and "popular welfare [*Volkswohlfahrt*]" which she helped create in the decades before the First World War.[166]

The "Cult of Motherhood" versus "The Cult of Domesticity"
In seeking control of women's reproductive rights, the Nazis were following a general European trend. This trend included republican countries, like France, where abortion and contraception were made illegal during the 1920s (to little avail).[167] The Nazis too were never able to eliminate abortion or reduce contraception.[168] But unlike France and nearly every other country in Europe, the Nazis *were* moderately successful in raising the birth and marriage rate in the middle of the Great Depression. They did this, as Timothy Mason suggests, *despite* their unsuccessful attempts to penalize contraception and abortion.[169] In fact there was a considerable element of voluteerism in creating a "cult of motherhood," a voluteerism that drew, on the one hand, from long-term biomaternalist continuities in the German women's movement and rejected, on the other, a privatized "cult of domesticity."[170]

We return here to the fact that a maternalist-oriented German feminism, though not necessarily more conservative than Great Britain's or Scandinavia's, was nonetheless different in its aspirations.[171] During the Wilhelmine and Weimar era some liberal women were reticent about asserting the claims of "first wave feminism" – that is, women's absolute political and legal equality with men.[172] Many supported laws which guaranteed illegitimate children "equal necessities for a material, intellectual and social development" without pushing for a constitutional amendment that would give single mothers the same rights as married ones (or unmarried fathers). Bäumer and some liberal colleagues were also uncomfortable about legalizing abortion.[173]

All the same, German liberalism incorporated a wide range of feminist perspectives. Democrats like Marie Elisabeth Lüders were above all interested in promoting the rights of single mothers. Lüders had her own illegitimate child, fathered by none other than the Jewish Democrat and erstwhile Vice-Chancellor Eugen Schiffer; her child's legal status would have become extremely precarious had his paternity ever been investigated by the state.[174] To be sure, Lüders disagreed with Nazi propaganda, which maintained that women were only useful insofar as they produced children.[175] She nonetheless appreciated the Nazis' apparently progressive attitude toward single motherhood. Lüders was elated to see articles from Heinrich Himmler's *Der Schwarze Korps* and Josef Goebbels's *Völkischer Beobachter* endorsing single mothers and criticizing obsolete bourgeois morality. Lüders likewise quoted an article by Deputy Führer Rudolf Hess insisting that the Third Reich would treat young, unmarried mothers just as well as any other mother who served the fatherland.[176] Emmy Beckmann agreed with Lüders, insisting that single mothers might have a positive impact on society without leading a conventional life.[177] Similarly Marianne Weber endorsed the concept of single motherhood and adoption – both elements of Heinrich Himmler's "fountain of life [*Lebensborn*]" program – which she felt bourgeois society had made too difficult.[178] Tentatively endorsing *Lebensborn*, which sought to produce as many Aryan children as possible regardless of a woman's marital status, is only the most notorious example of favoring single motherhood over conventional domesticity.[179]

Thus Lüders, Weber, and others applauded the extent to which children's "relation to the people's community [*Beziehung zur Volksgemeinschaft*]" now superseded conventional bourgeois mores in bestowing on children (and their mothers) social legitimacy.[180] The real dilemma was the question of a single mother's custody of her child. According to existing laws, the minute a father's identity was established, he could theoretically claim sole custody. Lüders advocated a form of shared parental rights instead, which "permitted the father to interact with the child" without a mother ceding custody. Every eighth child in Germany was born out of wedlock. What would happen if either party, mother or father, remarried? Or if no one accepted paternity, was the responsibility divided among all likely candidates? One might dispel this confusion by leaving children with the mother in all but the most exceptional cases. Giving rights to the father, on the other hand, could break apart the existing family, whatever its organization, and thereby undermine the social and familial bonds preserving the *Volksgemeinschaft*.[181]

Though Bäumer agreed with Lüders that Germany's patriarchal custody laws should be repealed, she felt that unmarried fathers had a greater obligation than merely to provide child support. As Gretchen said to Faust of their child, "Was it not granted to me and you; to you as well?"[182] Thus, whereas Lüders insisted on the full recognition of mothers' rights, Bäumer stressed the fathers' responsibility. Both favored a less traditional conception of the family, a vision they shared with some members of the Nazi regime.

One finds a similar convergence of Nazi and feminist attitudes toward marriage. In 1935 Camilla Jellinek applauded the Third Reich for allowing women greater agency in determining grounds for divorce. Nevertheless, as a Jew who had married a "non-Aryan" (Georg von Jellinek) herself, she complained that the Nazis did not change the 1913 provision by which women lost their citizenship when they married a foreigner. Lest she undermine the argument by mentioning the plight of Jews directly, Jellinek used the example of "racial" Germans to clinch her case, remarking upon the countless women, married to so-called "foreigners," who lost their citizenship after Versailles (e.g. Alsatians, Upper Silesians, North Schleswigers). The obvious solution was to delete the 1913 paragraph depriving women of citizenship when they married a foreigner. Of course this would also protect gentile women (or men) who married Jews.[183] Dr Agnes Martens-Edelmann was less qualified in her praise. Marriage could now be dissolved from either side based on the "principle of irreconcilability [*Zerrüttungsprinzip*]," while an extramarital affair (*Ehebruch*), committed by either partner, was no longer automatic grounds for divorce. Most importantly, the new laws held equally for women and men.[184]

From a liberal perspective the greatest strides occurred with regard to maternity leave. Bäumer lauded the new German law for "Protecting Mothers [*Mütterschutz*]" of 17 May 1942. Although pregnant women had to leave any work that involved dangerous chemicals or strain, they were now protected from losing their job regardless of tenure. Women with state insurance (*gesetzliche Krankenversicherung*) were also paid their full salary for the six weeks before and after birth. An employer could not release a worker while pregnant and for four months after delivery. This applied to women employed in rural work as well. For Bäumer the German law presented a model for other European welfare states.[185]

Whilst embracing the Third Reich's "liberal" attitude to single mother-hood, sexuality, and economic activity, in other spheres such as marriage loans, prostitution, and abortion liberal women remained skeptical.[186] Bäumer regretted that the concept of marriage loans deprived marriage "of its spiritual content, of the seriousness of reciprocal ties and the concept of loyalty." More troubling, Bäumer argued, was the fact that Nazi support for single mothers, along with their promotion of the *Lebensborn* program, "legitimized a second form of parenthood" that undermined the tradi-tional family structure.[187] Bäumer was disgusted by the Fascist glorifica-tion of motherhood as a kind of competition and blanched at Goering's Mother's Day speech praising Klara Hitler for giving birth to "the greatest son of all times." Hadn't the regime embarrassed German women enough?[188]

Eugenics was another troublesome issue. Despite her decades-long support for biological engineering in the interest of improving the health of the nation, Bäumer and her colleagues never endorsed widespread, state-enforced sterilization of the mentally or physically disabled.[189] Rather than defend sterilization, Bäumer tried to downplay its severity and distinctiveness: "I do not know to what extent births are controlled or regulated in Germany according to pseudoscientific principles. In terms of 'birth-control' [Bäumer employs the English phrase here] this term has signified in everyday parlance a very different tendency, of which the purpose was the 'un-birth [*Nichtgeburt*].' A legal framework for sterilizing those unworthy of reproducing, if that is what is meant, exists, as far as I know with women's approval, in almost all great democracies."[190] Bäumer had strong reservations regarding the indiscriminacy of the Nazi eugenics program, perhaps more so than some colleagues in "democratic" countries (Sweden and the United States spring quickly to mind).[191] Yet she expressed this reticence subtly, by redirecting the critique abroad.

The National Socialist view on prostitution presented less of a conun-drum. It had been made illegal in most northern European countries. Even several eastern and southern European nations, which, according to Bäumer, tended to be more tolerant of promiscuity, had begun to emulate this model: "There is no longer in Europe any determined defender of the *maisons de tolérance*, that are associated with the spirit of the Napoleonic Code. Whoever is familiar with the entire situation can observe only with great embarrassment how 'barracking' was being progressively reintro-duced in Germany." All one could do was hope for an inspired "opposi-tion" to prostitution, "all the more, when the Führer's book [*Mein Kampf*] takes so unambiguously clear a position [against it]."[192] That Himmler tolerated prostitution throughout the concentration camp system is well known. And by the mid-1930s his deputy Heydrich had set up his own, Gestapo-administered house of ill repute (the Salon Kitty) in order to spy on foreign diplomats and party rivals. In shining a light on these practices, Bäumer could not have endeared herself to Hitler or the SS.[193]

Marianne Weber also denounced the sexual licentiousness of the Nazi era. Weber was unhappy with recent work by a Nazi-affiliated academic, Otto Piper, who considered "extramarital affairs" perfectly natural, since "they now appear to occur with great frequency" and "God permits them in the interest of reproduction." Most offensive for Weber was Piper's contention that "even within the Christian Church 'hundreds of thousands' of young couples live together without getting married."[194] In December 1936 Weber answered Piper's criticisms by avowing that she was not a prude. But extra- and pre-marital sexual relations run rampant threatened to undermine "our highest ideal of community between the sexes, and the fact that it [marriage between a man and woman] has become the only permissible legal form in the West," not to mention "that the highest level of family life is only reached through the bond between a husband and his wife."[195] Though rejecting free love and sanctifying marriage, Weber was not necessarily promoting "conservative" values. She emphasized the intellectual and spiritual equality on which marriage ought to be based. Moreover, as Dorothee von Velsen noted in reviewing Marianne Weber's book *Die Frauen und die Liebe*, Weber affirmed that the deep platonic friendship between a husband and wife might extend to women like Helene Lange and Gertrud Bäumer. While hard to decode, such musings suggest that Weber and other liberal women tacitly accepted same sex relationships so long as they were built on lofty spiritual and intellectual foundations.[196]

If Weber, Bäumer, and van Velsen resisted some "liberal" aspects of Nazi family policy, especially legalized prostitution and unfettered sexual freedom, this was hardly indicative of the bourgeois sentimentality construed by their Nazi opponents. Decriminalizing prostitution in order to keep desperate women out of prison was one matter; condoning its proliferation, as Himmler seemed to, was quite another. Here Bäumer and her colleagues insisted on distinguishing between Nazi policies that encouraged women's liberation and those that simply introduced new forms of exploitation and oppression. For the Nazis, rehabilitating single mothers and normalizing sexual promiscuity were two sides of the same natalist coin; both policies encouraged more "Aryan" children. For liberal feminists the former was a vital pillar of women's liberation. But the latter would rob young women of their dignity and, if they became pregnant, their future. By insisting on the sanctity of marriage Weber and her colleagues hoped to bolster women's position as equal partners in German social and family life instead of sexual objects or baby machines.

Between the traditional cult of domesticity and a "first wave" feminism centered on political equality, between life as passive victims and as active collaborators, liberal women in the Third Reich sought to carve out a "third way," a "cult of motherhood" that facilitated female participation in social, political, and economic life.[197] Although Bäumer and her colleagues made certain concessions to a biologically essentialist conception of social reality, this emphasis on women's "natural" advantages over their male colleagues also encouraged women's entry into the health care industry, medical profession, and education.[198] Unlike their conservative counterparts, they defended the rights of women, families, the poor, and the sick by introducing liberal elements of "nurture" and natural rights into the debate.[199] For all its contradictions, then, this progressive biomaternalism reveals less the political bankruptcy of the German women's movement than the ideological resilience and allure of German liberalism's Naumannite traditions, traditions which Bäumer and her colleagues played so great a role in shaping.[200]

V

For many historians Gertrud Bäumer remains a "collaborationist" who sought "a *modus vivendi* with the Nazi regime," who always insisted that *Die Frau* "abstain from open criticism . . . and political comment of any kind."[201] If this chapter proves anything, however, it is that Bäumer and her colleagues never refrained from pointed criticism or trenchant analysis. "The problem," Bäumer wrote in 1936, was not that *Die Frau* had lost its edge, but "that women themselves continue *voluntarily* to refuse to engage intellectually in the most pressing issues of the day."[202] Bäumer considered her activities in the Third Reich a matter of negotiation, not collaboration. Even in Nazi Germany, she wrote Marianne Weber, there were always new spheres and new ways in which one could promote women's rights and responsibilities.[203] Indeed, the Gestapo and Propaganda Ministry called Bäumer in for questioning several times, at one point striking her from the "list of those permitted to edit magazines for almost two years."[204] When the Nazi sympathizer Frances Magnus von Hausen left the publishing board of *Die Frau* in 1937, Bäumer used her newfound freedom to sharpen, not tone down, its social and political edge. That she solicited articles from fellow Democrats like Beckmann, Lüders, von Velsen, Weber, and "non-Aryans" like Baum and Jellinek hardly suggests excessive professional caution or ideological complicity.[205]

Bäumer's success in providing succor to the women's movement – and a kernel of liberal feminism within it – should not be underestimated. As late as May 1940, in the midst of war, Bäumer could announce proudly that many women from the old (liberal) "associations" would like to have a readers' letters section in *Die Frau* in order to reinvigorate the sense of intellectual community that existed before 1933.[206] *Die Frau* was doing so well in fact that Bäumer could afford to print more editions than most other wartime periodicals.[207] When the Reichspropaganda Ministry (RPM) discontinued 200 periodicals in spring 1941 – ostensibly because of a shortage of paper – *Die Frau* survived with only the modest sacrifice of four pages in length.[208]

Of course sustaining *Die Frau*'s economic viability was merely the means to an end, namely "to maintain the intellectual level that was achieved across wide circles of women" before 1933.[209] After her books were burned in Leipzig and *Die Frau* was "temporarily suspended" in 1944, Bäumer persisted, much to the Gestapo's chagrin, in lecturing on women's and religious issues and working toward renewing the periodical as soon as the war was over.[210]

Bäumer and her liberal colleagues demonstrated a greater attraction to aspects of National Socialism than survival required. But this ideological engagement, it bears repeating, did not necessarily mean uncritical accommodation.[211] It reflects, rather, a cautious intellectual investment in a movement that, for all its faults, seemed capable of fulfilling elements of Friedrich Naumann's National-Social vision in a way that the Republic could not.[212] Where affinities did not exist – such as in the Nazi penchant for violence, in biological determinism, and in a repudiation of basic civil rights – even a superficial survey of *Die Frau* shows the extent to which Democrats were willing and able to question the gap between Nazi rhetoric and reality.[213] In negotiating the Third Reich liberal women drew upon a Naumannite tradition that, while preoccupied with race and biology, ultimately rejected, in the words of Bäumer, a "National Socialism without personal freedom, without ties of civility . . . propaganda instead of honesty – in truth the diabolical perversion of that which Naumann strove for as a political and social goal."[214] This complex reality, reflecting profound continuities as well as breaks, makes easy distinctions between resistance and accommodation, between victims and collaborators, impossible.

CHAPTER FOUR

Hitler's War?
Liberal Nationalism and Nazi Foreign Policy

I

In addition to demanding tens of billions in reparation payments, the 1919 Versailles Treaty – which blamed Germany for the First World War – robbed the fledgling Republic of significant territory in the north (North Schleswig), west (Alsace, Eupen-Malmédy, the Saarland), and east (Upper Silesia, Posen, Danzig). In clear contradiction of the liberal principle of self-determination afforded all combatants in Woodrow Wilson's Fourteen Points, the Treaty thereby separated hundreds of thousands of ethnic Germans from the Reich and explicitly forbade the inclusion of millions more in Austria, Bohemia, and northern Italy. Germany was also deprived of her colonies and excluded from the League of Nations. To add insult to injury, her army was reduced to 100,000 men, her western border demilitarized, and her navy and air force were, to all intents and purposes, abolished.[1]

Little wonder that the most universally popular aspect of the Nazi program prior to the Second World War was Hitler's successful abrogation of the Versailles Treaty. When Hitler repudiated reparations; exited the League of Nations over failed disarmament talks; signed a Non-Aggression Pact with Poland and a Naval Treaty with Great Britain; regained the Saarland by plebsicite and remilitarized the Rhineland through fiat, his achievements were celebrated by the vast majority of Germans.[2] If Hitler's brusque methods in incorporating Austria and the Sudetenland made even some military leaders uneasy, his foreign policy continued to enjoy support well into the Second World War.[3] Does this widespread approbation suggest that Nazi foreign policy was more reason-able, more pragmatic, indeed more "liberal" than we are usually led to believe? Or is it yet another example of the Germans' proclivity for unabashed ethnic nationalism and imperialism?[4]

Who better to answer these questions than German liberals? No party contributed more to the peaceful, multilateral direction of German diplo-macy between the end of the First World War and the collapse of the Weimar Republic. At the same time, no party did more over the previous century to propagate the German national idea that reached its apotheosis under Hitler.[5] This chapter will begin by looking briefly at liberal foreign policy views before 1933, with a particular focus on Germany's two most influential liberals, Friedrich Naumann and Gustav Stresemann. It proceeds by surveying liberal responses to the major foreign policy questions of the 1930s and Second World War. Did Weimar Democrats always view Hitler as an ideological fanatic, bent on war, genocide, and destruction? Or did they perceive commonalities, at least initially, between Nazi foreign policy and their own? When and where did liberal views diverge from Hitler's? And what alternative vision, if any, did German Democrats have for a postwar Europe?[6] Addressing these questions sheds light not only on the character and complexity of German liberalism, but also on the reasons for Hitler's popularity and unprecedented diplomatic successes.

II

The Contradictions of *Völkisch* Liberalism

Readers will recall that liberalism and nationalism were inextricably linked for most of the nineteenth century. Liberating nations from a foreign, usually monarchical yoke was after all perfectly compatible with a univer-salist belief in freeing the individual from feudal oppression. Only in the later Victorian era, with the rise of "scientific" racial theories and the apotheosis of the nation–state, did the implicit contradictions between ethnic (*völkisch*) nationalism and universalist liberalism begin to manifest themselves.

While present across Europe, these contradictions were never as profound in post-revolutionary states like France or Great Britain. Britain had its eugenicists and France had its Dreyfus Affair. But both nations' geographic integrity was more or less established prior to the rise of modern racism, their universalist constitutional principles more firmly entrenched. For a new state like Germany there was greater uncertainty as to whether universalism would win out over the competing particularisms of the time. Among these particularisms – from Catholic ultramontanism and Hanoverian separatism to the East Elbian aristocracy – there emerged a powerful strain of ethnic nationalism.[7]

The Wilhelmine epoch would see this wave of ethnic nationalism come to challenge liberal universalism across the political spectrum, from the Social Democratic left to the moderate right.[8] Already during the 1860s and 1870s Bismarck had exploited the liberal desire to construct a formidable nation–state to postpone the democratization of German politics and society. The delayed onset of mass politics until the 1890s did nothing, however, to quell the widespread popularity of ethnic nationalism. And the left liberals, despite their universalist moorings, were complicit in its success. Numerous members of Friedrich Naumann's National-Social Association, which later merged with the left liberal Radical Union, supported higher taxation and government spending, a worker-friendly social policy (unemployment and disability insurance, collective bargaining, strong unions), and women's rights. Many also believed the state should take a more active role in the biological health of the nation while promoting an imperialist projection of German culture in Eastern Europe, Africa, and Asia.[9]

The primary issue that differentiated *völkisch* members of Naumann's National Social movement like Max Maurenbrecher or Gottfried Traub from the Wilhelmine right was their social progressivism. Mainstream National-Socials like Naumann, Heuss, Heile, Bäumer, Rohrbach, and Stresemann were more conflicted, vacillating between *völkisch* and universalist poles.[10] A universalist minority of Naumann's supporters, led by Anton Erkelenz and Helmuth von Gerlach, opposed imperialism, ethnic nationalism, and anti-Semitism in no uncertain terms. Nevertheless, even Gerlach supported a union with Austria.[11] Meanwhile many leaders of the ostensibly anti-imperialist Radical People's Party – individuals like Otto Fischbeck, Julius Kopsch, and Otto Wiemer – were positively inclined toward *völkisch* nationalism. It should come as no surprise that the Progressive People's Party, which united both left liberal factions in 1910, supported a race-based citizenship law, advocated naval and colonial expansion, and did little to pull Germany back from the brink of war.[12]

Few of these nationalist and imperialist traits were unique to Germany. The British Liberals and French Radical Socialists occupied thousands of square miles of territory in Africa and Asia, brutally oppressed native peoples, and spent hundreds of millions on armaments. Conversely, the German Progressives were probably more socially liberal and less fascinated with colonialism than their French and British counterparts. Yet there *was* a qualitative difference between the *völkisch* creed prevalent across much of German-speaking Central Europe, which tacitly dismissed the possibility that Africans, Jews, or Poles could ever "become" Germans, and the universalist ethos widespread in France and Great Britain, which expected the assimilation of ethnic minorities through strenuous adherence to political, cultural, and linguistic norms.[13] The distinction between German and "western" liberalism (some would say Socialism as well) lay not in the former's peculiarly "conservative" social or political vision, but in the pervasive role of ethnic nationalism, a *völkisch*, exclusionary element which was present but never preeminent in French or Anglo-Saxon liberalism.[14]

The sudden, war-induced transformation from a flourishing Pan-Germanic Empire to a tottering, cosmopolitan Republic only exacerbated these *völkisch* proclivities. Liberals had little more to accomplish in the area of domestic reform: the Republic had achieved everything outlined in the Progressive Party program of 1912. But the liberals were more divided than ever on nationality and foreign policy.[15] The growing disparity between *völkisch* and universalist liberalism, between "national" and "rational democracy" in the words of Gertrud Bäumer, provides the first of three conceptual axes around which this chapter is organized.[16]

Friedrich Naumann's Mitteleuropa

In 1915 Friedrich Naumann published his most famous, influential, and controversial work, *Mitteleuropa* (Middle Europe). Naumann was not the first liberal to propose a German-led Central European Union; liberal revolutionaries put forward the idea in the 1840s, while the future DDP Foreign Minister Walther Rathenau gave it concrete shape in the early months of the First World War.[17] But Naumann expanded noticeably upon Rathenau's conception of a primarily economic union between Germany and Austria–Hungary. According to Naumann, a soon-to-be-victorious Germany would fulfill its geopolitical destiny by unifying Central Europe through her economic might, superior civilization, and political will, more closely incorporating – if not necessarily annexing – the land of many adjacent peoples along the way.[18]

By Naumann's frank admission *Mitteleuropa* could only be "the fruit of war." And, like Hitler's later vision of a "Greater Germany [*Großdeutschland*]," inclusive of all ethnic German territories, it privileged German hegemony in continental Europe over the traditionally imperialist "world policy [*Weltpolitik*]" prevailing in most liberal nationalist circles. Rather than challenge British rule at sea or focus on acquiring colonies in Africa and Asia, Germany was to extend her influence in Central and Eastern Europe, uniting all Germans in one state, displacing the multiethnic Russian and Austro-Hungarian empires, and superseding France as Europe's greatest power.[19]

Nevertheless, despite the geopolitical parallels between *Mitteleuropa* and *Mein Kampf*, Naumann's program was fundamentally liberal at heart. As the historian Henry Cord Meyer observes, the idea of *Mitteleuropa* was taken up by Wilhelmine liberals like Schacht, Bosch, Heuss, Rohrbach, Eugen Schiffer, and Gustav Stolper – all future Weimar Democrats – as a distinct counterpoise to the annexationist demands of the pan-Germans.[20] Instead of imposing her might on weaker neighbors, Germany would serve as the political, economic, and cultural bridge between East and West, Russia and Great Britain, a consensus-building "honest broker" in the most enlightened Bismarckian tradition. Naumann's conception of Central European community differed considerably from that of right-wing liberals and nationalist conservatives who believed that only German Protestants deserved full and active citizenship. Anyone who wished to create a functional *Mitteleuropa*, the Lutheran pastor asserted, must embrace Jews, Slavs, and Catholics as viable, equal, "state-supporting [*staatsbildend*]" members. More remarkable is Naumann's assertion, in the midst of war, that France and Germany were natural partners who needed to overcome their historical antagonism for the good of Europe. He likewise suggested that Turkey might join the union if it could achieve the necessary level of political and economic modernity.[21]

Naumann's book contained extensive criticism of the Wilhelmine Reich's intolerant policies on minorities in Alsace and Denmark, where "many things have occurred of which we should be ashamed." In the largely Polish regions of eastern Prussia, meanwhile, the government had employed "force . . . and desires equanimity in return," but this policy could never hope to win over "the soul of the Polish people." In order for *Mitteleuropa* to succeed, Naumann concluded, "there will have to be a significant revision of all such methods, a dissociation from forced Germanization . . . the administration will have to be flexible in matters that can be allowed without endangering the state! A friendlier attitude toward national minorities is necessary everywhere in Central Europe . . . Sober, perceptible liberalism must become apparent across linguistic borders! This must be if we wish to avoid bleeding to death in nationality conflicts."[22] In short, Naumann's *Mitteleuropa* may be construed as a liberal adumbration of the postwar European Community.[23]

Still, like the contemporary American concept of "manifest destiny," which Hitler greatly admired, *Mitteleuropa* was infinitely flexible and equally susceptible to appropriation by *völkisch* nationalists.[24] Given a more favorable outcome to the war, many Germans would surely have been satisfied with the kind of liberal, multilateral, primarily economic union Naumann proposed. The war did not turn out well, however, and the Versailles Treaty caused even many Democrats to fall back on a more chauvinist and irredentist vision of *Mitteleuropa*, a "Greater Germany [*Groß* or *Gesamtdeutschland*]" that sought the (re)incorporation of Europe's ethnic Germans, with little regard for their Slavic or Baltic neighbors. This vision bore more than a surface resemblance to the foreign policy conceptions of the NSDAP.

Gustav Stresemann and Liberal Revisionism

After a brief flirtation with Naumann's National-Social movement in the early twentieth century, Stresemann took a circuitous route back to liberal democracy. Having completed a dissertation on the growth of the bottled beer industry, the young liberal married Käthe Kleefeld, the beautiful daughter of a wealthy Jewish industrialist, founded his own trade association, and rose quickly in Saxony's National Liberal Party. Elected to the Reichstag in 1907, Stresemann came into conflict with the heavy industrial right wing of the NLP over his advocacy of social welfare issues. Though losing his seat in 1912 – in part due to his unacceptability to the NLP's right wing – he was reelected as an eloquent advocate of territorial annexations in December 1914. Stresemann quickly became the leading figure in the National Liberal Party, replacing his mentor Ernst Bassermann upon the latter's death in 1917. He remained a domestic reformer, supporting the elimination of the three-class voting system in Prussia and demanding a greater role for parliament. But Stresemann gained greater notoriety as one of the most uncritical defenders of territorial annexations in Eastern Europe and of unrestricted submarine warfare. Because of this "pan-German" reputation, Stresemann was excluded from negotiations to merge the Progressives and National Liberals in November 1918. Unwilling to play a secondary role in the DDP, he formed the right liberal German People's Party (DVP) a few weeks later.[25]

During its first eighteen months of existence, the DVP was a virulently nationalist, monarchist, and anti-republican party that stopped just short of abetting a right-wing *coup d'état* in March 1920. Led by Stresemann, the party leadership gradually came to acknowledge the immense challenges faced by all Weimar parties in the wake of the Versailles Treaty, and began to modulate its opposition to the Republic.[26] In August 1923, at the height of the Ruhr crisis and hyperinflation, Stresemann was able to convince his party to seek political responsibility and form a grand coalition with the Catholics, Socialists, and Democrats. During a chancellorship that lasted a mere one hundred days, Stresemann managed to clear French and Belgian troops from the Ruhr and to stabilize the currency. As Foreign Minister in subsequent cabinets, he pursued a "diplomacy of understanding [*Verständigungspolitik*]" that did much to revise the Versailles Treaty without the threat of military force. In 1926 Stresemann was awarded the Nobel Peace Prize.[27]

Stresemann was not the first Weimar Foreign Minister to choose the path of international understanding in the interest of long-term treaty revision. His Democratic predecessor Walther Rathenau understood the economic and geopolitical value to be played by Germany in stabilizing postwar Europe and the readiness of the Entente to ensure her survival. As early as 1922, the liberal industrialist worked out the Treaty of Rapallo, which provided a multilateral basis for future territorial revisions in the East as well as Germany's secret military training on Russian soil. After Rathenau's assassination in the same year, it fell to Stresemann to apply these principles consistently and to lasting effect.[28]

His chief long-term goals were to do away with reparations and to revise the eastern border of 1919, to reclaim Upper Silesia and the Polish Corridor from Poland, and to incorporate German Austria in the so-called *Anschluss* (a liberal demand going back to the nineteenth century).[29] In the meantime Stresemann was willing to settle for the restoration of Germany's sovereignty over its western borders, a downward revision of reparations, and the gradual rebuilding of the German military, illegally if necessary. These modest short-term aspirations and conciliatory methods, such as accepting the Dawes Plan (1924), which helped finance reparation payments, and signing the Locarno Treaties (1925–26), which permanently relinquished Alsace-Lorraine to France, evoked considerable right-wing recrimination, even within Stresemann's own party. The Dawes and Young Plans (1929) nevertheless eased Germany's financial burden and helped revive the economy culminating in a 1931 moratorium on reparations. Meanwhile the Locarno Treaties led to Germany's admission to the League of Nations in 1926, the evacuation of French troops from the left bank of the Rhine in 1930, and the tacit admission that Germany's eastern borders, unlike those in the west, were open to future revision. This last concession would prove crucial in paving the way for Hitler's successful incorporation of Austria, the Sudetenland, and the Memel twelve years later. Stresemann's modest short-term gains had far-reaching consequences, without which Hitler could never have pulled off his greatest diplomatic coups.[30]

In the wake of the Great Depression, France, Britain, and the United States tended to withdraw further from world affairs, opening a greater space for Hitler's aggressive revisionism. Indeed, some historians wonder whether the Stresemann's multilateralism in the 1920s was merely a pragmatic response to Germany's military and diplomatic weakness, a policy he would have readily discarded if presented the same opportunities as Hitler.[31] While the Nobel Peace Prize winner's premature death precludes any definitive answer to this question, we would do well to examine the attitudes of Stresemann's Democratic colleagues, who endorsed his liberal nationalist conception of multilateral revisionism most devoutly.

III

Initial Liberal Responses to Nazi Foreign Policy

The failure of German democracy to resist National Socialism, Hans Robinsohn observed in 1933, was the result of a nationalist tendency informing the whole of German history. "For historically and psychologically understandable reasons the desire for unity is very lively among Germans," Robinsohn explained, while "anti-Semitism supplements this national mystique well."[32] Of course many liberals, Robinsohn added, refused to endorse the more radical *völkisch* underpinnings of Nazi foreign policy. Most rejected the idea of a master race destined to spread its seed across Central and Eastern Europe.[33] Still, Robinsohn touched upon a fundamental reason for Nazi popularity, one which is sometimes underestimated in histories of the Third Reich: even dedicated anti-Fascists were hardly immune to the excitement that accompanied Hitler's headlong assault on the Versailles Treaty.[34]

In September 1934, for example, Germany's leading pacifist, the Nobel Peace Prize winner and Democrat Ludwig Quidde, initiated a controversy when he defended the main lines of Hitler's foreign policy at Locarno. According to Quidde, Germany was justified in denouncing the territorial provisions of the Versailles Treaty and walking out of the League of Nations' sponsored Disarmament Conference. Why should Germany adhere to limits on armaments that France and Great Britain refused to abide by? How could a treaty that guaranteed the right of national self-determination expressly forbid an *Anschluss* that was overwhelmingly popular in Austria as well as Germany? Accused in the émigré press of supporting "the unification of Austria with murderous Germany," "reclaim[ing] the Polish corridor," and opposing "the borders in the West" (i.e. Alsace's return to France), Quidde responded simply that his speech was perfectly compatible with being a "pacifist and Democrat."[35]

As Quidde explained in an equally controversial article in the pacifist journal *Friedens Warte*, "from the perspective of practical politics, National Socialism has taken over the principles and demands of pacifism." One could not ignore the hypocrisy of the western powers or abandon one's critique of the Versailles Treaty simply because Hitler had replaced Stresemann as Germany's chief advocate in world affairs. Quidde cited the January 1934 Non-Aggression Pact with Poland, which, in the best Stresemannian tradition, represented an historic, bilateral step towards German–Polish reconciliation and might culminate in a peaceful revision of the disputed eastern borders.[36]

His pacifist colleagues were livid. The old Naumannite imperialist turned pacifist Helmuth von Gerlach wrote Quidde that it "is for me incomprehensible how you could interpret the incredibly illegal rearmament of Hitler as an acceptance of the principles and demands of pacifism."[37] Quidde's Democratic colleague Alfred Falk was equally incensed:

> Since no one can be forced into the role of martyr, if someone lives within the infamous straitjacket of the Nazis one has the discretionary right to purchase some relative peace through absolute silence . . . If one can, however, live outside the criminal Reich one has the requisite duty as a pacifist and democrat to do, on the one hand, everything wherever and with any means possible to undermine the land of barbarians and their system; on the other, one must repeatedly and at every opportunity raise his voice on behalf of our imprisoned and badly mishandled friends and make the world aware of German terrorism . . . In contrast to the laughable Democrats and heavily compromised Social Democrats our pacifist crest was pure and unsullied. It has particularly infuriated me that you, the old fighter, have tiptoed out of the ranks at a time that gangsters rule *our* Berlin.[38]

Liberals who chose to remain silent, Falk suggested, could be absolved of complicity. But anyone who *volunteered* support, whether or not he lived in Germany, was a collaborator. More troubling, Falk argued, were Democrats like Quidde, who lent legitimacy to Hitler's regime by publicly betraying their principles.

Falk's frustrated missive indicates how crucial it is to historicize the liberals' first responses to National Socialism. If perspicacious Democrats might refer to the Nazis as "gangsters" and "terrorists" in 1933, Hitler and his henchmen had yet to become mass murderers. Falk's complaint that it would not pay to grant Hitler's "criminal" regime any legitimacy, no matter the cause, seemed impractical to patriotic Germans exasperated by fifteen years of Allied hypocrisy. Selectively backing German foreign policy was also a matter of liberal principle insofar as it challenged Great Britain and France to match their own rhetoric with disarmament. Quidde had nothing to gain personally. He remained one of the Gestapo's leading *personae non gratae*, was exiled in 1933, and would publish highly critical attacks on National Socialism throughout the 1930s.[39] Quidde endorsed aspects of Hitler's foreign policy because he saw them as a continuation of the revisionist goals pursued by Stresemann.

Quidde was not the only anti-Fascist Democrat to sanction Hitler's assault on Versailles.[40] After witnessing the new Chancellor's early diplomatic achievements and signs of economic recovery, Robert Bosch declared, "I am convinced that Hitler wants reconciliation . . . We should still hope that we will one day experience peace on earth."[41] In the mid-1930s Alfred Weber visited the Czech Prime Minister Masaryk to discuss the peaceful incorporation of the Sudetenland.[42] Though they would risk their lives to resist Nazism, Otto Gessler, Hans Robinsohn, Theodor Tantzen, and Wilhelm Külz all supported a union with Austria, the annexation of the Sudetenland, and a revision of the eastern border with Poland.[43] No liberal was oblivious to the fact that Hitler's protestations "against the accusation that he is pushing for [conflict]" contradicted earlier assertions "that there will be a new war, and that Germany will emerge victorious."[44] Seduced by the promise of further revision, however, few Democrats could marshal much principled opposition.[45]

Indeed, where Democrats were dissatisfied with German foreign policy, this often had to do with the *modest* scope of Hitler's early successes. Marie Lüders and the former Weimar Justice Minister, Heinrich Gerland, pined away for the return of Alsace-Lorraine even as the Third Reich officially denied any desire to overturn the western borders determined at Locarno.[46] For the Baltic German Democrat Elisabeth Bronner-Höpfner, Hitler's seeming lack of interest in restoring the German Memel region constituted a personal slight. Equally frustrating to many Democrats was the government's unwillingness to discuss the German Tyrol – a delicate issue because it now belonged to Mussolini's Italy.[47] Among Weimar liberals, Bäumer and Lüders were hardly alone in wondering why Hitler wasn't moving faster to unite all ethnic Germans "under one scepter."[48]

Keenly aware of the easy elision of Democratic and Nazi revisionism, Heuss worked intensely after 1933 to dispel claims that Naumannite left liberalism was little different to National Socialism.[49] For Naumann and his liberal compatriots, Heuss wrote in 1937, "nationalism and socialism appeared as two sides of the same task . . . nationalism not as unrestricted German self-love, but as an impetus for German self-determination . . . the will to infuse the life of the nation with a system of practical laws and legal order, so that the optimum was attained in terms of health, the pursuit of happiness, human rights, and civil freedom."[50] A country without a navy or colonies would never have the resources to ameliorate social inequalities. But healthy nationalism, Heuss continued, was not supposed to supersede the central liberal tenets of liberty and equality for all peoples:

> Naumann's Germanness was elementary and unprogrammatic. Certainly he was always moved by and claimed to have a "German" political mentality . . . But the knowing respect for all that was foreign and its singular character was for him a part of having a proud, unabashed national consciousness. Even in the midst of the imperialist influence that defined his being, he lacked that nationalist hubris that indicated a feeling of impotence. He was motivated by the belief that the eternal task had been placed before the Germans to conceive of and achieve solutions for the rest of the world in the intellectual, in the religious, and also in the sphere of social and economic solidarity, to which order and freedom were close relatives.[51]

Bäumer also insisted that the concept of national self-determination, which infused so much of Naumann's thinking, was "a liberal, a democratic idea" that had been twisted to serve the interests of the radical right.[52]

Nevertheless, when Heuss wrote her in February 1933 to indict the fanatical nationalism that facilitated Hitler's victory, Bäumer was noticeably silent.[53] Paul Rohrbach was likewise forced into a struggle between his cosmopolitan love of foreign cultures and the ethnic nationalist views he had imbibed as a young Baltic German.[54] This delicate balancing act between *völkisch* and liberal nationalism, between the subjugation of ethnic minorities and a multilateral "Central Europe [*Mitteleuropa*]," became increasingly difficult to maintain as the remnants of the Versailles Treaty fell by the wayside.

For this reason it is vital to differentiate, wherever possible after 1933, between Naumann's liberal nationalism and the race-obsessed chauvinism at the core of Hitler's National Socialism.[55] Distinguishing these tendencies is not always easy. Most Democrats fell somewhere between racist and universalist poles, while even liberal pacifists like Quidde might temporarily share some of the same objectives as Hitler. Based in part on the ideological continuum described above, we might nevertheless divide liberal democrats into four camps: those liberals who opposed Nazi foreign policy in principle regardless of the circumstances; those who agreed with many of Hitler's goals but quickly repudiated his methods; those who supported Nazi foreign policy throughout the early and middle years of the regime, becoming disillusioned after 1936 as Hitler took greater risks for seemingly more fanatical reasons; and those whose own ideological obsessions with ethnic nationalism and *Lebensraum* made it possible for them to rationalize Nazi foreign policy well into the Second World War.

Into the first camp one might place liberal émigrés and pacifists like Helmuth von Gerlach, Friedrich Wilhelm Förster, Walther Schücking, and Anton Erkelenz. These quintessentially universalist liberals, most of whom left the Democratic Party before 1933, consitute an exceedingly small minority. Quidde, Robinsohn, Gothein, and Tantzen, who represented the Democratic "left wing" in foreign policy terms, fit the profile of the second group. Bosch, Külz, Heuss, Dietrich, Lüders, and Schacht belong to the third, which epitomizes the "mainstream" of liberal democratic opinion. Finally Rohrbach, Bäumer, Winschuh, and Obst might fall into the *völkisch*-inclined fourth group, whose foreign policy views most often (but not always) overlapped with Hitler's. Although such general distinctions sometimes dissolve in the face of sociopolitical reality, they do provide a rough conceptual framework for understanding the complex relationship between liberal and Nazi foreign policy.

Territorial Revision, Rearmament, and the Rhineland

As the dust settled on Hitler's early foreign policy successes, most patriotic liberals faced a profound ethical dilemma: how to work toward Germany's diplomatic and economic resurgence without appearing to sanction the regime's illiberal policies in other ways. Heuss articulated this problem precisely in defending his colleague Georg Gothein against the absurd accusation that he was, according to Anton Erkelenz, a "criminal destroyer of the Republic." To be sure, unlike more radical pacifists, Gothein accepted the use of military force as a last resort, mainly to preserve one's national sovereignty or prevent egregious human rights abuses. He also disagreed with the Versailles Treaty's hypocritical application of the principle of self-determination, which deprived defeated powers of territory so that the Entente could cobble together ethnically heterogeneous states like Czechoslovakia and Yugoslavia. While he acknowledged the need for adequate national defense and self-determination, however, Gothein supported Germany's decision to leave the Geneva Disarmament Conference for the same reasons as Quidde: in order to highlight French and British hypocrisy, not as an endorsement of Hitler's designs for European conquest or accelerated rearmament. Now, after enduring right-wing charges of treason for opposing territorial annexations during the First World War, Gothein was censured by the left merely for upholding the same 1914 borders. In 1915 Naumann had fended off nationalist attacks on his party colleague; two decades later it was Naumann's protégé Heuss who jumped to Gothein's defense. What had Gothein done to betray the Republic? By acquiescing in some aspects of Hitler's foreign policy while denigrating the Nazi domestic program, Gothein only proved that he was a free-thinking Democrat.[56]

Just a few weeks after this exchange, Gothein echoed Walther Rathenau – and no doubt antagonized Hitler – by proposing the idea of "incorporat[ing] Russia" and other East European countries "into an economically united Europe." This "tariff union" would be mutually beneficial in providing Soviet raw materials for West and Central Europe and in supplying in return finished goods for the vast Russian market.[57] The Soviet Union, one may recall, was National Socialism's arch-enemy in 1934. A year later, the seventy-seven-year-old Democrat went further, rebuking Schacht's "Keynesian" economic policy, which Gothein felt would yield inflation instead of growth. In some ways anticipating the clearing arrangements that Schacht's "New Plan" worked out with East European client states, Gothein called for mutually beneficial trade agreements that encouraged German exports and lowered the cost of imports. But instead of creating a ring of Central and East European satellites, as Schacht envisioned, Gothein advocated a multilateral economic union along the lines of Naumann's *Mitteleuropa*.[58]

Gothein next turned his sights on Germany's future ally, Japan. Having brought Korea, Formosa, and Manchuria "under its bidding," the Asian superpower wanted "to make China exclusively into an object of exploitation." When the League of Nations denounced its occupation of Manchuria, the longtime "pacifist" recalled, Japan responded by brutally invading Shanghai and cynically abandoning the League (a subtle swipe at Hitler's decision to do the same). Now it followed up with designs on Beijing and with imperialist economic policies across Asia, which included "dumping" in client states (policies similar to those propagated by the Third Reich in Central and Eastern Europe). Gothein concluded by reiterating his 1934 demand for a "world coalition against Japan." Although the Axis alliance was a few years off, there could be no mistake about the analogies to the Third Reich embedded in Gothein's campaign against Japanese imperialism and ethnic cleansing.[59]

Liberals were less critical when it came to rearmament. Democrats like Rathenau, Otto Gessler, and most of all Stresemann labored – both legally and illegally – to erase the military constraints of the Versailles Treaty. It is difficult to imagine Stresemann walking out of the Disarmament Conference or unilaterally announcing plans to rearm. But these decisions by Hitler in many ways merely represented the public acknowledgement of the secret rearmament promoted by Weimar liberals since the early 1920s.[60] Most liberals greeted these moves as liberating, not warmongering. And while Hitler's decision to institute general conscription in March 1935 was a blatant abrogation of what was left of Versailles, Heuss, Bäumer, Lüders, and others justified it by pointing out France's own accelerating rearmament.[61]

Only the Rhineland occupation a year later changed some qualified Democratic supporters into nascent critics. Claiming that Franco-Soviet *rapprochement* nullified the military constraints of the Versailles Treaty, Hitler ordered a small number of German troops to remilitarize the Rhine on 7 March 1936. Vastly outnumbered by heavily armored French divisions massed along the border, Hitler faced the imminent collapse of his regime. When the French, preoccupied by domestic strife and the Italian invasion of Abyssinia, determined to do nothing, Hitler's popularity soared.[62]

Democrats reacted more skeptically than the population at large. Hans Robinsohn reported that the remilitarization of the Rhineland alienated important military leaders and split the officer corps.[63] Infuriated by the regime's eagerness to sacrifice German lives, Külz's enthusiasm for "Greater Germany" quickly dissipated and Bosch immediately approached his contacts in Great Britain, in the hope of deterring Hitler from taking any further unilateral actions.[64] After the Rhineland occupation even enthusiastic Naumannites like Bäumer warned against the consequences of Hitler's *va banque* foreign policy: "Every day the market niche for technology of mass murder [*Massentodes*] is being advanced in numerous laboratories, factories, and training fields . . . a European war in which all these 'advances' are really employed will ultimately recognize only the 'defeated [*Besiegte*].' "[65]

Lacking a viable alternative to Hitler, however, Democrats still looked to the Third Reich to remove the last teeth from the Versailles Treaty: to regain Danzig, the Polish Corridor, and Upper Silesia; to achieve the

Anschluss with Austria; and perhaps to incorporate Austria's lost German territories in Czechoslovakia (the Sudetenland) and Italy (the Tyrol).[66] Stresemann had advocated Germany's secret remilitarization and most Democrats could see no objective reason why Germany, nearly a generation after the war, should be deprived of the right to self-determination afforded other peoples by the Versailles Treaty.[67] A mounting fear of Soviet Communism, exacerbated by the Spanish Civil War and Anglo-French diplomatic feelers toward Stalin, also helped to hold liberal skepticism at bay.[68]

At the same time the methodological differences between liberal nationalist and Nazi diplomacy were becoming apparent. The Rhineland episode was the clearest departure yet from Stresemann's policy of revision through multilateral negotiation. Universal conscription and the remilitarization of the Rhineland were likewise essential catalysts in dissipating liberal enthusiasm for Hitler's foreign policy. If most Democrats shared Hitler's desire to eliminate the Versailles Treaty and unite Europe's ethnic Germans, few were ready to risk war or flout international law to do it. Meanwhile, there remained a vital foreign policy question, which divided many Weimar Democrats from the Nazis: Germany's former colonies.

Paul Rohrbach and the Colonial Question

No Weimar Democrat is more emblematic of the fraught relationship between liberal nationalism, imperialism, and National Socialism than Paul Rohrbach. Like many interwar German liberals who fail to fit the procrustean Anglo-Saxon model, Rohrbach has received little attention from historians. Those few who have examined his long and fascinating life tend to characterize Rohrbach as a closet conservative, whose worldview reflected the "ideological contradictions and social motivations that were represented by the bourgeois right." In typically dismissive fashion, Horst Bieber insists for example that "common-sense republicans [*Vernunftrepublikaner*]" like Rohrbach "were in reality outspoken anti-Democrats."[69]

This refusal to acknowledge Rohrbach's liberal pedigree is unjustified. A devoted Naumannite and Wilhelmine Progressive, Rohrbach articulated an "ethical imperialism" in which a liberal Germany, dedicated to freedom, capitalism, and democracy, would insinuate itself into countries across Europe and Africa, bringing civilization, economic growth, and good government to "benighted" peoples everywhere. Unlike some liberals who believed that Germany's future lay exclusively in Central and Eastern Europe (*Mitteleuropa*), Rohrbach was a fervent adherent of Chancellor

Bernhard von Bülow's "world policy [*Weltpolitik*]" and served for three years under Bülow as a commissioner in German Southwest Africa. This experience reinforced Rohrbach's conviction that Germany, a highly cultured nation of poets and thinkers, was better suited to colonizing than Great Britain, France, or Belgium, for whom economic exploitation was the only motivation. Like Naumann, he believed that Germany could spread her influence peacefully, through the wonders of German culture, industry, and technology.[70]

Rohrbach's "ethical imperialism" – a close variation on Britain's "White Man's Burden" or France's "Civilizing Mission" – profoundly influenced Heuss, Bäumer, Heile, and other National-Socials' foreign policy views. In domestic matters Rohrbach was a Progressive, encouraging greater democratization, civil rights, and social reform. He supported the Reichstag's Peace Resolution against the demands of the pan-Germans and helped create the German Democratic Party in November 1918.[71] "Only on the foundation of democracy," Rohrbach wrote a few weeks later, is it "possible to unite the unconditionally national and decisively social perspective." Rohrbach was pleased that his old friend Naumann was named DDP chairman and used his prominent role as publicist and editor of the widely read *Leitartikel-Korrespondenz* to promote a liberal nationalist foreign policy agenda.[72]

Rohrbach's relations with the DDP soured after Naumann's death, however. First the DDP national committee withdrew its promise to place Rohrbach on the Reichstag ballot. A year later his protégé Theodor Heuss scoffed at Rohrbach's belief that morality might still play a role in foreign policy. In 1924 he butted heads with the new DDP chairman Koch-Weser, whose willingness to expropriate East Elbian aristocrats and rebuild a coalition with the Socialists, Rohrbach believed, would alienate the DDP's bourgeois electorate at a time when liberal loyalties were on the wane. Rebuffed at every turn, Rohrbach flirted briefly with the Conservative People's Party before reluctantly joining the NSDAP in 1933.[73]

Rohrbach remained deeply ambivalent about the Hitlerian version of National Socialism.[74] While one could not deny how powerful "the national dynamic had become in the new state," he wrote, it was worrying to think what might happen in a Germany where, "in contrast to England, there was no leading class, produced through a long period of political acculturation, with a sober, consensus view of what one can tolerate politically and what one cannot, what one can permit to happen and what one cannot."[75] Despite his bitter resentment of the Versailles Treaty, he also urged the regime to make conciliatory advances toward Britain and

France. Regaining German land and honor was possible, Rohrbach argued, without inviting a second world war.[76]

From the perspective of Nazi foreign policy, which focused on acquiring *Lebensraum* in Eastern Europe, Rohrbach's views were iconoclastic. Hitler generally grounded his demands for eastern border revision in assurances that Germany had no desire to challenge British hegemony in Africa or Asia. Rohrbach, in contrast, lost no opportunity in demanding the return of Germany's African colonies and pointing out the abuses of Anglo-French colonial policy.[77] Rohrbach's "defense" of Italy's foray into Abyssinia in 1935 focused on British duplicity, for example, not on the dubious merits of Mussolini's grounds for invasion. Had the British not been prepared to instigate a global conflict over Fashoda a mere generation before? Did they not dominate Middle Eastern and African politics and commerce more than any European power? How could the British make a moral case against Italy?[78] This typical English casuistry was apparent in regard to Germany as well. Thus Albion repudiated Versailles by negotiating a Naval Pact with Hitler, while formally denying Germany her right to colonies, conscription, or rearmament.[79]

Though exasperated by British hypocrisy, Rohrbach's frustration with Hitler's colonial policy – or lack thereof – was equally palpable.[80] The material disadvantage in not regaining the colonies, Rohrbach contended, was exacerbated by the fact that "we have to stand by as onlookers as others work on cultivating and rationalizing an unimaginably immense part of the world."[81] Rohrbach spent much of the early to mid-1930s traveling across Africa and reporting back to Germany about the wonders of her lost colonies.[82] Far from reinforcing the genocidal racism of the Third Reich, these emotion-laden missives reflect the legacy of Naumann's liberal imperialism.[83] Like Naumann before him, Rohrbach yearned to "liberate" and "civilize" Africans, Asians, and East Europeans, not to enslave or exterminate them. Rohrbach likewise condemned the rise of racial pseudoscience in the Third Reich, at least indirectly, by taking the "liberal" French and British to task for employing similar stereotypes in their treatment of native Africans and Asians.[84]

He noted in particular British capriciousness in snubbing German, Italian, and Japanese colonial demands while refusing to liberate India, the largest colonial empire in the world.[85] In a January 1937 article titled "Magna Carta of Slavery," Rohrbach praised Jawaharal Nehru's criticism of the new Indian constitution. He issued similar condemnations of British policy in Palestine and took the French Prime Minister Léon Blum to task for not addressing political and cultural oppression in

Algeria. We will remember that Nehru and the Franco-Jewish Blum were both Socialists and neither was "Aryan." French Algerians, whose participation in the 1923 Ruhr occupation offended even moderate Germans, were "subhuman" according to Nazi race laws.[86]

Rohrbach's ethnocultural magnanimity did not preclude certain natalist, eugenicist, and paternalist sentiments prevailing across Europe in the 1930s. Like his French counterparts, Rohrbach lamented the fact that Germany's population was declining, a natural result of limited resources and insufficient *Lebensraum*. Like many Anglo-Saxon social theorists, he worried about "*nationale Vermassung*" – ethnosocial deracination of the German people as a result of industralization – and thought that National Socialism might be able to correct the "underappreciation of national feeling."[87] And, like many liberals across Europe, he referred to Japanese aggression as the "yellow peril" while mocking fears of Africa's growing population (with "a half dozen airplanes" one could deal easily with any African uprising).[88] If not necessarily racist in the biological sense propounded by the Nazis, Rohrbach's attitudes to Africans and Asians were replete with prejudice and cultural insensitivity.[89]

Yet he shared with his longtime collaborators Naumann, Schacht, Jäckh and other liberal imperialists a respect and admiration for non-Germanic peoples.[90] When describing the Chinese or Japanese, Rohrbach praised their ancient cultures, intellectual sophistication, and increasingly liberal attitudes to women. He enthused over the socially progressive and well-organized anti-imperialist movements in Korea, Vietnam, and India.[91] And by supporting German self-determination and eastward expansion on the continent he revealed little of the racial prejudice toward Slavs so widely shared among Nazis. Rohrbach claimed to recognize equally the rights of all "oppressed" peoples, be they German, Indian, Arab, or African.[92]

In a 1939 book written with his son Justus, *Africa Today and Tomorrow*, the Rohrbachs insisted on the role of culture, geography, economy, and history in shaping African peoples, dismissing questions of "blood and soil" as immaterial. First condemning the European introduction of the slave trade, which they blamed for many of Africa's ills, they exhorted Europeans to help lower the infant mortality rate and improve living conditions across the continent. In conclusion, they underscored Africa's ethnocultural diversity and great industrial potential, making a case for greater economic assistance and integration into world trade. This would have been a remarkably forward-thinking book for "liberal" Great Britain or America in the 1930s, much less Nazi Germany.[93] Thus Rohrbach's imperialist vision, despite its typical Edwardian prejudices, was markedly more progressive than Nazi conceptions of Africans as irredeemably, biologically inferior.[94]

By the late 1930s, Rohrbach had become visibly estranged from the regime. He resented in particular the dismissal of well-trained economic experts and colonial enthusiasts like Schacht and Goerdeler in favor of Nazi parvenus like Goering and Funk. Henceforth Rohrbach removed himself from all government organizations and worked to pursue an independent line as a freelance journalist and travel writer.[95] He continued to justify Germany's revisionist path, but through resort to international law and mutual understanding.[96] According to Heuss, Rohrbach also began to meet regularly with members of "one of the moral opposition cells in the Reich capital" which nurtured "personal ties to Dr Goerdeler" and "Bonhoeffer, with whom Rohrbach was friends." That Rohrbach belonged to the NSDAP was well known, Heuss added, which "only made it more dangerous for him as the circle's only active civil servant." "Regarding the upright opposition of Dr Rohrbach to the 'ideology' and politics of National Socialism," Heuss concluded, "there can be not the slightest doubt."[97]

IV

The Path to War

In 1936 most liberals still believed that Hitler and the Nazis had similar ambitions: a strong national defense; the return of Danzig, the Polish Corridor, and Upper Silesia; union with Austria: annexation of the Sudetenland and perhaps even the German-speaking Tyrol, which Hitler had so far downplayed to avoid a rift with Italy. Hermann Dietrich and the Democratic economist Gerhard von Schulze-Gävernitz felt nothing but reproach for Nazi domestic policies, but both insisted that it was "the failure of the Versailles Treaty" and not a German appetite for conquest that gave Hitler the platform for his diplomatic successes and created the preconditions for the Second World War.[98] Just before departing for England, August Weber likewise conceded that Hitler "had a good nose for foreign policy . . . he recognized with alacrity the weaknesses of western statesmen and exploited them in his favor, which explains his immense diplomatic achievements."[99] The liberal diplomat and Stresemann devotee, Werner von Rheinbaben, also praised Hitler's energetic revisionism. Early support for Hitler was hardly indicative of blind fanaticism, Rheinbaben maintained, but reflected the "conflicts of conscience, misdirected idealism, [and] disappointed hopes" of a generation burdened with Versailles.[100]

The ample correspondence between Gothein and his liberal colleague Joseph Williger illustrates well this "conflict of conscience" between revising Versailles on the one hand and averting war on the other. At first Williger took Hitler to account in November 1933 for failing to act on his promises to restore the Polish territories to Germany (which was, of course, the proximate cause of the Second World War six years later). As Hitler began to build his case for annexing the Sudetenland in 1937, Williger hoped that Germany would help revise the Hungarian borders as well. When Gothein referred to foreign press reports blaming international tensions on Hitler, Williger countered that the British were rearming just as quickly and that their newspapers were equally prone to propaganda and xenophobia. Finally, in the wake of Schacht's dismissal as Finance Minister in September 1937, Williger worried not that Hitler was consolidating his dictatorship, but that Germany had lost its best advocate for regaining German colonies in Africa.[101] Williger condemned Hitler's risk-taking in the same letter. He also took the occasion of 'universal' conscription to mock Hitler's race laws and denounce Germany's incursion into the Spanish Civil War.[102] But lest we discount these criticisms as liberal contrarianism, it bears repeating that Williger was disappointed by the *slow pace* of Hitler's revisionism.[103]

For similar reasons many Democrats continued to vacillate between criticism and approbation after 1936. Marie Lüders extolled the benefits of multilateral diplomacy and the gospel of international understanding. Unlike her more pacifistic colleagues, however, Lüders was genuinely committed to ensuring women's full participation in any future war.[104] She wrote two books which insisted on the historical necessity of women's integration into the armed forces and wartime economy. Though the first book about women's (lack) of participation in the First World War, *Die Unbekannte Heer* (The Unknown Army), invited mixed reviews, her follow-up *Frauen in der Kriegswirtschaft* (Women in the War Economy) was well received even in conservative military and Nazi circles.[105] Meanwhile there was a group of business-oriented liberals, including Bosch, Schacht, and Höpker-Aschoff, "who rejected a war, but who spoke of a power political expansion" in Central Europe for economic reasons.[106] To be sure, by early 1938 many of these hopes had been dashed. No Democrat relished the accelerating trend toward economic autarchy or the Nazification of the diplomatic corps, Finance Ministry, and General Staff in winter 1937–38.[107]

Still, few liberals could easily abandon their century-old territorial ambitions in Central and Eastern Europe, least of all when the Third Reich remained smaller than the Second and when millions of ethnic Germans were still separated from their countrymen, constituting unwanted minorities in majority Slavic countries. Naumann's earlier conception of *Mitteleuropa* lingered in the minds of many, supplemented by an underlying *völkisch* belief in uniting all Germans in a "Greater German Reich." After the Rhineland occupation, the Four Year Plan, accelerated rearmament, and the reorganization of the diplomatic and military corps, there could be no more illusions about Hitler's Stresemannian patrimony. But the injustices of Versailles remained.

The Dilemma of Self-Determination: Austria and the Sudetenland

The year 1938 was an enormously successful one for Hitler. It began with the deft incorporation of Austria (*Anschluss*) and concluded with the peaceful annexation of the Sudetenland.[108] The *Anschluss* was neither planned nor expected. Displeased with the continuing prohibition of the Austrian Nazi Party after a failed 1934 coup, Hitler insisted in January 1938 that the ban be lifted and that a Nazi be installed as Prime Minister. When Austrian Chancellor Kurt von Schusnigg demurred, calling instead for a plebiscite on Austro-German unity, Hitler massed troops on the border and ordered the Nazi-sympathizing Minister of the Interior Arthur Seyss-Inquart to prepare a coup. On 12 March 1938 German forces marched into Austria on Seyss-Inquart's invitation and Hitler, seeing no real domestic or foreign opposition, spontaneously announced the incorporation of Austria into the Greater German Reich.[109] The Munich Agreement was of course the last-minute September 23rd arrangement, brokered by the British Prime Minister Neville Chamberlain to prevent a European war, which subsequently ceded the ethnic German part of Czechoslovakia known as the Sudetenland to the Third Reich.[110]

Both these foreign policy coups were goals promoted in the 1920s and 1930s by German Democrats. Otto Gessler, for example, a Weimar Minister of War and future member of the anti-Hitler resistance, was chairman of the German-Austrian Cooperative Society (Deutsch-Oesterreichsiche Arbeitsgemeinschaft), to which numerous German and Austrian Nazis also belonged. As late as 1937, Gessler hoped that "the homogeneity of race" between the two countries would finally lead to political integration.[111] Heinrich Gerland was also a vocal supporter of the *Anschluss*, cooperating with Nazi colleagues to create a "Greater Germany."[112] In fact many moderate liberals, including the Jewish

Democrats Gustav Stolper and Eugen Schiffer, were emotionally wedded
to the idea of Austro-German unity.[113] If a liberal minority worried about
Hitler's unilateral methods – and the international community's failure to
respond to them – most rejoiced that the "phantom [of Versailles] is gone.
Greater Germany exists."[114]

Liberals registered more trepidation concerning Hitler's demands for the
Sudetenland. Like Austria, this mountainous, heavily fortified territory
along the Czechoslovakian border had never belonged to imperial
Germany, but was a former province of the Habsburg Empire. Hence, while
the incorporation of the Sudetenland appeared logical in the wake of the
Anschluss – and while most liberals empathized with the embattled German
minority – few viewed the Sudetenland as a casualty of Versailles or believed
it was worth a world war. Rohrbach alleges that no one trusted Hitler's
peaceful intentions in this regard and only the capitulatory stance of the
British at Munich prevented a coup.[115] Rheinbaben likewise recalls how the
Allies undermined the anti-Nazi opposition by playing into Hitler's hands:
France was "lacking in energy" and there were "errors and poor decisions on
both sides."[116] Allied passivity, Lüders later recalled, played a greater role in
encouraging Hitler than any premeditated plans for war.[117]

But the primary reason for this lack of resistance, both within Germany
and without, was the problematic tenet of self-determination. Neither
France nor Great Britain was willing to risk war over the territorial
integrity of Czechoslovakia, a recently cobbled together, multinational state
that contradicted the liberal nationality principle outlined in the Versailles
Treaty.[118] Furthermore, unlike Stalin's Soviet Union, Nazi Germany was
not a totalitarian state, at least not before the Second World War. The
Third Reich was a "participatory dictatorship," replete with public opinion
polls, plebiscites, and firmly entrenched interest groups. Anti-Nazi forces,
both at home and abroad, had to take account of (and were themselves
susceptible to) German public opinion.[119] Hitler invited risks that put
Germany on the precipice of war, but he succeeded in granting the vast
majority of liberals something they desperately desired: a "Greater
Germany," inclusive of Austria. Subsequently his burgeoning "approval
rating," not to mention the liberals' own guilty pleasure in Hitler's diplomatic conquests, rendered immediate political resistance superfluous.[120]

Matters became more complicated when Hitler's post-Munich foreign
policy began to outstrip the basic liberal premise of self-determination. In
March 1939 German troops occupied Bohemia and Moravia, granting
Slovakia nominal independence. The pretext for the invasion – that the few
thousand remaining ethnic Germans faced physical danger from angry

Czechs – appeared flimsy even to liberal nationalists. Democrats in particular registered the hypocrisy of incorporating Czech lands when the philosophical premise of German revisionism was national self-determination. More pragmatically, the last decades of the Austro-Hungarian Empire indicated the difficulties of suppressing minorities while building democracy and normalizing relations with Slavic neighbors. For these reasons, Hans Robinsohn suggested, "the occupation of Czechoslovakia is actually a monumental defeat for Germany."[121]

The catalyst for this unfortunate turn of events, Robinsohn observed, was a "nationality principle" run amok. Embraced by all signatories of the Versailles Treaty, the principle of self-determination provided Hitler with ample rhetorical ammunition for the division of Czechoslovakia. In the infinitely complex ethnoterritorial reality that was interwar Central Europe, one people's self-determination – in this case the Czechs' – almost always meant another's subjugation, in this case that of the Slovaks, Hungarians, Germans, and Poles.[122] Perhaps "the most crucial consequence [of this occupation] for Europe," Robinsohn continued, "is the recognition of what repercussions will follow if one leaves everything to the schematic principle of nationality." He concluded:

> Everywhere in Europe there are groups at work that play the role of national minorities in order to exaggerate their own importance or to serve the interests of their "Führer." One observes the events in Belgium, and one turns to look at Alsace-Lorraine and even at Brittany. There is no ethnographic slice of territory, no matter how meaningless, that is not a breeding ground for microcephalic but nonetheless all the more profound nationalism.[123]

By dismantling Czechoslovakia, Hitler had deprived Germany of its last moral high ground (if any remained after Munich). But he had also burdened an already divided anti-Nazi opposition with an impossible debate over whether to retain Bohemia and Moravia in a post-National Socialist Germany. Most importantly, Hitler's move demonstrated once and for all that liberal adherence to the easily manipulable principle of national self-determination would have to be discarded if the Democrats ever wished to propose an ideological alternative to National Socialism.[124]

War for Danzig?

This was the title chosen by the Oxford historian A.J.P. Taylor for the final chapter in his controversial book on the *Origins of the Second World*

War. Anticipating the so-called "functionalist" argument of a generation later, Taylor insisted that Hitler was an opportunist, acting as would any German statesmen under the circumstances. War broke out in September 1939 due to a series of misunderstandings resulting from Hitler's quite reasonable assumption that neither France nor Britian would unleash a world war to defend another dubious aspect of an already defunct treaty. In addition to the diplomatic evidence provided by Taylor, later functionalist historians have cited Germany's insufficient military and economic preparations to illustrate that a long, imperialist war for *Lebensraum* was never in the offing.[125] The alternative "intentionalist" view is that Hitler was already preparing for conquest in 1933, biding his time until he could unleash a war for *Lebensraum* in the East. The Second World War was not the cumulative result of rising stakes and miscalculations by multiple actors, but the inevitable outcome of a Nazi foreign policy bent on conquest.[126] Some historians accept the functionalist position that the Third Reich lacked clear objectives and failed to prepare adequately for war, but they simultaneously stress the role of Hitler's ideology – the so-called "primacy of politics" – in pushing events inexorably toward military conflict.[127]

If we examine the position of liberal democrats in the six months between the occupation of Bohemia and the invasion of Poland, it is this latter view that prevails: namely that Hitler's provocative foreign policy belied Germany's lack of economic, military, or strategic preparation for war. The lessons of the First World War, Georg Gothein wrote in early 1939, reveal that any total "war brings many greater losses than profits even for the victorious powers" and that the "demands that a future war would place on the exploitation of goods and people" were incalculable. Germany was no more ready for a long war in 1939 than it was in 1914. No systematic plan was in place to employ women to replace the millions of male workers heading to the front. Germany and Italy also lacked sufficient men and materiel to wage an extended war against the French and British empires, not to mention the Soviets.[128] Air power was the most effective weapon in modern warfare, Gothein noted, but a lost plane was nothing compared to the loss of a skilled pilot: "In this regard the western powers have an immense advantage insofar as the United States could supply them with extensive materials [including manpower]. The Berlin–Rome Axis should harbor no illusions about the fact that the USA would throw its strength in their favor should the situation of the western powers become critical." If the United States intervened, Gothein predicted, Germany's fate would be sealed.[129]

Hans Robinsohn agreed. Reporting on a confidential discussion with members of the Reichswehr in spring 1939, Robinsohn remarked: "it is astounding to assert that the preparations [for war] have for a long time been less masterfully carried out than one had assumed." There was such a "scarcity of food, life necessities and raw materials" that parts of Germany were experiencing a resurgence of the Depression-era black market. In order to underscore the combination of ideological fanaticism and inadequate short-term planning that characterized Nazi foreign policy, Robinsohn pointed out that the once conciliatory British ambassador Neville Henderson had come to take Hitler's plans for *Lebensraum* seriously, while Chamberlain, once bitten at Munich, had committed to military intervention in case of further aggression. Hitler's blind fanaticism, Robinsohn concluded, would be Germany's undoing.[130]

Regardless of their sympathy with various aspects of the Nazi program, many Democrats shared Gothein and Robinsohn's concern about the disparity between Germany's poor state of military preparedness and its ambitious foreign policy. Theodor Tantzen was certain that Hitler's "catastrophic diplomacy" would end in war. As he related to Werner Stephan in spring 1939, "In a few years Germany will be reduced to half its size. Better to be small but integrated into a peaceful community than be a constant source of unrest that threatens other countries and peoples." Stephan recalls how he was taken aback by Tantzen's "defeatist" views. Another Democratic colleague, Ernst Meyer, remembers a conversation in Tantzen's house around this time: "Those present saw Germany's only possible salvation in a quick invasion by the western powers . . . Better defeat in honor than shame; this was the common view, for such a regime, Tantzen exclaimed, 'is a pestilence.' "[131]

Gothein, Robinsohn, and Tantzen were more skeptical and principled than most. But many liberals expressed grave concern about the direction of German foreign policy after Munich. Though he had justified Hitler's every move since exiting the League of Nations, Rheinbaben confessed that Hitler was driving toward a war that Germany could not win.[132] Robert Bosch and Hans Walz were so thoroughly convinced of the inevitability of defeat that they began discussing plans for a post-Nazi Germany six months before the outbreak of hostilities.[133] Still technically a minister in the Reich Government, Schacht quietly sought out contacts in the bourgeois opposition.[134]

Liberal nationalists like Rohrbach and Bäumer were, typically, more ambivalent. When news of the Polish invasion broke on 2 September, Rohrbach felt none of the excitement and anticipation he displayed in

August 1914. Nor, however, did he wish for a repeat of November 1918.[135] Bäumer too was prepared "to recognize the injustice of war and yet not be able to wish for total defeat. The letters from this time reflect how earnestly she struggled with this inner conflict, how profoundly affected she was by the need of the people, and how much she wanted to help carry the suffering of those who were robbed of their sons."[136] Recalling the liberal crisis of conscience during the First World War, Theodor Heuss declared that German Democrats would once again have to straddle the line between the "distorted worldview" of pacifists on the one hand and radical nationalists who "considered the mere discussion of peace . . . as treason" on the other.[137] This time the stakes would be even higher.

V

Liberation or Conquest?

In September 1939 the impression predominated in liberal circles that Germany was fighting a "war of liberation [*Befreiungskrieg*]," even among those who believed Hitler had provoked it. The Versailles Treaty had ceded larges swaths of German territory to Poland between 1918 and 1921. And despite the open-ended wording of the Locarno Treaty, which admitted the possibility of future border revision, Poland had shown absolutely no desire to bargain any of it back.[138] No Democrat advocated territorial revision through military means, but, like Stresemann at Locarno, they refused to accept the postwar settlement as permanent. Erasing the Polish border was not a "Nazi" idea, after all. It was a concept shared by many "who were dedicated to the liberal ideas of the nineteenth-century German bourgeoisie" and who "could rely on a broad societal consensus in the interwar period that intended a revision of the Polish borders laid out in the Versailles Treaty."[139] Following the enormously successful German Offensive, which lasted a mere six weeks, many could not help but betray enthusiasm for the "liberation" of German minorities.[140]

Paul Rohrbach defended the occupation by arguing that the Poles had garnered far more land to the east and west than they deserved on the basis of the nationality principle.[141] Signs around Danzig and the Corridor, he wrote at the end of October, had duly been changed back to German, with new, well-built German houses finally crowding out the "dirty" Polish hovels that had proliferated in the interwar decades.[142] Unaware of Hitler's incipient plans for attacking the Soviet Union, Rohrbach criticized the cession of the Baltic countries to Stalin per the

Nazi-Soviet Pact. He was especially unhappy with Himmler's policy of moving Germans from their homes on the Weichsel and giving the province to the Russians. Visiting the Baltic states, he urged minorities who were "at least partially racial Germans" to preserve their *Volkstum* (ethnicity) in the face of Soviet barbarism and Nazi indifference.[143]

If Rohrbach's fervor for restoring Germany's ethnoterritorial integrity appeared greater than Hitler's in some regards, in other ways he tried to draw a line between Germany's "just" claims to Polish territory and Hitler's unnecessarily brutal methods. Notwithstanding his deep-seated resentment of British imperialism, Rohrbach praised an older generation of English statesmen who knew when to employ diplomacy rather than force. Concerned about the oppressive measures being taken against the Polish population, Rohrbach advised that Hitler follow a British "Commonwealth" model in occupied territories.[144] Rohrbach recognized that Germany's invasion of Yugoslavia was essential to stabilize the mess created by Italy's failed invasion of Greece, but urged restraint in dealing with the Greek and Slavic peoples.[145] Japan's occupation of China and Southeast Asia, Rohrbach added, was defensible only in reaction to Anglo-Saxon imperialism and American economic warfare (including a partial oil embargo from July 1940). As soon as the war was over, Germany's allies had an obligation to respect the rights of sovereign nations.[146]

Bäumer wrestled similarly with the tension between her enthusiasm for territorial revision and her disdain for the Nazi regime's oppressive methods. Pleased by the quick victory over Poland, Bäumer had enough compassion to worry about the casualties on both sides. She confessed to Marianne Weber how moving it was to read a soldier's letter from the Battle of Warsaw describing how "everyone had come together, Germans and Poles, men and women, to help the wounded." "I sacrifice myself not for the government," Bäumer wrote three weeks later, "I sacrifice myself for Germany."[147] In May 1941, after Hitler's deputy Rudolf Hess flew to Scotland and made a tragicomic attempt to negotiate peace with Great Britain, Bäumer grumbled to Emmy Beckmann: "A greater moral defeat is hard to imagine and it touches the entire German people. I at least must say that I am embarrassed." Hess was a "dumb fanatic" typical of the Nazi Party leadership. Equally problematic, however, was the way in which Hess's flight had undermined Germany's reputation abroad. Nazi rule was regrettable, Bäumer seemed to be saying, but that did nothing to dampen her German national pride or desire for victory.[148]

Some liberals were less qualified in their criticisms. In conquering Poland, wrote Hans Robinsohn, Hitler had finally revealed his megalomaniacal desire for acquiring unlimited *Lebensraum* and conducting an unwinnable war on two fronts. With remarkable foresight Robinsohn warned against Hitler's plans to resettle Germans in the East, expelling the Poles and Jews into an ersatz province, where they were apparently "supposed to beat each other to death."[149] Ricarda Huch found nothing hopeful in the outbreak of war. What did the ideological struggles between Fascism and Communism matter to the millions of men, women, and children perishing in their name?[150] Robert Bosch was visibly depressed and could think of nothing other than the regime's downfall.[151]

Most liberals, however, were hesitant to abandon their long-dreamt-of "Greater Germany." As Bäumer conceded to the Allies in 1946, "I saw the possibility of a revision of the Versailles Treaty and my belief in such an opportunity was strengthened by the armistice with France."[152] Hermann Dietrich took advantage of Hitler's early victories to obtain a Polish slave laborer to help maintain his family farm in Baden, writing his brother Waldemar in 1940 that he "had *ordered* a second one [emphasis mine]."[153] And though Erich Koch-Weser was forced to emigrate to Brazil because of his non-Aryan background, he wrote Dietrich emotionally in January 1941: "The more we are expressly removed from the events in Europe, the greater is our inner empathy with Germany's heroic struggle and its fate. We hope that it continues to turn out well." Dietrich responded optimistically: "our momentous military successes and the absolute indomitability of the German army will soon bring us peace."[154] By the end of June 1940, with the rapid defeat of France, few could restrain their enthusiasm.[155]

Operation Barbarossa

The first two years of the Second World War witnessed a stunning series of German victories, costing relatively few casualties or resources. First Poland fell; then Norway, Belgium, the Netherlands, and France in quick succession. Portentous only in retrospect, the Battle of Britain – when the Royal Air Force held off Goering's Luftwaffe – was more a draw than a defeat. And by the end of August 1941, Greece and Yugoslavia were subdued, German armies were at the gates of Leningrad, and the British were on the run in North Africa. Few could have imagined the immense reversal of fortune that would occur over the next eighteen months, all because of Hitler's ill-considered invasion of the Soviet Union.

"Operation Barbarossa" represented more than a military operation. It marked the beginning of an ideologically charged total war that would claim the lives of some twenty-five million soldiers and civilians. Poorly conceived from the start, Barbarossa began on 22 June 1941, six weeks late due to Germany's last second intervention in Greece and Yugoslavia. Only days after the first German Offensive, Himmler's SS special task forces (*Einsatzgruppen*) began murdering thousands of Communists and Jews, followed by mass shootings of otherwise sympathetic (that is, anti-Communist and anti-Semitic) Poles and Ukrainians. Within months, Reinhard Heydrich would outline the "Final Solution to the Jewish Question," which envisioned the extermination of every European Jew, and the gradual death by attrition of millions more East European Slavs. The war for *Lebensraum* and ethnic cleansing that began with the Polish invasion now took on a larger, more radical dimension.[156]

Despite the ideological fanaticism that helps to explain Barbarossa, there were pragmatic grounds for the operation. With America openly supporting Great Britain – the Lend-Lease Act was passed just weeks before the invasion – Hitler wanted to force a decision before the United States could impose its immense economic might in Britain's favor and possibly enter the war, as it had to devastating effect in 1917. Conversely, obtaining access to the Soviet Union's unlimited natural resources, from the Ukraine's wheat fields and millions of potential slave laborers to the oil of the Donets basin, was crucial for the economically overmatched Third Reich.[157] The liberals had not wanted a two-front war, but they had never been shy about their desire for additional land in the East or their virulent hatred of Soviet Communism. Insofar as Operation Barbarossa exemplified a growing disso-nance between liberal and Nazi revisionism, particularly in terms of ethnic cleansing, there remained geopolitical affinities that would have to be surmounted before Democrats could develop an alternative vision of German foreign policy.

Lebensraum

Many liberals saw the Third Reich as a vehicle for making the decades-old dream of *Mitteleuropa* into a reality. In the years after Naumann's death in 1919, myriad Democrats – from former National Socials like Rohrbach, Bäumer, and Heile to erstwhile National Liberals like Schacht, Dietrich, Winschuh, and Schiffer – expressed the desire for a political and/or economic union comprising much of Central Europe and spearheaded by a Greater Germany, inclusive of Austria. Some already employed the term *Lebensraum* in the 1920s.[158] Democratic irredentism, indeed expansionism, was buttressed by the work of liberal academics like Obst, Theodor Schieder, Werner Conze, and Hermann Freymarck, who argued that obtaining larger markets and additional *Lebensraum* in the Slavic East was an essential precondition for preserving a healthy German *Volkstum*.[159]

Freymarck, Gothein's colleague in the Breslau Chamber of Commerce, wrote a number of books in the 1930s and early 1940s giving credit to Hitler for discussing Silesia's importance as the center of a new, German-dominated *Mitteleuropa*.[160] Two decades after Germany lost thousands of square miles of territory and millions of people in a plebiscite to Poland, on 25 November 1941 the liberal geographer Obst gave a fascinating speech, alternately nationalist and post-nationalist, pan-German and pan-European. He admired Germany's territorial gains in Poland and Russia, but also hoped that Silesia might finally become the "central cog of major European commerce" as well as the decisive medium between the "Greater German Empire and the East" that it once was in the time of the Habsburg Empire. For Obst German political hegemony in Central and Eastern Europe did not have to mean ethnic cleansing or economic subjugation.[161]

To that end, in early 1942 Obst and Freymark published *The Foundations of the Development of Silesian Commerce and the Origins of the Silesian Railroad Network*, a brief but popular volume that went through multiple editions. Commissioned by the Third Reich, the book was adorned with the Nazi eagle and swastika. But its message was more redolent of Naumann than Hitler. It portrayed Silesia as the "natural medium between West and East, North and South" and as the foundation "of the Greater European Community that we are currently experiencing."[162] "Under the leadership of the Axis powers," Obst wrote, "the Greater European Realm is being welded together into an economic bloc that is voluntarily and happily accepted by the international community; that eradicates tariff walls in the immense region from the Atlantic coast to the Black Sea, from Scandinavia to the Mediterranean countries." Forward-looking Europeans, Obst concluded, understood the "necessity of a powerful, goal-oriented and wide-ranging Eastern colonization; for which the German state is not merely the friend and sponsor, but is itself, with its entire strength, the carrier and guarantor of this momentous . . . cultural and economic colonization!"[163]

Another influential Weimar Democrat, Josef Winschuh, was no less enthusiastic in his endorsement of a German-led *Mitteleuropa*. Seemingly oblivious to the genocidal policies developing on the eastern front, Winschuh presented the case for a federally organized European community. Germany would act as the "lead state [*Leitstaat*]," while the Reichsmark would become the common currency in every participating nation. The labor market might need to be regulated at first, as companies would naturally want to employ cheaper East Europeans to the detriment of German workers. Nevertheless, it was up to German entrepreneurs to work in concert with their industrious Slavic neighbors in order to build a "Greater German Economic Sphere [*großdeutschen Wirtschaftsraum*]" that, alongside post-Soviet Russia, could create a true European community.[164] According to Winschuh, the only impediment to this Greater German Economic Sphere – and its Japanese counterpart in Asia – was the outdated imperialism of the Anglo-Saxon powers, loath to relinquish control of the world economy.[165]

Obst and Winschuh were not the only Democrats to draw parallels between *Mitteleuropa* and Hitler's conquests. So too did Naumann's closest acolytes. In 1938 Heuss characterized Hitler's incorporation of Austria and the Sudetenland as the "consolidation of *Mitteleuropa*," which he believed would expand its reach over time.[166] Bäumer advocated a Germanocentric *Mitteleuropa* as necessary and inevitable, whether it occurred through war or peace.[167] Bäumer's co-editor at *Die Hilfe*, Wilhelm Heile, was likewise unable to contain his excitement at the prospects of a German-dominated European community.[168] Even Hans Robinsohn, a Jewish Democrat now living in exile, favored some kind of German-led European federation which reintegrated her lost eastern territories. Similarly to Naumann, Robinsohn saw a future union in which the "voluntary limitation of the sovereignty of individual states will be realized." Like Naumann, he singled out the pivotal nature of the Franco-German relationship in making this union possible. But Robinsohn had no greater desire to relinquish German land, culture, or influence than liberal nationalists like Winschuh, Obst, or Bäumer.[169]

Certainly one can understand why historians tend to conflate calls for a "Greater European Economic Community" (Obst) or "Greater German Economic Sphere" (Winschuh) with Nazi plans to colonize the East. The liberal vision of a German-dominated *Mitteleuropa* was likewise informed by cultural and to some extent racial prejudices that differed from National Socialism more in degree than in kind.[170] There are nevertheless salient points of discontinuity that indicate the persistence of universalist values within the liberal nationalist worldview. Obst and Freymarck avoided the typical Nazi references to the racial inferiority of the Slavic peoples and repeatedly emphasized the need to "work toward reconciliation after the victory of the Axis powers" if the aim was to "produce the anticipated economic upsurge." Though resentful of Polish territorial acquisitions after 1918 and unapologetic about Germany's right to take back such territories in 1939, most Democrats supported an independent Poland extending from Cracow to Lvov. Perhaps it is no coincidence that the most detailed liberal plans for a European community began to appear in late 1941, following news of the atrocities carried out on the eastern front. For, despite their nationalist designs and ethnic preoccupations, German Democrats saw themselves not as genocidal occupiers, but as "culture-bearing" liberators.[171]

Anti-Communism

Liberals never possessed the fanatical hostility to Marxist socialism endemic in right-wing circles. The German Democrats had worked closely with the Majority Socialists (SPD) after 1919, collaborating on the Weimar constitution, negotiating the Versailles Treaty, and battling the extreme nationalist right as well as the Communist left. Nevertheless, the DDP always abhorred Soviet-style "Bolshevism," which most liberals viewed as more dangerous than National Socialism. Nazism may have undermined democracy and the rule of law, but the Communists wished to add German nationality and private property to the list. No liberal had sought war with the Soviet Union. All the same, no liberal could hope for a Communist victory in the way some secretly wished for an American or British one.[172]

In fact liberal justifications for destroying the Bolshevik regime after 1941 are similar to arguments put forward by Great Britain and the United States four years later. In barely two decades, Paul Rohrbach observed, Soviet Russia had doomed millions to starvation and "brought the peasantry, 80 percent of the East European people, into an ever deteriorating condition of state supported slavery." The leading classes of Russian society, "the so-called intelligentsia, were murdered and starved to death." Despite Stalin's ambitious five-year plans, the Soviet Union had not succeeded in catching up with the West, but built gigantic, inefficient factories that produced far less than the regime claimed.[173] In March 1944, long after Rohrbach had relinquished any hope of German victory, he warned that an Allied victory could unwittingly surrender continental Europe to the Russians.[174] Such anti-Communist anxieties hardly make Rohrbach a Nazi fellow traveler. Only eighteen months later, Great Britain and the United States would repeat the same critique in order to justify western policies of containment.[175]

Bäumer also published a series of articles stressing the dangers of Soviet Communism. "Bolshevization" meant (even greater) loss of cultural and intellectual freedom and would lead to (further) subjugation of women and minorities.[176] Under Soviet occupation, Bäumer also feared the disintegration of the family and a rise in sexual licentiousness and violence, which virtually all Germans associated with Bolshevism.[177] "Atheistic"

Bolshevism threatened to wipe out Christian values and German culture, Bäumer reasoned, as one witnessed in Soviet-occupied Poland, Finland, and the Ukraine. Starvation and genocide could not be far behind.[178] In a controversial article titled "Europe Betrayed," Bäumer chastised Britain and America for encouraging a criminal Soviet regime to run roughshod over Europe. How could Churchill and Roosevelt profess to seek Germany's liberation while Stalin destroyed all vestiges of democracy and civil rights in every country he conquered?[179] Even in late 1943, though she harbored no more illusions about the viability of National Socialism, Bäumer averred that anything was better than Bolshevism.[180] Heuss, Winschuh, and Rohrbach expressed similar sentiments.[181]

Liberal fears of Bolshevization, both real and imagined, do nothing to justify the aggressive expansionism of the Third Reich, much less the annihilation of millions of East European Jews or Russian prisoners of war.[182] We should nonetheless be careful before accepting the argument that those who supported the German offensive against the Soviet Union were uncritical nationalists, indirectly complicit in the atrocities on the eastern front.[183] Left liberals maintained a cordial relationship with German Social Democracy before and after the Third Reich. It was simply inconceivable for a Democrat, no matter how badly she or he desired Hitler's demise, to countenance German defeat on the eastern front.[184]

Turning Points

The enormous impact of America's entry into the Second World War in December 1941 was not lost on German liberals. But unlike three years earlier (1938) or later (1944), few took the perceived change in Germany's military prospects as an incentive for redoubling their opposition to the regime. From Bäumer's perspective, the Americans were clearly not interested in a negotiated peace, having already prolonged the war through Lend-Lease and contributed to the mounting casualties and privations on both sides. Roosevelt's unqualified defense of Anglo-American interests in Asia and strangulation of Japanese oil supplies, Rohrbach added, had only contributed to military escalation and brutalization on all fronts. After Versailles no German could trust America's good intentions. Indeed, history showed that any sign of weakness would only ratchet up Allied demands.[185] Resistance to Hitler was further undermined by Roosevelt's announcement in early 1943 that the Allies would seek unconditional surrender. This anxiety was compounded by rumors, fed by Goebbels's propaganda machine, of Allied designs to divide up postwar Germany and turn it into a rump agrarian state.[186]

Under these circumstances even determined opponents of the regime put forward stringent preconditions indicating their reticence to capitulate on Allied terms. According to Hans Robinsohn, a "revolution" was necessary as "salvation from threatening catastrophe!" – namely from defeat and occupation by the Soviet Union. Restoring freedom and democracy were valuable aims, Robinsohn continued, but Hitler's overthrow was most pressing because it would help to broker a favorable peace before the Allies – or, worse, the Bolsheviks – were in a position to dictate another Versailles Treaty. "Without denying the responsibility of the Nazi regime for the origin of the Second World War," Robinsohn reasoned, *"we must refuse to acknowledge* with steady insistence *any sole or total responsibility* for the German people [my italics]." In a clear reference to the infamous "war guilt clause," Article 231 of the Versailles Treaty, Robinsohn averred: "the attitudes of all enemy governments from at least 1933 had made possible the developments that led to war. That goes for Poland in 1934, France and England from 1933 to 1938 and Russia in 1939." Finally, Robinsohn asserted that any peace negotiations must recognize the difference between "Hitlerdom and Germandom [*Hitlertum und Deutschtum*]," between National Socialist and liberal conceptions of a Greater German Reich.[187]

Robinsohn believed that a total German defeat would burden any postwar democracy the same way as it had Weimar. Even in the wake of Hitler's unprovoked invasions of Poland and the Soviet Union, he refused to acknowledge Germany's sole responsibility for initiating and prosecuting the war. In fact Robinsohn wished to retain many of the territorial acquisitions made by the Third Reich, including Austria, Danzig, and the Sudetenland.[188] Coming from a left-wing Jewish Democrat, one ardently opposed to Hitler and cognizant of the "Final Solution," these are astounding claims, illustrating the depth and pervasiveness of liberal nationalism three years into the Second World War.

Yet liberals were quicker than most to see the writing on the wall and perceptive enough to realize that negotiating surrender to the western Allies was better than strangulation by attrition, culminating in Soviet occupation. Bäumer first began to articulate these concerns privately in December 1941. Regaining Germany's old eastern borders was hardly worth the mounting destruction of her civilization and youth. How to celebrate Christmas, she wondered, when Hitler was drafting seventeen-year-old boys into military service and workers were laboring seven-day weeks for meager pay.[189] Given that Germany's modest living standards were similar to prewar levels and the military prospects relatively promising, this was a remarkable admission.[190] For his part Robinsohn was one of the first Democrats to detail the mass murders of Polish and Soviet civilians. With considerable insight he suggested that this kind of ideological fanaticism was proof that a Hitler-led Germany would eventually self-destruct.[191] Robinsohn welcomed (and expected) the failure of the Blitzkrieg in the winter of 1942, which he saw as a golden opportunity to overthrow Hitler.[192]

The final straw that broke the tenuous bond between liberal and Nazi foreign policies appeared some months later, with the Soviet counteroffensive at Stalingrad. The disastrous encirclement of General Paulus's Sixth Army in November 1942, combined with the landing of US troops in French North Africa, left little doubt that Germany had reached the beginning of the end.[193] Ricarda Huch cited Stalingrad as proof that Germany's long-term prosecution of the war was unfathomable. "Another year of war," she wrote in 1943, "then Germany will lie in ruins, and the Germans are a people of homeless beggars."[194] Despite the threat of censorship, Bäumer's *Die Frau* expressed a similarly pessimistic view, punctuated by moving accounts of individual tragedies.[195] "War appears sweet," Reinhold Maier wrote a few weeks after Paulus's surrender, "only to those who do not experience it."[196] After Stalingard no amount of rationalization could reconcile liberal nationalism with the Wagnerian nihilism of Nazi true believers.

Toward a Post-Nationalist Germany?

Passionate opponents of the regime, confessed Marie Baum, nonetheless found it difficult to "wish for a defeat of one's own fatherland rather than a victory under Hitler's rule." In spring 1943 some liberals still hoped for a miracle, believing that a post-Hitlerian Germany might sue for peace without relinquishing her pre-1939 borders.[197] Yet the brutality of terror bombing at home and mounting casualties abroad persuaded most Democrats, for pragmatic as well as ideological reasons, to begin formulating a post-nationalist foreign policy. Such a policy would shift its focus away from acquiring *Lebensraum*, recovering colonies, or preserving Germany's great power status. The purpose was rather to build a secure and peaceful Europe with Germany at the center. In some ways, this was a return to the pre-Weimar geopolitical conceptions of Naumann, Rathenau, and Rohrbach. But few liberals any longer believed the struggle for German hegemony was worth the extinguishing of what was left of German social, economic, and cultural life.

This evolution in outlook was no mere opportunism. Gertrud Bäumer had sacrificed much in her efforts to justify Nazi foreign policy, severing long-term contacts with liberal colleagues abroad, trying friendships with

1 Steering Committee of the newly founded German State Party, 1930: (*seated, from left to right*) Gertrud Bäumer, Hermann Dietrich, Alfred Weber, Hermann Höpker-Aschoff, (*standing, from left*) Theodor Heuss, Hermann Fischer and Albert Jäger.

2 Hermann Dietrich (*front center*) meeting British Prime Minister Ramsey MacDonald (*second from left*), flanked by the liberal scientists Max Planck (*left*) and Albert Einstein (*right*) in 1931.

3 (*From left to right*) Ernst Jäckh, Hjalmar Schacht, Otto Gessler, and Carl Petersen at historian Hans Delbrück's eightieth birthday party, 1929.

4 Marianne Weber, 1920.

5 Robert Bosch (*center*) and Adolf Hitler attending the international auto show in Berlin, 1936.

6 Wilhelm Külz, 1927.

7 Theodor Heuss delivering a eulogy on the tenth anniversary of Friedrich Naumann's death, 1929.

8 Katharina von Kardorff-Oheimb and Siegfried von Kardorff with their family, 1929.

9 Alfred Weber (*center*) talking with his Heidelberg colleague, the liberal historian Hans von
Eckardt (*right*) at a sociological conference in Berlin in about 1930.

10 DDP Women's leaders in 1919: Elisabeth Brönner-Hoepfner (*seated left*), Gertrud Bäumer (*seated center*), and Marie Baum (*standing left*).

11 Marie Lüders, 1930.

12 Friedrich Naumann delivering a speech against the Versailles Treaty only a few months before his death (1919).

13 Gustav Stresemann and his bride Kathé (Kleefeld) Stresemann around the time Stresemann left Friedrich Naumann's National Social movement (1903).

14 Erich Koch-Weser (left) and Eugen Schiffer, 1919.

15 Fritz Elsas, 1931.

16 Reinhold and Gerta Maier casting votes in a plebiscite on merging Baden and Württemberg into one state in the new Federal Republic of Germany (1950).

pacifist colleagues at home, and compromising thirty years of work toward *rapprochement* with the international women's movement.[198] Her changing attitudes to German nationalism after Stalingrad were equally sincere. Having frequently impugned liberal cosmopolitanism in the past decade, in July 1943 Bäumer wrote Marianne Weber about the need to return to the more humanistic values of the Weimar years. Writing Heuss a few weeks later, Bäumer described the horrors of war in a fashion that Nazi censors would have found highly unpatriotic. Disposing of her typically phlegmatic nationalism, she cited the number of under-age soldiers being killed and maimed, families being torn apart and cities being destroyed as proof that the regime had lost touch with reality.[199] When she attempted to publish articles describing the refugee situation and the bottlenecks in armaments production, Goebbels would not allow it. Writing Dorothee van Velsen in early 1944, Bäumer saw nothing worth salvaging in Hitler's Third Reich: "Everywhere a prison, and that is bitter. Everywhere barbed wire, and that is a shame [*Überall ein Gitter, und das ist bitter. Überall ein Draht, und das ist schad*]." In September 1944, *Die Frau* was discontinued. No doubt Bäumer's change in tone contributed to the measure.[200]

The normally taciturn Wilhelm Heile was energized by the prospects of defeat. Frightened by early bouts with the Gestapo and in desperate financial straits, Heile had been wary of attacking the regime. Now, only two weeks after the Normandy landing, he expressed his optimism at the imminent downfall of the Third Reich. Owing to "the catastrophe of 1918" and fear of economic ruin, many Germans had backed Hitler. The German people, however, were not "eternally naïve and dumb and there-fore susceptible to the Führer principle." They would learn from their mistakes and construct a better Germany on the ruins of the Third Reich.[201] Although Maier sympathized with "good Germans [who did] not want to lose the war," he believed the Third Reich had to die in order for Germany to live on.[202] For Heuss the war had accomplished precisely the opposite of what liberals intended in tentatively supporting Hitler. Rather than liberate Germany from the bounds of Versailles, it introduced levels of repression and destruction that were inconceivable in peacetime. Only defeat could reverse this process.[203]

Most Democrats acknowledged the need to continue fighting the Soviet Union; many feared a second Versailles.[204] Nevertheless by 1943 even Bäumer and Rohrbach were articulating the need for a post-nationalist, pan-European peace. In a series of articles published during the last two years of the war, Rohrbach instructed his readers that people were diverse and could not be easily divided along ethnocultural lines. Racist stereotypes propagated by the Nazis, Rohrbach observed, were no truer of France or Great Britain than the negative stereotypes of "German character" broadcast by the Allied powers. In January 1945, as the last German offensive dissipated in the Netherlands, Rohrbach published a controversial article ("The Writing on the Wall") urging readers to conceive of a post-National Socialist political and social order. Again Rohrbach insisted that the Nazi obsession with racial exclusivity be replaced by a socially inclusive view that accepted the commonalities in all peoples.[205] These articles nearly led to his arrest.[206]

The Gestapo, we must remember, became no more merciful or less efficient in the final months of the war. Many longtime prisoners of the concentration camps were murdered at this time. Others who had avoided arrest suddenly found themselves detained. In March 1945, only weeks before liberation, Reinhold Maier was compelled to attend a local "party celebration" on pain of arrest. In April, he commented that the only freedom left to a German was turning off the radio when Goebbels was speaking.[207] Having survived detention in various concentration camps, the Democratic diplomat Count Bernstorff was assassinated by SS guards in April 1945, just days before the armistice.[208] Under these circumstances, the perceptible shift in liberal attitudes should be taken at face value, indicating the importance of the Second World War in dissociating German liberalism from the *völkisch* nationalism and imperialism that always threatened to undermine its core values in the decades before the Nazi seizure of power.

VI

After 1945 many Democrats were quick to acknowledge their role in abetting Europe's destruction. The collapse of the Republic and the rise of Hitler owed much to the liberal obsession with eliminating Versailles and building a Greater German Reich.[209] For Weimar liberals were never merely parroting Nazi ideas in an effort to accommodate the regime. Nor were they fulfilling the role of bourgeois reactionaries which left-wing contemporaries and later German historians have imputed to them. On the contrary, the Nazis had in many ways appropriated (and perverted) liberal concepts (*Mitteleuropa, Volksgemeinschaft, Anschluss,* treaty "revision") and arguments (self-determination, opposition to western imperialism, the need for *Lebensraum*) developed and defended by Weimar Democrats before and after the First World War.[210]

Undoubtedly the liberals were too slow to recognize the adverse consequences of using Nazi means to accomplish liberal nationalist ends. As in other areas of German social, political, and intellectual life, Democrats recognized certain affinities between liberalism and National Socialism: obtaining German parity in armaments, regaining the Saarland from France, remilitarizing the Rhineland, achieving a union with Austria, revising the eastern borders with Poland, and reincorporating German minorities abroad. Even the proximate cause of the Second World War, restoring German sovereignty over Danzig and the Polish Corridor, was an aspiration widely shared by Weimar Democrats. All these demands fit in perfectly well with the "liberal" principle of national self-determination propagated by Wilson at the Paris Peace Conference and paradoxically denied Germany and Austria in the wake of Versailles. While one might have wished that Stresemann and not Hitler had orchestrated Germany foreign policy after 1933, there is no denying its liberal antecedents.

These continuities between liberal and Nazi revisionism, between Naumannite and Hitlerian worldviews, were systematically shattered after Munich. Frustrated by Hitler's penchant for risk-taking, purge of the civilian and military leadership, and blatant repudiation of self-determination in occupying Bohemia, Democrats began to juxtapose a universalist, multilateral conception of European community to a Germanic empire based on exclusionary, annihilatory nationalism. Although some hope for a Pax Germanica based on Naumann's *Mitteleuropa* returned with Hitler's string of early victories, it quickly dissolved after Barbarossa. Thus, just as it had encouraged German revisionism in the interwar period, Naumann's malleable concept now came to define a liberal vision of European community.

CHAPTER FIVE

"Neither Jews nor Anti-Semites":
The Liberal Answer to Hitler's "Jewish Question"

I

In the introduction to his seminal volume on Jewish life in the Third Reich Peter Pulzer stresses the degree to which Germans, gentile and Jewish alike, viewed Nazi anti-Semitism as part of "a cyclical phenomenon that flared during crises but would normally lie fairly dormant . . . the principal reason why German Jews underestimated the significance of Hitler's coming to power was . . . their familiarity with prejudice and discrimination."[1] This statement holds true for German liberals as well. The year 1933 hardly marked a decisive caesura before which "liberal" attitudes to German Jewry predominated and after which emerged a new paradigm of racial exclusion. German liberals, like Germans in general, had a close but fraught relationship with German Jewry, a product of the liberals' equally contradictory affinities with the *völkisch* creed that helped to generate and reinforce racial anti-Semitism in the second half of the nineteenth century.[2]

Most liberals hoped to resolve the "Jewish Question" – namely the issue of what to do with Germany's visible Jewish minority – through assimilation. This seemingly "universalist" philosophy did not preclude underlying anti-Semitic assumptions similar to those on the radical right.[3] Since the role of anti-Semitism lies at the center of current debates on the origins of the Holocaust, the attitude of a party with such close and contradictory ties to German Jewry provide a unique perspective on the evolution of the "Final Solution to the Jewish Question" after 1933.

Until recently the so-called functionalist explanation dominated historiography on the "Final Solution." Functionalists reject the traditional ("intentionalist") view that Hitler and the Nazi leadership, motivated by fanatical anti-Semitism, planned the Holocaust from the moment they took power. For functionalists Hitler's anti-Semitism, not to mention the highly variegated anti-Jewish sentiments of the German people, was a necessary but not sufficient cause of the cumulative radicalization that led to the "Final Solution." Functionalist scholars have pointed instead to a combination of escalating internal pressures (overlapping responsibilities, bureaucratic chaos, and a general competition among rival party and state agencies for power and resources) and external circumstances (war, brutalization, limited resources, and the drive for *Lebensraum* in Eastern Europe) to explain the evolution of genocidal policy.[4]

This interpretation has been challenged in recent years by a modified version of the "intentionalist" argument, one that incorporates elements of a functionalist approach but refuses to overlook the central role played by an all-pervading racist ideology. David Bankier and Peter Longerich, for example, have reinforced the view that a fanatically anti-Semitic Nazi leadership played *the* decisive role in pushing forward ever more radical measures against the Jews. At the same time, they contend that the German population, while skeptical regarding the Nazis' more brutal anti-Jewish measures, was at least passively anti-Semitic and ultimately acquiesced in the exclusion and murder of their Jewish fellow citizens.[5] More controversially, historians like Daniel Goldhagen, Michael Wildt, and to a lesser extent Peter Fritzsche have insisted on the active complicity, indeed enthusiasm, of "ordinary" Germans in removing the Jews from the German *Volksgemeinschaft*. In their reading of events, Nazi persecution of the Jews was only possible because "ordinary" Germans, including those with no particular affinity to other aspects of National Socialism, shared elements of Hitler's "eliminationist" anti-Semitism.[6]

Hence the question: did German liberals embrace the anti-Semitic assumptions of their Nazi opponents and their "ordinary" German brethren? What were their reactions to the first wave of anti-Jewish legislation, the Nuremberg Laws, *Kristallnacht* ("The Night of the Broken Glass"), or the "Final Solution"? Were liberal attitudes to official anti-Semitism characterized by a pattern of growing indifference and eventual acquiescence, as the new "intentionalism" contends? To the extent that they empathized with Jewish colleagues, the question remains as to whether liberals could resist Nazi Jewish policy without themselves becoming victims.[7] And how did "non-Aryan" liberals respond to similar challenges? What do their experiences say about the nature and pervasiveness of (liberal) anti-Semitism in the Third Reich? Before we begin to answer these queries, we ought to discuss briefly the relationship between liberalism and anti-Semitism before 1933.

II

Liberalism and the "Jewish Question" to 1933

From the moment in 1879 when the liberal historian Heinrich von Treitschke declared, "The Jews are our misfortune," German liberalism has had a Janus-faced relationship with the "Jewish Question." Treitschke's infamous pronouncement would be taken up by "eliminationist" anti-Semites for generations to come, eventually bedecking the arena at Hitler's annual Nuremberg Rally. But before we dismiss German liberalism as hardly less anti-Semitic than National Socialism, we should remember that Treitschke, who was on the extreme right wing of the National Liberal Party, concluded his original polemic by urging the Jews to assimilate into, not leave, the German Reich. Indeed, Theodor Mommsen, Treitschke's main opponent in the so-called "Berlin Anti-Semitic Controversy," claimed little disagreement in principle.[8] From the nationalist right to the cosmopolitan left, most Wilhelmine liberals expected Jewish assimilation in return for combating state-sponsored racial or religious discrimination.[9]

When discussing liberalism and the "Jewish Question," it is therefore important to distinguish between "anti-antisemitism" and "philosemitism." "Anti-antisemitism" connotes a typically liberal resistance to discrimination against individuals on a racial or religious basis. Outright "philosemitism" endorses what we might anachronistically call a "multicultural" paradigm, fostering the existence of German Jewry as a distinct cultural and religious entity.[10] Right-wing insinuations to the contrary, very few liberals, even Jewish liberals, embraced "philosemitism." Among "anti-antisemites" one might differentiate rather between *völkisch* liberals, who publicly defended the Jews' equal right to participate in society but privately denigrated their "alien" national character, and univeralist liberals who saw little point in preserving religious or racial particularism of any kind.[11] Notwithstanding these subtle ideological differences, all liberal "anti-antisemites" wished the "Jewish Question" would soon be resolved so they might stop spending time and energy defending their party against accusations of "philosemitism."[12]

Yet erroneous allegations of philosemitism only multiplied after the First World War, as right-wing parties tried to exploit the fact that Jews tended overwhelmingly to support the left liberal Democrats. The DDP faced a dilemma. On the one hand, Jews provided a vital reservoir of financial support, political talent, and intellectual dynamism. On the other hand, in many constituencies a reputation for philosemitism meant political suicide.[13] The Democratic Party Secretary Otto Fischbeck actively dissuaded Jewish liberals, including Weimar's brilliant Foreign Minister Walther Rathenau, from running for public office.[14] And in 1930 the Democrats merged with the racist paramilitary organization known as the Young German Order, which had its own "Aryan paragraph" opposing Jewish membership. Though the Young Germans eventually agreed to delete this provision, many cosmopolitan and Jewish liberals withdrew from the new German State Party in protest.[15]

The merger surely did not turn Democrats into Nazis. Jewish liberals like Fritz Elsas and Erich Koch-Weser, the DStP's first chairman, continued to play a leading role. Nevertheless, even Democrats who earnestly resisted National Socialism proved notably ambivalent regarding Nazi anti-Semitism.[16] After the State Party organized a Silesian assembly in defense of the Republic, the Democratic official Marcel Mitschke wrote the DDP/DStP co-chairman Hermann Dietrich with indignation. In contrast to the provincial liberal dailies, the *Berliner Tageblatt* devoted only "26 lines" to the assembly, "including a wholly misleading title and entirely unnecessary complaints . . . that really don't interest anyone" but that "one percent Jewish minority that is supposedly 'oppressed' in Germany!!!" It was obvious, Mitschke added, that "the State Party could thank these repugnant '*Weltblatt*'-methods for its going to the dogs; that is not only my conviction, but that of many who still stand by democracy!"[17] Another left liberal conceded various Nazi transgressions, but implored his party to acknowledge the Nazi achievements in diminishing "the destructive role of the Jewish boulevard press."[18] Even Heuss protested when his name was included on a "list of shame" alongside "the rootless Jewish literati, against whom I have fought for these many years and with whom it is hardly pleasant to go down in history." These sentiments appear all the more offensive when one considers that they derive from private correspondence with a liberal colleague from whom Heuss had nothing to gain or fear.[19]

Equally revealing is the explanation of a longtime Democrat for why he was leaving the party in early 1933: "If I soon leave the party it is not because I'm changing with the wind . . . but because I really do not want to be alone in one party with the pariah [*verscheuchten*] Jews. Politically I am no anti-Semite, but I'm also no Jew."[20] Such statements hardly clinch the case for an "eliminationist anti-Semitism" ingrained across the sociopolitical spectrum. But, to borrow from Chinua Achebe's comments on Joseph Conrad's *Heart of Darkness*, while German Democrats may have condemned the Nazis' anti-Semitic excesses, many were indifferent to "the racism on which it sharpened its iron tooth."[21]

Initial Liberal Responses to Nazi Anti-Semitism

Generally hesitant to attack the *völkisch* underpinnings of Nazi anti-Semitism, Democrats were nonetheless quick to point out anti-Semitic injustices against longtime political friends and colleagues.[22] The liberal (DVP) physicist Max Planck protested the dismissal of Jewish colleagues by declining to lecture.[23] On another occasion the entire Heidelberg Medical Faculty petitioned the Ministry of Culture on behalf of Jewish scholars.[24] Most Democrats continued to meet with Jewish friends, knowing that this would hardly endear them to the regime.[25] Theodor Heuss, Hermann Dietrich, and August Weber, whose wife was Jewish, convened a farewell party for Erich Koch-Weser at the Deutsche Gesellschaft, a republican club on Berlin's Schadowstrasse. Dozens of Democratic colleagues attended.[26] Jewish Liberals like Robinsohn and Elsas became close confidants of high-ranking generals and politicians, while Eugen Schiffer received frequent visitors during his internment in Berlin's infamous Jewish Hospital.[27]

Christian religious devotion was an important factor in marshalling liberal opposition to Nazi Jewish policies. Karl Barth delivered a number of public declarations denouncing anti-Semitism in no uncertain terms.[28] "Christ belonged to the people of Israel," Barth declared in a December 1933 sermon. "The blood of this people coursed through his veins . . . Jesus Christ was a Jew." Barth wrote a colleague in January 1934: "anyone who believes in Christ, who was himself a Jew . . . simply *cannot* be involved in the contempt of Jews and ill-treatment of them which is the order of the day."[29] For Hans Walz anti-Semitism was nothing other than the "precursor to a later anti-Christianity."[30] Wilhelm Külz added that "a party built up on hate and intolerance can never retain the 'spiritual commitment' of the German people" and reassured the chairman of the Central Association of Germans of Jewish Confession (CVDJG): "Now as before I will belong to those who openly oppose anti-Semitism, no matter where and in what way it appears, because it is unworthy of a cultured and Christian people."[31] Marie Lüders likewise attacked the Nazis' unwarranted "interventions into the rites of a world-recognized religious community."[32] None of these liberals was persecuted for such "philosemitic" statements.

Georg Gothein and Joseph Williger were among the few Democrats to condemn *völkisch*, anti-Semitic ideology outright, independently of its theological implications.[33] Commenting on a Nazi official in charge of restricting Jewish involvement in the economy, Williger wrote Gothein:

"I'm thinking it is Otto Hiedt . . . who must indeed be an Aryan, even if he stutters." "What does an Aryan cow look like?" Williger quipped in May 1935. "Brunette like Hitler, fat like Goering, a mouth like Goebbels, and all milked out like the German people." Williger and Gothein did not confine their outrage to sarcastic dismissals of Nazi race laws. Both men rejected the "Aryan Declaration" required of individuals who wished to join or remain members of state-sanctioned associations. Their refusal to sign this document constituted no small sacrifice in a country where bourgeois life was embedded in an extraordinary network of political clubs, social fraternities, and economic organizations. Williger went so far as to rebuff a government request to submit his wife's racial origins.[34]

These admittedly atypical examples suggest that liberal reticence in commenting on the "Jewish Question" had less to do with fear of recrimination than with a decades-long habituation to *völkisch*, anti-Semitic discourse.[35] Gustav Stolper, though himself Jewish, was quick to highlight Heuss's "pure Aryan" character in attempting to find his friend a teaching position in Switzerland.[36] Born to Jewish parents, the liberal jurist Walter Jellinek praised the Nazi regime for overcoming Germany's social and political divisions and approved the July 1933 Law for the Prevention of Genetically Diseased Offspring. Of course Jellinek's American contemporary, Chief Justice Oliver Wendell Holmes, advocated eugenics as well. But Holmes was neither Jewish nor living in Hitler's Germany. The Democrat Josef Winschuh also approached the first phase of anti-Jewish legislation with unsettling equanimity. For Winschuh the rise of National Socialism signified the end of the liberal "bourgeois era [*bürgerliche Zeitalter*]," hence Jewish era, since "the bourgeois lifestyle had become a welcome camouflage" by means of which Jews might garner influence.[37]

Gertrud Bäumer's views on the "Jewish Question" were equally complex. Already in the 1920s some liberal feminists were complaining that Bäumer was only reelected chair of the BDF over the gifted Alice Salomon because of her successful exploitation of anti-Semitic stereotypes.[38] In defending the merger with the Young Germans Bäumer wrote Emmy Beckmann: "they [the Young Germans] . . . will bring us out of the one-sided asphalt-democratic Jewish atmosphere." In the pages of *Die Frau* Bäumer also "employed racist argumentation and thereby sanctioned it."[39] This included articles instructing women on how to contribute to building a "racial community" and why Hitler should unite German "peoples and races under one scepter."[40] As she witnessed the consequences of Nazi anti-Semitism, however, Bäumer frequently contradicted this *völkisch* creed. After the regime fired a Jewish colleague, she condemned the Law for the Protection of the Civil Service. She also made an extra effort to correspond with Jewish colleagues and solicit articles from non-Aryans like Marie Baum and Camilla Jellinek.[41] In 1936 Bäumer published a lead article in *Die Frau* arguing that an individual's intellect and moral values were more important in determining her worth than "composing heredity charts and maintaining the purity of the blood."[42] For Bäumer and her colleagues there was no contradiction in criticizing Nazi anti-Semitism while still accepting elements of the *völkisch* ideology on which anti-Semitic persecution was based.[43]

Democrats appeared most ready to attack Nazi discrimination on a case-by-case basis, especially where friends or colleagues were involved. Thus Camilla Jellinek, herself Jewish, contributed a fascinating article to the March 1935 issue of *Die Frau*, "The Martyrdom of a German Who Was No Longer Permitted to be German." Wary of its implications, but not about to censor her colleague, Bäumer published the article with a disclaimer. *Die Frau* was not taking a position on such a sensitive issue, merely reporting on some legal inconsistencies in marriage laws with foreigners that caused consternation abroad (a typical trope employed by liberal critics, which absolved the author of responsibility for raising an uncomfortable issue). Based on the 1913 Reich Citizenship Law, Jellinek began, a German woman who married a Pole in 1922 but separated from him only a year later had lost her citizenship, since she became "Polish" upon marriage. Not only did the 1913 law deem her stateless, it did not permit her to end her marriage. Jellinek used this example to demand that the law be changed so that women who marry "aliens" would not lose their citizenship. Given that Camilla herself had married a Jew, this article would prove remarkably prescient. Six months later Jews would lose their citizenship.[44]

The Nuremberg Laws

In terms of Nazi Jewish policy, 1934 was a deceptively quiet year. After the flurry of anti-Semitic legislation, boycotts, emigration, and abuse that characterized the first few months of Nazi rule, the regime appeared to settle into a tacit agreement with German Jews. The Nazis left no doubt that the latter would do well to leave Germany; those who could or would not leave found their political, economic, and cultural influence severely curtailed. But physical acts of violence became less frequent. Vitriolic attacks in propaganda and the press tended to subside. Jewish businessmen and professionals were permitted to earn a living through interaction with Aryans, if often brokered through middlemen or on a restricted basis.[45] Although moderate anti-semitic persecution continued, the Nazis focused in 1934 on the final phases of coordination of party and state, securing the administrative and police apparatus and working out a *modus vivendi* with the German armed forces. This relationship was cemented by Hitler's and Himmler's decision to assassinate the SA leader Ernst Röhm, who had called for a "second revolution" in order to eliminate the plutocratic elites with whom Hitler shared power. Within weeks of this bloody 30 June purge – known to posterity as "The Night of the Long Knives" – Hitler assumed command of the army and, on the death of Hindenburg, merged the offices of Reichsführer, Chancellor, and President into one office. The Nazi dictatorship was complete.[46]

By the early months of 1935, millions of SA stormtroopers were becoming restless. Their social radicalism had been shackled by Hitler's pact with the military–industrial complex, and their leaders had been murdered in the Röhm purge. With most Communist and Socialist leaders already imprisoned, the SA turned to the ranking scapegoat: the Jews. Throughout the spring and summer uncoordinated assaults on Jewish businesses and occasionally on individual Jews picked up across the Reich. The rabid anti-Semite Julius Streicher called for brutal measures in his pornographic weekly, *Der Stürmer*, and attacked Jews with a bullwhip in broad daylight. Soon the escalating property damage and bad press caused by such attacks began to alienate the very business and military elites the regime had worked so hard to mollify. It was in this context of regulating "wild" anti-Semitism that the Third Reich would inaugurate a new phase in Jewish policy: the Nuremberg Laws.[47]

For some time political moderates, including the liberal Schacht, had urged the regime to intervene to quell the uncoordinated violence of the preceding months. But Hitler only decided to issue legislation regulating relations between Germans and Jews at the last minute, after determining that the program for the annual Nuremberg party rally lacked gravity. Hence the infamous Law for the Protection of German Blood and German Honor and Reich Citizenship Law were developed quickly, on an *ad hoc* basis, by a small group of government bureaucrats. Though improvised, the laws' implications were clear enough: Jews were stripped of their citizenship, could no longer marry or maintain sexual relations with Germans, and could only work for gentiles in exceptional situations. Still, there persisted some uncertainty as to who or what constituted a Jew. The result was a compromise between the most ardent anti-Semites and the most pragmatic administrators. Anyone with six or more Jewish great-grandparents was treated as Jewish. Anyone with one Jewish great-grandparent would be considered

German. Anyone with one or two Jewish grandparents would be considered a *Mischling*, a person of "mixed race," *unless* the individual in question was raised in the Jewish religion or was otherwise politically unreliable, in which case that individual would be considered a full Jew.[48] Deemed German in some cases – for example, in being recruited for military service – such individuals were not allowed access to higher political office and not always permitted to marry. By introducing "non-racial" factors like religious and political affiliation, not to mention specific clauses for Jewish veterans and those married to gentiles, the Nuremberg Laws complicated as much as they clarified.[49] Indeed, few Democrats viewed the Nuremberg Laws as a watershed, perhaps because they believed, like many Germans, that the government had merely created a legal settlement "which would make it possible for the German people to be able to seek a tolerable relationship with the Jewish people."[50]

Some were more skeptical. The laws did nothing to quell the growing wave of anti-Semitism, Williger wrote Gothein, but quite a lot to undermine the German *Rechtsstaat*. To hear German academics give lectures on "racial lessons [*Rassenlehre*]" was as shocking as it was distasteful. More discouraging was the fact that respected Protestant theologians seemed to embrace the laws despite the fact that Christianity was so obviously a product of Judaism. Both liberals lamented that Jewish colleagues experienced renewed attacks despite the legislation, while being simultaneously deprived of the right to make a living. The persecution of the Jews might not spur German exports or alleviate unemployment, Williger concluded sarcastically, but at least the soldiers were becoming more handsome.[51] Emmy Beckmann made the same argument in *Die Frau*, albeit more delicately: "race is merely an instrument, while it is the intellect that decides."[52] Another eminent liberal contributor to *Die Frau*, Ricarda Huch, spoke out publicly against the Nuremberg Laws, while Heuss and Höpker-Aschoff managed to publish critical articles in *Die Hilfe*.[53]

Notwithstanding these concerns about codifying racial discrimination, most Democrats did not recognize an "eliminationist" impulse in Nazi Jewish policy, much less did the population at large.[54] "Alongside the view that there are too many Jewish attorneys (doctors, journalists . . . etc.)," wrote Hans Robinsohn in 1936, there was also "a sharp condemnation of the chicaneries against the Jews, and sometimes even a condemnation of the race laws."[55] Even the SS and Gestapo routinely dismissed charges of racial miscegenation (*Rassenschande*), Robinsohn recalled, and ordered local police "to stop carrying out temporary incarcerations" in such cases, since the unpleasant conditions made the "confessions of such prisoners" useless.[56] Local policies, Robinsohn believed, were largely motivated by political or economic opportunism: "If the district governor is a rabid anti-Semite, then the Jews there have it bad . . . As soon as the pressure [from above] lets up, one detects moderation shortly thereafter. Typical in this regard are the experiences encountered in the wake of the boycott against Jewish businesses . . . after the cessation of the propaganda customers once again found their way into Jewish shops."[57] If many liberals still appeared indifferent to Nazi anti-Semitism in the mid-1930s, this was because they genuinely believed the situation was stabilizing and the worst was over.[58] This seeming equanimity was belied, moreover, by the Democrats' dedication to helping Jewish colleagues in everyday life.[59]

III

Resisting Anti-Semitism in Everyday Life

The two pillars of Nazi Jewish policy after Nuremberg and before the Second World War were "Aryanization" (the legal expropriation or forced sale of Jewish property) and emigration. The two policies were inextricably linked in the sense that the former helped finance the latter. Deprived of their citizenship, livelihood, and the better part of their capital, the majority of German, Austrian, and Bohemian Jews emigrated in the four years between the Nuremberg Laws and the beginning of the Second World War. That is, despite the claims of intentionalist historians who argue that Hitler always planned to exterminate European Jewry, the vast majority of Nazi leaders and institutions sought to "assist" Jews in emigrating. The problem was that Hitler's obsession with economic autarchy and Goering's characteristic rapacity made financing emigration more difficult than it had to be. Due to legal restrictions related to Aryanization many Jews were stripped of the capital that was necessary to obtain entry into foreign countries during the Great Depression. From 1935 the Jews were also subject to a harsh regime of foreign exchange controls, which made the transfer of any German currency, jewelry, or precious metals abroad nearly impossible.[60]

We should not confuse enthusiasm for Jewish emigration with "philosemitism," or even with a more moderate "anti-antisemitism." Initially the Nazis also hoped that Jews would settle elsewhere, even if that meant a Jewish state in Palestine, which is one reason why Adolf Eichmann studied Hebrew and developed ties to Zionists.[61] The difference between Democrats and Nazis is that liberal engagement in Aryanization and emigration, with few exceptions, was indicative of a concerted effort to ameliorate, not worsen, the situation of Jews in the Third Reich.[62] It is the ubiquitous willingness of gentile Democrats to represent, subsidize, and socialize with Jewish colleagues that reveals the presence of an alternative discourse to Nazi anti-Semitism, one that ran counter to the escalating anti-Jewish measures of the regime. Here it is essential to remember that, in a totalizing if not necessarily totalitarian regime, even small private initiatives had great public resonance. Criticizing anti-Semitism in print or speaking out publicly against Nazi Jewish policy took courage. Helping Jewish colleagues negotiate the arcane legal and economic terrain of the Third Reich might result in interrogation and arrest. Even retaining Jewish employees in the wake of the Nuremberg Laws was dangerous.[63] Despite this, Hjalmar Schacht, Hermann Dietrich, and Theodor Heuss, each in their own way, embody the remarkable possibilities for liberal resistance to Nazi anti-Semitism.

Liberal *"Anti-Antisemitism"* in Power:
The Case of Hjalmar Schacht

Emblematic of the liberal response to Nazi anti-Semitism in the middle years of the Third Reich is Hitler's Reichsbank President and Finance Minister, Hjalmar Schacht. Ever since the erstwhile Democrat was acquitted at Nuremberg historians have debated the assertion by the "Old Wizard" that he tried "to prevent the worst excesses of Hitler's policies," anti-Semitism in particular. Early on, most scholars agreed with the verdict, arguing that the "business world was . . . a so-called refuge in which . . . the Jews were able to continue comparatively unmolested until the second half of the thirties, almost until Schacht stepped down as Minister of Economics."[64] More recently historians have insisted that Schacht, who had already abandoned the Democratic Party before the Nazi "seizure of power," was never as sympathetic toward Jews as he claimed. Some even blame Schacht, in restoring the German economy and facilitating the expropriation of Jewish property, for Hitler's long-term popularity and, indirectly, for the Holocaust.[65]

This revisionist approach ignores vital aspects of historical context. Before Auschwitz moderate anti-Semitism was acceptable across Europe, even among "anti-antisemitic" Democrats. Schacht saw no contradiction in befriending and mentoring Jewish colleagues while simultaneously propagating anti-Semitic stereotypes.[66] His position on the "Jewish Question" is exemplified in a letter he wrote to a colleague regarding the Socialist Reichspresident Ebert's decision not to invite a representative of the Jewish religious community to speak at a celebration in honor of the new Weimar Republic. The Jewish community's repeated insistence on "equal" representation with Protestants and Catholics, Schacht suggested, was one of the reasons for the rise in anti-Semitism after the First World War. "No one denied the Jews human or political equality," Schacht concluded, "but their religious values were certainly not worth 50 or 100 times those of other beliefs."[67] Schacht's letter reflects the struggle of many Democrats between a classical liberal view that Jews deserved equal rights as individuals and a lack of patience, verging on anti-Semitism, with the influence ostensibly demanded by Jews as a collective ethnoreligious entity.

There are superficial continuities between Schacht's moderate anti-Semitism and Nazi policies on the Jews in the early years of the Third Reich. Schacht accepted the reduction of Jewish influence in finance and the professions. He also reluctantly endorsed the 1935 Nuremberg Laws, which he hoped might finally resolve the eternally nettlesome "Jewish Question."[68] And Schacht rarely utilized his power to restrain the tide of Aryanization.[69] But what was the point of opposing the expropriation of Jewish property in the wake of the Nuremberg Laws? The Jews, Schacht reasoned, were stripped of their citizenship rights and Germany was in the midst of the Great Depression. Why expend one's limited political capital protecting the financial interests of individuals who were no longer citizens and who possessed, on average, considerably more assets than the average German? As cynical as these considerations may have been, even Schacht's most prominent critics note that he did nothing to accelerate the process and may have prevented its worst excesses.[70]

Of course it is crucial to distinguish between purely pragmatic "anti-antisemitism" designed to serve the German economy and genuinely magnanimous efforts to curb Nazi persecution of the Jews. When Schacht urged Goebbels to refrain from anti-Jewish boycotts and advised Hitler to tone down the regime's anti-Semitic propaganda in the early 1930s, German economic policy was based on increasing exports to major world markets. The regime could ill afford to alienate western consumers by unproductive and largely symbolic attacks on Jews. While Schacht's warnings before 1936 might be dismissed as pragmatic, however, they were nonetheless courageous and flew in the face of party dogma. With the acceleration of Jewish persecution and the turn toward economic autarchy in 1936, it is virtually impossible to view these "anti-antisemitic" exertions as utilitarian. Quite the contrary: even where Schacht framed his complaints in practical terms, he compromised himself ideologically.[71] Like many Democrats who made concessions to the prevailing winds of anti-Semitism, Schacht never completely shed his liberal antipathy to virulent race hatred.

Thus Schacht invested substantial political capital and personal energy to prevent anti-Semitic excesses at the precise time when such actions promised the least return.[72] He castigated the infamous anti-Semitic pornographer Julius Streicher and attacked SA stormtroopers for their lack of civility toward Jews. In one particularly "anti-antisemitic" speech at Königsberg only a month before the Nuremberg Laws, he chastised Nazi fanatics, "who under the cover of darkness 'heroically' deface the windows [of Jewish shops], who portray every German that frequents a Jewish shop as a betrayer of the people, who declare that all erstwhile Freemasons are scum." Schacht received multiple warnings from Nazi officials.[73]

Though Goering's appointment as plenipotentiary for the Four Year Plan in September 1936 confirmed Schacht's decline in power and influence, he continued to question Nazi policies. Schacht actively purged Nazis from his Economics Ministry as well, employing devout republicans in their stead. Even Hans Robinsohn, always cool toward Schacht during their time as party colleagues, acknowledged that the "Old Wizard" represented a liberal beacon in an otherwise bleak Nazi storm.[74] In his unpublished memoirs, August Weber, another Democrat who condemned Schacht's opportunism after 1933, nonetheless recalls the quiet assistance Schacht gave to Jewish liberals at the height of Nazi persecutions; that Weber's "non-Aryan" family had to flee to England in 1938 lends poignancy to these recollections.[75]

For all these reasons it remains difficult to accept the contention that, in Jewish matters, "there was no discord between Schacht and Hitler."[76] Hitler made no secret of these ideological differences when he relieved Schacht of his duties as Reichsbank President in January 1939: "You simply do not conform to the general National Socialist framework" and "you have refused to allow your civil servants to be evaluated by the party."[77] As Robinsohn noted further, there was a palpable "strengthening of the political opposition" in the wake of Schacht's dismissal.[78] Schacht was personally close, before and after his retirement, to members of the Kreisau and Goerdeler Circles. Suspected of complicity in the 20 July conspiracy, he spent the last ten months of the Third Reich in Ravensbrück, Flossenburg, and Dachau concentration camps – ten months more than most of his Democratic colleagues.[79] Whether Schacht could have done more with his ample if ultimately transient influence is an interesting matter for speculation. But there is little doubt that he preserved an uncommon degree of liberal moderation and compassion in an otherwise virulently anti-Semitic Reich.

Hermann Dietrich and the Everyday Opportunities for "Anti-Antisemitism"

As Schacht's career illustrates, the experience of Jewish persecution could turn even the most ambivalent "anti-antisemites" into opponents of Nazi Jewish policy. Like Schacht, the State Party chairman Hermann Dietrich was never known for his "philosemitic" views during the Weimar Republic. Though hardly an anti-Semite, he expressed few reservations about the DDP's merger with the *völkisch* Young Germans and voted for the Enabling Law along with his State Party colleagues. Dietrich would nevertheless become one of the most notable "anti-antisemites" in the Third Reich, doing more than most Democrats to insulate Jewish colleagues from the evolving "Final Solution."[80] Throughout the 1930s we find letters from Jewish associates, sometimes once or twice removed, requesting financial assistance, jobs, or legal advice.[81] Rarely did he disappoint. Already in 1933, as the major Jewish-owned publishing firms were forced to release scores of writers and editors, Dietrich helped many Jewish colleagues move into other jobs.[82] In 1934, always on the lookout for Jewish employment opportunities, Dietrich instructed a colleague to investigate a rumor that "a paper will appear in the Mosse Verlag that is supposedly produced by non-Aryan people."[83] In 1936 a former Ullstein employee, Alexander Weinstein, contacted Dietrich for help in obtaining a visa. Encouraged that Weinstein had spent three years training to be a mechanic, Dietrich promised to mine contacts to find him a job abroad.[84]

Dietrich frequently took Jewish clients in cases of Aryanization and emigration. Neither was terribly remunerative. According to the Aryanization laws, any income made by representing Jews was taxed an *additional* 40 percent over the usual rate.[85] Yet Dietrich devoted an immense amount of time to assisting Jewish acquaintances in selling their businesses in order to finance their emigration. Even after the war began Dietrich managed to help at least a dozen Jewish men and women emigrate to Great Britain, America, or Palestine.[86]

Dietrich's motives were not purely altruistic. When a former DDP colleague, Ernst Mayer, wrote looking for employment, Dietrich facilitated Mayer's purchase of a soon-to-be Aryanized real estate business. Mayer undoubtedly paid the Jewish owner a more favorable price than that offered by the Nazi government.[87] All the same, he still worked out an exceptional deal thanks to Dietrich, who subsequently used Mayer as his real estate agent.[88] Dietrich was also cautious. He does not appear to have defended Jewish firms *against* Aryanization, for example. Still, many gentile lawyers refused to represent Jews altogether; others exploited their vulnerable situation.[89] Dietrich, to the contrary, treated his Jewish clients with the utmost respect, in many cases offering free counsel.[90]

On a more personal level, Dietrich retained his Jewish secretary, Käthe Zolki, long after it was safe to do so. As we will recall, when the Reich Legal Association first inquired why Dietrich continued to employ a non-Aryan secretary in 1937, Dietrich argued that her expertise was needed to finish up a particular case, and then only at his home office in Berlin-Steglitz. It is nonetheless obvious that he was using her services for a great many duties.[91] After Dietrich moved permanently to his home office in July 1940, he dismissed his "Aryan" secretary Charlotte Bein, and Ms Zolki took over *all* formal secretarial duties.[92] Dietrich likewise permitted her to handle both delicate financial correspondence and the most intimate personal matters. One might assume this opened his practice to Gestapo intervention and compromised his friends and colleagues. Yet dozens of Dietrich's colleagues wrote Zolki back personally, wishing her happy holidays, thanking her for gifts sent on Dietrich's behalf, and encouraging her "to remain brave," no doubt referring to the difficulty of being Jewish in wartime Nazi Germany.[93] Dietrich himself kept in close touch with erstwhile Jewish associates long after it was wise to do so.[94]

Dietrich worked equally hard to sponsor Jewish emigration. As the last chairman of the Defense League Against Anti-Semitism, Georg Gothein had more experience than his junior colleague in dealing with Jewish persecution, yet he still turned to Dietrich to intervene in the case of the Hamburg Democrat Felix Waldstein. Dietrich responded skeptically. In the seven weeks since *Kristallnacht*, he had contacted the American consulate repeatedly on behalf of Jewish colleagues, but the conversation inevitably "ended in a very depressing fashion." The Americans, Dietrich complained, were hardly more favorable to Jewish émigrés than the Third Reich. Nevertheless, only a few weeks after Gothein's missive to Dietrich, Waldstein managed to emigrate to London.[95] August Weber likewise singles out Dietrich in his memoirs, noting that no former Democrat played a greater role in assisting Jewish colleagues.[96]

Dietrich could only do so much. He was neither particularly well connected to Reich officials nor extraordinarily wealthy. But that is why his example is so illuminating. Dietrich's co-chairman of the DStP Reinhold Maier, also a lawyer with a small practice (though much less real estate), found himself in similar circumstances. The only real difference is that Maier had a Jewish spouse instead of a Jewish secretary. After his wife and children emigrated in 1936, however, Maier remained incapable of mustering the least resistance to National Socialism. Afraid that the

Gestapo might take away his law practice, he even filed for divorce in 1943.[97] Meanwhile Dietrich managed to find employment for Jewish colleagues, help others sell their businesses, and facilitate emigration wherever possible, all the while protecting his Jewish secretary and refusing to participate in the Reich Legal Association in any appreciable way. While modest in its impact, Dietrich's long-term non-conformity indicates the remarkable degree to which Democrats might resist Nazi Jewish policy without compromising their safety or their livelihood.

Theodor Heuss and "Individualist" Anti-Antisemitism

Heuss was not immune to the underlying anti-Semitism pervading German political culture in the 1920s and 1930s. Like many gentile colleagues, he was uncomfortable with the disproportionate number of Jews in the DDP. And though loyal to Jewish friends like Gustav and Toni Stolper and Fritz Elsas – his son Ernst Ludwig would marry Elsas's daughter Hanne – he always tried to distance himself from the "rootless Jewish [elements]" in the party.

But as the Third Reich commenced and Heuss witnessed at first hand the practical consequences of Nazi anti-Semitism, his fundamental liberal convictions triumphed over his darker *völkisch* inclinations. As Breslau's Chief Rabbi Leo Baeck put it, Theodor Heuss gave Jews hope in otherwise hopeless times.[98] One of the few Democrats to criticize Nazi anti-Semitism before Hitler came to power, Heuss provided succor to numerous Jewish colleagues after 1933.[99] Toni Stolper, August Weber, and others would recall Heuss's unconditional friendship during the initial anti-Semitic onslaught as well as his efforts to meet Jewish colleagues after their emigration.[100] Heuss did not confine his efforts to friends. In June 1934 he wrote the Reich Press Chamber on behalf of the conservative Anna von Gierke who, owing to her non-Aryan (Jewish) background, was not allowed to continue her journal *Soziale Arbeit*. In spite of his dislike of Gierke's politics, Heuss insisted that her journal be continued because it was indispensable "for the maintenance and continued professional training of female welfare workers."[101]

Equally considerate, on the occasion of the seventieth birthday of the former Colonial Secretary and Jewish Democrat Bernhard Dernburg, in 1935, Heuss wrote the "right" liberal (DVP) President of the German Colonial Society, Heinrich Schnee. Given Dernburg and his family's advancing isolation, Heuss inquired whether Schnee might send him a semi-official greeting in recognition of his many years of government service. Schnee did exactly that. There can be little doubt that Heuss intended such official approbation to help shield Dernburg and his family from mounting persecution. That Schnee and Heuss both pointed to this exchange at the former's denazification trial indicates how noteworthy this simple gesture must have been.[102]

At the time Heuss was completing his Naumann biography in early 1937, Werner Stephan, the former Democrat cum press attaché in Goebbels's Propaganda Ministry, forwarded Heuss an advance copy of Nazi Agricultural Minister Walther Darré's bizarre and virulently anti-Semitic book *Schweinemord* (Pig Slaughter). Outlandish even by Nazi standards, the book claimed that Jews had undermined the German economy in the First World War by orchestrating the unnecessary slaughter of all the nation's pigs. Both men expressed bemusement and disgust.[103]

In contrast to this absurd brand of anti-Semitic literature, which centered on Jewish maliciousness and venality, Heuss highlighted Jewish virtues. He seized in particular on Naumann's friendship with the "important Jewish philanthropist" Charles Hallgarten. "Hallgarten was a great do-gooder, often willingly exploited because he took human weaknesses into account, wholly objectively and humbly, with a feeling for the helpful purpose of wealth . . . Naumann called him 'a virtuoso of practical humanity.'" According to Heuss, Naumann admired the fact that Hallgarten was a "self-conscious and proud Jew, engaged with the social problems of the Jewish people (but nonetheless not a Zionist)."[104] Naumann was hardly an anti-Semite before meeting Hallgarten, but Hallgarten helped dispel the last of those "clichéd conceptions" that Naumann had picked up in the company of the right-wing Christian Socialist Adolf Stöcker. Hallgarten's example, Heuss explained, had taught Naumann to view all Jews as individuals, not collectively as Zionists or socialists. Making "[b]lanket judgements regarding entire groups," Heuss concluded, "was not [Naumann's] style."[105]

Here Heuss articulates a quintessentially liberal "anti-antisemitism," focused primarily on respecting the rights of the individual before the law. Like most of his peers, Heuss was unprepared to view the Jews' dilemma as a special problem and unwilling to dismiss the "kernel of truth" in some anti-Jewish stereotypes (e.g. economic striving, tendencies toward socialism, internationalist inclinations). Rather than combat anti-Jewish prejudices of any kind, something one sees only among a few so-called "philosemites," Heuss preferred to emphasize the dangers of making "blanket judgements regarding entire groups."

There were some liberals with philosemitic sympathies. Georg Gothein, a co-founder and the last chairman of the Defense League Against Anti-Semitism, repudiated the claim that there was a "kernel of truth" to racial anti-Semitism and acknowledged the unique challenges facing Jews as a distinct community in the Third Reich. Katharina von Kardorff was a founding member of the German Committee for a Jewish Palestine (Deutsches Komitee Pro Palästina), which included Max Weber, Thomas Mann, Albert Einstein, Leo Baeck, and Martin Buber among other prominent (Jewish) Democrats. In the 1930s Kardorff single-mindedly wielded her considerable gifts of persuasion to improve the situation of German Jews.[106] She assisted numerous Jewish colleagues financially and politically, and complained to Nazi authorities about anti-Semitic measures on more than one occasion. She even wrote eloquent letters denouncing the desecration of Jewish graves in Berlin, Mannheim, and Frankfurt. To facilitate Jewish emigration to England and Palestine, Kardorff carried on a running correspondence with the future President of Israel, Chaim Weizmann, and his wife Vera. And though she had no legal training, Kardorff studied the Aryanization laws in order better to assist Jewish friends. In 1937 the wealthy heiress and her husband held a reception for Jews and Germans with Jewish friends to which she invited diplomats, including the French, British, and Russian ambassadors to Germany, in order to help Jews find asylum abroad.[107]

These exceptions, among whom we might include Marie Baum below, prove the general rule that most Democrats failed to propose a conceptual alternative to the Nazi "Jewish Question." This reluctance had less to do with their own inherent anti-Semitism than with a liberal inclination to privilege the rights of the individual over the special status (or victimhood) of a particular ethnic or religious group.[108] This response to Nazi anti-Semitism was grounded in a nineteenth-century, universalist ethos that viewed racial and religious prejudice as a function of ignorance and irrationality, not as the core of a fanatical, modern, and totalizing ideology. For many Democrats, dispelling anti-Semitism was a matter of mutual enlightenment. Anti-Semitism would disappear as Germans dispensed with their view of the Jews as a collective "alien" entity, which was in any case economically and diplomatically impractical. The Jews in turn would shed their own ethnoreligious particularity and special claims to victimhood. The first five years of the Third Reich – in fact, much of the Weimar Republic – illustrated the inadequacy of this classical liberal response to Nazi anti-Semitism. It would take *Kristallnacht* and its aftermath to bring this realization home.

From **Kristallnacht** *to the Final Solution:*
The Bosch Circle and the Limits of Liberal "Anti-Antisemitism"
On the night of 9–10 November 1938 Joseph Goebbels ordered a nationwide pogrom against the Jews. Days earlier a disgruntled Polish Jew, angry

that his parents had been incarcerated and deported back to Poland by the Nazi government, had assassinated a German diplomat in Paris. Anxious to find a resolution to the nagging "Jewish Question" and always on the lookout for dramatic ways to reinforce the racial *Volksgemeinschaft*, Goebbels seized the moment to impress upon German Jewry the necessity of leaving the Third Reich. Burning synagogues, breaking the windows of Jewish-owned businesses, injuring and arresting thousands of others, the brown-shirted stormtroopers unleashed an unprecedented reign of terror on Greater Germany's Jewish community. The next morning hundreds of millions of dollars in property, Aryan as well as Jewish, had been destroyed. Almost one hundred Jews had been killed. A new phase in Nazi Jewish policy had begun.

What has come to be known as the Night of Broken Glass (*Kristallnacht*) did not inaugurate the Holocaust. It did, however, indicate once and for all the barbarity, destructiveness, and utter ineffectuality of pogrom-like attempts to intimidate Jews into leaving Germany. In the wake of this devastation Hitler, Goering, and Goebbels (reluctantly) agreed that the enormously efficient Reichsführer SS Heinrich Himmler, supported by Reinhard Heydrich and the Gestapo, should proceed to "solve" the "Jewish Question." Impressed by his efforts to promote Jewish emigration in Vienna, Heydrich sent the young Adolf Eichmann to Berlin to set up a Central Office of Jewish Emigration. From that point forward, eliminating the Jews from Germany came under the purview of the SS.[109]

Liberals understood that Nazi Jewish policy had crossed the Rubicon. For reasons pragmatic as well as ethical, Schacht was outraged, sending a memorandum to his entire staff expressing the hope that "none of you took part; otherwise I would advise him to quickly resign from the Reichsbank."[110] For Külz, *Kristallnacht* was a galvanizing event, pushing the eminently bourgeois Democrat to the left and in part explaining his cooperation with the East German Socialists a decade later.[111] Upon leaving Gestapo custody for the fifth time in five years, August Weber, with Dietrich's help, immediately set to work engineering his own emigration to London (his children had left years before).[112] After November 1938 Koch-Weser, though an ardent patriot, refused to return to Germany.[113]

No Democrat was affected more than Robert Bosch. Well before the events of *Kristallnacht*, Bosch had taken a hand in resisting Nazi Jewish policy. Bosch was a member of Gothein's Defense League Against Anti-Semitism before 1933, and Nazi abuses against Jews were central to the rationale behind the Bosch Circle. Between 1934 and 1936 Bosch employed his connections abroad to facilitate the emigration of Jewish colleagues. He was also able to enlist the help of Jewish financiers who would otherwise have boycotted economic interaction with the Third Reich.[114] He developed ties with Jewish leaders across the Reich, like Breslau's Chief Rabbi Leo Baeck, while providing funds to help finance emigration.[115] Bosch's goodwill and ample resources were indispensable in the wake of *Kristallnacht*, when both the regime and its victims evinced an urgency which was often lacking during the first six years of the Third Reich. Between 1938 and 1940 he secreted "considerable sums" in a fund to assist Jews who found themselves in dire straits after their assets were frozen in the wake of *Kristallnacht*. Bosch was no Oskar Schindler, but his actions illustrate "the opportunities for assistance in the time of a dictatorship."[116]

While Bosch concentrated on providing Jews with financial backing, his employee Carl Goerdeler focused on undermining Nazi policies outright. As mayor of Leipzig Goerdeler had already garnered a reputation for philosemitism, defending the rights of Jewish physicians and dentists to treat Aryan patients. In 1936 he urged Hitler to countermand his deputy's request to remove a statue of the famous composer (and Marie Baum's great-uncle) Felix Mendelssohn-Bartholdy from the Leipzig town square. When he nevertheless found the statue gone upon returning from a trip to Finland, Goerdeler resigned his post in protest.[117] Soon hired by Bosch, Goerdeler proceeded to transfer 1.2 million Reichsmarks to Leo Baeck "for saving Jewish lives." He also began a propaganda campaign to draw American and English attention to the accelerating persecution of the Jews. Only three days before the *Kristallnacht* pogrom, Goerdeler met with the British financier A.P. Young in Switzerland to discuss, among other things, the "Jewish Question." "There is not yet in evidence any strong reaction among the democracies," Goerdeler complained, "in the press, the Church, and in parliament, against the barbaric, sadistic, and cruel persecution of 10,000 Polish Jews in Germany." Shortly after *Kristallnacht* he met with Young again to deplore the "senseless persecution of the Jews" and "the way in which the Nazi leaders enriched themselves by stealing Jewish property," urging the British government "to save the world from this terrible catastrophe."[118]

Given its ties to the armaments industry, officer corps, and German-Jewish community, the Bosch Circle was probably the best placed among liberal "resistance groups" to understand and influence the course of the "Final Solution." Until his death in March 1942 Bosch exchanged ideas with Baeck about the most effective way to help the German Jewish community in the wake of the "Final Solution." Bosch and Baeck ultimately

agreed – similarly to Roosevelt and Churchill – that overthrowing the Nazi
regime was the only sure way to halt the policy of extermination. While this
did raise the delicate matter of whether to limit the role of Jews in a post-
Nazi Germany, for tactical reasons Baeck accepted Hans Walz's and
Goerdeler's proposal to introduce a *numerus clausus* regarding the number of
Jews permitted to hold leading positions. By limiting Jewish participation,
the logic went, Goerdeler would be able to create the widest conceivable
resistance movement, one that could move as quickly as possible.[119]

Because Goerdeler's 1941 memo on the "Jewish Question" referred to
Jews as a separate race and proposed they be resettled in Palestine if their
families had not lived in Germany before 1871, some historians contend
that even the "liberal" elements in the German resistance movement shared
the Nazis' racial anti-Semitism. There is no question that Goerdeler had
imbibed many of the prevailing prejudices regarding the "preponderance"
of Jews in German culture, politics, and finance.[120] Walz too was at least as
motivated by Christian altruism as he was by a liberal belief in the equality
of all Germans, regardless of ethnicity or confession.

But there are two crucial qualifications to be made in assessing
Goerdeler and the plotters' attitude to the "Jewish Question." First, we
must differentiate between the typical, moderate anti-Semitism characteristic of most bourgeois Europeans (and Americans) in the 1930s and a
willingness to eliminate the rights, livelihoods, and ultimately the lives of
fellow Jewish citizens.[121] One ought to read Goerdeler's or Walz's qualified defense of Jewish rights as a necessary concession to the former, as
Baeck did, and not a precursor to the latter. Second, in the highly charged
anti-Semitic atmosphere of the Third Reich deeds speak louder than
words. Goerdeler resigned his mayoral post, we will recall, in protest at the
removal of the Jewish composer Felix Mendelssohn-Bartholdy's statue
from Leipzig town square. Goerdeler also worked intimately with his
Jewish colleague Fritz Elsas in drafting plans for a post-Nazi government.
He even made the left-wing Democrat chief of his shadow Reich
Chancellery.[122]

Most compelling is the fact that Goerdeler took the "Jewish Question"
seriously in the first place. As we have seen, few liberals and fewer conservatives were preoccupied by the situation of the Jews. Hans Robinsohn,
himself a Jewish resistance leader, acknowledged that privileging the
"Jewish Question" over other matters of post-Nazi reconstruction would
alienate otherwise sympathetic Germans.[123] Goerdeler, Bosch, and
company nevertheless insisted on developing a position on the "Jewish
Question" that would allow German Jews to retain their citizenship and

sponsor the creation of a Jewish state in Palestine.[124] Finally, Goerdeler's last will and testament, "Thoughts about the German Future by One Condemned to Death," described the impact that the "Final Solution" had on his decision to overthrow the Nazi regime. We must recognize, he wrote, that Hitler's hands were "dripping with the blood of innocent Jews, Poles, Russians and Germans who were murdered and starved to death, with the blood of millions of soldiers of all nations who are on his conscience . . . We must not deny the Jews the rights which God gave to all humans." According to Nazi secret police (SD) reports, the prisoner "again and again expressed his outrage about the great massacres of Jews in Poland."[125]

In fact "at least fifteen members of the anti-Hitler conspiracy stated during interrogation that their main motive, or one of their main motives for their opposition to National Socialism, was the persecution of the Jews." These included the liberal economist Adolf Lampe and jurist Franz Sperr, who, according to the Gestapo, "stubbornly take the liberal position of granting to the Jews in principle the same status as every German."[126] All made sincere efforts to shield Jews from deportation after the killing operations began in summer 1941. Goerdeler, Walz, and Bosch's private secretary Willy Schloβstein, whose wife was half Jewish, were intent on finding jobs for Jewish colleagues in order to shield them from deportation.

Such endeavors threatened to run aground on the single-minded enthusiasm with which the SS pursued the "Final Solution." Hans Walz was called into the local Gestapo office when he tried to prevent the deportation of a Jewish doctor who worked in the company clinic. After that, he made sure Jewish employees were transferred to different divisions to protect their identity, not only from the authorities, but from possible betrayal by their own co-workers. The dozens of letters from German Jews thanking Walz for his efforts indicate how significant such small acts of kindness could appear at the height of the Holocaust.[127]

Bosch, Walz, and Goerdeler were unable to put a significant brake on the "Final Solution," due in no small measure to the continual postponement and ultimate implosion of the 20 July plot. Yet their failure signifies less the weakness of liberal opposition to the Holocaust than the immensity and drive of the Nazi extermination machine. The conflicts and contradictions that characterized Hitler's prosecution of the war after 1941 seem to have dissipated with regard to the "Final Solution", one of the few examples in the Third Reich of virtually unadulterated totalitarianism. Except for a successful *coup d'état* backed perhaps by a general strike of the army and labor, there was little that *any* German could have done to stave off the "Final Solution."[128] The Bosch–Beck–Goerdeler group provided a clear, well-articulated "liberal" solution to the "Jewish Question," which soundly rejected the "eliminationist" impulse in Nazi anti-Semitism. Few Democrats approached this combination of thought and action.

At the same time, we must be careful about interpreting the "absence of evidence of overt manifestations of opposition to anti-Jewish policies . . . as evidence of antisemitism."[129] Like most Germans, liberals did not immediately understand the nature of the "Final Solution." Marie Baum, herself a quarter Jewish, later reported that one heard "authentic reports of the murdering of Jews in the Baltic, in Poland and Russia, [but] without any inkling as to their extent."[130] Hans Robinsohn was Jewish, enjoyed contacts with high-ranking military officials, and had himself predicted in October 1939 that Nazi resettlement policy would end in extermination. But he remained oblivious to the true nature of the "Final Solution" for many months after it began.[131] Evidence from the diaries and testaments of gentile liberals like Katharina von Kardorff, Ricarda Huch, and Paul Freiherr von Schoenaich confirm Baum and Robinsohn's recollections.[132]

One might condemn German liberals for their apparent indifference to so-called "Jewish Questions" and typical myopia in realizing the wider implications of the "Final Solution." Indeed, by propagating the concept of *Lebensraum*, virulent anti-Bolshevism, and the apotheosis of the German race, some liberals abetted wartime resettlement policies that resulted in genocide.[133] There is little evidence, however, that any of these liberals countenanced the logical extension of those policies: the extermination of ethnic minorities. On the contrary, it looks as if knowledge of the mass murders in the East was the decisive step in jarring many nationalist Democrats to their senses.[134] In the wake of the German invasion of the Soviet Union, Bäumer, Obst, Winschuh, and Rohrbach worked to differentiate their liberal nationalist pretensions from the race-based imperialism of Hitler. If many failed to understand the terrible magnitude of the Nazi "Final Solution," most German Democrats responded to Nazi anti-Semitism by affirming liberal-universalist traditions of individual equality before the law and the sanctity of human life.

IV

The Jewish Liberal Experience in the Third Reich

In *Eichmann in Jerusalem*, Hannah Arendt famously suggested that German Jews were complicit in their own destruction; not only in the

Jewish Councils' willingness to send their brethren to Auschwitz, but, implicitly, in the Jews' less than energetic reaction to Nazi persecution, whether through fight or flight. This accusation is misplaced insofar as it fails to take account of the extraordinarily difficult professional, familial, and emotional choices confronting German Jews after 1933. Many Jews, liberal and otherwise, did what they could to resist the Third Reich.[135] But the mere fact that Arendt and other Jewish émigrés might hold such negative views of their co-religionists reminds us of the complex relationship between Jewish liberals and the Third Reich.[136]

Although it was never easy to emigrate, the vast majority of German Jews *did* have a choice about whether to leave. And while Jews faced greater risks than gentiles in opposing National Socialism, as we shall see, they enjoyed opportunities for resistance, active as well as passive. Furthermore, one cannot assume that Jewish Democrats were uniquely resistant to National Socialism or preternaturally aware of the long-term dangers of staying in Germany. Like their gentile colleagues, liberals of Jewish descent were generally patriotic Germans loath to abandon their country. Having experienced multiple waves of anti-Semitism in the past, many Germans Jews dismissed Nazi propaganda as merely a more virulent incarnation of traditional right-wing anti-Semitism. Most believed the situation would improve with the return of political and economic stability.[137]

When Jewish liberals did emigrate – and they certainly left at a higher rate than their gentile colleagues – few did so as a matter of conscience. Personal and professional reasons played a greater role. A liberal past did not make it impossible to negotiate the Third Reich successfully, but being liberal *and* Jewish made the odds more daunting; the regime more immediately threatening.[138] The first wave of Jewish emigration, for example, occurred in the wake of the Reichstag fire, when the Gestapo began to assert extra-legal control of German society and the Reichstag began passing anti-Semitic legislation. The most influential Jewish liberals in the publishing world, like the *Berliner Tageblatt's* Theodor Wolff and the *Vossische Zeitung's* Georg Bernhard, emigrated immediately for fear of their lives.[139] Jewish academics were often the next to leave. Less engaged in politics than their colleagues in the press and initially protected by tenure, many survived the early phases of *Gleichschaltung*.[140] Nevertheless, they "faced a range of humiliations, such as boycotts, disruptions of their classes, and house searches. Some were eventually restricted from travel to scholarly conferences abroad, prevented from publishing, or denied access to the university's library. Others had their pensions reduced." Few Jewish liberals were able to hold their academic position beyond 1936, after the Nuremberg Laws initiated a new flood of purges.[141]

Finally there were Jewish liberal politicians. In fact, the roll-call of aspiring émigrés who went to Heuss, Dietrich, and other gentile colleagues for assistance gives the impression that rank-and-file Democrats were more likely to have financial difficulties in emigrating than their colleagues in business or academia. Still, those who left did so reluctantly. The case of Gustav Stolper is illustrative. Unlike Bernhard and Wolff, Stolper did not belong to the "cosmopolitan" left wing of the party. Like his mentor Schacht, Stolper was a free market capitalist and liberal nationalist who demanded a complete revision of the Versailles Treaty, including an *Anschluss* with Austria. A German first and foremost, Stolper's Jewish confession was incidental. And, like Robinsohn and Koch-Weser, Stolper did not believe that Germans were peculiarly anti-Semitic. Only weeks before his departure, he highlighted the skeptical reaction of gentile Berliners to Goebbels' boycott of Jewish businesses on 1 April 1933, blaming Nazi anti-Semitism on the unhealthy influence of the "Bohemian Hitler," not the German people. He took the future Minister of War Blomberg at his word when the latter assured Stolper in early 1933 that the "army would never allow the old [Weimar] flag to be replaced by the swastika." By his wife's own admission, so intent was Stolper on displaying his German national feeling that he voluntarily dismissed a few left-leaning writers from his magazine, *Der Volkswirt*, in a futile attempt to conciliate the regime.[142]

Everything changed in the aftermath of the anti-Jewish boycott. *Der Volkswirt*, according to Stolper, "was fundamentally transformed." One could "no longer publish a critical word," which made the journal's existence "not only intellectually intolerable and morally suspect, but financially impossible in the long run." At the end of April Stolper therefore threw caution to the wind, publishing his last lead article in *Der Volkswirt*. Banned by the Reich Press Association, the piece denounced the ideological capitulation of so-called liberal economists like "[Hans] Luther and Schacht" to National Socialism.[143] Emigrating temporarily to Zürich, Stolper sold his paper for one-third of its market value, promising not to return until Hitler was out of office. He landed in New York City a few months later.[144]

Stolper would always claim that his departure was due principally to philosophical differences with the regime. But his personal sentiments at the time indicate how much his decision was based on necessity. As he wrote Schacht in July 1933: "you can imagine what the departure from

Germany means, and still more the departure from a Germany whose future fills me with the greatest concern, from a Germany, to which I, in spite of everything that has happened to me, remain bound by heart and soul. I leave this country because no one will let me live here, though I will never feel like an emigrant but a German citizen."[145] One can only speculate on the effect this emotional missive might have had on Schacht's evolving attitude to the "Jewish Question."

Erich Koch-Weser's reasons for leaving in 1933 were equally complex. Few liberals of Jewish descent – though baptized Protestant, Koch's mother was Jewish – were more influential. As Reich Interior and Justice Minister in multiple cabinets and chairman of the DDP from 1924 to 1930, he helped shape both the Republic and the Democratic Party. A devoted patriot and pragmatist, Koch also single-handedly engineered the DDP's merger with the *völkisch*-nationalist Young Germans. If nothing else, Koch's enthusiasm for the project illustrates his relative equanimity about the potential dangers of late Weimar anti-Semitism.[146]

So why would Koch leave his homeland so quickly? One might assume Koch's "Jewishness" was the decisive factor. Despite his visibility as a Weimar Minister, "Jewish" liberal, and DDP chairman, however, Koch does not appear to have stood as high on the list of "enemies of the Reich" as fellow "non-Aryans" like Wolff, Stolper, or even gentile liberals like Heuss and Maier. He was also a Protestant *Mischling* (of mixed race), many of whom, like Marie Baum, negotiated the twelve years of the Third Reich successfully. Anti-Nazi politics played a part in his decision. But Koch was certainly more nationalist than Maier or Baum. Rather, as in Stolper's case, personal and professional considerations were paramount. First, it is important to remember that Koch was blamed by his Democratic colleagues for the failure of the State Party experiment and resigned from the party in disgrace in November 1930. Three years later Koch still had not repaired the damage to his personal and professional life. Like many attorneys in the midst of the Depression, Koch-Weser's practice was hardly thriving. His prospects took an additional downturn with the March 1933 laws restricting Jewish representation in the professions. Having contemplated a life in South America since his ignominious retirement from politics, and already struggling to attract clients, Koch viewed the Nazi seizure of power as the final straw: negotiating the purchase of a cattle ranch, he moved to Brazil.[147]

Thus like their "full-Jewish" brethren, liberals of half-Jewish descent rarely relinquished their ties to Germany for "moral" reasons. According to Koch, in fact, liberals of "mixed race" had a more difficult time coming to terms with post-1933 conditions than "full" Jews. In contrast to self-consciously Jewish Germans, Koch observed, "[c]ountless people of mixed blood" only "discovered" their Jewishness upon being "forcibly removed" from their jobs. For liberal nationalists who never considered themselves Jewish, some of whom openly sympathized with aspects of the Nazi "revolution," this revelation was hard to accept. And lest we forget that anti-Semitic stereotypes prevailed among Jews as well as gentiles, Koch insisted that liberals of "mixed-race [*Mischlinge*]" couldn't call upon the same sympathies at home or connections abroad "since they lacked those international ties that Jews are apt to have if only through their religion."[148] Liberal *Mischlinge*, it seems, felt more betrayed by Hitler than their "fully" Jewish brethren.[149]

At least Koch, safely relocated to South America, could afford to be open in his repudiation of the regime, publishing a scathing appraisal of the Third Reich shortly before his death in 1944. For Jewish Democrats determined to live and work in Nazi Germany, life was virtually impossible without making multiple daily concessions to the regime. Sometimes these accommodations, in an environment of political paranoia and economic desperation, were self-destructive. Hermann Dietrich found himself arbitrating one such situation when the chair of the Central Association of Germans of Jewish Confession (CVDJG), Paul Liebig, accused a Jewish publishing firm of price gouging at a time, in mid-1934, when neither had any funds. There is little doubt that financial difficulties brought out the worst on both sides, as Liebig accused the Jewish publisher, Fürst, of perpetuating through exorbitant prices the very anti-Semitic stereotypes the CVDJG fought against. Although this was a common trope before 1933, employed by Jew and gentile alike, it nonetheless illustrates the Darwinistic political and economic pressures which even Jewish Democrats faced in opposing anti-Semitism.[150]

The case of the eminent Jewish historian Hans Rothfels is instructive. Rothfels was a liberal nationalist typical of the right wing of Stresemann's DVP. Whilst he disliked the Weimar Republic and despised the Versailles Treaty, he refused to support the elimination of the former in order to achieve the destruction of the latter. Still, when the Nazis came to power, Rothfels was, like many nationalists, genuinely enthusiastic about the early achievements of the NSDAP.[151] More interesting is the fact that he and another non-Aryan historian, Hans Herzfeld, were "protected" at first by the local Nazi administration in Königsberg because both were technically *Mischlinge* and "supporters of the 'national Revolution.'" A decorated veteran, Rothfels had lost a leg in the First World War. He was also friendly with the "progressive" Nazi and Danzig Senate President, Hermann Rauschning, who generally resisted the NSDAP's more extreme racial policies. Rothfels's Nazi defenders pointed out his tireless work on behalf of Germany's colonization of the East and reasoned: "racial conceptions are good as far as it goes, but here an exception needs to be made." His opponents countered that, although Rothfels's record was impeccable, permitting a Jew to lecture Germans about *Lebensraum* at the Reich's easternmost academic outpost might confuse students about the necessity of racial purity. The resulting compromise was that Deputy Führer Rudolf Hess had Rothfels transferred to cosmopolitan Berlin, where he might work on questions of *Ostpolitik* without the distractions of full-time teaching and far removed from the sensitive border regions of the Reich.[152] For all the anti-Semitic crudeness and hypocrisy of this episode, one can perhaps understand how nationalist Jews might be ready to develop a *modus vivendi* with the Third Reich.

According to Hans Robinsohn, "non-Aryan" liberals were hardly more reliable ideologically than their gentile colleagues. "They would doubtless happily have let themselves be coordinated," Robinsohn writes, "if that had only been possible. The Jews are in this regard essentially no different from the gentiles, so uncomfortable as this acknowledgment might momentarily be . . . for the self-concept of the Jews."[153] This observation is borne out by the claims of non-Aryan liberals, reflected in Hermann Dietrich's party correspondence, who asserted that they were "German" not "Jewish."[154] The Liberal Erich Welkow likewise reported with regret that some Hessian Jews felt pressure to support the Nazi Party in order to affirm their patriotism.[155] We also have the comment of Richard Merton, a Jewish liberal executive at I.G. Farben who was eventually forced to resign in 1938:

> That I in the years after 1933 did not, like so many others, slide into the sins of National Socialism was . . . not a special accomplishment on my part; I owe it to the fact that I was protected by my four Jewish grandparents from damaging my soul. I was *forced*, as I said already then many times, to make a virtue of necessity. Others, like you . . . had the option to cooperate, to make compromises, to build bridges. The great majority did that under the compulsion of maintaining their positions. . . . To be sure, toward all of those who were not in this situation but still wanted to take part, I always felt a certain skepticism, but also understanding. One *wants*, indeed, to take part. The drive for prestige is a very powerful impulse in all people of all social classes.[156]

These forthcoming observations are hard to ignore. Like most of their gentile colleagues, German Jews found anti-Semitism patently offensive and wrong-headed. But in other respects, as Robinsohn, Welkow, and Merton suggest, liberal Jews were susceptible to National Socialism. The point is not that Jews were necessarily complicit in their own destruction, only that assessing (Jewish) liberal "resistance" to Nazi anti-Semitism is a challenging undertaking, one that eludes simplistic binaries such as "anti- or philo-Semitism", "intentionalism or functionalism", "resistance or collaboration."[157]

Jewish Liberal "Non-Conformity"
At the same time that liberals of Jewish descent worked to retain their German identity, the Nazis tried equally hard to force Jews to reclaim their "Jewishness."[158] In fact there existed an "apparent Nazi tolerance of the communal and organizational dimension of Jewish life in Germany, as distinct from the lives of Jews as individuals." The CVJDG, to which many liberal Jews belonged, existed until early 1939, outliving many impeccably "Aryan" and Christian interest groups. To be sure, such Jewish organizations never "challenged the constitutionality of the discriminatory paragraphs – the so-called *Arierparagraphen* – of the antisemitic legislation of spring 1933, nor did they ever call into question the legality of the infamous Nuremberg Laws." They did however seek out legal loopholes and sympathetic officials on an individual basis in order to combat the worst aspects "of everyday Jewish life in Germany before the war: antisemitic signs and posters, offensive songs, economic boycotts, arbitrary dismissals, exclusion of Jews from the professions, individual outrages, discrimination in schools, administrative harassment, religious libel." The decision to combat Nazi race laws in the courts rather than emigrate "was at the opposite pole of accommodation to the regime. It went against the grain of mainstream Nazi policy and could entail considerable personal sacrifice and risk – as is amply attested by the repeated arrests of its leading members and their incarceration in concentration camps. Indeed, it may arguably even be regarded as a form of Jewish resistance."[159]

These remarks highlight the stark contrast in liberal nationalist and Nazi approaches to the "Jewish Question" before the Second World War. In the interest of reversing the emancipaton process and of encouraging emigration – thus for entirely cynical reasons – the race-obsessed Nazis recognized the Jews' "rights" as a community, even encouraging Jewish cultural, religious, and ethnic self-determination in order to separate them more thoroughly from the German *Volksgemeinschaft*.[160] Conversely,

German liberals, even those with *völkisch* concerns, generally defended the rights of individual Jews before the law. They seemed reticent, meanwhile, perhaps even theoretically unable, to conceive of German Jews as a distinct community facing singular challenges that could not be resolved on an individual basis.

Jewish liberals had similar difficulties viewing their own social or juridical situation as unique. They frequently treated the "Jewish Question" that played so central a role in Nazi ideology as subordinate to more "pressing" questions of politics, economy, and society. Neither Elsas nor Robinsohn, for example, accepted the Nazi "equation of National Socialism with Germanness," nor did either cite his own "Jewishness" as crucial in shaping his oppositional attitude to the regime. As Robinsohn explained later when asked to describe his experience "as a Jew" in the Third Reich, "my peripheral position regarding Jewish problems makes me less than suitable for work on specific Jewish matters . . . I never lived as 'a Jew' in Germany, but as a man born in Germany who was immensely interested in German political problems."[161] One reason for their ability to see themselves as "Germans" was their "privileged" status *vis-à-vis* other Jewish Democrats. Both were independently wealthy, well assimilated – Elsas was a converted Protestant – and enjoyed the "protection" of ranking liberals like Hjalmar Schacht and Werner Stephan.[162] Perhaps the knowledge of many émigré colleagues' negative experiences abroad contributed to the sublimation of their Jewishness.[163] Whatever the reason, both men were genuinely preoccupied by an ecumenical desire to rescue a liberal Germany from the throes of Hitlerism. Surviving a pending Holocaust was the least of their concerns.[164]

This universalist perspective was tested in the wake of *Kristallnacht*. Even the position of "privileged" Jews like Elsas and Robinsohn became precarious. Without Schacht's protection, Robinsohn's textile factory was "Aryanized" and with it the remainder of his fortune. Robinsohn's conviction that emigration was the wisest course was reinforced when 30,000 Jews were sent to concentration camps in November 1938.[165] Many of his Jewish colleagues followed a similar path.[166] Looking back a year later, Robinsohn remarked that the war and subsequent radicalization of the "Jewish Question" had indeed made life intolerable for German Jews. But in tracking the first resettlements of Jews to "special reservations" in occupied Poland he cautioned that matters would only get worse in the years to come, possibly culminating in mass extermination. For the first time, the "Jewish Question" began to take pride of place in Robinsohn's reports.[167]

Observations of Jewish (liberal) émigrés like Robinsohn are essential in gauging contemporary attitudes to the emerging "Final Solution."[168] Equally interesting are the perspectives of Jewish liberals who stayed. For, unlike their gentile colleagues, liberals of Jewish descent could hardly ignore the "Jewish Question" after September 1939. To be sure, during the war Jewish liberals shared a typical German unwillingness to discuss the "Final Solution." But the sources are rich enough to reconstruct the experiences and outlook of three of the most prominent "Jewish" liberals to remain in Germany after 1939: Fritz Elsas, the erstwhile mayor of Berlin and leading member of the anti-Nazi resistance; Eugen Schiffer, the former Weimar Vice-Chancellor, Finance, and Justice Minister and co-founder of the East German Liberal Democratic Party; and Marie Baum, Democratic parliamentarian, Heidelberg professor, and Weimar women's leader.

Fritz Elsas

A legal scholar by training, Fritz Elsas entered politics during the First World War as a Progressive (FVP) member of the Stuttgart city council.[169] As a DDP *Landtag* (provincial parliament) representative and mayor of Berlin, Elsas rose to become one of the most influential Democrats in the last years of the Weimar Republic. Like many colleagues in the Robinsohn–Strassmann Group, Elsas was a socially radical, left-wing liberal. Yet unlike Robinsohn or Strassmann, he followed Koch-Weser into the *völkisch*-inflected DStP because he felt it was necessary to combat National Socialism by any means possible. With this in mind, Elsas supported a temporary "dictatorship of the center" as the most pragmatic response to a dictatorship of the extreme right or left. He likewise co-founded the journal *The State Is You* alongside such liberal luminaries as Thomas Mann, Ernst Jäckh, and Ricarda Huch.[170] As a converted Protestant married to an "Aryan," Elsas was protected by a "privileged mixed-marriage [*privilegierte Mischehe*] and could easily have retreated into "inner emigration." Nevertheless, instead of following the path of least resistance, Elsas joined the incipient Robinsohn–Strassmann Group in 1934.[171]

Among all liberal democrats – and certainly Jewish liberals – Elsas may have taken the greatest risks and had the greatest impact. Until 1937 his main professional activity was advising Jews how to negotiate the complex currency controls, Aryanization laws, and other legal restrictions that stood in the way of emigration. In July 1937 the Gestapo appeared at his door and proceeded to rifle through his cabinets; finding nothing incriminating, they nonetheless sent Elsas to the Berlin Moabit prison for a month of interrogation.[172] Elsas subsequently lost his secretary and much of his clientele and was evicted from his apartment, which was owned by the widow of the Jewish artist Max Liebermann and therefore "Aryanized" after *Kristallnacht*. Elsas emerged from these travails a changed man. Shaken to the core, he also seemed stirred to more active resistance. Moving into a modest apartment in Berlin-Dahlem, Elsas tended his garden, helped Jewish colleagues emigrate, and began to contemplate Hitler's demise.[173]

Not only did Elsas join the Robinsohn–Strassmann Group and Solf Circle (see Chapter 1), but he enjoyed ties – much closer than Robinsohn's or Strassmann's – to Carl Goerdeler and other high-ranking members of the 20 July conspiracy. After war broke out, Elsas expanded his work for the resistance. When he met the ardent Nazi general Walter von Reichenau, who apparently intimated Hitler's plans for an invasion of the Low Countries, Elsas forwarded this information on to Holland through contacts in Copenhagen and Stockholm.[174] He also collaborated with the shadow Chancellor Goerdeler on plans for a post-Nazi government and was eventually designated to replace Hans Lammers as head of the Reich Chancellery. Given the profound trust that must have developed between the two men, it is hardly surprising that Goerdeler sought refuge with Elsas after the failed assassination attempt.[175] Unfortunately this led the police to Elsas, who was incarcerated and tortured. Refusing to betray any of his accomplices, he was transferred to Sachsenhausen concentration camp in December 1944. At some point in mid-January 1945 Elsas was murdered by the Gestapo.[176]

Elsas's involvement in the 20 July plot is compelling for three reasons. First and foremost, Elsas was apparently not arrested in 1937 and 1944 (or murdered in 1945) *because* he was Jewish, but because of his direct complicity in the plot. It is nonetheless astounding that a left-wing Jewish liberal who composed the bulk of the plotters' proclamation to the German people and occupied a leading position in Goerdeler's shadow government should survive the first wave of executions when so many "Aryan" generals and politicians did not. While his marriage to a gentile no doubt protected Elsas prior to his involvement in the resistance, it cannot have played a major role thereafter. Finally, Elsas's close relationship with Goerdeler, Beck, and other leading conservatives suggests the simplicity of any assertions about the pervasiveness of anti-Semitism – much less its "eliminationist" variant – throughout German society. Many of Germany's leading generals, aristocrats, and businessmen clearly trusted Elsas with their lives, not to mention Germany's future. His is a singular example of the potential for active Jewish resistance, the skepticism of German elites toward Nazi anti-Semitism, and perhaps even the lingering respect for the law of *Rechtsstaatlichkeit* of the German justice system described by Robinsohn above.

Eugen Schiffer

Born in 1860, Eugen Schiffer was a widely respected jurist and politician before the turn of the twentieth century. Joining the Prussian House of Representatives in 1903, Schiffer built a reputation as a "conservative" National Liberal. He supported the Hohenzollern monarchy, defended the Prussian Three Class Electoral Law (which gave greater weight to wealthier voters), and advocated German imperialism. Finally sent to the Reichstag by his Magdeburg constituents in 1912, the fifty-two-year-old migrated to the liberal left, becoming a founding member of the German Democratic Party six years later.[177]

Some historians explain this shift in loyalties as typical of Schiffer's political opportunism.[178] But it is equally clear that Schiffer, a converted Jew, genuinely wished to distance himself from the *völkisch*, annexationist forces that emerged within the National Liberal Party during the First World War.[179] As Weimar's first Finance Minister, Vice-Chancellor, and later Justice Minister, the strong-willed jurist helped rescue the Republic from collapse, defending it against revolutionary sallies from the left and right. More classical liberal than Naumannite progressive, Schiffer never took National Socialism seriously, dismissing Hitler's movement as a crackpot perversion of Communism. Schiffer was disappointed by the inability of German liberalism to remain relevant during the middle years of the Republic, advocating a DDP merger with his former National Liberal colleagues in the DVP. When this idea of a unified liberal party failed, Schiffer withdrew from politics, only reentering public life twenty years later, in the aftermath of the Second World War.[180]

Like many Democrats, Jewish and gentile alike, Schiffer barely discusses the Third Reich in his memoirs. Fortunately we have the ample reminiscences of friends and colleagues, who attest to the incredible stoicism and verve with which the aging liberal confronted Nazi persecution. We also have Schiffer's significant correspondence to and from fellow Democrats, which helps illuminate his everyday reality.

As a "non-Aryan," Schiffer's pension was reduced by 30 percent in April 1933 and he lost many of the honorary titles he had accumulated since the late nineteenth century. Schiffer nevertheless managed to weather the first six years of the Third Reich successfully, existing in a state of active retirement.[181] He saw little contradiction between his slowly deteriorating personal situation and Germany's return to great power status. Like many gentile colleagues, he spoke approvingly of Hitler's aggressive revision of the Versailles Treaty. And though he deplored the more egregious Nazi abuses of German *Rechtsstaat* tradition, Schiffer believed, like Robinsohn, that many jurists operated constitutionally and that legal debates about rolling back Jewish emancipation were hardly unique to the Third Reich.[182]

It was *Kristallnacht* that undermined Schiffer's relative complacency. In its aftermath Schiffer had to accept the name "Israel" (his daughter Marie the name "Sarah") and give up a portion of his property to pay Goering's billion-mark "fine" for "fomenting" the damage.[183] Schiffer was circumspect enough to avoid open criticism of a policy that appeared so central to the Nazi *Weltanschauung*, but he didn't shy away from expressing his feelings of growing isolation and betrayal. As early as in 1935, Schiffer was comparing (Jewish) Democrats to castaways in lifeboats screaming to each other across dark, stormy seas. Although desperate to meet, both feared the noise might attract predators.[184] After *Kristallnacht*, Schiffer's normally allegorical observations became more frequent and less oblique. In June 1939, he related to Heinrich Gerland the bittersweet feeling of seeing his only son Hans, who had secured release from Sachsenhausen with the help of an SS colleague, off to London. For the father and daughter who remained, Schiffer observed wryly, "life corresponded to the actual state of affairs."[185]

A few months later he announced that "writing and decoding hieroglyphic script is too tiring" and endeavored to paint a picture of the everyday challenges facing a Jewish family in wartime Germany: cobbling together temporary living quarters when the Air Ministry commandeers one's apartment; obsessing about everyday life's "insignificant details" to avoid an oppressive reality; poring over Weimar's missed opportunities; bemoaning one's faith in the political maturity of the German people.[186] Writing Gerland on Christmas Eve 1941, following the initial deportations of German Jews, Schiffer explained that for the first time in many years he had decided not to "walk the empty streets at twilight in order to see the flickering Christmas lights through the windows and hear the sound of joy and jubilation" from neighboring houses. In Germany it was no longer possible to hear "the sounds of Angels' wings" in "the still of [Christmas] night." "But I am convinced," Schiffer concluded, "that angels still fly over mankind. Even if one cannot see or hear them – they are there."[187]

Despite steadily deteriorating circumstances, Schiffer never lost his intellectual buoyancy. He helped organize a "Wednesday Society," to which he invited intellectuals of all political stripes. The Gestapo decided the group was ultimately harmless, but one must give Schiffer credit for organizing any "political" activity, which drew attention to his non-Aryan status.[188] He also began work on a biography of Bismarck. After reading the manuscript, Heuss promised to recommend the book to Hans Bott Verlag and was cautiously optimistic about the chances for publication. He added only that Hans Bott was disappointed at the sales of Höpker-Aschoff's *Our Way through the Epoch* and was reticent to publish another work by a leading figure of the Weimar Republic, "no matter how objective and loyal the work might be."[189] This seemingly innocuous exchange is interesting because neither party suggested that Schiffer's "Jewishness" might be a problem. The same disregard for Nazi anti-Semitism can be seen in Gerland, Meinecke, Gessler, Noske, Fischbeck, and other Weimar Democrats' determination to include Schiffer in their inner circle, to write and visit frequently, and to refer to the former Justice Minister and Vice-Chancellor by his lofty title ("His Excellence").[190]

Even after the "Final Solution" took its murderous course in summer 1941 Schiffer and his daughter carried on with grace and aplomb. The first real indignity was their accession to wearing the yellow star in September 1941. The Schiffers' names appeared on a list of putative deportees in August 1942, yet for some reason they were never picked up. The Schiffers had another close call in January 1943, when two Gestapo men showed up at the door to arrest a visiting Jewish colleague, Dr Max Fleischmann. Fleischmann promptly committed suicide in the bathroom. Angered by this display of defiance, the Gestapo ordered Marie Schiffer to come in for questioning. She was released at the behest of her brother-in-law, the liberal academic and future DDR politician Waldemar Koch, who explained that she needed to care for her elderly father.[191]

Matters now escalated. A couple of weeks after the Fleischmann incident, both Schiffers received instructions from the Berlin Jewish community to vacate their apartment and move into a small room in a Jewish nursing home. In April 1943 they were relocated again to the abandoned Jewish Hospital in Berlin-Wedding, an infamous destination mentioned in numerous memoirs of the Holocaust. Although ostensibly reserved for "protected [*geschützten*]" Jews, conditions in such domiciles were terrible. For all but the most basic necessities of life, the Schiffers depended on friendly visitors. No one could leave without the express permission of the SS guards, which was rarely granted. From March 1944 the Jewish

Hospital was the only location for the collection and centralized deportation of the remaining Berlin Jews. This building had served not only as a residence, then, but as a detention center for various Jewish "criminals"; as the office for the New Reich Association of German Jews; as a Gestapo station and prison; and had eventually become a woefully understaffed hospital. Its conditions were not enhanced by the constant ebb and flow of deportees or the frequent and devastating Allied bombing attacks. After two years in "hell" the Schiffers were liberated by the Russians in April 1945.[192]

According to his former National Liberal colleague Paul Moldenhauer, himself something of an anti-Semite, Schiffer possessed remarkable "indomitability" and "intellectual elasticitity."[193] He appears never to have internalized the anti-Semitism around him. Schiffer acknowledged that the twelve years of the Third Reich were an "exceedingly horrible matter," but he described them as an aberration. National Socialism's defeat was inevitable, Schiffer wrote; its brutality and fanaticism could never extinguish the urbane, civilized Germany he had known for seventy years before 1933.[194] Far from breaking Schiffer's will or dissolving his patriotism, the Third Reich only spurred his sardonic sense of humor, literary genius, and political ambition.[195] Within weeks of Hitler's suicide the buoyant eighty-five-year-old ended his two-decade political hiatus to co-found the East German Liberal Democratic Party (LDPD) and serve as President of the Ministry of Justice in the nascent GDR.[196]

Marie Baum

Like Elsas and Schiffer, the Democratic social reformer Marie Baum refused to accept her legal marginalization. Baum was a great-niece of the Jewish composer Felix Mendelssohn-Bartholdy and granddaughter of the renowned *salonnière* Rebecca Lejeune Dirichlet, a close friend of Alexander von Humboldt and wife of the famous mathematician Johann Lejeune Dirichlet. Baum's parents, both of whom were active in the late nineteenth-century women's movement, encouraged their daughter to carry on this intellectual legacy. In 1896, when women were still not permitted to obtain doctorates at most German universities, Baum obtained a Ph.D. in Chemistry at the University of Zurich. As one of the few female chemists in all of Germany, Baum went to work as a factory inspector and became an expert on industrial organization and labor issues. Possessing a unique professional pedigree and enjoying unparalleled connections to the central figures in the antebellum women's movement, Baum emerged as a leading Democratic politician after the First World War. She served briefly as a

Reichstag deputy, worked in the Reich Ministry of Labor, and regularly contributed articles on social welfare and labor reform to Bäumer's *Die Frau*. In 1928 she became the first female faculty member to join Alfred Weber's Institute for Social and Political Science at the University of Heidelberg.[197]

Baum's initial experience of Nazi anti-Semitism occurred during the 1 April 1933 boycott, when a group of stormtroopers forbade her – as a putative "Aryan" – from entering a Jewish store. Ironically, Baum was simultaneously relieved of her lectureship at the University of Heidelberg and lost her civil service position in the Foreign Office owing to her Jewish heritage. By her own admission, Baum considered this "accusation" a defamation of her German character and repeatedly referred in her memoirs to "Jewish friends and wards [*Schützlingen*]," as if she herself belonged in a different category. Also indicative of the *Mischling*'s struggle with identity to which Koch-Weser alludes above, Baum stressed how many of these non-Aryan victims "belonged to the Christian community."[198]

A reluctance to identify with the German Jewish community was not unique to *Mischlinge*, however. As we have seen, Elsas, Schiffer, and Robinsohn – all "full-blooded" Jews – systematically distanced themselves from their own Jewishness, viewing the regime's anti-Semitic nastiness from the perspective of persecuted German patriots.[199] Given Baum's greater "distance" from her Jewish roots, it is all the more striking that she became preoccupied with the "Jewish Question."[200] Baum would spend hours recording the fates of every Jewish friend and colleague. "Little Lisa H," who faced every tragedy with "lively piety," was murdered in the gas chambers immediately after her arrival in Auschwitz. Her neighbor, a "72-year-old military physician, who lost a leg in the First World War," died in Theresienstadt, shortly after his nonagenarian mother. Two sisters, "one a chemist, the other a botanist," were lucky enough to emigrate to California before deportation. But emigration, Baum recalls, was not always salvation. After having to separate from two of his four children, a Jewish doctor died abroad of "heartbreak and homesickness." This "shared experience of Jewish need," as Baum later described it, was uncommon among both Jewish and gentile Democrats.[201]

Such stories nevertheless moved Baum, in her words, to join the " 'other Germany' [that had] come together at that time in smaller or larger groups, in order to help the persecuted and sponsor emigration, especially of children and young people." At the beginning, Baum recalls, the assistance of gentile samaritans was permitted, even encouraged by the regime, which sought to rid Germany of as many Jews as possible. After the outbreak of war, and especially with the "Final Solution" in 1941, assisting Jews became much more dangerous. Baum remembers how many kept up their efforts in illegal ways. While the majority of Germans were indifferent, Baum acknowledged, the largest obstacle to overcome was "the lack of preparedness of foreign countries to accept refugees." Too many times well-meaning Germans had managed to help Jews clear all the financial and bureaucratic hurdles, only to be told by the western democracies that there was no place that would take them. "How much unmentionable horror," Baum laments, "could have been prevented by a generous settlement policy on free land, of which the earth is never poor."[202]

Baum also believed that the intermittent harassment she experienced was primarily a result of her "work [improving] the lot of Jewish people," not of her "non-Aryan" background. The Gestapo first interrogated her when they intercepted telegrams from Switzerland regarding the illegal acquisition of foreign currency for emigrants. Although the police threatened to deprive Baum of her pension if she did not reveal more information, Baum insisted that she had never broken or advised anyone to break a law, and was released. Another time an "eel smooth" Gestapo man appeared at her apartment, again to discuss her knowledge of illegal currency dealings. Frustrated with Baum's constant demurrals and insistence that "her negotiations had always stayed within the bounds of legality," the policeman finally demanded to know "why I did not emigrate myself, since the government appeared so unpalatable to me." Baum responded coolly: "because I'm 67 years old and have always served my country loyally." Embarrassed, the Gestapo man left her apartment.[203]

Her worst police encounter occurred on 21 November 1941, only a few weeks after Heydrich called the Wannsee Conference, which would convene in January 1942 to plan the "Final Solution."[204] This time four Gestapo officials proceeded to ransack Baum's apartment, sifting through her library, files, and letters for hours. Baum notes that she was extraordinarily fortunate in three ways. First, she had only just forwarded to a friend a letter from Bishop August von Galen who, a day earlier, had attacked the genocidal policies of the regime in a now famous sermon. Second, upon glimpsing a Gestapo man at her desk as she approached her apartment she quickly read and destroyed a letter she had received from a Jewish friend in that day's mail. Third, she stashed a number of "seriously incriminating letters with her handkerchief and gloves in the previously designated place." She did this so instinctively that for days she worried whether the Gestapo might have had these materials in their possession. Still, the Gestapo officers behaved properly, confiscating only some

suspicious note cards and correspondence that Baum depended on to
assist Jewish émigrés. The most "outrageous" thing they did was to appropriate a few dozen books from Baum's personal library that "had nothing
really to do with their investigation" and were no doubt headed to the
cash-strapped "libraries of the SS order castles' (basically retreats where
young SS recruits were trained)."[205]

Notwithstanding the relative civility of her interactions with the
Gestapo, Baum was one of a few liberal contemporaries to acknowledge
the magnitude and utter depravity of the Nazi "Final Solution." She was
also one of the few Democrats to risk her life repeatedly on Jews' behalf.
Yet Baum, herself a *Mischling*, claims not to have fully grasped what was
happening until late in the process:

> the shared experience of Jewish need was for me the impetus for that
> inner transformation that has probably affected all those capable of
> change during these twelve terrible years. It is an indescribable experi-
> ence, to be confronted by naked violence, in which Satan, the most
> radical evil, becomes perceptible . . . The experience did not occur to me
> suddenly; it demanded time and strength. For years I felt a heavy pres-
> sure, a spiritual reality, that could not be grasped or illuminated, until
> slowly rays of light began to break through . . . It followed step by step:
> erecting and expanding the concentration camps, whose brutalities I first
> discovered . . . during a last visit to Switzerland in May 1939 . . . [but]
> the extent and the much more horrible kind of methods were unknown
> to me and many others . . . Buchenwald, Dachau, Ravensbrück,
> Theresienstadt, and Auschwitz are the only camps whose names I knew
> before 1945, but whose actual purpose was until that time kept in the
> dark from us.[206]

Baum was obviously no apologist for Nazi transgressions. In addition to
her left liberal politics, non-Aryan background, and selfless efforts on
behalf of Jewish émigrés, she wrote a preface to the first German edition
of *The Diary of Anne Frank* – a decade before the Holocaust became
a topic of polite conversation. Still, she never saw the Holocaust as a
peculiarly German crime.[207]

One question remains. Why was Baum – or for that matter the "fully"
Jewish Schiffer and Elsas – able to survive when most Jews were not?
Dietrich Goldschmidt speculates that Schiffer's connections to notable
politicians and intellectuals played a decisive role, from the Prussian
Finance Minister Johannes Popitz and Reich Finance Minister Count

Schwerin von Krosigk to the eminent liberal historian Friedrich Meinecke.[208] Elsas and Baum also had well-placed family and friends. All three were technically Protestants; Baum was only a quarter Jewish and Elsas belonged to a privileged, mixed marriage. Advancing age played a role as well. The primary aim of the "Final Solution" was to eliminate younger Jews who might provide "the seed of a new Jewish revival."[209] Thus Schiffer was left at home after Dr Fleischmann's suicide, to be cared for by his already middle-aged daughter. Baum appears to have gained some leverage by citing her age.

Still, none of the three Jewish liberals fitted the conventional definition of inner emigration. Elsas was a leading member of the 20 July resistance, and ultimately paid the price for "treason" (not "race"). Baum labored passionately to ameliorate Jewish suffering, facilitating emigration, publishing critical articles in the pages of *Die Frau*, and developing close relationships with numerous members of the 20 July plot. She survived unscathed.[210] Though less actively engaged than Elsas or Baum, Schiffer convened his own "oppositional" discussion circle while speaking openly of his hostility to the Third Reich. The experiences of all three Democrats reflect the potential for Jewish non-conformity and the durability of German liberal values, even in the wake of the "Final Solution".

V

During the course of their voluminous correspondence Karl Jaspers and his star pupil, the German-Jewish émigré Hannah Arendt, eventually turned to Jaspers's analysis of the German resistance. Arendt wrote Jaspers that his assessment was quite good, but that "you have completely forgotten about the Jews." The liberal philosopher responded matter-of-factly. Since the Jews were no longer citizens according to the Nuremberg Laws of 1935, it didn't make sense to include them in a discussion of the "German" resistance. That Jaspers was an ostensible "philosemite" whose own wife was Jewish makes Arendt's observation and Jaspers's insensitive response all the more telling.[211] For, as another putative "philosemite" Theodor Tantzen put it after the war, "The murder of the Jews was for them [members of the resistance] not the central problem. They viewed this crime together with other crimes."[212] Even Heuss, who made an immense effort as Federal President to raise awareness of the Holocaust, rarely mentioned the persecution of the Jews between 1933 and 1945.[213]

Given the risks that many liberals, gentile and Jewish alike, took in other ways, one cannot write off the seeming uninterest in the "Jewish Question" as fear of persecution. Latent anti-Semitism played a role. As we have seen, some Democrats acquiesced in the 1933 laws limiting Jewish involvement in the civil service, education, and the professions. As the persecution worsened and Nazi legal restrictions became more illiberal, however, even *völkisch*-inclined Democrats did what they could to defend or assist individual Jewish friends or colleagues in need.[214] The case of non-Aryan liberals like Elsas, Baum, and Schiffer does little to dispel this impression of initial indifference to "Jewish Question(s)" followed, gradually, by growing political, legal, and ideological non-conformity.[215] All three were equally susceptible to the patriotic fervor of their Democratic colleagues.[216] All three viewed themselves as German national Protestants and declined to see their marginalization as peculiarly "Jewish." If Jews faced greater challenges than Catholics or even Communists, they were never merely victims. That Jewish liberals might persevere as they did, organizing discussion circles, helping colleagues escape, even plotting the downfall of the regime, indicates significant Jewish agency in the midst of the Holocaust.[217]

At the same time we must recall the difficulties liberals encountered in helping individual Jews. Although collective action appears to have checked some Nazi measures, in no aspect of the Third Reich was *individual* dissent more difficult than in relation to the so-called "Jewish Question."[218] As war ensued and the "Final Solution" developed its murderous logic, helping Jews became a dangerous business, one that forced many liberals – even Jewish liberals – to make unpleasant choices. As we have seen, Reinhold Maier divorced his Jewish wife out of fear of the Gestapo. When asked to hide a Jewish child for a few days while his adopted parents endured an impending Gestapo visit, the humanitarian Anna von Gierke, herself part Jewish, confessed that "for the first time in her life, she was compelled to refuse someone in need of help." Marie Baum's colleague Elisabeth von Thadden was executed by the Gestapo in part for her "illegal" assistance to impoverished Jews.[219] These dangers did not dissuade Democrats from assisting Jews in retaining their assets or employment, emigrating, or evading deportation.[220] But liberals could only provide minor remedies, disregarding Nazi laws in everyday life and trying to improve the situation of individual Jews as best they could.[221]

Though liberals were generally "anti-antisemitic" on an individual basis, rarely did they contemplate challenging Nazi anti-Semitism at a conceptual level.[222] After 1933 Democrats continued to view the right-wing (as well as Zionist) obsession with the *collective* fate of German Jewry as antithetical to universal claims of equality for all individuals before the law.

From Treitschke to Elsas, most liberals, whether Jewish or gentile, shared a general conviction that the Jewish Question would resolve itself only through assimilation, not through greater ethnoreligious particularism. This reticence to privilege shared Jewish suffering over the problems facing all Germans can hardly be equated with "eliminationist anti-Semitism." But, to paraphrase the Democrat Mayer-Pantenius from the beginning of this chapter, the vast majority of liberals "were also no Jews."[223] Lacking the benefit of hindsight, preoccupied with survival, and distracted by larger questions of domestic and foreign policy, German Democrats reacted similarly to their liberal colleagues in France, Great Britain, and the United States. On an individual basis they expended substantial time, money, and effort in helping Jewish colleagues. Ultimately, however, they failed to provide an alternative answer to Hitler's "Jewish Question."[224]

Conclusion

I

Democrats worked harder than any bourgeois party to prevent the collapse of the Weimar Republic. But after fourteen years of turmoil and three years of rule by presidential decree, few liberals were passionate enough about democracy to make it the chief platform for their opposition to Nazism. Some were cautiously optimistic that a majority coalition led by Hitler might restore a sense of order and authority to the rudderless Weimar state. Democrats were less sanguine about the mounting Nazi assault on German civil society. Freedom of conscience, freedom of expression, and freedom of assembly had long traditions in German liberalism, harking back to Kant, Schiller, and von Humboldt. Whether operating as private individuals, through informal discussion circles, or within elaborate networks of resistance, no Democrats were willing to give up these fundamental liberties easily.[1]

It is in this sphere of cultural and intellectual life that one witnesses the greatest contrast between liberal democrats and National Socialists as well as the greatest passion for non-conformity. One is hard pressed to find a liberal whose journalistic activity or literary output conformed to the prevailing *Zeitgeist*, who did not criticize Nazified cultural or intellectual norms, whose publications were never censored. Despite long-standing traditions of anti-Catholicism and distrust of religion in public life, liberals made no secret of their support for the Confessing Church, non-conforming Catholics or confessional freedom. Finally, liberal intellectuals seem to have preserved (and utilized) a considerable level of autonomy,

both within and without the academy. To the extent that they "collaborated," they did so on ideological terms that were already familiar to liberal
nationalists in the Weimar Republic.

The relationship between the liberal women's movement and National
Socialism was more complex. On the one hand Democratic women saw a
number of similarities between Nazi social policy and biomaternalist
trends latent within German feminism. On the other hand Bäumer and
company rejected the extreme racism, chauvinism, and authoritarianism
that frequently accompanied such policies. Of the aspects of Nazi ideology
that they endorsed, few were traditionally "conservative." In terms of
social welfare, occupational training, universal health care, a more "liberal"
attitude to female sexuality and single motherhood, and women's "biological destiny" to control certain "feminine" spheres and occupations, there
were obvious affinities between liberal ("Naumannite") feminism and
National Socialism. Notwithstanding these affinities, nearly all members
of the liberal women's movement vocally opposed Nazi attempts to
discourage co-education, dissuade women from university study, or
remove them from public and professional life.

In no arena were liberal and Nazi views initially more similar than in
foreign policy. Before the outbreak of war in September 1939 there is a
near-perfect overlap in liberal demands from the Weimar period and
Hitler's stated goals. Admittedly some Democrats refused to countenance
the Führer's foreign policy on principle, no matter what its conceptual
similarities to Naumann's *Mitteleuropa* or Stresemann's revisionism. Still,
many shared the opinion that the importance of eradicating the Versailles
Treaty outweighed any moral qualms about Hitler's bellicose rhetoric.
After the Rhineland occupation in March 1936, which was the first time
Hitler truly seemed to risk war, one begins to perceive greater dissent in
liberal circles. At first this opposition was inchoate, having more to do
with Hitler's confrontational means than nationalist ends. Even after
the occupation of Bohemia in March 1939 and the outbreak of war,
liberals could hardly muster a coherent alternative to Hitler's *va banque*
foreign policy. It was the terrible experience of war on the eastern front,
punctuated by Allied terror bombing, which finally caused German
liberals to break from their historically fraught relationship with ethnic
nationalism and promote a modified version of Naumann's *Mitteleuropa*, a
vision not dissimilar from the European Community embodied in the
Treaty of Rome.[2]

This held doubly true where anti-Semitism was concerned. Despite
its reputation as an "anti-antisemitic" organization, the Democratic Party

had often proved unwilling to combat racism before 1933. Many gentile Democrats shared some of the Nazis' anti-Semitic tenets, while even Jewish liberals showed little interest in so-called "Jewish Question(s)." Others were simply embarrassed by the "philosemitic" reputation of their party. No one imagined, much less countenanced, what would occur in the next decade. This went for *völkisch*-inclined liberals such as Bäumer, Obst, and Rohrbach, ardent patriots like Dietrich, Heuss, and Lüders, and for Jewish Democrats like Schiffer, Robinsohn, and Elsas. Thus, if there is one area where one sees almost no long-term accommodation, it is the "Final Solution." Of course liberals were able to effect little real change in Nazi Jewish policy, not only because they lacked sufficient influence, but also because they underestimated the magnitude of the atrocities and were themselves preoccupied by other matters of domestic and foreign policy. At the same time, it is no exaggeration to suggest that the Holocaust would have been nigh impossible had all Germans held the same attitudes and made the same sacrifices as their liberal brethren.

II

The question of what course these Democrats took after 1945 constitutes a book in itself, one very different from the type of story *Living With Hitler* has tried to tell. Just as liberalism had ceased to exist as a party political institution in 1933, many liberals returned to public life in 1945. Some played significant roles in rebuilding German democracy, none more so than Heuss, who became the Federal Republic's first President. Any useful discussion of German liberalism after 1945 must therefore be approached in terms of political history, with all the complex party permutations and negotiations this entails. That kind of undertaking, which other historians have begun to address, lies beyond the scope of these pages.[3] But given the emphasis we have placed on continuity, on the relationship between pre-1933 trends in German liberalism and National Socialism, it is fitting to conclude with a brief look at the paths these liberals followed after 1945 as well.

The "Old Wizard" Hjalmar Schacht found it absurd that someone who left office in January 1939, never employed slave labor, and spent ten months in Flossenburg and Dachau concentration camps could be tried for war crimes. Most of his colleagues agreed, acting as witnesses on the Reichminister's behalf. Schacht might have embellished somewhat in describing his participation in the Third Reich as primarily an attempt to prevent "Hitler's worst excesses," but he remains the most influential "opponent" of the regime in the erstwhile Democratic ranks. Suffice it to say that Schacht parlayed his reputation as a financial genius, his proximity to Hitler, and the publicity of his trial into worldwide fame.[4]

Reinhold Maier was a founding member, alongside Heuss, of the short-lived Democratic Party (DVP/DPD) and its more durable successor, the Free Democratic Party (FDP) in 1949. For nearly eight years he served as Minister President of Baden-Württemberg. After remarrying his émigré wife in 1946 he became an outspoken opponent of radical nationalism and anti-Semitic discrimination, which he discussed in depth in his 1962 memoir *Bedrängte Familie* (Family under Siege). He also opposed the nationalist right wing of the FDP that gained strength in the early 1950s, demanding that the liberals remain a left-center republican party between the SPD and CDU. Elected to the Bundestag in 1953, he succeeded Dehler as FDP chairman from 1957 to 1960.[5]

In Russian-occupied East Berlin, Wilhelm Külz co-founded Germany's first postwar Liberal Democratic Party (LDPD) and served briefly, with Heuss, as co-chairman of the united German Democratic Party (DPD). Külz worked selflessly to prevent Germans from being drawn into the incipient struggle between Communism and capitalism, East and West. As the fiction of free elections and civil liberties in the Russian zone became apparent in 1947, tensions arose between western and eastern liberals. In early 1948, against Heuss and Maier's wishes, Külz decided to participate as DPD co-chair in a Communist (SED)-led Congress for German Unity. He was promptly sacked from the DPD party leadership, which seceded to form the Free Democratic Party. Külz passed away a few months later, never having to witness the official division of Germany in 1949.[6]

Released from his Berlin detention center by Soviet troops, the eighty-five-year-old Eugen Schiffer veritably leapt back into the political fray. He co-founded the LDPD and began a three-year term as Justice Minister for the Russian-occupied zone. When he could no longer tolerate the Socialist Unity Party (SED)'s emerging dictatorship in East Germany, Schiffer moved to the West.[7] There he rejoined his Weimar colleagues Heuss and Maier in the FDP and settled into composing a lively pre-1933 memoir, *A Life for Liberalism* (1951). Now in his nineties, Schiffer rekindled his long-smoldering relationship with the widowed Katharina von Kardorff, recently arrived from East Germany. Having each spent nearly half a century in public life, the two confided in each other about love, poetry, and the collapse of the Weimar Republic. Both agreed that democracy would not survive in postwar Germany without a greater commitment to liberal values across the political spectrum.[8]

Liberated from rural exile and relative penury, Wilhelm Heile began organizing a new liberal party shortly after Germany's surrender. One of the first Democrats invited to govern by the Allied authorities, he served as Minister President of Lower Saxony until the end of 1946, when he left office to pursue party political matters.[9] Despite a history of personal friction with Heuss, the two old co-editors of *Die Hilfe* worked closely to rebuild German democracy. In the face of a renewed Socialist left, Heile wrote Heuss in February 1946, it was crucial "to achieve the coordination of all liberal democratic forces in Germany" regardless of the name of the party. Because Heile could abide neither the Christian nor the Socialist direction of the CDU/CSU, he co-founded the liberal German People's Party (DVP), which soon coalesced into the FDP.[10] A devoted Naumannite, Heile continued to believe in the "close relationship of national and social ideas on the basis of a liberal-freedom-oriented idea of the state" and hoped that a democratic Germany, restored to Great Power status, could pave the way for European unification.[11]

The unsinkable Hermann Dietrich joined the FDP and accepted an appointment as Minister for Food and Agriculture in the American occupation zone. As he had during the Third Reich, Dietrich continued to assist former colleagues, sometimes to clear their name with the occupation authorities.[12] But he was uncommonly sharp with those who were willing to make unnecessary concessions. Dietrich criticized Marie Lüders, for instance, when she recommended that the Americans employ a former SS man as economic administrator. No matter how effective, Dietrich reasoned, this was not the kind of person who should hold responsibility in a democratic Germany. He likewise opposed Lüders's suggestion that peasants be relocated to underpopulated areas, which smacked too much of "Nazi methods" of population policy. Dietrich reserved considerable criticism for the incipient Christian Social Party (CSU), calling it "nothing more than a well-camouflaged stockpot for old Nazis of every stripe and the worst kind of particularists."[13] A year after the war Dietrich published a short book, *In Search of Germany*, examining the reasons for Weimar's failure. He assigned significant responsibility to the weaknesses of the Weimar constitution and Germans' inexperience of democracy. All the same, Dietrich concluded, few republics – and fewer liberal parties – could have withstood the lethal combination of military defeat, a Draconian peace, and the Great Depression.[14]

After participating in the Berlin LDPD and helping refound the Federation of German Women (BDF), Marie Lüders emigrated to West Germany and, at the age of seventy-five, was elected to the Bundestag as an FDP representative in 1953.[15] She served for nine years, passing important legislation that guaranteed German women citizenship rights if they married a non-German. Like many Weimar Democrats chastened by their experience of the Third Reich, Lüders proved especially sensitive to Jewish issues after 1945. She took a leading role in publicizing and combating the rise in anti-Semitic incidents in the late 1950s and helped organize a special session of the Bundestag condemning anti-Semitism. For Lüders the lesson of the Third Reich was, in the words of her colleague Hans Lenz, never again to let "overheated national feeling" stifle democracy in Germany.[16]

Gertrud Bäumer remained close to Heuss, Baum, and other Weimar Democrats, often discussing how best to salvage Naumann's National-Social legacy from the ruins of Hitler's National Socialism.[17] In fact Bäumer joined the CDU because she felt the FDP was neither Christian nor social enough.[18] Like Schacht and Rohrbach, Bäumer resented the denazification proceedings, to which she personally was also subjected. Responding to accusations of collaboration, Bäumer noted how many lower-ranking Nazis had slipped through the cracks, heel-clicking and Hitler-saluting in beer halls across Germany, while state officials who joined the party out of pure pragmatism faced extended prison sentences.[19] Although she was eventually cleared of charges, the Allied authorities never allowed Bäumer to recommence publication of *Die Frau*. The German women's movement, which Bäumer did so much to sustain before and after 1933, would take two decades to recover its Weimar-era strength.[20]

Theodor Heuss served in the immediate postwar administration, co-founded and chaired the FDP, and in 1949 was elected the first President of the Federal Republic. Reinvigorated by the collapse of the Third Reich, Heuss evinced none of the mixed feelings shared by Bäumer, Schacht, or Heile. He was optimistic about Germany's prospects for democracy and more committed to public service than he had been in the Weimar Republic. He agreed with Bäumer and Weber that an "ethically minded" political culture would be useful in anchoring the new German democracy. But he demanded a firm separation of church and state, which he felt was necessary for maintaining intellectual pluralism.[21] Like Dietrich and Maier, both of whom had also voted for the Enabling Law, Heuss was prepared to acknowledge the Germans' shared complicity in Hitler's rise to power, in the rampant destruction of the Second World War and, more remarkably for the late 1940s, in the implementation of the "Final Solution." He was careful, however, to stress the importance of rebuilding a unified Germany, free of the mistakes committed in 1919. "Germany's

Life is Europe's Peace," Heuss wrote in January 1947. Demanding reparations or delaying Germany's political and economic renewal, Heuss warned, would only restore the climate of resentment that hamstrung Germany's first democracy.[22]

The surviving members of the Robinsohn–Strassmann Group generally supported the work of their senior FDP colleagues.[23] With the exception of Dehler, they were not the key players. Rather, most of the early leaders of postwar liberalism – Külz, Schiffer, Heuss, Maier, Heile, Lüders, Tantzen, Dietrich, Höpker-Aschoff – had matured politically during the *Kaiserreich* and were already national figures in the Weimar Republic. That this coterie of Weimar Democrats had helped build Germany's first republic, weathered the Nazi storm, and seemingly learned from their mistakes was attractive to the Allied occupation authorities, who feared employing too many Nazi fellow travelers but were equally reluctant to cede influence to Kurt Schumacher's SPD. Hence the FDP, despite its relatively low proportion of the vote, became a vital reservoir of postwar leadership.[24]

Nevertheless, as Weimar Democrats yielded to the younger generation, old ideological differences slowly reemerged. By the early 1950s disagreements in national and social policy threatened once again to split the FDP, much as they had thirty years earlier. While the Weimar generation, led by south-west Democrats like Heuss, Maier, and Dehler, fought to make the party a left-center bridge between SPD and CDU, the Westphalian chapter of the FDP coalesced around two former Nazis – the Propaganda Chief Werner Naumann and SS leader Werner Best – to oppose "denazification," defend the interests of capital, and rein in democracy. Even after the departure of this second so-called "Naumann Circle," Heuss and company had to marshal all their moral and organizational strength to ensure that "National Socialism" would not make a comeback.[25]

Indeed, while distinctions in regional political culture played a role, the varied paths of leading Weimar Democrats after 1945 – including the fact that Bäumer, Lemmer, Nuschke, and Brammer chose the CDU; Alfred Weber, Baum, Landahl, and Eric Lüth the SPD – can be explained in part by the perception that the FDP was but a hollow shell of Weimar left liberalism. Many former Democrats made the case that the social liberal, Naumannite worldview which had developed in the *Kaiserreich*, found resonance in the 1920s, and was recast by the liberal experience of National Socialism would be better served in the CDU or SPD than in the increasingly laissez-faire, anti-democratic FDP.[26] That Baum first joined the CDU on Naumannite ("Christian Social") grounds and then migrated to Alfred Weber's incipient "Free Socialist" party shows the social liberal affinities that existed between the two major German parties in the late 1940s, especially in the South and West.[27]

Finally, a minority of Democrats who figure prominently in this story retired from the scene due to age, temperament, or political unreliability. After barely enduring "denazification," Rohrbach withdrew to write his memoirs. Marie Baum tired of politics, as did her friend Ricarda Huch, who died shortly after the war. Theodor Tantzen served briefly as Minister President of Lower Saxony, likewise passing away in 1947. Alfred Weber made an unsuccessful attempt to found a regional SPD party affiliate based on "liberal [*freie*] socialism," then returned to teaching alongside his colleague Jaspers.[28] Frustrated by the East German LDPD's apparent hostility to female politicians, Kardorff moved to Düsseldorf and slowly withdrew from public service.[29] The last chairman of the German Democratic Party, Erich Koch-Weser, died in Brazil in 1944. He was never able to return to his Lower Saxon *Heimat*.

III

What lessons might be gleaned from the experience of liberal democrats in the Third Reich? First, I hope we have gained a better understanding of the ideological resilience of German liberalism. German liberals, for all their contradictions, were never merely ciphers of the reactionary right. Aside from the *völkisch* proclivities embraced by many Democrats before 1933, they shared a clear set of "liberal" values, based on common political and intellectual traditions, which were constantly negotiated with the National Socialist regime. As Horst Sassin puts it, "despite its organizational disintegration in the last phase of the Weimar Republic . . . liberalism as a political idea was capable [of providing] a humanitarian response to the excesses of National Socialism" as well as "a fundamental alternative" to the Third Reich. Hence the "regenerative power of democratic and social liberalism was able to hold out all those many years . . . during the seemingly futile struggle against the National Socialist system."[30]

Where I would disagree is in the implication that the experience of National Socialism had little impact on the character or depth of liberal values; that is, that there was a more or less unbroken continuity between the liberalism of Weimar and Bonn. Built in the dynamic incubator of the *Kaiserreich*, left liberals had their first chance to govern in 1919. While Democrats contributed as much as any party to building the Republic, they also did much to undermine it. The Naumannite, social liberal program that displaced laissez-faire economic doctrines within the DDP before

1933 accounts to some extent for the affinity some Democrats felt with the "progressive" elements of National Socialism. More salient in explaining the transition of many liberals from democracy to Fascism is Naumann's profound legacy of ethnic nationalism and imperialism. Naumann, Max Weber, and a few other far-sighted colleagues had begun to renounce these elements of the National-Social creed as early as the First World War; but most liberal nationalists had to witness for themselves the consequences of favoring ethnicity over universality, pan-German nationalism over international understanding, order and security over democracy.

It was the radical restructuring – and ultimately destruction – of Weimar politics and society brought on by National Socialism that caused German left liberalism to mature into the foundational ideology of the Federal Republic. Only the horrors of the Second World War could jolt the vast majority of Weimar Democrats into shedding their imperialist and nationalist proclivities once and for all, in the name of European peace and stability.[31] Now that the hoary "national question," which had divided German liberalism for a century, was subsumed in the name of democracy, liberals could finally turn to the pressing social questions that divided all modern industrial societies.

The winner in 1945 was neither Communism nor Fascism, Socialism or conservatism; it was Naumannite social liberalism, the same liberalism that appeared to fail so miserably in 1933. It is no coincidence that Weimar Democrats played a role in the Federal Republic so far out of proportion with their party (the FDP)'s single-digit vote totals or eventual drift to the right. The Democrats' pre-1933 successes and failures, and, equally importantly, their experiences in the Third Reich, prepared them for the challenges of rebuilding liberal democracy, of balancing the rights of the individual and the collective, secular humanism and Christianity, of integrating capitalism and social welfare, securing women's and minority rights, and of seeking national greatness without eschewing international understanding. The Democrats were the natural leaders of the second German Republic, just as they were of the first.

If the FDP was hardly more successful electorally than its Weimar predecessor, it was for entirely different reasons. For while the DDP's decline in the 1920s mirrored a precipitous loss of faith in liberal democratic and laissez-faire values across the political spectrum, the FDP's marginalization in the Federal Republic reflected precisely the opposite: the pervasiveness of a social liberal, Naumannite consensus towards which both great postwar parties – the SPD and CDU – had moved.[32] In its national, social, and liberal diversity, the Weimar DDP already contained within it nearly the full spectrum of West German democracy. Willy Brandt, Helmut Schmidt, and Gerhard Schröder would have felt perfectly at home with Anton Erkelenz, Helmut von Gerlach, and Ludwig Quidde on the DDP's cosmopolitan "left." Ludwig Erhard, Helmut Kohl, and Angela Merkel have much in common with Theodor Heuss, Reinhold Maier, and Gertrud Bäumer on the more nationalist, economically liberal, but likewise socially progressive "right." No longer an embattled minority fighting off the twin specters of Fascism and Communism, left liberalism's internal contradictions would finally come to define the political stakes for Germany's next generation of Democrats, Christian and Social alike. That is why Heuss and Maier's center-left FDP eventually transformed over the course of the Federal Republic into a right-center, laissez-faire interest group. The collective experience of Fascism, war, and occupation made Naumann's social liberalism ideologically hegemonic but politically obsolete, the victim of its own success.[33]

Indeed, if we confine ourselves to the level of Gramscian hegemony, many would argue that liberal democracy, in Germany and elsewhere, has emerged from the twentieth century more secure than ever.[34] Yet liberalism is a fragile commodity. It remains vulnerable to the irrational and authoritarian tendencies inherent to all modern democracies, never more so than when they face internal crises and external threats. As Richard Steigmann-Gall has suggested, while we "are given to presuming that the things we tend to dislike in modern society must have reigned triumphant in Nazism," the contrary was often the case. "The corollary to such an admission," Steigmann-Gall continues, "is not that Nazism is somehow redeemable, but rather that it is much closer to us than we dare allow ourselves to believe."[35]

With notable exceptions, National Socialism and Naumannite left liberalism shared a commitment to capitalism and imperialism; deficit-financed job creation, social welfare, universal health care, and education; science, technology, and eugenics; the separation of church and state; and a Greater Germany based on the principle of national self-determination. Despite these affinities, it took the experience of millions of deaths in a futile war, a punitive peace treaty costing billions, and economic dislocation on an unprecedented scale to push German liberals down a National Socialist path. It has taken much less than that to bring other democracies to the brink. Given the increasingly global challenges facing liberal democracy in the twenty-first century, such dangers have scarcely disappeared.

Notes

Introduction

1. Hauptmann to Wolff, 11.29.33; Wolff to Hauptmann, 12.04.33, in NL Theodor Wolff, BAK: N 1207, #11. A moving encomium to impoverished textile workers, published at the height of Kaiser Wilhelm II's autocratic reign, *The Weavers* was a politically controversial work.
2. Martina Neumann, *Theodor Tantzen: Ein widerspenstiger Liberaler gegen der Nationalsozialismus*, Hannover: Hansche, 1998, 14–15; Dieter Langewiesche, *Liberalism in Germany*, Princeton: Princeton University Press, 1999, 282–285.
3. See Horst R. Sassin and Rainer Erkens, eds, *Dokumente zur Geschichte des Liberalismus in Deutschland*, St Augustin: COMDOK, 1989, 397–406; Carlheinz von Brück, *Bürger gegen Hitler: Demokraten im antifaschistischen Widerstand*, Berlin: Der Morgen, 1986, 18–84; Hans-Georg Lehmann, *Nationalsozialistische und akademische Ausburgerung im Exil: Warum Rudolf Breitscheid der Doktortitel aberkannt wurde*, Marburg: Pressestelle d. Phillips-Universität, 1985, 4–6; Marie-Dominique Cavaillé, *Rudolf Breitscheid et la France 1919–1933*, Frankfurt: P. Lang, 1995, 298–305; also see Volker Ebersbach, *Heinrich Mann: Leben, Werk, Wirken*, Leipzig: P. Reclam, 1978; Rudolf Wolff, ed., *Heinrich Mann: Werk und Wirkung*, Bonn: Bouvier, 1984; Seger to Quidde, 7.14.34, Gerlach to Quidde, 11.04.34, 11.22.34, in NL Quidde, BAK: N 1212, #28; Quidde to Villard, 6.14.33, 10.17.33, Villard to Quidde, 9.14.33, in NL Quidde, BAK: N 1212, #80.
4. As quoted in Neumann, *Tantzen*, 416–417; Dietrich to Koch-Weser, 5.19.41, NL Dietrich, N 1004, #149; Barthold C. Witte, "Liberaler in schwierigen Zeiten – Werner Stephan (15 August 1895–4 Juli 1984)," in *Jahrbuch zur Liberalismusforschung* (*JzLF*), 18 (2006); Horst Sassin, *Widerstand, Verfolgung und Emigration Liberaler 1933–1945*, Bonn: Liberal-Verlag, 1983, 24–25.
5. Joachim Scholtyseck, *Robert Bosch und der liberale Widerstand gegen Hitler 1933 bis 1945*, Munich: C.H. Beck, 1999, 190.
6. Langewiesche, *Liberalism*, 284.
7. See, for example, Eric Kurlander, "Negotiating National Socialism: Liberal Non-Conformity and Accommodation in the Period of *Gleichschaltung*," *JzLF*, 17 (2005), 59–76; Neumann, *Tantzen*; Scholtyseck, *Bosch*; Knut Hansen, *Albrecht Graf von Bernstorff*, Frankfurt: Peter Lang, 1996; Horst Sassin, *Liberale im Widerstand: Die Robinsohn–Strassmann-Gruppe, 1934–1942*, Hamburg: Hans Christians, 1993;

Angelika Schaser, *Helene Lange und Gertrud Bäumer: Eine politische Lebensgemeinschaft*, Köln: Böhlau, 2000; Armin Behrendt, *Wilhelm Külz*: Berlin: Der Morgen, 1985; Albert Fischer, *Hjalmar Schacht und Deutschlands "Judenfrage": Der "Wirtschaftsdiktator" und die Vertreibung der Juden aus der deutschen Wirtschaft*, Cologne: Böhlau, 1995.

8. Sassin, *Liberale*, 9; Jürgen Froelich, "Nur Versagt? Das liberale Bürgertum und der Nationalsozialismus," *Mut*, 446 (October 2004), 66.

9. See, for example, Hans Mommsen, "Resistance", in Christian Leitz, ed., *The Third Reich: The Essential Readings*, Oxford: Blackwell, 1999, 263; Scholtyseck, *Bosch*, 15; Geoff Eley in Eley, ed., *Society, Culture, and the State in Germany, 1870–1930*, Ann Arbor: Michigan, 1996, 87; Jürgen C. Heβ, *Theodor Heuss vor 1933*, Stuttgart: Ernst Klett, 1973, 203–204; Richard J. Evans, *The Feminist Movement in Germany, 1894–1933*, London: Sage, 1976, 274; Friedrich Sell, *Die Tragödie des Deutschen Liberalismus*, Baden-Baden: Nomos, 1981; Hans Rosenberg, *Bureaucracy, Aristocracy and Autocracy: The Prussian Experience 1660–1815*, Cambridge, Mass.: Harvard University Press, 1966; Fritz Stern, *The Failure of Illiberalism*, New York: Columbia University Press, 1992; *The Politics of Cultural Despair: A Study in the Rise of German Ideology*, Berkeley: University of California Press, 1974; Georg Mosse, *The Crisis of German Ideology*, New York: Howard Fertig, 1998; Hans-Ulrich Wehler, *The German Empire 1871–1918*, Providence: Berg, 1993. For more on the "collaboration" of industrial and commercial elites, see Scholtyseck, *Bosch*, 7–9, 546–549; Henry Turner, *German Big Business and the Rise of Hitler*, New York: Oxford University Press, 1985; Peter Hayes, *Industry and Ideology: IG Farben in the Nazi Era*, Cambridge: Cambridge University Press, 1987; David Abraham, *The Collapse of the Weimar Republic: Political Economy and Crisis*, New York: Holmes & Meier, 1986; Reinhard Neebe, *Grossindustrie, Staat und NSDAP 1930–1933: Paul Silverberg und der Reichsverband der Deutschen Industrie in der Krise der Weimarer Republik*, Göttingen: Vandenhoeck & Ruprecht, 1981; Paul Erker, *Industrieeliten in der NS-Zeit: Anpassungsbereitschaft und Eigeninteresse von Unternehmen in der Rüstungs- und Kriegswirtschaft, 1936–1945*, Passau: Wittenschaftsverlag Rothe, 1994; Werner Plumpe, *Betriebliche Mitbestimmung in der Weimarer Republik: Fallstudien zum Ruhrbergbau und zur Chemischen Industrie*, Munich: Oldenbourg, 1999; Heinrich August Winkler, *Mittelstand, Demokratie und Nationalsozialismus: Die politische Entwicklung von Handwerk und Kleinhandel in der Weimarer Republik*, Cologne: Kiepenheuer & Witsch, 1972; Hans-Jürgen Pühle, *Agrarische Interessenpolitik und preussischer Konservatismus in Wilhelminischen Reich 1893–1914: Ein Beitrag zur Analyse des Nationalismus in Deutschland am Beispiel des Bundes der Landwirte und der Deutsch-Konservativen Partei*, Bonn: Neue Gesellschaft, 1975.

10. Eric Kurlander, *The Price of Exclusion: Ethnicity, National Identity and the Decline of German Liberalism, 1898–1933*, New York: Berghahn, 2006; Alistair Thompson, *Left Liberals, the State, and Popular Politics in Wilhelmine Germany*, Oxford: Oxford University Press, 2000; Kevin Repp, *Reformers, Critics, and the Paths of German Modernity: Anti-Politics and the Search for Alternatives, 1890–1914*, Cambridge, Mass.: Harvard University Press, 2000; Jennifer Jenkins, *Provincial Modernity: Local Culture and Liberal Politics in fin-de-siècle Hamburg*, Ithaca, NY: Cornell University Press, 2003; Jan Palmowski, *Urban Liberalism in Imperial Germany: Frankfurt am Main, 1866–1914*, Oxford: Oxford University Press, 1999; Larry Jones, *German Liberalism and the Dissolution of the Weimar Party System*, Chapel Hill: University of North Carolina Press, 1988; Bruce Frye, *Liberal Democrats in the Weimar Republic: The History of the German Democratic Party and the German State Party*, Carbondale: Southern Illinois University Press, 1985; Lothar Albertin, *Liberalismus und Demokratie am Anfang der Weimarer Republik: eine vergleichende Analyse der Deutschen Demokratischen Partei und der Deutschen Volkspartei*, Düsseldorf: Droste, 1972; Werner Stephan, *Aufstieg und Verfall des Linksliberalismus 1918–1933: Geschichte der demokratische Partei*, Göttingen: Vandenhoeck & Ruprecht, 1973; Werner Schneider, *Die Deutsche Demokratische Partei*

in der Weimarer Republik, 1924–1930, Munich: Wilhelm Fink, 1978; Jürgen C. Heß, *Das ganze Deutschland soll es sein: Demokratischer Nationalismus in der Weimarer Republik am Beispiel der Deutsche Demokratische Partei*, Stuttgart: Klett-Cotta, 1978.

11. See, for example, Günter Grau, ed., *Hidden Holocaust? Gay and Lesbian Persecution in Germany 1933–45*, London: Cassell, 1995; Ian Kershaw, *Hitler Myth: Image and Reality*, Oxford: Oxford University Press, 1987; Günter Lewy, *The Catholic Church and Nazi Germany*, New York: McGraw-Hill, 1964; Kevin P. Spicer, *Resisting the Third Reich: The Catholic Clergy in Hitler's Berlin*, DeKalb: Northern Illinois University Press, 2004; Robert Gellately, *Backing Hitler: Consent and Coercion in Nazi Germany*, Oxford: Oxford University Press, 2001; Paul Weindling, *Health, Race, and German Politics: Between National Unification and Nazism, 1870–1945*, Cambridge: Cambridge University Press, 1989; Mark Roseman, *A Past in Hiding: Memory and Survival in Nazi Germany*, New York: Picador, 2001; Jill Stephenson, *Women in Nazi Germany*, New York: Longman, 2001; Irene Gunther, *Nazi Chic: Fashioning Women in the Third Reich*, New York: Berg, 2004; Shelley Baranowski, *Strength through Joy: Consumerism and Mass Tourism in the Third Reich*, Cambridge: Cambridge University Press, 2007; Frank Bajohr, *"Unser Hotel ist Judenfrei." Bäder-Antisemitismus im 19. und 20. Jahrhundert*, Frankfurt: Fischer, 2003; Lora Wildenthal, *German Women for Empire, 1884–1945*, Durham, N.C. Duke University Press, 2001; Cynthia Crane, *Divided Lives: The Untold Stories of Jewish-Christian Women in Nazi Germany*, New York: St. Martin's Press, 2000; Elizabeth Heineman, *What Difference Does a Husband Make? Women and Marital Status in Nazi and Postwar Germany*, Berkeley: University of California Press, 1999; Claudia Koonz, *Mothers in the Fatherland: Women, the Family and Nazi Politics*, New York: St. Martin's Press, 1987; Michael Kater, *The Twisted Muse, Musicians and their Music in the Third Reich*, Oxford: Oxford University Press, 1997; Detlev Peukert, *Inside the Third Reich,* New Haven: Yale University Press, 1987; Richard Plant, *The Pink Triangle: The Nazi War against Homosexuals*, New York: Holt, 1986; Peter Stachura, *Nazi Youth in the Weimar Republic*, Santa Barbara: Santa Barbara, 1975; Guenter Lewy, *The Nazi Persecution of the Gypsies*, Oxford: Oxford University Press, 2000; Robert Gellately and Nathan Stolztfus, eds., *Social Outsiders in the Third Reich*, Princeton: Princeton University Press, 2001.

12. Scholtyseck, *Bosch*, 189–191; "Even if German liberalism had been reduced to a negligible force in power political terms," adds the historian Horst Sassin, "the question remains whether liberals were predestined to be opponents of the Nazi state out of ideological or humanitarian grounds." Sassin, *Liberale*, 9–10.

13. Konrad H. Jarausch and Larry Eugene Jones, "German Liberalism Reconsidered: Inevitable Decline, Bourgeois Hegemony, or Partial Achievement?" in Jarausch and Jones, eds, *In Search of a Liberal Germany*, New York: Berg, 1999.

14. More than fifteen years ago, Horst Sassin concluded that "a theoretical discussion of the concept of resistance" was no longer required, since it "has been so widely addressed in recent years." See Sassin, *Liberale*, 14; Eric Kurlander, "New Approaches to Bourgeois Resistance in Germany and Austria," *History Compass*, 4 (2006), 1–18; Hans Mommsen, *Alternatives to Hitler: German Resistance under the Third Reich*, London: I.B. Tauris, 2003; Klemens von Klemperer, *German Resistance against Hitler: The Search for Allies Abroad, 1938–1945*, Oxford: Clarendon Press, 1992; Peter Hoffmann, *German Resistance to Hitler*, Cambridge, Mass.: Harvard University Press, 1985; Fabian von Schlabrendorff, *The Secret War against Hitler*, Boulder, Col.: Westview Press, 1994; Walter Schmitthenner and Hans Buchheim, eds., *Der deutsche Widerstand gegen Hitler*, Cologne: Kiepenheuer & Witsch, 1966; Hans-Adolf Jacobsen, ed., *20. Juli 1944: Die deutsche Opposition gegen Hitler im Urteil der ausländischen Geschichtsschreibung*, Bonn: FRG Press and Information Office, 1969; Bodo Scheurig, ed., *Deutscher Widerstand 1938–1944: Fortschritt oder Reaktion?* Nordlingen: DTV, 1969; Gerhart Binder, *Irrtum und Widerstand: Die deutschen Katholiken in der Auseinandersetzung mit dem Nationalsozialismus*, Munich: Pfeiffer,

1968; Lewy, *The Catholic Church*; Karl-Heinze Jahnke, *Weiße Rose contra Hakenkreuz. Studenten im Widerstand 1942/43*, Rostock: Koch, 2003.

15. Leonidas Hill, "Towards a New History of the German Resistance to Hitler," *CEH*, 14 (1981), 369–399; Martin Broszat, Ele Fröhlich, and Anton Grossman, eds., *Bayern in der NS-Zeit. Soziale Lage und politisches Verhalten der Bevölkerung im Spiegel vertraulicher Berichte*, München: Oldenbourg, vols I–IV, 1977–1983; Hans Medick, " 'Missionare im Ruderboot'? Ethnologische Erkenntnisweisen als Herausforderung an die Sozialgeschichte," *Geschichte und Gesellschaft*, 10 (1984), 296–319; Alf Lüdtke, *Alltagsgeschichte: Zur Rekonstruktion historischer Erfahrungen und Lebensweisen*, Frankfurt: Campus, 1989; Jane Caplan, ed., *Nazism, Fascism and the Working Class: Essays by Tim Mason*, Cambridge: Cambridge University Press, 1995; Timothy W. Mason, *Sozialpolitik im Dritten Reich*, Opladen: Westdeutscher, 1978; Kershaw, *Hitler Myth*; David F. Crew, ed., *Nazism and German Society, 1933–1945*, London: Routledge, 1994; Thomas Childers and Jane Caplan, eds, *Reevaluating the Third Reich*, New York: Holmes & Meier, 1993; David Clay Large, ed., *Contending with Hitler: Varieties of German Resistance in the Third Reich*, Cambridge: Cambridge University Press, 1991.

16. Richard Löwenthal and Patrick von der Mühlen, eds, *Widerstand und Verweigerung in Deutschland, 1933 bis 1945*, Berlin: Dietz, 1984; Allan Merson, *Communist Resistance in Nazi Germany*, London: Lawrence & Wishart, 1986, 4–5; Peukert, *Inside*, 3–23.

17. Sassin, *Liberale*, 18.

18. See again Klemperer, *Resistance*; Hoffmann, *Resistance*; Schlabrendorff, *The Secret War against Hitler*; Lothar Kettenacker, ed., *The "Other Germany" in the Second World War*, Stuttgart: Klett, 1977; Gellately, *Backing Hitler*; Joachim Fest, *Plotting Hitler's Death*, London: Weidenfeld & Nicolson, 1996; Theodore S. Hamerow, *On the Road to the Wolf's Lair*, Cambridge, Mass.: Belknap, 1997.

19. Peukert, *Inside*, 25. It is after all easy to establish cases of "resistance" among those minorities or target populations whose pre-1933 status in German society was antithetical to Nazi ideals. For subaltern groups, preserving some semblance of normality after 1933 – in some cases simply surviving – constituted an act of "non-conformity." While this kind of research is indispensable in helping us to outline the contours (and extremity) of repression, often on the fringes of the Reich, it tells us less about the nature of ordinary social, political, and intellectual life for the majority of Germans who were neither threatened with arrest nor targeted for deportation. This makes liberal non-conformity all the more interesting and illustrative of the everyday limits of coercion and consent.

20. Robert Gellately, *The Gestapo and German Society: Enforcing Racial Policy 1933–1945*, Oxford: Clarendon, 1990; Gellately and Stolztfus, eds, *Social Outsiders*; Reinhard Mann, *Protest und Kontrolle im Dritten Reich: Nationalsozialistische Herrschaft im Alltag einer rheinischen Großstadt*, Frankfurt: Campus, 1987; Eric A. Johnson, *Nazi Terror: The Gestapo, Jews and Ordinary Germans*, New York: Basic Books, 1999.

21. Neumann, *Tantzen*, 16–20, 25–27.

22. Peukert, *Inside*, 244.

23. "Because National Socialism was double-sided, the resistance against National Socialism must reflect this characteristic . . . To deny this would be an injustice to the people who stood before an almost insoluble dilemma, to pursue opposition out of their liberal [. . .] convictions on the one hand while sustaining an armament and forced labor system on the other." Scholtyseck, *Bosch*, 188–189, 548–549.

24. See Ludwig Elm, *Zwischen Fortschritt und Reaktion: Geschichte der Parteien der liberalen Bourgeoisie in Deutschland, 1893–1918*, Berlin: Akademie, 1968, 3–9; Langewiesche, *Liberalism*; Kurlander, *Price*.

25. See Albertin, *Liberalismus und Demokratie*; Hartmut Shustereit, *Linksliberalismus und Sozialdemokratie in der Weimarer Republik. Eine vergleichende Betrachtung der Politik von DDP und SPD 1919–1930*, Düsseldorf: Schwann, 1975; Jones, *German*

Liberalism; Kurlander, *Price*, 77–93; Jonathan Wright, *Gustav Stresemann: Weimar's Greatest Statesman*, Oxford: Oxford University Press, 2002, 111–125.

26. These included Hugo Preuss, Weimar's first Interior Minister (1918–19) and "father of the constitution," as well as the Heidelberg Law Professor Gerhard Anschütz, its chief legal defender and interpreter. See Hugo Preuss, *Deutschlands republikanische Reichsverfassung*, Berlin: Neuer Staat, 1923; Gerhard Anschütz, *Die Verfassung des deutschen Reichs vom 11. August 1919*, Berlin: Stilke, 1921.

27. Most influential in this regard were Eugen Schiffer, Weimar's first Finance Minister (1919); Walther Rathenau, Minister for Reconstruction (1921); Eduard Hamm, Economic Minister (1923–25); Hjalmar Schacht, Weimar Currency Commissioner (1923) and Reichsbank President (1924–30); Hermann Dietrich, Economic Minister (1930), Vice-Chancellor (1930–32), and Minister for Food and Agriculture (1930–32); and Hermann Höpker-Aschoff, the longtime Prussian Finance Minister (1925–31).

28. Eugen Schiffer, Justice Minister (1919–21) and Vice-Chancellor (1919–20); Erich Koch-Weser, Interior Minister (1919–21) and Justice Minister (1928–29).

29. Wilhelm Abegg, Prussian Police President (1923–26) and State Secretary of the Interior (1926–32).

30. Otto Gessler, Defence Minister (1920–28).

31. Walther Rathenau, Foreign Minister (1922).

32. For example, Theodor Wolff, *Berliner Tageblatt*; Heinrich Simon, *Frankfurter Zeitung*; Georg Bernhard, *Vossische Zeitung*; Paul Rohrbach, *Leitartikel-Korrespondenz*; and Hellmut von Gerlach, *Welt am Montag*.

33. Max Weber, Thomas Mann, Albert Einstein, Gerhart Hauptmann, and Friedrich Meinecke, to name only a few.

34. Helene Lange, Gertrud Bäumer, Alice Salomon, Marie Elisabeth Lüders, Marianne Weber, and Else Ulrich-Beil, among others.

35. Ludwig Quidde.

36. Quidde, Gerlach, Anton Erkelenz.

37. Schacht, Gessler, Rohrbach.

38. Schiffer, Koch-Weser, Theodor Tantzen.

39. Despite a tendency in the literature to dismiss the Democrats as a party of aging notables, it is important to note that four of the five Democratic Reichstag deputies in March 1933 – Theodor Heuss (1884), Reinhold Maier (1889), Heinrich Landahl (1895), and Ernst Lemmer (1898) – belonged to the same generation as Adolf Hitler (1889), Hermann Goering (1893), and Joseph Goebbels (1897). Gertrud Bäumer (1873), Marie Lüders (1878), and Hermann Dietrich (1879) were decades younger than Reich President Paul von Hindenburg (1847) and virtually the same age as Konrad Adenauer (1876), who would retire as Chancellor of the Federal Republic in 1963. Ludwig Luckemeyer, *Föderativer liberaler Rebell in DDP und FDP und erster liberaler Vorkämpfer Europas in Deutschland*, Korbach: W. Bing, 1981, 28; Scholtyseck, *Bosch*, 192–193.

40. Ernst Lemmer, as quoted in Hans Bott, ed., *Begegnungen mit Theodor Heuss*, Tübingen: Wunderlich, 1954, 69; Jürgen Froelich, " 'Die Hilfe' im Nationalsozialismus," in Christoph Studt, ed., *"Diener des Staates" oder "Widerstand zwischen den Zeilen,"* Berlin: LIT, 2007, 120.

41. In contrast to prosopography, a tendency in the literature to focus on individual biography has worked to the detriment of comparative political, cultural, and ideological history. By privileging the biographies of predominantly male liberals who helped to build the Federal Republic much of this work is also insufficiently critical and implicitly chauvinist. See Angelika Schaser, "Liberalismus-Forschung und Biographie. Ein Beitrag aus geschlechtergeschichtlicher Perspektive," *JzLF*, 15 (2003), 185–198; A. Schaser, "Erinnerungskartell: Der Nationalsozialismus im Rückblick der deutschen Liberalen," in A. Schaser, ed., *Erinnerungskartelle: Zur Konstruktion von Autobiographien nach 1945*,

Bochum: Winkler, 2003, 49–80; Neumann, *Tantzen*; Scholtyseck, *Bosch*; Fischer, *Schacht und Deutschlands "Judenfrage"*; Schaser, *Lange und Bäumer*; Hansen, *Bernstorff*; also see limited discussion of the period 1933–45 in Modris Eksteins, *Theodor Heuß und die Weimarer Republik*, Stuttgart: E. Klett, 1969; Karl Dietrich Bracher, *Theodor Heuß und die Wiederbegründung der Demokratie in Deutschland*, Tübingen: Wunderlich, 1965; Eberhard Demm, ed., *Alfred Weber als Politiker und Gelehrter*, Stuttgart: Steiner, 1983; E. Demm, *Von der Weimarer Republik zur Bundesrepublik: Der Politische Weg Alfred Webers, 1920–1958*, Düsseldorf: Droste, 2000; Reinhard Blomert, *Intellektuelle im Aufbruch: Karl Mannheim, Alfred Weber, Norbert Elias und die Heidelberger Sozialwissenschaften der Zwischenkriegszeit*, Munich: Hanser, 1999; Manfred Schmid, ed., *Fritz Elsas: Ein Demokrat im Widerstand*, Gerlingen: Bleicher, 1999; Joachim Ramm, *Eugen Schiffer und die Reform der deutschen Justiz*, Darmstadt: Luchterwand, 1987; Thilo Ramm, ed., *Eugen Schiffer: Ein nationalliberaler Jurist und Staatsmann, 1860–1954*, Baden-Baden: Nomos, 2006.

42. Jarausch and Jones, "German Liberalism Reconsidered," 13.
43. Wright, *Stresemann*, 111–201; Kurlander, *Price*, 122–127; Ursula Susanna Gilbert, *Hellmut von Gerlach (1866–1935): Stationen eines deutschen Liberalen vom Kaiserreich zum "Dritten Reich"*, Frankfurt: P. Lang, 1984; Peter Pistorius, "Rudolf Breitscheid 1874–1944," (Cologne diss.), 1970.
44. Maurenbrecher to Naumann, 5.14.13, NL Naumann, BAB: N 3001, # 105; Theodor Heuss, *Friedrich Naumann: Der Mann, das Werk, die Zeit*, München: Siebenstern, 1968, 526–527.
45. *"Wahlzeitung #5, Demokratische Vereinigung Breslau*, 12.01.11.
46. Rather, the "Nazi synthesis of Darwinism and national community bore more than a surface resemblance to the discursive terrain" of Wilhelmine progressive milieu. Repp, *Reformers*, 322–325; or, as Rudolf Heberle writes in his masterful study of Nazism in Schleswig-Holstein, "one can, in the ideology of the progressive Liberals in the region, discern certain attitudes and sentiments which later on facilitated the conversion of broad masses of middle class elements to National Socialism: There was a combination of anti-capitalistic, anti-plutocratic sentiments with anti-imperialistic attitudes, and of an emphatic rejection of proletarian Socialism with an attitude of social solidarity that favored progressive labor legislation or *Sozialpolitik*." R. Heberle, *From Democracy to Nazism: A Regional Case Study on Political Parties in Germany*, New York: Howard Fertig, 1970, 28–29. Also see Kurlander, *Price*, 27–85; Peter Theiner, *Sozialer Liberalismus und deutsche Weltpolitik: Friedrich Naumann im Wilhelminische Deutschland (1860–1919)*, Baden-Baden: Nomos, 1983, 5–10; Karl Heinrich Pohl, "Der Liberalismus im Kaiserreich," in Rüdiger von Bruch, ed., *Friedrich Naumann in seiner Zeit*, New York: De Gruyter, 2000, 65–66; Oded Heilbronner, *"Freiheit, Gleichheit, Brüderlichkeit und Dynamik". Populäre Kultur, populärer Liberalismus und Bürgertum im ländlichen Süddeutschland 1850 bis 1930*, Munich: Martin Meidenbauer, 2007; Reinhard Opitz, *Der deutsche Sozialliberalismus, 1917–1933*, Cologne: Pahl-Rugenstein, 1973; James J. Sheehan, *German Liberalism in the Nineteenth Century*, Chicago: Chicago, 1978; Thompson, *Left Liberals*; Repp, *Reformers*; Jenkins, *Provincial Modernity*; Jones, *German Liberalism*; James Retallack, *Germany in the Age of Kaiser William II*, New York: St. Martin's Press, 1996; Sell, *Die Tragödie*; Langewiesche, *Liberalism*.
47. See Baümer's speech, 3.14.31, in BAK: R 45 III 49, 48. Heuss, *Hitlers Weg*, Stuttgart: Union deutscher Verlagsgesellschaft, 1932; Heuss, *Naumann*, 529. "They say: what attracts the masses? The national idea! And then they say: From now on, we will also push these national ideas somewhat more into the foreground . . . Or they say: it is perhaps the opposition to the modern democratic system! And if it is necessary, quintessential old Democrats go forth and declare: that is the old party, those are the old names and then arrives a State party – that is, the Democratic Party – which is responsible for Germany's entire misfortune and has become so obsolete as a party that it no longer dares to carry its name; it goes out and says: people, get rid of the

old party; German people, the old parties have failed; give your voice to the State Party." Adolf Hitler, as quoted in the *Schleswiger Nachrichten*, 9.23.30.

48. See Kurlander, *Price*, 347–354; Wolfgang Schivelbusch, *Entfernte Verwandschaft: Faschismus, Nationalsozialismus, New Deal, 1933–1939*, Munich: Hanser, 2005; Götz Aly, *Hitlers Volksstaat: Raub, Rassenkrieg, und Nationalsozialismus*, Frankfurt: Fischer, 2005; Edward Ross Dickinson, *The Politics of German Child Welfare from the Empire to the Federal Republic*, Cambridge, Mass.: Harvard University Press, 1996; David F. Crew, *Germans on Welfare: From Weimar to Hitler*, New York: Oxford, 1998; Daniel P. Silverman, *Hitler's Economy: Nazi Work Creation Programs, 1933–1936*, Cambridge, Mass.: Harvard, 1998; Young-Sun Hung, *Welfare, Modernity, and the Weimar State, 1919–1933*, Princeton: Princeton, 1998; Anthony Nicholls, *Freedom with Responsibility: The Social Market Economy in Germany, 1918–1963*, Oxford: Clarendon, 1994; Michael Burleigh, *The Third Reich: A New History*, New York: Hill & Wang, 2000; Dagmar Herzog, *Sex after Fascism: Memory and Morality in Twentieth Century Germany*, Princeton: Princeton, 2005; Peukert, *Inside*; Repp, *Reformers*; Weindling, *Health, Race and German Politics*; Woodruff Smith, *The Ideological Origins of Nazi Imperialism*, New York: Oxford, 1986; W. Smith, *Politics and the Sciences of Culture in Germany, 1840–1920*, New York: Oxford University Press, 1991.

49. See Wehler, *German Empire*; Winkler, *Mittelstand*; Pühle, *Agrarische Interessenpolitik*; Sell, *Die Trägodie*; Fritz Fischer, *Griff nach der Weltmacht*, Düsseldorf: Droste, 1967; Rosenberg, *Bureaucracy*; Stern, *Illiberalism*; Mosse, *The Crisis of German Ideology*.

50. See again Jones, *Liberalism*; D. Peukert, *The Weimar Republic: The Crisis of Classical Modernity*, New York: Penguin, 1991; Abraham, *Collapse*; Sheehan, *German Liberalism*; Charles Maier, *Recasting Bourgeois Europe*, Princeton: Princeton, 1988; Stanley Suval, *Electoral Politics in Wilhelmine Germany*, Chapel Hill, N.C.: University of North Carolina Press, 1985; Dan S. White, *The Splintered Party: National Liberalism in Hessen and the Reich, 1867–1918*, Cambridge: Cambridge University Press, 1976; Geoff Eley, *Reshaping the German Right: Radical Nationalism and Political Change After Bismarck*, Ann Arbor: Michigan University Press, 1990; David Blackbourn and Geoff Eley, *The Peculiarities of German History: Bourgeois Society and Politics in Nineteenth-Century Germany*, New York: Oxford University Press, 1984; Brett Fairbairn, *Democracy in the Undemocratic State*, Toronto: Toronto University Press, 1997; James Retallack, *Notables of the Right: The Conservative Party and Political Mobilization in Germany, 1876–1918*, Boston: Unwin Hyman, 1988; David Blackbourn, *Class, Religion and Local Politics in Wilhelmine Germany*, New Haven: Yale University Press, 1980; Thompson, *Left Liberals*; Margaret Anderson, *Practicing Democracy: Elections and Political Culture in Imperial Germany*, Princeton: Princeton University Press, 2000; Frye, *Democrats*.

51. Repp, *Reformers*, 316.

52. See Kurlander, *Price*. Or, as Repp himself observes, any "study which follows the careers" of Wilhelmine social reformers "into the Third Reich" must stress their "contribution to the second, fatal experiment in National Socialism." Repp, *Reformers*, 325.

53. For more on the central role of the "Volksgemeinschaft" in defining interwar German mentalities, see Kurlander, *Price*; Peukert, *Inside*; Burleigh, *Third Reich*; Aly, *Hitlers Volksstaat*; David Schoenbaum, *Hitler's Social Revolution*, New York: Norton, 1997; Alf Lüdtke, "The Appeal of Exterminating 'Others': Workers and the Limits of Resistance," in Leitz, ed., *The Third Reich*, 155–177; Steffen Bruendel, *Volksgemeinschaft oder Volksstaat: Die "Ideen von 1914" und die Neuordnung Deutschlands im Ersten Weltkrieg*, Berlin: Akademie Verlag, 2003; Michael Wildt, *Volksgemeinschaft als Selbstermächtigung: Gewalt gegen Juden in der deutschen Provinz 1919 bis 1939*, Hamburg: Hamburger, 2007; Peter Fritzsche, *Life and Death in the Third Reich*, Cambridge, Mass.: Harvard University Press, 2008; Helmut Walser Smith, *The*

Continuities of German History: Nation, Religion, and Race Across the Long Nineteenth Century, Cambridge: Cambridge University Press, 2008.

54. See Franz Neumann, *Behemoth: The Structure and Practice of National Socialism 1933–1944*, New York: Oxford University Press, 1944; also see Heilbronner, *"Freiheit, Gleichheit, Brüderlichkeit und Dynamik"* and Eksteins, *Left Liberal Press*, 175, 201, 230; *Breslauer Zeitung*, 7.25.32, 7.28.32. Reports on speeches by Neumann in Trebnitz and Bayer in Prausnitz, 11.02.32, in DVP protocols, BAB: R 45 II, 53129; Rüdiger vom Bruch, "Sozialer Liberalismus und deutsche Weltpolitik," in Bruch, ed., *Friedrich Naumann*, 9–10; Repp, *Reformers*; Kurlander, *Price*.

Chapter One: "A Gift to Germany's Future?"

1. Jeremy Noakes and Geoffrey Pridham, eds, *Nazism: The Rise to Power*, vol. I, Exeter: Exeter, 1998, 123–124; Evans, *Power*, 12–14.
2. Evans, *Power*, 122–123; Broszat, et al., eds, *Alltag und Widerstand*; Ian Kershaw, *Popular Opinion and Political Dissent in the Third Reich*, Oxford: Oxford University Press, 2002; Gellately, *Gestapo and German Society*.
3. See allied questionnaire in letter to Dietrich, 2.05.47, in NL Dietrich, BAK: N 1004, #458.
4. See "Auszug aus den Verhandlungen des Reichstages," 3.23.33, in NL Dietrich, BAK: N 1004, #458.
5. Frye, *Democrats*, 161–167.
6. See Robinsohn to Dehler, 12.02.56, in NL Robinsohn, BAK: N 1296, #2; Jürgen C. Heß, *Das ganze Deutschland*; Kurlander, *Price*.
7. Dieter Fricke, *Die Bürgerlichen Parteien in Deutschland*, vol. I, Leipzig: Bibliographisches Institut, 1968, 326; Huber, *Bäumer*, 371–376; S. Remy, *The Heidelberg Myth*, Cambridge, Mass.: Harvard University Press, 2002, 25; Froelich, "He Served the German People Well," 633–634.
8. Heß, *Theodor Heuss vor 1933*, 205. Jürgen C. Heß, " 'Die Nazis haben gewußt, daß wir ihre Feinde gewesen und geblieben sind': Theodor Heuss und der Widerstand gegen den Nationalsozialismus," *JzLF*, 14 (2002), 143–148; J. C. Heß, " 'Die deutsche Lage ist ungeheuer ernst geworden': Theodor Heuss vor der Herausforderungen des Jahres 1933," *JzLF*, 6 (1994), 65–136.
9. Albertin and Wegner, *Linksliberalismus*, 205.
10. Höpker-Aschoff in *Vossische Zeitung*, 2.26.33, in NL Höpker-Aschoff, BAK: N 1129, #7.
11. Günther Wirth, "Publizist, Politiker, und Parlementarier: Zum Wirken von Otto Nuschke," *Berlinische Monatsschrift*, 2 (1999), 30–31; Brammer article in *Demokratischer Zeitungsdienst*, 3.03.33, in NL Külz, BAK: N 1042, #19.
12. Böckling to Dietrich, 3.01.33, in NL Dietrich, BAK: N 1004, #143.
13. Letter from Dietrich, Maier, and Petersen to DStP members, 2.11.33, in NL Külz, BAK: N 1042, #19.
14. Fricke, *Parteien*, 327–329; Burleigh, *Third Reich*, 142–155.
15. Koch to Dietrich, 3.07.33, in NL Dietrich, BAK: N 1004, #149; See official letter, 3.28.33, in NL Dietrich, BAK: N 1004, #142; Dietrich to Mitschke, 2.20.33, in NL Dietrich, BAK: NL 1004, #150.
16. See letters from Borkmann to Dietrich, 2.23.33, 3.02.33, in NL Dietrich, BAK: 1004, #143.
17. Heuss, *Erinnerungen*, 428–430; Heß, " 'Die Nazis haben gewußt," 149–154; Heß, "Die deutsche Lage ist ungeheuer ernst geworden," 86–92; Külz speech in NL Külz, BAK: N 1042, #19.
18. Ablass to Dietrich, 3.09.33; Dietrich to Ablass, 3.28.33, in NL Dietrich, BAK: N 1004, #142; Mitschke to Schütt, 2.11.33, Mayer-Pantenius to Dietrich, 6.16.33, in

212 *Notes to pp. 16–17*

NL Dietrich, BAK: N 1004, #150; Berghaus to Dietrich, Höpker-Aschoff, 5.15.33, in NL Dietrich, BAK: NL 1004, #143.

19. Wilms to Dingeldey, 4.24.33, in NL Dingeldey, BAK: N 1002, #98.

20. Winter to Dingeldey, 4.09.33, in NL Dingeldey, BAK: N 1002, #98; Dietrich to Koch, 3.15.33, in NL Dietrich, BAK: N 1004, #149; H. Dietrich, *Creating a New State: German Problems – 1945 to 1953*, n.p.: n.pub., 8; Schacht, *Schlusswort*, 9.06.50, in NL Traub, BAK: N 1059, #67.

21. These were criticisms the former laissez-faire liberal would discard completely in the wake of Schacht's successful "Keynesian" economic reforms. Höpker-Aschoff, "Das Ermächtigungsgesetz," *Vossische Zeitung*, 3.19.33. BAK: N 1129, #7; See MS [1936] in NL Höpker-Aschoff, BAK: N 1129, #3; Schacht, *Schlusswort*, 9.06.50, in NL Traub, BAK: N 1059, #67.

22. Fricke, *Parteien*, 328–329.

23. Ibid.

24. "Fragment von Erinnerungen aus der NS-Zeit," in Eberhard Pikart, ed., *Theodor Heuss: Der Mann, das Werk, die Zeit: Eine Ausstellung*, Tübingen: R. Wunderlich, 1967, 177–178.

25. Ibid. Adelheid von Saldern, *Hermann Dietrich: Ein Staatsmann der Weimarer Republik*, Boppard: Harald Boldt, 1966, 198; Luckemeyer, *Rebell*, 15, 112; Hans Heinrich Welchert, *Theodor Heuss. Ein Lebensbild*, Bonn: Athenäum, 1959, 77–78; Lemmer, *Manches war anders. Erinnerungen eines dt. Demokraten*, Munich: Herbig, 1996, 174–185; Lückemeyer, *Heile*, 112.

25a. Heuss, *Erinnerungen*, 406–407.

26. Ibid.

27. Frye, *Democrats*, 186–190; Herbert Bertsch, *Die FDP und der Deutsche Liberalismus*, Berlin: Deutscher, 1965, 146–149; Lothar Albertin, "Die Auflösung der bürgerlichen Mitte und die Krise des parlamentarischen. Systems von Weimar," in Eberhalb Kolb and Walter Mülhausen, eds, *Demokratie in der Krise: Parteien im Verfassungssystem der Weimarer Republik*, Munich: Oldenbourg, 1997, 59–111; Barthold C. Witte, "Liberaler in schwierigen Zeiten," see Heß, "Die deutsche Lage ist ungeheuer ernst geworden," 86–94.

28. See Adolf Hitler, *25 Punkte Program*, Munich: Franz Eher, 1920, 2.24.20; Burleigh, *Third Reich*, 133–136; Richard Evans, *The Coming of the Third Reich*, New York: Penguin, 2004, 195–212; Detlef Mühlberger, *Hitler's Followers: Studies in the Sociology of the Nazi Movement*, New York: Routledge, 1991, 202–209.

29. Gerald Feldman, *The Great Disorder: Politics, Economy, and Society in the German Inflation, 1914–1924*, Oxford: Oxford University Press, 1997, 131–198, 211–250, 302, 754–821; Frye, *Democrats*, 88–101; Maier, *Recasting Bourgeois Europe*, 350–355; Jones, *Liberalism*, 50–67, 151–164, 246–304.

30. The NSDAP was "an expressly socialist party," wrote the former Weimar Treasury Secretary Georg Gothein in 1933, "which was openly hostile to business." According to Gothein, National Socialism meant "eliminating the currency, nationalizing banking and large industries, expropriation of all income above 12,000 RM and increasing social expenditures to a financially insupportable level." See Gothein articles from 1933, primarily in *Vossische Zeitung*, "Aussischlose Sanierungspläne," "Hebt die allgemeine Kaufkraft," "Die brennende Not des Hausbesitzes," "Sorgen eines Steuerzahlers," in NL Gothein, BAK: N 1006, #64; also see see Höpker-Aschoff, "Totaler Staat und Rechtstaat," 1.06.34, *Die Hilfe*, in NL Höpker-Aschoff, BAK: 1129, #9.

31. Fricke, *Parteien*, 326; Huber, "Bäumer," 371–376; Albertin und Wegner, *Linksliberalismus*, 464–471; Frye, *Democrats*, 88–101, 157–177; Froelich, "He Served the German People Well," 633–634; Josef Winschuh, *Männer Traditionen Signale*, Berlin: F. Osmer, 1940; Maier to Schmid, 5.26.33, in Reinhold Maier, *Briefwechsel mit seiner Familie 1930 bis 1946*, Stuttgart: Kohlhammer, 1989, 35–38; Stephan, *Linksliberalismus*, 483; See MS [1936] in NL Höpker-Aschoff, BAK: N 1129, #3.

32. Kurlander, *Price*, 214–219, 271–274; Heuss to Dietrich, 5.09.32, in NL Heuss, BAK: N 1221, #58; Heuss to Mück, 5.07.33, in NL Heuss, BAK: N 1221, #648; also see Monika Faßbender, "Zum Briefwechsel zwischen Anton Erkelenz und Gertrud Bäumer, 1933," *JzLF*, 2, (1990), 150–156; Guido Müller, "Theodor Heuss: Deutscher Bildungsbürger und ethischer Liberalismus. Problemen und Aufgaben einer Heuss-Biographie in der Spannung zwischen politischen-gesellschaftlichen Strukturen und selbstverantworteter Individualität (1884–1963)," *JzLF*, 15 (2003), 210–211; Heß, *Das ganze Deutschland*; Heß, *Theodor Heuss vor 1933*, 207; Frye, *Democrats*, 118–145, 187–190; Heuss to Dietrich, 5.09.32, in NL Heuss, BAK: N 1221, #58; Maier to Schmid, 5.26.33, in Maier, *Briefwechsel*, 35–38. For a recent work that emphasizes the prevalence of ethnic nationalist feeling across the political spectrum, see Fritzsche, *Life and Death*.

33. See Dietrich letter, 3.28.33, in NL Dietrich, BAK: N 1004, #142; Heß, "Die deutsche Lage ist ungeheuer ernst geworden," 86–94, 130–134; Lothar Albertin, "Die Auflösung," 59–112.

34. Letter from Dietrich to Ablass, 3.28.33, in NL Dietrich, BAK: N 1004, #142.

35. 3.31.33 Sitzung und Parteivorstand Berlin: Die Dt. Volkspartei zur Lage, quoted in Eberhard Kolb and Ludwig Richter, eds, *Nationalliberalismus in der Weimar Republik: die Führungsgremien der Deutschen Volkspartei, Quellen zur Geschichte des Parlamentarismus 1918–1933*, Düsseldorf: Droste, 1999; Dingeldey to Meissner, 11.18.32; Dingeldey to Schleicher, 12.30.33, in NL Schleicher, BAF: N 1042, #31, #77; Dingeldey to Wrochem, 11.17.33, in NL Dingeldey, BAK: N 1002, #98; Dingeldey to von Seeckt, 3.15.33, in NL von Seeckt, BAF: N 1247, #189; Heuss, *Erinnerungen*, 445; Hans Mommsen, *The Rise and Fall of Weimar Democracy*, Chapel Hill, N.C.: University of North Carolina Press, 1996, 456; Wright, *Stresemann*, 520; Ludwig Richter, *Die Deutsche Volkspartei, 1918–1933*, Düsseldorf: Droste, 2002.

36. Zapf to Dingeldey, 4.01.33; Dingeldey to Zapf, 4.18.33; Zapf to Dingeldey, 4.21.33, in NL Dingeldey, BAK: N 1002, #98.

37. Welkow to Dingeldey, 2.24.33; Dingeldey to Welkow, 3.22.33, in NL Dingeldey, BAK: N 1002, #103; Uthoff to Dingeldey, 4.25.33, in NL Dingeldey, BAK: N 1002, #98.

38. Ibid.

39. Uthoff to Dingeldey, 4.25.33, in NL Dingeldey, BAK: N 1002, #98.

40. Wilms to Dingeldey, 4.24.33, in NL Dingeldey, BAK: N 1002, #98.

41. Ibid.

42. Goetz in 14.5.1933 Sitzung des Gesamtvorstandes, in Albertin und Wegner, eds, *Linksliberalismus*; Wolf Volker Weigand, *Walter Wilhelm Goetz*, Boppard: Harald Boldt, 1992, 311–315.

43. Schnell to Dingeldey, 5.15.33, BAK: N 1002, #63.

44. Ibid.

45. On Schnell's career as a Nazi doctor, see http://www.catalogus-professorum-halensis.de/schnellwalter.html. Also see Frye, *Democrats*, 190–193; Albertin, "Die Auflösung," 107; Welkow to Dingeldey, 6.26.33, in NL Dingeldey, BAK: N 1002, #103.

46. Dingeldey to Arps, 11.01.33, in NL Dingeldey, BAK: N 1002, #96.

47. Dingeldey to Welkow, 11.07.33, in NL Dingeldey, BAK: N 1002, #103.

48. Ibid.

49. Dingeldey to Wrochem, 11.17.33; Welkow to Dingeldey, 12.09.33, in NL Dingeldey, BAK: N 1002, #98.

50. Dingeldey to Lammers, Hitler, 7.25.33; Königsberg office to Dingeldey, 10.19.33, NL Dingeldey, BAK: N 1002, #63.

51. Theodor Heuss, *Robert Bosch: His Life and Achievements*, New York: Henry Holt, 1994, 294–320. Wilhelm Treue, "Widerstand von Unternehmen und Nationalökonomen," in Jürgen Schmädeke and Peter Steinbach, eds, *Der Widerstand gegen den Nationalsozialismus*, Munich: Piper, 1985, 928–929.

52. Scholtyseck, *Bosch*, 109–114.
53. Heuss, *Bosch*, 534–543.
54. Scholtyseck, *Bosch*, 144–146, 168–174, 191–192.
55. Paul Rohrbach, *Um des Teufels Handschrift: Zwei Menschenalter erlebter Weltgeschichte*, Hamburg: H. Dulk, 1953, 345.
56. Scholtyseck, *Bosch*, 190–191.
57. Ibid., 135–144; J. Scholtyseck, "Robert Bosch: Ein Liberaler im Widerstand gegen Hitler," *JzLF*, 15 (2003), 170–172.
58. Scholtyseck, *Bosch*, 211–218; Sell, *Die Tragödie*, 436–439; Scholtyseck, "Bosch," 176–178.
59. Treue, "Widerstand," 929–932; Klemperer, *German Opposition*, 151; Heuss, *Bosch*, 543–552; Scholtyseck, *Bosch*, 193.
60. Peter Hoffmann, *The History of the German Resistance*, Cambridge, Mass.: MIT Press, 1977, 34; Scholtyseck, *Bosch*, 192–193.
61. Scholtyseck, *Bosch*, 200–201.
62. Treue, "Widerstand," in Schmädeke and Steinbach, eds, *Widerstand*, 929.
63. Scholtyseck, *Bosch*, 195–199; Heuss, *Bosch*, 575; Hans Rothfels, *The German Opposition to Hitler*, Chicago: Henry Regnery, 1963, 84–85.
64. Treue, "Widerstand," in Schmädeke and Steinbach, eds, *Widerstand*, 932–934; Scholtyseck, *Bosch*, 189–190; Klemperer, *Resistance,* 21.
65. Scholtyseck, *Bosch*, 205–209; Hans Mommsen, "Die Widerstand gegen Hitler und die deutsche Gesellschaft," in Schmädeke and Steinbach, eds, *Widerstand*, 15.
66. Scholtyseck, *Bosch*, 188.
67. Cf. Bärbel Meurer, ed., *Marianne Weber: Beiträge zu Werk und Person*, Tübingen: Mohr Siebeck, 2004; Katja Eckhardt, *Die Auseinandersetzung zwischen Marianne Weber und Georg Simmel über die "Frauenfrage"*, Stuttgart: Ibidem, 2000; Christa Krüger, *Max und Marianne Weber: Tag- und Nachtgeschichten einer Ehe*, Zürich: Pendo, 2001.
68. See Weber articles in *Die Frau* (DF), March 1933 (3/33).
69. Marianne Weber, *Lebenserinnerungen*, Bremen: Johannes Storm, 1948, 215–233.
70. Ibid., 215; Remy, *Myth*, 110–111.
71. Remy, *Myth*, 20–21.
72. Weber, *Lebenserinnerungen*, 215.
73. Remy, *Myth*, 29, 111; for an allegorical critique of Fascism, see Hans von Eckardt, *Ivan the Terrible*, New York: Knopf, 1949.
74. Remy, *Myth*, 110–111. August Weber, *Erinnerungen*, in BAK: KLE 384 Weber, August, 215–229; Charles R. Wallraff, *Karl Jaspers: An Introduction to his Philosophy*, Princeton: Princeton University Press, 1970, 8–9.
75. Gerhard Besier, ed., *Die Mittwochs-Gesellschaft im Kaiserreich: Protokolle aus dem geistigen Deutschland, 1863–1919*, Berlin: Siedler, 1990; on the more famous Wednesday Society, the 20 July 1944 plot and resistance in the Third Reich, see Klaus Scholder, ed., *Die Mittwochs-Gesellschaft: Protokolle aus dem geistigen Deutschland 1932 bis 1944*, Berlin: Severin & Siedler, 1982. Neumann, *Tantzen*, 195–196.
76. Armin Behrendt, *Wilhelm Külz. Aus dem Leben eines Suchenden*, Berlin: Der Morgen, 1968, 132–147; Neumann, *Tantzen*, 191–192. Thomas Kübler, "Wilhelm Külz als Kommunalpolitiker," *JzLF*, 18 (2006), 110–111.
77. See Gothein to Dietrich, 12.04.33; Dietrich to Gothein, 12.12.33; Dietrich to Hans Bott and Rainer Wunderlich (publisher), 1.24.54, in NL Dietrich, BAK: N 1004, #145, #155. Neumann, *Tantzen*, 195–198; August Weber, *Errinerungen*, 112–113, in KLE Weber, BAK: KLE 384.
78. Neumann, *Tantzen*, 31, 51–58, 91, 107–111, 205–208.
79. Ibid. Heß, " 'Die Nazis haben gewußt," 143–211; August Weber, *Erinnerungen*, 163–170, 179–185.

80. Von Schlabrendorff, *The Secret War against Hitler*, 165–166; Neumann, *Tantzen*, 188–189, 198–199.
81. Sassin, *Liberale*, 19–26, 33–34; Neumann, *Tantzen*, 353–354: Frye, *Democrats*, 94–95, 137–144; Karl Holl, *Ludwig Quidde (1858–1941): Eine Biographie*, Düsseldorf: Droste, 2007, 423–510.
82. Sassin, *Liberale*, 14.
83. Scholtyseck, *Bosch*, 189, 249; Sassin, *Liberale*, 34–36, 249.
84. Sassin, *Liberale*, 36–39, 56, 67.
85. Ibid., 71–76, 88, 108–119, 329–331.
86. Ibid., 43–45, 66–79, 85–95, 161–167; Neumann, *Tantzen*, 353–354; Scholtyseck, *Bosch*, 189.
87. Sassin, *Liberale*, 50–57, 114, 156–157, 194–195, 214–215, 262.
88. Hansen, *Bernstorff*, 235–277; Baum, *Rückblick*, 309–312; Heuss article, "Wilhelm Solf," 2.09.46, in NL Heuss, BAK: N 1221, #48; Neumann, *Tantzen*, 353–354; Sassin, *Liberale*, 247–248. Also see Sharon Blair Brysac, *Resisting Hitler: Mildred Harnack and the Red Orchestra*, New York: Oxford University Press, 2002; Karl Heinz Roth and Angelika Ebbinghaus, eds, *Rote Kapellen, Kreisauer Kreise, Schwarze Kapellen: Neue Sichtweisen auf den Widerstand gegen die NS-Diktatur 1938–1945*, Hamburg: VSA, 2004; Stefan Roloff und Mario Vigl, eds, *Die "Rote Kapelle": Die Widerstandsgruppe im Dritten Reich und die Geschichte Helmut Roloffs*, Munich: Ullstein, 2002.
89. Sassin, *Liberale*, 122–123, 147, 247–249; Klemperer, *Resistance*, 159.
90. Neumann, *Tantzen*, 163–166.
91. Heuss to Gestapo, 10.11.33, to telephone company, 7.1.33; Heuss to Dr. Schütt, 1.10.34, to Dietrich letters, 2.05.34, 2.19.34, 6.18.34, in NL Heuss, BAK: N 1221, #79, #146.
92. Scholtyseck, *Bosch*, 126.
93. August Weber, *Erinnerungen*, 179–205.
94. Kübler, "Wilhelm Külz, 110–111.
95. Lüders, *Fürchte Dich Nicht: Persönliches und Politisches aus mehr als 80 Jahres*, Köln: Westdeutscher, 1963, 128–136; Baum, *Rückblick*, 308–318; Bäumer to Heuss, 10.18.43; to Beckmann, 11.22.43, in Beckmann, ed., *Band*, 208–211; Eugen Diesel, as quoted in Bott, ed., *Begegnungen*, 391; Weber, *Erinnerungen*, 182–183.
96. Gellately, *Gestapo and German Society*, 51–63.
97. Neumann, *Tantzen*, 166. Cf. Barry A. Jacksich, "Continuity and Change on the German Right: The Pan-German League and Nazism, 1918–1939," paper presented at Annual Meeting of the German Studies Association, 2005.
98. Neumann, *Tantzen*, 164–171; Heinz Höhne, *Order of the Death's Head*, New York: Penguin, 2001, 238–260.
99. Neumann, *Tantzen*, 229–239.
100. Saldern, *Dietrich*, 190–208; Frye, *Democrats*, 159–164. For an alternative view, see Jürgen Froelich, "He Served the German People Well," 619–640.
101. Dietrich to Koch, 3.15.33, in NL Dietrich, BAK: N 1004, #149; Heuss to Goetz, 12.31.37, in NL Heuss, BAK: N 1221, #80; Froelich, "He Served the German People Well," 629–634.
102. Letter to Brodauf, 1.30.41, in NL Dietrich, BAK: N 1004, #143.
103. Neumann, *Tantzen*, 188–189.
104. See correspondence from 1936 to 1940 in NL Dietrich, BAK: N 1004, #s 143, 145, 147, 163. August Weber, *Errinerungen*, 203–204, in KLE Weber, BAK: KLE 384.
105. Neumann, *Tantzen*, 220–221.
106. Behrendt, *Külz*, 152–155; Külz to Dietrich, 3.18.35, 11.03.36, 5.19.38, 5.27.38, 4.12.39, 10.12.39, 5.16.40; Dietrich to Külz, 3.19.35, 12.04.36, 12.16.36, 4.25.37, 6.03.38, 11.01.39, 5.15.40, in NL Dietrich, BAK: N 1004, #149.

107. Nuschke to Dietrich, 2.15.36, and from Dietrich to Nuschke, 6.01.40, 6.03.40, 6.21.40, in NL Dietrich, BAK: N 1004, #152.
108. Heuss to Ablaß, 9.10.40; Ablaß to Heuss, 9.12.40, in NL Heuss, BAK: N 1221, #72.
109. Maier to Dietrich, 5.09.34; Dietrich to Maier, 11.09.36, in NL Dietrich, BAK: N 1004, #150.
110. Dietrich to Schmidthals, 5.29.37, 10.07.39; Dietrich to Rönneberg, 10.18.40, 10.14.35, in NL Dietrich, BAK: N 1004, #s 154–155.
111. Correspondence between Dietrich and Himmel, Brönner-Höpfner, 10.08.40, 4.14.38, 12.05.38 in NL Dietrich, BAK: N 1004, #147.
112. Dietrich letters to Brönner-Hoepfner, Else Hoffmann, 12.05.38, 8.23.37 in NL Dietrich, BAK: N 1004, #147.
113. Joens to Dietrich, 12.09.38; Dietrich to Joens, 12.10.38, in NL Dietrich, BAK: N 1004, #148.
114. See correspondence between Dietrich and NSRB, 8.06.36, 2.03.37, 2.05.37, 3.01.37 in NL Dietrich, BAK: N 1004, #367.
115. Correspondence between Dietrich and NSRB, 6.22.39, 6.27.39, 7.05.39, in NL Dietrich, BAK: N 1004, #367.
116. Ibid., 5.15.37, 5.22.37, 4.28.38, 3.29.39, 4.30.39, in NL Dietrich, BAK: N 1004, #367.
117. See correspondence between Dietrich and NSRB, 4.27.39, 4.29.39, 5.02.39, 5.12.39, 5.15.39, 5.16.39, 6.05.39. NL Dietrich, BAK: N 1004, #367.
118. Ibid., 6.17.39, 6.20.39, 6.26.39. NL Dietrich, BAK: N 1004, #367.
119. See correspondence between Dietrich and NSRB, 9.09.39, 9.26.39, 3.11.40, in NL Dietrich, BAK: N 1004, #367.
120. See correspondence between Dietrich and NSRB, 3.15.40, 7.01.40, 7.24.40, 7.02.24, in NL Dietrich, BAK: N 1004, #367.
121. Ibid., 1.08.41, 2.17.41, 2.20.41, 2.21.41, 5.27.41, in NL Dietrich, BAK: N 1004, #367.
122. Correspondence between Dietrich and NSRB, 5.15.41, 6.27.41, in NL Dietrich, BAK: N 1004, #367.
123. Ibid., 5.20.41, 6.27.41, 9.30.41, 12.01.41, 2.18.42, 3.05.02, 3.28.42, 3.27.42, 8.03.42, 9.01.42, 11.06.42, 11.09.42, in NL Dietrich, BAK: N 1004, #367.
124. Invitation to hear speech by Reich Minister of Justice, 11.20.42 and Dietrich response, 11.30.42, in NL Dietrich, BAK: N 1004, #367.
125. Dietrich to Reich authorities, 3.30.42, 5.05.42, in NL Dietrich, BAK: N 1004, #365.
126. See Dietrich letters, 6.10.37, 7.19.40, in NL Dietrich, BAK: N 1004, #364; Klemperer, *The German Opposition*, 59–67, 164–167.
127. Letter, 7.22.44, asking for permission to travel to Baden semi-permanently since the Berlin-Steglitz office is mostly destroyed and his Baden property needs help. NL Dietrich, BAK: N 1004, #365.
128. Froelich, "He Served the German People Well," 635–636.
129. See Gerhard Ritter, *Carl Goerdeler und die deutsche Widerstandsbewegung*, Stuttgart: Deutsche Verlags-Anstalt, 1954; F.L. Carsten in Carsten, ed., *The German Resistance to Hitler*, Berkeley: California, 1970; Eberhard Zeller, *The Flame of Freedom: The German Struggle against Hitler*, London: Oswald Wolff, 1967; Schlabendorff, *The Secret War against Hitler*; Ger van Roon, *German Resistance to Hitler: Count von Moltke and the Kreisau Circle*, London: Van Nostrand Reinhold, 1971; Hoffmann, *History*; also see http://www.gedenkstaette-ploetzensee.de/13_e.html.
130. Neumann, *Tantzen*, 266–267, 277–278, 284–285, 297–299; H. Sassin, "Ernst Strassmann und der 20. Juli 1944: Anmerkungen zu Klemens von Klemperer und Joachim Scholtyseck," *JzLF*, 13 (2001), 193–199; Frye, *Democrats*, 192–194; Hugo Stehkämper, "Protest, Opposition und Widerstand im Umkreis der (untergegangenen) Zentrumspartei," in Schmädeke and Steinbach, eds, *Widerstand*, 901; Hoffmann, *History*, 356–358.
131. Sassin, *Liberale*, 49, 73; Hoffmann, *History*, 36–53.
132. Scholtyseck, *Bosch*, 205–206, 547–553.

133. Neumann, *Tantzen*, 269–277, 299–301, 343–345; Rothfels, *Opposition*, 89; Klemperer, *Opposition*, 59, 164–167; Hoffmann, *History*, 356–358.
134. Remy, *Myth*, 110; Heuss, *Aufzeichnungen, 1945–1947*, 13–14; Sassin, *Liberale*, 222–234; Scholtyseck, *Bosch*, 355–356. Heß, " 'Die Nazis haben gewußt,' " 192–195; Gessler to Heuss, 5.10.38, 1.19.39, NL Heuss, BAK: N 1221, #79; Jaenicke to Beck, 8.25.39; Beck to Jaenicke [Nov. 1942], in NL Beck, BAF: N 1028, #7.
135. Sassin, *Liberale*, 226–234; Neumann, *Tantzen*, 302.
136. Sassin, "Ernst Strassmann;" Sassin, *Liberale*, 173–202; Neumann, *Tantzen*, 353–354.
137. Heß, " 'Die Nazis haben gewußt,' " 192–195.
138. Sassin, *Liberale*, 226–234; Neumann, *Tantzen*, 296–302; Frye, *Democrats*, 192.
139. Klemens von Klemperer, *Der einsame Zeuge: Einzelkämpfer im Widerstand*, Passau: Richard Rothe, 1990, 8–11.
140. Hansen, *Bernstorff*, 271–277.
141. Frye, *Democrats*, 193–194; Klemperer, *Resistance*, 167; Sassin, *Liberale*, 227–230.
142. Baum, *Rückblick*, 309–312; Neumann, *Tantzen*, 299–300.
143. Heuss, *Aufzeichnungen, 1945–1947*, 15–16.
144. See Michael Stolleis, *The Law under the Swastika: Studies on Legal History in Nazi Germany*, Chicago: Chicago University Press, 1998; Christian Hilger, *Rechtsstaatsbegriffe im Dritten Reich. Eine Strukturanalyse*, Tübingen: Mohr Siebeck, 2003; Neumann, *Tantzen*, 341.
145. In discussing the 20 July plot on Hitler's life, Hans Mommsen writes: "Politicians such as Konrad Adenauer or Theodor Heuß, while detached from the regime, did not see a starting-point for any effective opposition. Nearly all resistance groups agreed in their opposition to a return to Weimar conditions." Mommsen in Leitz, ed., *The Third Reich*, 263; also see Luckemeyer, *Rebell*, 15; Scholtyseck, *Bosch*, 351.
146. In "so-called 'bourgeois' circles," the Gestapo observed, "a certain lack of participation, perhaps even covert opposition, has made itself apparent . . . in the refusal to respond to the German greeting [Hitler salute] and furthermore in the efforts to distance oneself and to be 'among themselves.' " Sassin, *Liberale*, 18–19; Sassin and Erkens, eds, *Dokumente*, 350–361.
147. Sassin, *Liberale*, 247–248; Neumann, *Tantzen*, 260; Scholtyseck, *Bosch*, 189–190.
148. See also Eric Kurlander, "Negotiating National Socialism: Liberal Non-Conformity and Accommodation in the Period of *Gleichschaltung*," *JzLF*, 17 (2005), 59–76.

Chapter Two: "Writing between the Lines"

1. Sassin, *Liberale*, 283.
2. Kater, *Muse*, 6–7. Also, see Alan Steinweis: "One of the most persistent generalizations to have emerged from almost five decades of postwar research on Nazi Germany is the notion of a German artistic and cultural establishment at the mercy of a totalitarian regime determined to mobilize the arts in pursuit of its own ideological ends." A. Steinweis, *Art, Ideology, and Economics in Nazi Germany*, Chapel Hill, N.C.: University of North Carolina Press, 1993, 1–3. For an earlier interpretation, see Peter Gay, *Weimar Culture: The Outsider as Insider*, New York: Harper & Row, 1968; Mosse, *Nazi Culture*.
3. Kater, *Muse*, 6–10. For an excellent local study of the interplay of culture, politics, and the marketplace in the Third Reich, see Christoph Schmid, *Nationalsozialistische Kulturpolitik im Gau Westfalen-Nord: Regionale Strukturen und locale Milieus (1933–1945)*, Paderborn: Ferdinand Schöningh, 2006. "Having taken insufficient account of institutional continuities," Steinweis suggests, "historians have not been prompted to evaluate the connections between the goals and policies of the pre-1933 professional organizations and those of their Nazi-era successors . . . a plethora of urgent problems that confronted the German art world both before and after 1933

have been examined only superficially. These problems included severe unemployment among professional artists in all fields, uneven and insufficiently rigorous
systems of professional education and certification, and a social insurance system that
was fragmentary at best." Steinweis, *Art*, 2–3; Paquet to Heuss, 1.26.34, in NL
Heuss, BAK: N 1221, #91.

4. Kater, *Muse*, 6–7. See, in particular, Jonathan Huener and Francis R. Nicosia, eds,
    The Arts in Nazi Germany: Continuity, Conformity, Change, Oxford: Berghahn, 2006;
    Clemens Zimmermann, *Medien im Nationalsozialismus: Deutschland, Italien und
    Spanien in den 1930er und 1940er Jahren*, Vienna: Böhlau, 2007.

5. Sassin, *Liberale*, 18.

6. As Heuss remarked sardonically: "he could thank the Führer" for his great biogra-
    phies of the liberal leaders Naumann and Bosch. Heuss, *Aufzeichnungen 1945–1947*,
    Stuttgart, 1966, 17–18; also see Sassin and Erkens, *Dokumente*, 376–378; Remy,
    Myth, 10–11.

7. "Scholars, having embraced National Socialism to varying degrees, did so out of a
    variety of personal and professional motives, including a clear desire to reconceptu-
    alize the nature of scholarly inquiry itself and a related desire to alter the purpose and
    structure of the university. They didn't 'betray' academic culture but sought to reshape
    it." Remy, *Myth*, 13–21, 234–245. For a fascinating collection of articles analysing the
    collaboration of (liberal) intellectuals in the Third Reich, see Winfried Schulze and
    Otto Gerhard Oexle, eds, *Deutsche Historiker im Nationalsozialismus*, Frankfurt:
    Fischer, 1999.

8. Steinweis, *Art*, 17–18; Magnus Brechtken, "Die Existenz der Journalisten unter den
    Bedingungen der Diktatur 1933–1945," in C. Studt, ed., *"Diener des Staates" oder
    "Widerstand zwischen den Zeilen." Die Rolle der Presse im "Dritten Reich,"* Münster:
    LIT, 2007, 75–98.

9. Ibid. Lemmer, *Manches war doch Anders*, 195–202; also see Christoph Studt,
    Introduction," in C. Studt, ed., *"Diener des Staates"*, 3–9.

10. Gustav Stolper to Joseph Schumpeter, quoted in Toni Stolper, *Ein Leben in
    Brennpunkten unserer Zeit: Gustav Stolper 1888–1947*, Tübingen: R. Wunderlich,
    1954, 317–318.

11. "Absurd: if someone hopes for better times; Character: not necessary for a career;
    Feuilleton: that which is still worth reading; Hocus Pocus: see Politics; Journalism:
    walking the tightrope [*Seiltanz*] between the lines; Optimist: irredeemable;
    University: training ground for future civil servants." See Gothein copy of
    Westdeutscher Beobachter, 10.12.36, announcement banning paper, *Der Querschnitt*, NL
    Gothein, BAK: N 1006, #64.

12. Scholtyseck, *Bosch*, 154–155.

13. Ibid.

14. Birk to Dietrich, 2.14.34, in NL Dietrich, N 1004, #143.

15. See articles by Wolff, Häuber, in *Berliner Tageblatt* (*BTB*), 3.18.33, 7.16.33, 7.09.33;
    Dietrich to Nüschke, 5.05.35, in NL Dietrich, BAK: N 1004, #152; *BTB* to Dietrich,
    10.13.36, 10.22.36, NL Dietrich, BAK: N 1004, #143; Neumann, *Tantzen*, 157–158;
    Günther Gillessen, *Auf verlorenem Posten: Die Frankfurter Zeitung im Dritten Reich*,
    Berlin: Siedler, 1986, 56, 111–148, 186–193; Gotthart Schwarz, "Berliner Tageblatt
    (1872–1939)," in Heinz-Dietrich Fischer, ed., *Deutsche Zeitungen des 17.–20.
    Jahrhunderts*, vol. II, Pullach: Dokumentation, 1972, 315–327; Margaret Boveri, *Wir
    lügen alle: Eine Hauptstadtzeitung unter Hitler*, Olten: Walter, 1965; Werner Becker,
    "Demokratie des sozialen Rechts: Die Politische Haltung der Frankfurter Zeitung,
    der Vossischen Zeitung und des Berliner Tageblatts, 1918–1924" (Munich diss.),
    1965.

16. Werner Wirthle, *Frankfurter Zeitung und Frankfurter Societäts-Druckerei GMBH: Die
    wirtschaftlichen Verhältnisse, 1927–1939*, Frankfurt: Societäts-Verlag, 1976, 29–41;
    Hummerich, *Wahrheit*, 62–65; Gillessen, *Posten*, 111–133.

17. See Heß, " 'Die Nazis haben gewußt,' " 143–148; also see Heß," 'Die deutsche Lage ist ungeheuer ernst geworden,' " 65–136; Froelich, *"Die Hilfe* im Nationalsozialismus," in Studt, ed., *"Diener des Staates,"* 115–129.

18. Müller, "Theodor Heuss," 199–214; Ernst Wolfgang Becker, "Ein Haus voller Briefe für die deutsche Geschichte des 20. Jahrhunderts. Zum Stand der Edition 'Theodor Heuss. Stuttgarter Ausgabe,' " *JzLF*, 17 (2005), 215–234; Thomas Hertfedler and Christiane Ketterle, eds, *Theodor Heuss: Publizist–Politiker–Präsident*, Stuttgart: Klett, 2003; Heß, " 'Die Nazis haben gewußt,' " 155–170, 192–195.

19. Bracher, *Theodor Heuss*, 10–12.

20. Eksteins, *Heuss*, 119–120; Heß, *Theodor Heuss vor 1933*, 221–222.

21. Reinhold Maier in Josef Eberle, ed., *Abschied von Theodor Heuss*, Tübingen: R. Wunderlich, 1964, 31–32.

22. See Heuss letters from 5.10.33, 5.11.33 in NL Heuss, BAK: N 1221, #76; Heß, " 'Die deutsche Lage ist ungeheuer ernst geworden,' " 102–106; Eberle, ed., *Abschied*, 24–25.

23. Reiner Burger, *Theodor Heuss als Journalist*, Hamburg: LIT, 1998, 501–502.

24. "Gedanken über Revolution," *Deutscher Aufstieg*, 46, 4.04.33, in NL Heuss, BAK: N 1221, #76.

25. Heuss to Mück, 5.07.33, in NL Heuss, BAK: N 1221, #648; Heß, " 'Die Nazis haben gewußt' ", 143–148; Heß, " 'Die deutsche Lage ist ungeheuer ernst geworden,' " 82–101; Savelkouls to Heuss, 2.05.34, in NL Heuss, BAK: N 1221, #94; also see Froelich, *"Die Hilfe* im Nationalsozialismus," in Studt, ed., *"Diener des Staates,"* 117–119.

26. Leo Baeck, in Bott, ed., *Begegnungen*; Bracher, *Theodor Heuss*, 11.

27. Toni Stolper, in Eberle, ed., *Abschied*, 105–106; Stolper, *Begegnungen mit Theodor Heuss*, Tübingen: Hans Bott, 1954; Jürgen Heß, "Theodor Heuss aus der Perspektive des Counter Intelligence Corps der US-Army, 15. September 1949," *JzLF*, 17 (2005), 132.

28. "Gedanken über Revolution," *Deutscher Aufstieg*, Nr. 46, 4.04.33, in NL Heuss, BAK: N 1221, # 76.

29. See articles 6.04.33, 8.05.33, in NL Heuss, BAK: N 1221, #46, # 398. Heß, "Die deutsche Lage ist ungeheuer ernst geworden," 120–127.

30. Froelich, *"Die Hilfe* im Nationalsozialismus," in Studt, ed., *"Diener des Staates,"* 119–123; also see Robert Gellately, "Surveillance and Disobedience: Aspects of the Political Policing of Nazi Germany," in Francis Nicosia and Lawrence Stokes, eds, *Germans against Nazism: Nonconformity, Opposition and Resistance in the Third Reich (Essays in Honor of Peter Hoffman)*, New York: Berg, 1990, 17–18. Peukert, *Inside*, 64; Heß, "Die deutsche Lage ist ungeheuer ernst geworden," 111–124.

31. R. Dahrendorff, *T.Heuss: Zur geistigen Gestalt des Politikers und Publizisten*, Tübingen: R. Wunderlich, 1984, 240–241; Burger, *Heuss*, 294–297.

32. Paquet to Heuss, 2.05.36; Mommsen to Heuss, 7.08.33, 7.15.33; Heuss to Baeumer, 3.31.33, 4.4.33, in NL Heuss, BAK: N 1221, #s 91, 88, 396; Ziegenfuss to Heile, 12.04.44, NL Heile, BAK: N 1132, #1; Heß,"Die deutsche Lage ist ungeheuer ernst geworden," 128–130; Burger, *Heuss*, 291–294, 387–390.

33. Heuss to Bäumer, 6.12.33; Würtenberg to Heuss, 5.5.33; Oppenheimer to Heuss, 5.19.34, in NL Heuss, BAK: N 1221, # 396; Froelich, *"Die Hilfe* im Nationalsozialismus," in Studt, ed., *"Diener des Staates,"* 117–118.

34. Oppenheimer to Heuss, 5.19.34 in NL Heuss, BAK: N 1221, #396. Also see articles by Heuss, August Weber, and Hermann Höpker-Aschoff, 1.06.34 *Die Hilfe*, 1.06.34, in NL Höpker-Aschoff, BAK: 1129, #9. Hüber, "Bäumer," 353–354, 361–369; Froelich, *"Die Hilfe* im Nationalsozialismus," in Studt, ed., *"Diener des Staates,"* 117–118; Wolf Volker Wiegand, *Walter Wilhelm Goetz*, Boppard: Harald Boldt, 1992, 311–321.

35. Undated (1933) letter from Hans Bott Verlag; Author to Heuss, 10.9.33; Brönner to Heuss, 12.19.33, in NL Heuss, BAK: 1221, #396.

36. Heuss to the Reichspropaganda Ministry (RPM), 8.22.34; RPM to Heuss, 9.13.34, 12.17.34, 12.22.34 in NL Heuss, BAK: 1221, #644.
37. Jahnke to RPM, 7.18.34; RPM to Heuss, 3.31.36; Gauß to Heuss, 10.01.36, in NL Heuss, BAK: N 1221, # 396; Steinweis, *Art*, 38–45, 174–175; Burger, *Heuss*, 309–313.
38. Savelkouls to Heuss, 2.05.34, in NL Heuss, BAK: N 1221, # 94.
39. Ursula Krey, "Der Naumann-Kreis: Charisma und politische Emanzipation," in Bruch, ed., *Naumann*, 143–145; Dahrendorff, *Heuss*, 262–269.
40. Letter to Heuss, 2.05.36; Heuss to Wagner (1934), in NL Heuss, BAK: N 1221, #s 604, 396; Burger, *Heuss*, 309–310; Pikart, ed., *Heuss*, 185–187.
41. Letter to Heuss, 2.25.35; RPM to Heuss, 9.22.36, in NL Heuss, BAK: N 1221, #s 604, 396; also see Froelich, "*Die Hilfe* im Nationalsozialismus," in Studt, ed., "*Diener des Staates*," 122–123.
42. Hans-Bott-Verlag to Heuss, 1.07.36, 10.2.36, in NL Heuss, BAK: N 1221, #s 604, 396
43. Witte to Heuss, 5.24.33, NL Heuss, BAK: 1221, # 396; Heß, "Die deutsche Lage ist ungeheuer ernst geworden," 128–134.
44. Ibid. Muehle to Heuss, 2.21.33; Schneck to Heuss, 8.17.34, in NL Heuss, BAK: 1221, # 643, #96; Meyer to Heuss (1937), in NL Heuss, BAK: N 1221, #88; Stolper, *Begenungen mit Theodor Heuss*, Tübingen, 1954, 445.
45. Schabel to Heuss, 8.17.34, NL Heuss, BAK: N 1221, #96.
46. Dibelius to Heuss, 2.04.36, 3.05.36, in NL Heuss, BAK: 1221, #396.
47. Heuss to Dietrich, 1.13.36, in NL Dietrich, BAK: N 1004, #146.
48. Letter to Heuss, 2.25.35, in NL Heuss, BAK: N 1221, #604; Schmidthals to Dietrich, 2.22.37, in NL Dietrich, BAK: N 1004, #155; Froelich, " 'Die Hilfe' im Nationalsozialismus," in Studt, ed., "*Diener des Staates*," 127–128.
49. Heuss to Dietrich, 1.13.36, in NL Dietrich, BAK: N 1004, #146; Froelich, "*Die Hilfe* im Nationalsozialismus," in Studt, ed., "*Diener des Staates*," 127–128; Scholtyseck, *Bosch*, 124, 342–343; Burger, *Heuss*, 301–304.
50. See correspondence between Heuss and RVDP from 1.16.36, 5.11.36, 4.05.37, in NL Heuss, BAK: N 1221, #76.
51. See letters from RVDP to Heuss, 12.20.33, 8.18.33, 1.29.34; Heuss to RVDP, 6.15.34, in NL Heuss, BAK: N 1221, #92.
52. See Heß, " 'Die Nazis haben gewußt,' " 152.
53. RVDP to Heuss, 1.16.36, 11.19.36, 4.05.37; Heuss to RVDP, 11.5.36, 2.11.37, 3.20.37, in NL Heuss, BAK: N 1221, #92; Burger, *Heuss*, 315–318; Pikart, ed., *Heuss*, 192–194.
54. Wordemann to Heuss, 1.31.40, in NL Heuss, BAK: N 1221, #399; also see Krey, "Der Naumann-Kreis," 145, Scholtyseck, *Bosch*, 350–351; Froelich, "*Die Hilfe* im Nationalsozialismus," in Studt, ed., "Diener des Staates," 124–128; Letter to Beckmann, 5.15.41, in Beckmann, ed., *Band*, 146–147.
55. Heß, "Die deutsche Lage ist ungeheuer ernst geworden," 130–136.
56. Quote taken from Lemmer, *Manches war doch Anders*, 195–202; also see Studt, ed., "*Diener des Staates*."
57. Luckemeyer. *Rebell*, 15–28, 79, 111–114.
58. Although the Nazis tried to ban art and literary criticism in the middle 1930s, here too most attempts to control mainstream culture were half-hearted at best. Mosse, *Nazi Culture*, 162–163; Steinweis, *Art*.
59. Heile review in *Berliner Volkszeitung*, 1.24.39, in NL Heile, BAK: N 1132, #13.
60. Heile review in BVZtg, 1.04.39, in NL Heile, BAK: N 1132, #13.
61. Heile review in BVZtg, 1.17.39, in NL Heile, BAK: N 1132, #13.
62. Heile review in BVZtg, 10.28.38, in NL Heile, BAK: N 1132, #13.
63. Heile review in BVZtg, 6.03.38, in NL Heile, BAK: N 1132, #13. For more on Hitler's fascination with Sherlock Holmes, see William Cook, "Holmes, Sweet Holmes", *New Statesman*, 8.26.02.
64. Heile review in *Berliner Volkszeitung*, 8.30.38, in NL Heile, BAK: N 1132, #13.
65. Luckemeyer, *Rebell*, 15–20.

66. Heile to Prüfer, 5.19.38, speech by Heile, 1.12.41; Heile to Östermann, 8.01.42, NL Heile, BAK: N 1132, #1.
67. Luckemeyer, *Rebell*, 114–115; Letter to Heile, 6.03.44, in NL Heile, BAK: N 1132, #1.
68. The liberal Erich Welkow privately eviscerated the low quality of film and theater in the Third Reich as "dumb, pointless and unpleasant" but refused to "hurl his spear!" publicly for economic reasons. Welkow contacted Dingeldey, for example, to suggest to the former People's Party chairman, who did not have financial concerns, to write a book on the theme of "autocracy and democracy." Such topics were more interesting than the "shit one writes for money." Welkow to Dingeldey, 9.01.37, 11.12.37, in NL Dingeldey, BAK: N 1002, #103.
69. Bethmann to Kardorff, 3.02.36, in NL S. von Kardorff, BAK: N 1040, #8.
70. Boetticher to Kardorff, 4.09.42, in NL S. von Kardorff, BAK: N 1040, #8.
71. See series of letters from Marguerite Bismarck to Kardorff, in NL S.V. Kardorff, BAK: N 1040, #8.
72. See Moldenhauer speech honoring Kardorff's birthday, 2.07.43; Meinecke to S.V. Kardorff, 4.05.43, in NL S. von Kardorff, BAK: N 1040, #5, #11.
73. von Bülow to S. von Kardorff, 4.19.43; Hoetzsch to Kardorff, 12.31.35, 3.14.43, in NL S.V. Kardorff, BAK: N 1040, #10.
74. Thilo Ramm, "Der Fehltritt der Frauenrechtlerin: Bemerkungen eines Juristen," *JzLF*, 17 (2005), 245.
75. Karl Jarres, review of "Unser Weg durch die Zeit," *Kölnische Zeitung*, 1.12.36.
76. Ibid. Review from *Hochland* (April 1936) in NL Höpker-Aschoff, BAK: NL 1129, #12.
77. Office of Deputy Führer (Hess) to Hans Bott, 5.19.36, in NL Höpker-Aschoff, BAK: NL 1129, #12.
78. See Lüders, *Das unbekannte Heer. Frauen kaempfen fuer Deutschland*, Berlin: E.S. Mittler & Sohn, 1936; Lüders to Under, 10.18.36, NL Lüders, BAK: N 1151, #326.
79. Ibid.
80. Scholtyseck, *Bosch*, 351.
81. Schiffer to Gerland, 4.14.36, in NL Gerland, BAK: N 1010, #21.
82. Lüders to Velthuysen, 4.01.41; Velthuysen to Lüders, 5.05.41, in NL Lüders, BAK: N 1151, #326.
83. Schmid, *Nationalsozialistische Kulturpolitik*, 459–476; Sassin, *Liberale*, 376–377.
84. For more detail on the truly remarkable collection of politicians and intellectuals who participated in the Naumann circle, see Heuss, *Erinnerungen*, 28–64; Krey, "Der Naumann-Kreis," 128–144.
85. Kurlander, *Price*, 83–84, 111–112; Sell, *Die Tragödie* 286–298, 361–362; Sheehan, *German Liberalism*, 258–283; Langewiesche, *Liberalism*, 7–11; Frye, *Democrats*, 6–20, 88–101.
86. Krey, "Der Naumann-Kreis", 115–119.
87. See the numerous letters of Stapel to Heuss, BAK: N 1221, #98. Also see Heinrich Kessler, *Wilhelm Stapel: Als Politischer Publizist*, Nürnberg: Lorenz Spindler, 1967.
88. See letters Schwander to Heuss, 1939–42, in NL Heuss, BAK: N 1221, #97.
89. Letter to Heuss, 6.26.36, NL Heuss, BAK: N 1221, #644.
90. See excerpt from Heuss, *Erinnerungen*, in Pikart, ed., *Heuss*, 179–180; also see Steven D. Korenblatt, "A School for the Republic: Cosmopolitans and their Enemies at the Deutsche Hochschule für Politik, 1920–1933", *CEH*, 39 (2006), 394–430.
91. According to Heuss, "Spengler's preparing the way for the present political situation in Germany can not easily be overestimated, for his formulations made the liveliest impression on the academic youth in the early twenties." Heuss to Reck-Malleczewen, 5.16.36. NL Heuss, BAK: N 1221, #92; Heuss to Boene, 4.03.39, in NL Heuss, BAK: N 1221, #399.
92. J. Naumann to Heuss, 2.06.37, 5.07.38; Loew to Heuss, 1.24.35, 12.12.37, in NL Heuss, BAK: N 1221, #643.

93. Scholtyseck, *Bosch*, 349–351; Barthold C. Witte, "Theodor Heuss und Naumanns Nachleben in der Bundesrepublik Deutschland," in Bruch, ed., *Friedrich Naumann*, 361–362, 366.
94. Letter to Bahner, 10.12.37, in NL Heuss, BAK: N 1221, #73; Burger, *Heuss*, 323–324; Krey, "Der Naumann-Kreis," in Bruch, ed., *Friedrich Naumann*, 118.
95. Heuss, *Naumann*, 7. Also see Geoff Eley and James Retallack, eds, *Wilhelminism and its Legacies: German Modernities, Imperialism, and the Meanings of Reform, 1890–1930 – Essays for Hartmut Pogge von Strandemann*, New York: Berghahn, 2003.
96. Heuss, *Naumann*, 106–108.
97. Witte, "Theodor Heuss," in Bruch, ed., *Naumann*, 366–367.
98. Heuss, *Naumann*, 28–32.
99. Ibid., 113.
100. Ibid., 197; Hans Cymorek, "Das Werdende schon erleben, ehe es geworden ist," *JzLF*, 15 (2003), 133–145.
101. Heuss, *Naumann*, 198.
102. Ibid., 537.
103. Ibid., 527.
104. BAK: N 1221, #399, letters from Johannes Naumann to Heuss, 3.01.33, 4.11.35.
105. Alfred Weber to Heuss, 1.08.36, 1.25.37, 8.17.37, 7.26.45, in NL Heuss, BAK: N 1221, #103.
106. Schweizer to Heuss, 8.09.38, in NL Heuss, BAK: N 1221, #97.
107. Letter from Sachverlag für Wirtschafts- und Steuerrecht, 1.08.38, BAK: N 1221, #399.
108. Paula Anderson to Heuss, March 1938; Haebler to Heuss, 11.18.38; Liebmann to Heuss, 12.24.37; Sachverlag für Wirtschafts und Steuerrecht to Heuss, 1.10.38; Roser to Heuss, 12.28.37; Heuss to Tilgner, 12.13.37, in NL Heuss, BAK: N 1221, #s 398–399.
109. See excerpts from Hans Rothfels, Toni Stolper, Albert Schweizer, etc., in Bott, ed., *Begegnungen*, 386–387, 439–442; Naumann to Heuss, 6.10.37; Goetz to Heuss, 12.21.37; Bosch to Heuss, 12.31.37; Heile to Heuss, January 1938, in Pikart, ed., *Heuss*, 215–217; Boene to Heuss, 4.3.39; Woldt to Heuss, 1.23.41; Pechel to Heuss, 11.2.37, 5.2.39; Reichsarchiv to Heuss, 2.9.43, 3.09.43; Schoepflin to Heuss, 7.8.39; Stotz to Heuss, 2.11.38; Vossler to Heuss, 1.2.40; *Königsberger Tageblatt* to Heuss, 4.13.38. NL Heuss, BAK: N 1221, #399, #102, #92, #643.
110. Bäumer, *DF*, 3/38.
111. Nestle to Heuss, 2.20.38, 10.19.42; Heuss to Nestle, 12.05.42;10.19.42. NL Heuss, BAK: N 1221, #90.
112. Kaefer to Heuss, 5.14.41, BAK: N 1221, #643; Heuss, *Naumann*, 7.
113. Willinger to Gothein, 4.02.35. in NL Gothein, N 1006, #34.
114. Evans, *Power*, 241–242, 247–248.
115. See Richard Steigman-Gall, *The Holy Reich: Nazi Conceptions of Christianity, 1919–1945*, Cambridge: Cambridge University Press, 2003; Daniel Goldhagen, *A Moral Reckoning: The Role of the Catholic Church in the Holocaust and its Unfulfilled Duty of Repair*, New York: Vintage, 2003; Lewy, *The Catholic Church*; Kershaw, *Popular Opinion and Political Dissent in Bavaria, 1933–1945*, New York: Oxford, 1983; also see Binder, *Irrtum und Widerstand*; Jonathan Wright, *"Above Parties": The Political Attitudes of the German Protestant Church Leadership*, New York: Oxford University Press, 1974. For earlier, less critical work on the Christian "resistance" see, for example, John Conway, *The Nazi Persecution of the Churches, 1933–1954*, London: Weidenfeld & Nicolson, 1968; Ernst Wolf, *Die evangelischen Kirchen und der Staat im Dritten Reich*, Zürich: EVZ, 1963; Heinrich Huber, *Dokumente einer christlichen Widerstands-Bewegung: Gegen die Entfernung der Kruzifixe aus den Schulen*, Munich: Schnell & Steiner, 1948; Heinrich Hermelink, *Kirche im Kampf: Dokumente des Widerstands und des Aufbaus in der evangelischen Kirche Deutschlands von 1933 bis 1945*, Tübingen: R. Wunderlich, 1950.
116. David Blackbourn, *Marpingen: Apparitions of the Virgin Mary in a Nineteenth-Century German Village*, New York: Knopf, 1994, 85–92.

117. Margit Gottert in Meurer, *Marianne Weber*, 126, 146–150, 171; Bäumer to Marianne Weber, Berlin, 5.23.36. Beckman ed., *Band*, 92.
118. "The Nazi attraction to Protestantism was . . . often predicated on the same things that Protestants themselves heavily emphasized . . . the most enthusiastic of which were of a theologically liberal mien; it was also visible in the Nazi conception of the nonconfessional school, a means of bridging Germany's confessional divide that had first been devised by Kulturprotestanten for remarkably similar reasons." Steigmann-Gall, *Reich*, 85; also see Matthew D. Hockenos, *A Church Divided: German Protestants Confront the Nazi Past*, Bloomington: Indiana University Press, 2004, 15–17.
119. The relationship between Protestantism and Nazism, Shelley Baranowski observes, was one of "negotiation and coexistence rather than confrontation . . . not the unqualified rejection of National Socialism extinguished only by massive repression . . . but rather a series of occasional, partial and circumscribed acts directed towards limited ends." Baranowski, *The Confessing Church*, 4; Hübinger, *Kulturprotestantismus*; Matthias Wolfes, "Die Demokratiefähigkeit liberaler Theologen: Ein Beitrag zum Verhältnis des Protestantismus zur Weimarer Republik," in Bruch, ed., *Friedrich Naumann*; see Rohrbach, *Handschrift*, 407–408; Hockenos, *A Church Divided*, 15–19.
120. Hockenos, *A Church Divided*, 23–28.
121. Lindsay, *Covenanted Solidarity: The Theological Basis of Karl Barth's Opposition to Nazi Antisemitism and the Holocaust*, New York: Peter Lang, 2001, 249–251; Hockenos, *A Church Divided*, 172–173.
122. Wolfes, "Die Demokratiefähigkeit," in Bruch, ed., *Friedrich Naumann*, 295–299; Heuss to Dibelius, 3.15.33, in NL Heuss, BAK: N 1221, #76.
123. Bäumer, "Zum Schicksal des Christentums," *DF*, 4/34.
124. See Marianne Weber, "Drei zeitgeborene Fragen über Christentum und der Welt," *DF*, 3/40; Bäumer to Beckmann, 8.13.41, in Beckmann, ed., *Band*, 153; Konrad Löw, *Die Schuld. Christen und Juden im nationalsozialistischen und heutigen Urteil*, Gräfeling, 2002, 142–144.
125. Bäumer to Beckmann, 11.25.43, in Beckmann, ed., *Band*, 212.
126. For more on Himmler's hostile views on Christianity, see Himmler speech, 6.09.42, in Noakes and Pridham, eds, *Nazism, 1919–1945, Vol. 2: State, Economy and Society 1933–1939*, Exeter: Exeter, 2000, 304. Bäumer to Beckmann, 8.13.41, in Beckmann, ed., *Band*, 153.
127. Letter from Heuss to Dibelius, 3.15.33, in NL Heuss, BAK: N 1221, #76. Dibelius, after Ernst Troeltsch the foremost theologian in the DDP, "engaged willingly in informal propagandizing for the new regime" and belonged "to the group of theologians who because of their nationalism and disillusionment with the Weimar Republic had recognized that 'Germany was National Socialist and must remain National Socialist.' " Remy, *Myth*, 36–37, 110, 234–235. Also see Ingrid Wurtzbacher-Rundholz, ed., *Theodor Heuss über Staat und Kirche 1933 bis 1946- mit Materialenanhang über Konkordatsfragen 1927*, Frankfurt: P. Lang, 1986, 20–21; Dahrendorff, *Heuss*, 256; Heuss to Bäumer, 11.30.33, in NL Heuss, BAK: N 1221, #396.
128. Williger to Gothein, 7.03.33, in NL Gothein, BAK: N 1006, #34.
129. Neumann, *Tantzen*, 208–215.
130. Ehrich to Heuss, 3.24.35, in NL Heuss, BAK: N 1221, #76; Heuss to Riethmüller, 11.25.33, in NL Heuss, BAK: N 1221, #93; Heuss to Erdmann, 12.05.34, in NL Heuss, BAK: N 1221, #77.
131. Williger to Gothein, 5.07.35, 7.04.35, 2.10.37, 8.13.37, in NL Gothein, BAK: N 1006, #24; Kershaw, *Nemesis*, 40–42, 663–667; Burleigh, *Third Reich*, 712–728; Hockenos, *A Church Divided*, 28–30.
132. Schacht, *Rede des Reichbankpräsidenten und beauftragten Reichswirtschaftsminister Hjalmar Schacht auf der Deutschen Ostmesse. Königsberg, am 18. August 1935*. Berlin: Druckerei der Reichsbank, 1935.

133. Scholtyseck, *Bosch*, 164–167.
134. Sassin, *Liberale*, 184–185, 276–284.
135. Dietrich to Wittig, 9.01.37, in NL Dingeldey, BAK: N 1002, #95; Scholtyseck, *Bosch*, 165–167.
136. Kardorff to Frodel, 4.24.37; Galen telegrams/letters from 7.14.41, 7.17.41, 7.22.41, in NL K. von Kardorff-Oheimb, BAK: N 1039, #9a, #53.
137. Steigmann-Gall, *Reich*, 112–113, 153–155.
138. Huch to Baum, 7.24.44, in Baum, ed., *Briefe an Freunde*, Zürich: Manesse, 1986, 391; Matthias Wolfes, "Die Demokratiefähigkeit," in Bruch, ed., *Friedrich Naumann*, 293–294; Steigmann-Gall, *Reich*, 156, 216–218; Mosse, *Nazi Culture*, 262–263; Froelich, "*Die Hilfe* im Nationalsozialismus," in Studt, ed., "*Diener des Staates*," 120–121.
139. Baum, *Rückblick*, 290–292.
140. These included Gertrud Bäumer, Ernst Lemmer, Marie Baum, Otto Nuschke, and Karl Brammer, to name a few. See Theo Rütten, *Der deutsche Liberalismus 1945 bis 1955*, Baden-Baden: Nomos, 1984.
141. Sassin, *Liberale*, 275.
142. Ingo Haar, *Historiker im Nationalsozialismus. Deutsche Geschichtswissenschaft und der "Volkstumskampf" im Osten*, Göttingen: Vandenhoeck & Ruprecht, 2000, 361–367.
143. Remy, *Myth*, 1.
144. Ibid., 10–11. See essays in Schulze and Oexle, eds, *Deutsche Historiker im Nationalsozialismus*, Michael Fahlbusch, *Wissenschaft im Dienst der nationalsozialistischen Politik? Die "Volksdeutschen Forschungsgemeinschaften" von 1931–1945*, Baden-Baden: Nomos, 1999, 20–21, 785–788; Haar, *Historiker*, 11–12, 71–72.
145. "Despite looming defeat and increasing physical and material hardships," writes Steven Remy, "there is little evidence of opposition by university professors or students at Heidelberg or elsewhere (with the glaring exception of the 'White Rose' group in Munich)." Remy, *Myth*, 110; Fahlbusch, *Wissenschaft*, 788; Blomert, *Intellektuelle im Aufbruch*, 7–12; Haar, *Historiker*, 199–203.
146. Sassin und Erkens, eds, *Dokumente*, 377; Weigand, *Goetz*, 311–341.
147. Remy, *Myth*, 10–11; Mosse, *Nazi Culture*, 263–269; NSDAP to Gerland, 10.30.35, 12.07.35, in NL Gerland, BAK: N 1010, #12.
148. Blomert, *Intellektuelle in Aufbruch*, 7; Volker Kruse in Eberhard Demm, ed., *Geist und Politik im 20. Jahrhundert. Gesammelte Aufsätze zu Alfred Weber*, Frankfurt: P. Lang, 2000, 207–208; E. Demm, ed., *Soziologie, Politik und Kultur: Von Alfred zur Frankfurtschule*, Frankfurt: Lang, 2003, 8–13.
149. Peter Molt, "Der Beitrag Alfred Webers zur Begründung der Politikwissenschaft in Deutschland," in Demm, ed., *Geist und Politik im 20. Jahrhundert*, 236–237.
150. Blomert, *Intellektuelle in Aufbruch*, 16; Molt, "Der Beitrag Alfred Webers," in Demm, ed., *Geist und Politik im 20. Jahrhundert*, 238–242.
151. See Demm, *Von der Weimarer Republik zur Bundesrepublik*, 221–22; Fritz Ringer, *The Decline of the German Mandarins: The German Academic Community*, Hanover: Wesleyan University Press, 1969, 186–187; ibid., 186–187, 418–423.
152. Blomert, *Intellektuelle in Aufbruch*, 308–309.
153. Demm, *Politische Weg*, 223.
154. For these reasons, among others, Heuss would politely urge Andreas to retire in 1947. Remy, *Myth*, 28; Blomert, *Intellektuelle in Aufbruch*, 19; Andreas to Heuss, 11.07.34, 7.26.38; Heuss to Andreas, 7.18.47, in NL Heuss, BAK: N 1221, #72.
155. Letter to the editor of *Volksgemeinschaft*, 3.08.33, in NL Weber, BAK: N 1197, #32.
156. Letter to the editor of *Volksgemeinschaft*, 3.11.33, in NL Weber, BAK: N 1197, #32.
157. Remy, *Myth*, 28; Demm, *Politische Weg*, 225–229.
158. Demm, *Politische Weg*, 226.
159. Letter from Heidelberg to Weber, 4.18.33, Wagner to Weber, 4.27.33, in NL Weber, BAK: N 1197, #32.

160. Demm, *Politische Weg*, 227–229; Blomert, *Intellektuelle in Aufbruch*, 329–330.
161. Demm, *Politische Weg*, 224.
162. See Weber's handwritten response, 3.13.33; article titled "Der gleichberechtigte Bürger Weber," in the *Volksgemeinschadt*, 3.15.33, in NL Weber, BAK: N 1197, #32.
163. Remy, *Myth*, 21.
164. Weigand, *Goetz*, 311–321.
165. Demm, *Politische Weg*, 234–5; Demm, ed., *Alfred Weber, Politische Theorie und Tagespolitik (1903–1933)*. Marburg: Metropolis, 1999, 4–6; Welkow to Dingeldey, 6.26.33, in NL Dingeldey, BAK: N 1002, #1003.
166. Dingeldey to Wittig, 11.05.37, in NL Dingeldey, BAK: N 1002, # 95.
167. Willinger to Gothein, 3.08.34, 7.20.34, in NL Gothein, BAK: N 1006, #34.
168. Undated letter [1947]; letter to Heuss: 1.3.44, in NL Heuss, BAK: N 1221, #48, #101.
169. Baum, *Rückblick*, 264–280; Baum, "Gedanken zu Ernst Jüngers Werk," *DF*, 11/37.
170. Baum, ed., *Briefe* 240–246; James Skidmore, *The Trauma of Defeat: Ricarda Huch's Historiography during the Weimar Republic*, Frankfurt: P. Lang, 2005.
171. Baum, ed., *Briefe*, 290–296, 310–326.
172. NSDAP to Gerland, 10.30.35, 12.07.35; also see ample correspondence between Schiffer and Gerland, 1.07.29 to 12.26.41, in NL Gerland, BAK: N 1010, #12, #21.
173. Walter Goetz, *Historiker in meiner Zeit*, Cologne: Böhlau, 1957, 77–87, 259–263.
174. Weigand, *Goetz*, 312–315.
175. Ibid., 315–324.
176. Walter Goetz, *Die Rassenforschung*, in *Archiv für Kulturforschung* 22, 1932, 1; Otto Aichel, "Die Rassenforschung. Bemerkungen zu dem gleichnamigen Aufsatz von Walter Goetz," in *AfK* 22, 1932, 372; Walter Goetz, *Nachwort*, in *AfK* 22, 1932, 379; Goetz, *Intuition in der Geschichtswissenschaft*, München: C.H. Beck, 1935; Goetz, *Geschichte der deutschen Dante-Gesellschaft und der deutschen Dante-Forschung*, Weimar: Bohlau, 1940; Weigand, *Goetz*, 324–341; Burger, *Heuss*, 308.
177. Christopher Corneissen, "Die wiedererstandene Historismus – Nationalgeschichte in der Bundesrepublik der funfziger Jahre," in Konrad Jarausch and Martin Sabrow, eds, *Die historische Meisterzählung – Deutungslinien deutscher Nationalgeschichte nach 1945*, Göttingen, Vandenhoeck & Ruprecht, 2002; Remy, *Myth*, 23; also see Fahlbusch, *Wissenschaft*, 1999; Haar, *Historiker*; Klaus Hornung, *Hans Rothfels und die Nationalitätfragen in Ostmitteleuropa, 1926–1934*, Bonn: Kulturstiftung der deutschen Vertriebene, 2001; Notker Hammerstein, *Antisemitismus und die deutsche Universitäten, 1871–1933*, Frankfurt: Campus, 1995.
178. "The strong maintenance of collective resistance of all instructors would have been useful against the destruction of the self-administration of the universities and the arbitrary dismissal of numerous non-Aryan colleagues." Baum, *Rückblick*, 276–278.
179. See *Rundschreiben*, Otto Stoffregen to RVDP, 8.18.33; Stauß to Heuss, 12.02.39, in NL Heuss, BAK: N 1221, #92, #99; Heß, " 'Die Nazis haben gewußt,'" 148–151.
180. Deutsche Presse to Heuss, 11.18.38, NL Heuss, BAK: N 1221, #76; Kershaw, *Hitler: Nemesis*, 45–59.
181. RVDP to Heuss, 3.17.39, in NL Heuss, BAK: N 1221, #92; Walter von Keudell, 4.12.1939, in *Theodor Heuss, Der Mann, das Werk, die Zeit. Eine Ausstellung*, Tübingen, 1967, p. 222.
182. RSK to Heuss, 1.11.41, 2.08.41, in NL Heuss, BAK: N 1221, #92.
183. Heuss to Riezler 2.05.41, in NL Heuss, BAK: N 1221, #643.
184. Heuss to "Parteiamtliche Prüfungskommission zum Schutze des Nationalsozialistischen Schriftums", 2.14.41, in NL Heuss, BAK: N 1221, #92.
185. Article by Heuss on Poelzig's resignation, 2.04.33; Harvard University to Heuss, 5.2.38, in NL Heuss, BAK: N 1221, #s 46, 643. See "Vorwort zur Neue Ausgabe," in Heuss, *Hans Poelzig: Das Lebensbild eines deutschen Baumeisters*, Tübingen: Ernst Wasmuth, 1948.

186. Dahrendorff, *Heuss*, 245–248; Eberhard Pikart, ed., *Heuss: Aufzeichnungen*, 13–14.
187. NS Reichsleitung to Heuss, 4.24.41, Parteiliche Pruefungskommission zum Schutz des Nationalsozialistischen Schrifttums to Heuss [1941]; correspondence between Heuss and RVDP, 12.05.36, 2.11.37, 3.26.37, 5.13.41; RSK to Heuss, 3.01.41, in NL Heuss, BAK: N 1221, #s 643, 92.
188. Pikart, ed., *Heuss: Aufzeichnungen* 1945–1947, 13–14; Pikart, ed., *Heuss*, 197–198.
189. Heuss to Nestle, 12.05.42; Heuss to *Neuen Schau*, 11.27.42; Heuss to Gestapo, 7.18.42; Gestapo to Heuss, 9.19.42, in NL Heuss, BAK: N 1221, #s 90, 643.
190. See Werner Stephan, *Joseph Goebbels: Daemon einer Diktatur*, Stuttgart: Union, 1949, 9–11; Witte, "Liberaler in schwierigen Zeiten," 243–247.
191. Correspondence between Heuss and RVDP, 4.17.42, 7.12.42, in NL Heuss, BAK: N 1221, #92.
192. Dahrendorff, *Heuss*, 288. Heuss to *Neue Schau*, 11.27.42; *Neue Schau* to Heuss, 4.5.43, in NL Heuss, BAK: N 1221, #90; Beck to Heuss, 1.20.41, 6.13.44; Stenger to Heuss, 5.25.42; Societäts-Verlag to Heuss, 12.17.42, in BAK: N 1221, #s 73, 99, 644.
193. Heuss to Allmers, 5.01.42, in NL Heuss, BAK: N 1221, #72; Bosch to Heuss, 3.04.42; Heuss to Bosch, 3.06.42, in Pikart, ed., *Heuss*, 225–226; Scholtyseck, *Bosch*, 349–352.
194. Scholtyseck, *Bosch*, 353–354.
195. Reclam Verlag to Heuss, 3.23.43, in NL Heuss, BAK: N 1221, #92; Pikart, ed., *Heuss: Aufzeichnungen*, 13–16.
196. Gillessen, *Posten*, 131, 437, 505–518; Burger, *Heuss*, 353–358.
197. Heuss to RVDP, 6.09.42; Frankfurter Sol. Druckerei to Heuss, 2.14.40; Reichspropaganda Ministry (RPM) to Heuss, 6.25.42, Heuss to Verlag Philipp Reclam, 3.23.43, in NL Heuss, BAK: N 1221, #s 99, 643.
198. See Heuss articles, 3.09.43, 8.19.43, 6.16.43, 3.30.43, 7.18.44; *Frankfurter Zeitung* (*FrZtg*) to Heuss, 12.01.41; Heuss to *FrZtg* 4.01.42, on Dante Gesellschaft, 2.22.40; on Joseph Wirth, 7.05.41, in NL Heuss, BAK: N 1221, #s 46, 47, 644.; Burger, *Heuss*, 358–376.
199. Frankfurter Soc. Druckerei to Heuss, 9.22.43, in NL Heuss, BAK: N 1221, #92; NL Heuss, BAK: N 1221; Gillessen, *Posten*, 485–489; Hummerich, *Wahrheit zwischen den Zeilen*, 84–91.
200. RVDP to Heuss, April 1944, in NL Heuss, BAK: N 1221, #92.
201. Heuss to *Neue Wiener Tageblatt*, 4.28.44, Schoepflin to Heuss, 4.29.44, in NL Heuss, BAK: N 1221, #88, #102.
202. Firm Melliand Textilberichte to Heile, 11.20.44, in NL Heile, BAK: N 1132, #1; Heuss, *Aufzeichnungen 1945–1947*, 16–17.
203. Ziegenfuss to Heile, 3.14.44, 12.04.44, NL Heile, BAK: N 1132, #1.
204. Sissi Brentano to Heuss, 11.22.44, in NL Heuss, BAK: N 1221, #644.
205. Max Wiessner of Deutscher Verlag (Berlin) to Heile [late 1944] in NL Heile, BAK: N 1132, #1.
206. Sassin, *Liberale*, 18–19.
207. Schecker, "Die Eingliederung der Jugend in die Volksgemeinschaft," *DF*, 3/33; Welkow to Dingeldey, 8.14.37, NL Dingeldey, BAK: 1002, #103; Heuss articles, 2.09.46, 2.15.46, in NL Heuss, BAK: N 1221, #48.
208. Bäumer, "Bilanz 1934," *DF*, 1/35.
209. Wittig to Dingeldey, 9.01.37, 11.03.37, in NL Dingeldey, BAK: N 1002, #95; Schmidt, *Kulturpolitik*, 459–476; Tooze, *Ökonomie*, 375–379, 748–754.
210. See again Steinweis, *Art*; Huener and Nicosia, eds, *The Arts in Nazi Germany*; Zimmermann, *Medien*.
211. Emmy Beckmann, "Entwicklungen in der dramatischen Dichtung seit der Jahrhundert-wende," *DF*, 6/35, in NL Bäumer, BAK: N 1076, #5; Heuss to G. Schultze-Pfaelzer, 6.08.37, 6.16.37, in NL Heuss, BAK: N 1221, #97.
212. Hans-Bott-Verlag to Heuss, 7.04.33, NL Heuss, BAK: N 1221, #396.

213. Remy, *Myth*, 110–111.
214. Sassin, *Liberale*, 17–20, 247–248; also see Ralf Dahrendorf, *Society and Democracy in Germany*, New York: Doubleday, 1967.

Chapter Three: "The Woman" in the Third Reich

1. See Adelheid von Saldern, "Victims or Perpetrators? Controversies about the Role of Women in the Nazi State," in Christian Leitz, ed., *The Third Reich*, Oxford: Blackwell, 1999, 207–228; Stephenson, *Women*; Gisela Bock, *Zwangssterilisation im Nationalsozialismus: Studien zur Rassenpolitik und Frauenpolitik*, Opladen: Westdeutscher, 1986; Ann Taylor Allen, *Feminism and Motherhood in Germany*, New Brunswick: Rutgers University Press, 1991, 230–234. For a summary of this debate, see Attina Grossmann, "Feminist Debates about Women and National Socialism," *Gender & History*, 3 (Autumn 1991), 350–358.
2. See von Saldern, "Victims or Perpetrators?" 207–228; Koonz, *Mothers*; Evans, *Movement*; Barbara Greven-Aschoff, *Die bürgerliche Frauenbewegung in Deutschland 1894–1933*, Göttingen: Vandenhoeck & Ruprecht, 1981; Ute Planert, *Antifeminismus im Kaiserreich: Diskurs, soziale Formation und politische Mentalität*, Göttingen: Vandenhoeck & Ruprecht, 1998. Also see assorted essays in Renate Bridenthal, Atina Grossman, and Marion Kaplan, eds, *When Biology was Destiny*, New York: Monthly Review, 1984.
3. Kirsten Heinsohn, Barbara Vogel, and Ulrike Weckel, eds, *Zwischen Karriere und Verfolgung. Handlungsräume von Frauen im nationalsozialistischen Deutschland*, Frankfurt: Campus, 1997; Ilse Boroth and Barbara Serloth, eds, *Gebroche Kontinuitäten? Zur Rolle und Bedeutung der Geschlechtsverhältnisse in der Entwicklung des Nationalsozialismus*. Innsbruck: Studienverlag, 2000; Repp, *Reformers*; Wildenthal, *German Women*; Kathleen Canning, *Languages and Labor of Gender*, Ann Arbor: Michigan University Press, 2002; Kevin Passmore, *Women, Gender and Fascism, 1919–1945*, Manchester: Manchester University Press, 2003.
4. See Renate Bridenthal and Claudia Koonz, "Beyond *Kinder, Küche, Kirche*: Weimar Women in Politics and Work"; Attina Grossman, "Abortion and Economic Crisis: The 1931 Campaign Against Paragraph 218"; Elisabeth Meyer-Renschhausen, "The Bremen Morality Scandal"; Renate Bridenthal, " 'Professional' Housewives: Stepsisters of the Women's Movement," in *Destiny*, 33–108; also see Greven-Aschoff, *Frauenbewegung*; Heide-Marie Lauterer, *Parlamentarierinnen in Deutschland 1918/19–1949*, Königstein: Ulrike Helmer, 2002; Raffael Scheck, *Mothers of the Nation: Right-Wing Women in Weimar Germany*, Oxford: Berg, 2004; Julia Sneeringer, *Winning Women's Votes: Propaganda and Politics in Weimar Germany*, Chapel Hill, N.C.: University of North Carolina Press, 2002.
5. Ibid.; see also Edward Ross Dickinson, "Biopolitics, Fascism, Democracy: Some Reflections on Our Discourse about Modernity," *CEH*, 37 (2004), 1–46; Detlev Peukert, *The Weimar Republic*, 208–235; Repp, *Reformers*, 104–138, 300–312; Heide-Marie Lauterer, *Liebestätigkeit für die Volksgemeinschaft*, Göttingen: Vandenhoeck & Ruprecht, 1994; Ute Planert, ed., *Nation, Politik und Geschlecht. Frauenbewegungen und Nationalismus in der Moderne*, Frankfurt: Campus, 2000; Robert G. Moeller, *Protecting Motherhood: Women and the Family in Postwar Germany*, Berkeley: University of California Press, 1993, 8–20, 122–141; Crew, *Germans on Welfare*, 147–148; Hung, *Welfare*, 249–250.
6. Saldern, "Victims or Perpetrators?" For early work on the ambivalent nature of women's engagement after 1933, see Angelika Ebbinghaus, ed., *Opfer und Täterinnen: Frauenbiographien des Nationalsozialismus*, Nordlingen: Greno, 1987.
7. Evans, *Movement*, 153–158; Huber, *Bäumer*, 120–127.

8. Schaser, *Lange und Bäumer*; Margit Göttert, *Macht und Eros. Frauenbeziehungen und weibliche Kultur um 1900. Eine neue Perspektive auf Helene Lange und Gertrud Bäumer*, Königstein: Ulrike Helmer 2000; Repp, *Reformers*, 108–115.

9. Quidde to Naumann, 6.11.15; Naumann to Quidde, 6.11.17, in NL Naumann, BAB: N 3001, #23; Evans, *Movement*, 130–135, 166–167.

10. Evans, *Movement*, 153–158; Huber, *Bäumer*, 123–125; Greven-Aschoff, *Frauenbewegung*, 192–194.

11. Caroline Hopf, *Frauenbewegung und Pädagogik: Gertrud Bäumer zum Beispiel*, Bad Heilbrunn: Julius Klinkhardt, 1997, 227–235; Göttert, *Macht und Eros*.

12. See Repp, *Reformers*; Schaser, *Lange und Bäumer*, 314–332; Schaser, "Innere Emigration" als 'konformer Widerstand'. Gertrud Bäumer 1933 bis 1945," *Ariadne*, 32 (1997); Schaser, "Gertrud Bäumer, eine der wildesten Demokratinnen oder verhinderte Nationalsozialistin?" in Heinsohn, Vogel, and Weckel, eds, *Zwischen Karriere und Verfolgung*, 16–43; Greven-Aschoff, *Frauenbewegung*, 188–189.

13. Evans, *Movement*, 259–260; Greven-Aschoff, *Frauenbewegung*, 186.

14. Those Fascists who considered everything in the Weimar constitution an "error of baseless liberalism," Bäumer announced in March 1933, were equally mistaken in viewing "man as the single carrier of all decisive state power." See Bäumer article "Die Frauen in der Volks- und Staatskrisis," *DF*, 3/33, in NL Bäumer, BAK: N 1076, #13.

15. Greven-Aschoff, *Frauenbewegung*, 186; Repp, *Reformers*, 105–147; Canning, *Languages*, 170–217. See also Herzog, *Sex after Fascism*.

16. According to the *Evangelischen Frauenzeitung*, "We do not oppose National Socialism as a party, but only in its position vis-à-vis the woman." Greven-Aschoff, *Frauenbewegung*, 188. See essays in Stephanie Gilmore, *Historical Perspectives on Second-Wave Feminism in the United States*, Champaign: Illinois, 2008; Estelle B. Freedman, *No Turning Back: The History of Feminism and the Future of Women*, London: Ballantine, 2003.

17. Kathleen Canning, *Gender History in Practice*, Ithaca, N.Y.: Cornell University Press, 50–51.

18. Evans, *Movement*, 259–260.

19. See Gertrude Baumbart, "Vom Bildungsziel der Frau im Lichte des Nationalsozialismus und der Frauenbewegung" in *DF*, 11/33, in NL Bäumer, BAK: N 1076, #13.

20. Marianne Weber, "Persönliche Existenz und überpersonale Verantwortlichkeit"; Bäumer, "Ausstellung Berlin," *DF*, 11/33.

21. Bäumer, "Panik über den Frauenberufen," *DF*, 11/33.

22. Witte, "Liberaler in schwierigen Zeiten," 247.

23. See Gertrud Bäumer, *Im Licht der Erinnerung*, Tübingen: R. Wunderlich, 1953, 9–12, 138–164.

24. Huber, *Bäumer*, 30–34, 94–95; Schaser, *Lange und Bäumer*, 85–88.

25. Repp, *Reformers*, 108–115.

26. Bäumer, *Die soziale Idee*, 9.

27. See Faßbender, "Briefwechsel," 150–152; also see Gertrud Lohmann, *Friedrich Naumanns Deutscher Sozialismus*, Berlin: J. Särchen, 1935; Hans Voelter, *Friedrich Naumann und der deutsche Sozialismus*, Heilbronn: E. Salzer, 1950; Gertrud Theodor, *Friedrich Naumann*, Berlin: Rütten & Loerning, 1957.

28. "Pulled back and forth between individualistic motives and social motives of diverse shades, they [social theorists] have still not arrived at a unified and well-founded 'social ethos' and cultural policy." Bäumer, *Die soziale Idee*, 7.

29. Canning, *Languages*, 190; Repp, *Reformers*, 147.

30. Schaser, *Lange und Bäumer*, 92–115; Schaser, " 'Corpus mysticum.' Die Nation bei Gertrud Bäumer," in Frauen & Geschichte Baden-Württemberg, eds, *Frauen und Nation*, Tübingen: Silberburg, 1996, 118–132, 245–250; also see Bäumer, *Die soziale Idee*; G. Bäumer, *Die Frau in der Kulturbewegung der Gegenwart*, Wiesbaden: J.F. Bergmann, 1904; Helene Lange and Gertrud Bäumer, eds, *Die Handbuch der Frauenbewegung*, Berlin: W. Moeser, 1901.

31. Bäumer, *Die seelische Krisis*, Berlin: Herbig, 1924, 10, 17.

32. Bäumer, *Krisis*, 27, 33.

33. Huber, *Bäumer*, 351–355.

34. Bäumer, *Krisis*, 140–141.

35. Hüber, *Bäumer*, 148–169, 353–357; Greven-Aschoff, *Frauenbewegung*, 186.

36. "The German people are called upon to make decisions over general trends in plebiscitary fashion, but not over clearly articulated political questions." See Bäumer article, "Die Frauen in der Volks- und Staatskrisis," *DF*, 3/33, in NL Bäumer, BAK: N 1076, #13: Pikart, ed., *Heuss*, 178–179.

37. Marie Luise Bach, *Biographische Daten und Texte zu einem Persönlichkeitsbild*, Weinheim: Deutscher Studien Verlag, 1989, 4–5; also see Bäumer article "Die Frauen in der Volks- und Staatskrisis," *DF*, 3/33.

38. In the April 1932 presidential election, "women voted 56% for Hindenburg (versus 48% of the men), 33.6% for Hitler (versus 35.9 % of the men) and approximately 10.4 % for Thaelmann as opposed to 15.4% of the men." Bäumer, *Der neue Weg der deutsche Frau*, Stuttgart: Deutsche Verlags-Anstalt, 1946, 30–36.

39. Huber, *Bäumer*, 366–368.

40. Ibid., 360–361.

41. Ibid., 187–192, 292–295.

42. Neumann, *Tantzen*, 265.

43. Greven-Aschoff, *Frauenbewegung*, 187.

44. Allen, *Feminism*, 234–236.

45. See Schaser, *Lange und Bäumer*, 247–248; "Bürgerliche Frauen auf dem Weg in die linksliberalen Parteien (1908–1933)," *Historische Zeitschrift*, 263 (1996), 641–680; Lauterer, *Parlamentarierinnen*, 68–83; also see Greven-Aschoff, *Frauenbewegung*, 161–162; Huber, *Bäumer*, 364.

46. Huber, *Bäumer*, 365–369; Neumann, *Tantzen*, 264–265; Evans, *Movement*, 259.

47. Louise Otto-Peters, "Die Gefahr fuer die Frauen"; Bäumer, "Der Wille und die Bereitschaft zu einer gerechten Wuerdigung unbequemer Tatsachen ist unter der Herrschaft des Machtgedankens sehr gering geworden' "; Bäumer, "Die politische Arbeitsteilung," *DF*, 3/33.

48. Louise Otto-Peters, "Die Hemmungen," *DF*, 3/33; Bäumer, "Das Ende des Allg. Frauenvereins," *DF*, 9/33.

49. Ibid.

50. See Bäumer, "Die Frauen in der Volks- und Staatskrisis," *DF*, 3/33.

51. Ibid.

52. See Bäumer articles "Genf" and "Von Gestern zum Morgen," *DF*, 10/33. NL Bäumer, BAK: N 1076, #13.

53. Bäumer to Beckmann, 4.13.33, in Beckmann, ed., *Band*.

54. Bäumer to Koenig, 7.29.33, in Beckmann, ed. *Band*.

55. Ibid.

56. Neumann, *Tantzen*, 265; Schaser, *Lange und Bäumer*, 288.

57. Doherr, "Die Frauenwirtschaftskammer in Hamburg," *DF*, 11/33; Else Ulich-Beil, "Familie, Volk und Staat," *DF*, 3/33.

58. See Bäumer, "Fiat," *DF*, 12/34; Beckmann, "Emma Ender zum 60. Geburtstage," *DF*, 9/35; Bäumer, "Die Seniorin der europäischen Frauenbewegung," *DF*, 6/36; Bäumer, "Zur geschichtlichen Tiefe der Frauenfrage," *DF*, 7/35.

59. Bäumer, "Die Frau und die Geschichte," *DF*, 2/37; on the prominent role played by women in the Weimar welfare state, see Crew, *Germans on Welfare*, 47–66; Young-Sun Hung, "Gender, Citizenship, and the Welfare State: Social Work and the Politics of Femininity in the Weimar Republic," *Central European History*, 30 (1997), 1–24.

60. "Wer tritt das Erbe an? Nicht nur von der Sache, sondern vor allen Dingen auch von der Unbedingtheit und Furchtlosigkeit der Haltung." Bäumer, "Vom ersten Aufruhr in der Mädchenbildung," *DF*, 11/37.

61. Bäumer, "Frauen machen Geschichte," *DF*, 1/40.
62. Bäumer, "Zum 'Status' der deutschen Frau," DF, 9/37.
63. Ibid. According to Ann Taylor Allen, the lesser focus on individual rights and political equality in Germany *vis-à-vis* England preceded the Third Reich. See Allen, *Feminism and Motherhood in Western Europe, 1890–1970*, New York: Palgrave, 2005.
64. Stephenson, *Women*, 8.
65. Bäumer, "Zum 'Status' der deutschen Frau," *DF*, 9/37.
66. Ibid.
67. "Die Menschenrechte und die Frauen: 'A propos d'un anniversaire,'" *DF*, 7/39.
68. Ibid.
69. Ibid.
70. Ibid.
71. See Karen Hagemann and Stefanie Schüler-Springorum, eds, *Heimat-Front. Militär und Geschlechtsverhältnisse im Zeitalter der Weltkriege*, Frankfurt: Campus, 2002; Andrea Süchting-Hänger, *Das "Gewissen der Nation." Nationales Engagement und politisches Handeln konservativer Frauenorganisationen 1900–1937*, Düsseldorf: Droste, 2002.
72. See letters from Lüders to Hans Bott Verlag, 2.02.36, 6.16.36, to Blomberg, 5.04.37, 2.02.36. NL Lüders, BAK: N 1151, #326.
73. See Lüders 1935 draft of the article "Gesetz über Frauendienstpflicht," notes on the articles [1936/1937], "Betrifft Untersuchung der Möglichkeiten des maximalen und optimalen Einsatzes weiblicher Arbeitskräfte zum Ersatz von Männern in der Kriegswirtschaft," "Vormerkungen für die Beschaffung von Fach- und Ersatzarbeitern für die Durchführung des Vierjahresplanes," "Arbeitseinteilung Centrale," in NL Lüders, BAK: N 1151, #156.
74. See Lüders correspondence, 11.17.36, 11.20.36, NL Lüders, BAK: N 1151, #156.
75. Bäumer, "Das unbekannte Heer," *DF*, 12/35.
76. See Bäumer and Magnus von Hausen, "Wehrhaft und Friedensbereit"; Bäumer, "Wie entwickelt sich die Rechtstellung der deutschen Frau," *DF*, 6/35.
77. Bäumer, "Frauenaufgaben im Kriege," *DF*, 5/40; Bäumer, "Arbeitsdienstpflicht im Rahmen der deutschen Frauenerziehung," *DF*, 10/40.
78. Bäumer, "Internationale Frauenbewegung an der Wende," *DF*, 3/39.
79. Ibid.
80. Bäumer, "Die falsche Emanzipation: Zur Stellung der Frau in der Sowjet-Union," *DF*, 10–11/41.
81. Ibid.
82. Ibid.
83. Bäumer, "Frauen in der Tragödie Spaniens," *DF*, 9/38; Bäumer, "Die Frauen Finnlands im Volkstumskampf," *DF*, 2–3/42.
84. Bäumer likewise criticizes the Soviet struggle "not only against this or that religion, such as Christianity or Islam, but religion in general." Bäumer, "Die falsche Emanzipation: Zur Stellung der Frau in der Sowjet-Union," *DF*, 10–11/41.
85. Schoenbaum, *Hitler's Social Revolution*, 178–192; T. Mason, "Women in Nazi Germany, 1925–1940. Family, Welfare, and Work," in Caplan, ed., *Nazism*, 131–211; Jill McIntyre, "Women and the Professions in Germany 1930–1940," in Erich Matthias and Anthony Nicholls, eds, *German Democracy and the Triumph of Hitler*, London: Allen & Unwin, 1971, 175–213; Jacques Pauwels, *Women, Nazis and Universities. Female Students in the Third Reich 1933–1945*, San Francisco: Greenwood Press, 1984.
86. Ibid. Stephenson, *Women*, 10–14; Greven-Aschoff, *Frauenbewegung*, 173–175; Mason in *Nazism*, 178–207.
87. "Bäumer, "Zum 'Status' der deutschen Frau," *DF*, 9/37; also see Bäumer, "Einsatz der Frau in der Nationalwirtschaft," *DF*, 2/39.
88. Bäumer, "Else Kolshorn," *DF*, 10/33.

89. Annemarie Niemayer, "Zahlen sprechen," *DF*, 10/33.
90. Bäumer, "Panik über den Frauenberufen," *DF*, 11/33.
91. Ibid.
92. Bäumer, "Vom Gestern zum Morgen," *DF*, 10/33.
93. Bäumer, "Vom Bildungsziel der Frau im Lichte des NS und der Frauenbewegung," *DF*, 11/33.
94. Ibid.
95. Bäumer, "Panik über den Frauenberufen," *DF*, 11/33.
96. Bäumer, "Bilanz 1934," *DF*, 1/35.
97. Ibid.
98. Ibid.
99. Bäumer, "Berufsschicksal der Wohlfahrtspflegerin," *DF*, 9/35.
100. Ibid.
101. Bäumer, "Jugend- und Fürsorgeamt," *DF*, 12/35.
102. Stephenson, *Women*, 110–111, 143–144.
103. Mason, "Women", in Caplan, ed., *Nazism*, 182–190; Stephenson, *Women*, 90–91.
104. Stephenson, *Women*, 180–181.
105. Bäumer, "Der Freiwillige Frauenhilfsdienst," *DF*, 6/38.
106. Lüders, "Fabrikpflege," *DF*, 2/36.
107. Lüders, "Zu viel Arbeit – zu wenig Hände!" *DF*, 4/37.
108. Bäumer, "Einsatz der Frau in der Nationalwirtschaft," *DF*, 2/39.
109. Ibid.
110. Ibid.
111. Ibid.
112. "So long as men are motivated by professional jealousy instead of the people's welfare . . . woman will have only negligible prospects of being employed according to the measure of her abilities," ibid.
113. Bäumer, "Frauenschaffen 1938 und in Zukunft," *DF*, 1/39.
114. Ibid.
115. See also Schacht, *Abrechnung*; Mason, "Internal Crisis and War of Aggression, 1938–1939," in Caplan, ed., *Nazism*, 104–130; Richard Overy, "Germany, 'Domestic Crisis' and War in 1939," in Leitz, ed., *Third Reich*, 97–128.
116. Bäumer, "Fraueneinsatzin der Kriegwirtschaft," *DF*, 1/41.
117. Bäumer, "Frauenreserven," *DF*, 4/41.
118. See letter regarding "Frauenreserven" [1946] in NL Bäumer, BAK: N 1076, #5.
119. This disparity between men and women was never as great at the level of primary education. Stephenson, *Women*, 143–144; Patricia Mazon, *Gender and the Modern Research University, 1865–1914*, Stanford: Stanford University Press, 2003; Fritz Ringer, *Toward a Social History of Knowledge*, New York: Berghahn, 2000.
120. Lenore Kühn, "Geistige Fuehrung im Frauentum," *DF*, 1/34.
121. Schlüter-Hermkes, "Die Selbstbehauptung der Frau an den deutschen Hochschulen," *DF*, 1/34.
122. Stephenson, *Women*, 186–187. See also Mazon, *Gender*, 3–25.
123. Stephenson, *Women*, 4–6, 184–185.
124. "Zum 'Status' der deutschen Frau," *DF*, 9/37.
125. Bäumer and Frances Magnus von Hausen, "Zur Krisis des Frauenstudiums," *DF*, 1/34.
126. Bäumer, "Die Pflicht zur Wissenschaft," *DF*, 1/34.
127. Mosse, *Nazi Culture*, 40.
128. Bäumer, "Die Pflicht zur Wissenschaft," *DF*, 1/34.
129. Bäumer, "Frauendienstpflicht als Gegenwartsaufgabe," *DF* 10/35.
130. Ibid.
131. Beckmann, "Fragen der Mädchenbildung in der pädagogischen presse der letzten Monate," *DF*, 10/35; also see Helmut Stubbe-da Luz, "Emmy Beckmann

(1880–1967), Hamburgs einflußreichste Frauenrechtlerin," *Zeitschrift des Vereins für Hamburgische Geschichte*, 73 (1987), 97–138.

132. Ibid.
133. Beckmann, "Fragen der Mädchenbildung," *DF*, 1/37.
134. Bäumer, "Auswirkungen der Schulreform," *DF*, 5/37; also see Claudia Huerkamp: *Bildungsbürgerinnen. Frauen im Studium und in akademischen Berufen 1900–1945*, Göttingen: Vandenhoeck & Ruprecht, 1996.
135. Ibid.
136. Bäumer, "Bilanz 1934," *DF*, 1/35.
137. Bäumer, "Die Frauen in den Rechts- und Sozialwissenschaften," *DF*, 8/37.
138. Bäumer, "Studentin, Altakademikerin und Frauenwelt," *DF*, 10/37.
139. Bäumer, "Die höhere Schule im Lebensprozeß des Volkes," *DF*, 5/38.
140. Bäumer, "Zum Problem der Hochschulauslese," *DF*, 11/38.
141. Bäumer, "Frauenschaffen 1938 und in Zukunft," *DF*, 1/39.
142. Bäumer, "25 Jahre Frauenstudium in Deutschland," *DF*, 6/39.
143. Ibid.
144. Ibid.
145. See Peukert, *Inside*, 103–118; Timothy Mason, "The Containment of the Working Classes in Germany," in Caplan, ed., *Nazism*, 231–273; Lüdtke, "The Appeal of Exterminating 'Others' "; Fritzsche, *Life and Death in the Third Reich*; Wildt, *Volksgemeinschaft*.
146. Freedman, *No Turning Back*, 75–88, 177–279.
147. Bäumer, "Vom Gestern zum Morgen," *DF*, 10/33.
148. Herzog, *Sex after Fascism*, 11–65.
149. Edward Ross Dickinson, "Biopolitics," 43–46; Schoenbaum, *Revolution*, 234–288; Burleigh, *Third Reich*, 219–228. For two more controversial works that emphasize the similarities between liberal democratic and Nazi welfare states, see Aly, *Hitlers Volksstaat* and Schivelbusch, *Entfernte Verwandschaft*.
150. Repp, *Reformers*, 112–113.
151. "What makes Bäumer's enthusiasm for eugenics before the First World War so startling is precisely the fact that it seemed to her perfectly compatible with the deep commitment to liberal humanism – if not liberal individualism – motivating her efforts to overturn divisive categories of race, class, confession, and gender that stood in the way of social unity." Repp, *Reformers*, 128–133.
152. Bäumer, "Der Sinn der Wohlfahrtspflege und die Frauenarbeit," *DF*, 3/35.
153. Ibid.; Crew, *Germans on Welfare*, 68–75.
154. Bäumer, "Der Sinn der Wohlfahrtspflege und die Frauenarbeit," *DF*, 3/35.
155. Ibid.; Crew, *Germans on Welfare*, 137–155; For more on the Nazi use of "racism as social policy", see Peukert, *Inside*, 208–235.
156. "Eindrücke und Meinungen: Fragen einer Mutter. Zum Erbgesundheitsgesetz," *DF*, 3/35.
157. Bäumer, "Nächstenliebe und Fernstenliebe: Gedanken zum Winterhilfswerk," *DF*, 12/38; for more on the relative effectiveness of *Winterhilfswerk*, see Burleigh, *Third Reich*, 223–228.
158. Bäumer, "Nächstenliebe und Fernstenliebe: Gedanken zum Winterhilfswerk," *DF*, 12/38; also see Schoenbaum, *Revolution*, 152–177; Peukert, *Inside*, 86–100.
159. Ibid.
160. Bäumer, "Der Regierer muss klug sein, dass er der Liebe Raum lasse," *DF*, 11/33.
161. Bäumer, "Unser Bild vom Staat des lebendigen Volkstums," *DF*, 3/33.
162. Bäumer, "Hedwig Heyl," *DF*, 2/34.
163. Bäumer, "Frauen machen Geschichte," *DF*, 1/40.
164. Bäumer, "Zehn Jahre NS Volkswohlfahrt," *DF*, 8–9/42; Baumer, "Internationale Frauenbewegung an der Wende," *DF*, 3/39.

165. Bäumer, "Die internationale Bedeutung des deutschen Mutterschutzgesetzes," *DF* 10–11/42.
166. Repp, *Reformers*, 108–135; Crew, *Germans on Welfare*, 204–215; Hung, *Welfare*.
167. Stephenson, *Women*, 5.
168. Ibid., 70–71.
169. Mason, "Women," in Caplan, ed., *Nazism*, 162–178.
170. Report from *Völkischer Beobachter*, 5.27.36, quoted in Mosse, *Nazi Culture*, 42.
171. "It was, in fact, both backward- and forward-looking, seeking to preserve positive aspects of women's traditional work as well as to open up new possibilities for work in the professions and social reform. Discourses on public and private motherhood encompassed the most radical as well as the most conservative positions taken by feminists of this era." Allen, *Feminism*, 230.
172. Greven-Aschoff, *Frauenbewegung*, 168.
173. Ibid., 170.
174. Heide-Marie Lauterer, "Liebe Marquise von O.: Von den gesellschaftlichen Problemen liberaler Parlamentierinnen in der Weimarer Republik. Kommentar und Edition eines Briefes von Marie Elisabeth Lüders an Katharina v. Oheimb vom 26. Sept. 1924," *JzLF*, 16 (2004), 273–283.
175. Lüders, "Zur Reform des Unehelichenrechts," *DF*, 11/35.
176. See articles 2.29.40 from "Der Schwarze Korps" and 2.24.39–2.26.39 from *Völkisch Beobachter*, in NL Lüders, N 1151, #265. Also see Heide-Marie Lauterer, " 'Fürchte Dich nicht' – Marie-Elisabeth Lüders' Stellung zu den beiden deutschen Diktaturen," *JzLF*, 17 (2005), 91–98.
177. Beckmann, "Ein erfuelltes Frauenleben," *DF*, 12/33.
178. Weber, "Wahlmutterschaft," *DF*, 2/35.
179. "Finally, illegitimacy, a persistent stigma in socially and morally conservative circles, was wholly irrelevant to the Nazi view of childbirth. If the infant was racially pure and healthy, it did not matter at all whether its parents were legally married. The logical consequences of prioritizing breeding in this morally neutral way were carried to an extreme by Heinrich Himmler, who founded a series of maternity homes from 1936 under an SS-run association called the 'Well of Life' (*Lebensborn*). These were intended for racially approved unmarried mothers, who otherwise might not receive the facilities he thought they deserved. Infant mortality rates amongst illegitimate children were notoriously higher than the national average." Evans, *Power*, 521; see also Burleigh, *Third Reich*, 234; Gellately, *Gestapo and German Society*, 217–218.
180. Lüders, "Zur Reform des Unehelichenrechts," *DF*, 11/35; Lauterer, " 'Fürchte Dich nicht,' " *JzLF*, 17 (2005), 91–98.
181. Lüders, "Zur Reform des Unehelichenrechts," *DF*, 11/35.
182. Bäumer, "War es nicht Dir und mir geschenkt? Dir auch". "War es nicht Dir und mir geschenkt?" *DF*, 1/35.
183. Camilla Jellinek, "Zum Gesetz über die Anwendung deutschen Rechtes bei der Ehescheidung vom 24. Januar 1935," *DF*, 5/35; also see Klaus Kempter, *Die Jellineks 1820–1955. Eine familienbiographische Studie zum deutschjüdischen Bildungsbürgertum*, Düsseldorf: Droste, 1998.
184. Martens-Edelmann, "Vorraussetzungen der Ehescheidung," *DF*, 4/36.
185. Bäumer, "Die internationale Bedeutung des deutschen Mutterschutzgesetzes," *DF* 10–11/42.
186. See Herzog, *Sex after Fascism*, 10–17; Dr. jur. Anna Mayer, "Staat und Sittlichkeit in germanischer und romanischer Auffassung," *DF*, 11/33.
187. Bäumer, *Der neue Weg*, 14–18.
188. Bäumer to Borchers, 05.15.41 in Beckmann, ed., *Band*, 147–148.
189. Repp, *Reformers*, 125–126.
190. Baumer, "Internationale Frauenbewegung an der Wende," *DF*, 3/39.

191. Weindling, *Health, Race and German Politics*, 146–153, 388–392. Also see Luca Dotti, *L'utopia eugenetica del welfare state svedese, 1934–1975: il programma socialdemocratico di sterilizzazione, aborto e castrazione*, Soverio: Rubbettino, 2004; Astrid Ley, *Zwangssterilisation und Ärzteschaft: Hintergrunde und Ziele ärztlichen Handelns 1934–1945*, Frankfurt: Campus, 2004.

192. Bäumer, "Bilanz 1934," *DF*, 1/35.

193. As the Auschwitz inmate Hermann Langbein reminds us, "Himmler ordered the establishment of bordellos in the concentration camps. This was intended to combat homosexuality. On one occasion Himmler said that these brothels also were supposed to constitute an 'incentive for greater achievements'; an inmate had to pay for visits to the brothel with bonus coupons that were awarded for good work." Hermann Langbein, *People in Auschwitz*, Chapel Hill, N.C.: University of North Carolina Press, 2004, 405–406. Heydrich himself set up his own house of prostitution, Berlin's "Salon Kitty", named after its infamous Madame Kitty Schmidt, and trained his "employees" to extract sensitive information from prominent customers, which included the Italian Foreign Minister, Mussolini's son-in-law Count Ciano, and the SS commander Sepp Dietrich. Walter Schellenberg, *Hitler's Secret Service*, New York: Harper, 1974.

194. Weber, "Würdigung und Kritik einer evangelischen Sexualethik," *DF*, 4/36.

195. Weber, "Zur Ethik des Geschlechtstebens: Antwort an Herrn Professor D. Otto Piper," *DF*, 12/36; Weber, "Die Ehe als Daseinserfüllung," *DF*, 7/35; Krüger, *Max und Marianne Weber*; Barbel Meurer, ed., *Marianne Weber*; Marianne Weber, *Lebenserinnerungen*.

196. Velsen, "Marianne Weber: Die Frauen und die Liebe," *DF*, 11/35; Schaser, *Lange und Bäumer*, 17–20, 43–48.

197. Stephenson, *Women*, 110–111.

198. Bäumer, "Vom Gestern zum Morgen," *DF*, 10/33; Bäumer, "Der Sinn der Wohlfahrtspflege und die Frauenarbeit," *DF*, 3/35.

199. Süchting-Hänger, *Das "Gewissen der Nation,"* 399.

200. Schoenbaum, *Revolution*, 111–113.

201. Lüders to Veltchen, 3.29.33, BAK: N 1151, #326; Stephenson, *Women*, 193–194; Huber, *Bäumer*, 364; Evans, *Movement*, 273–275.

202. See Bäumer's letters to Helene König, 3.28.36 and Mai; Beckmann, 3.25.36, 10.19.36; Marianne Weber, 10.16.36, in Beckmann, ed., *Band*, 87–89, 95, 109, 119, 130.

203. See letters in Beckmann, ed., *Band*, 33–45, 194–195.

204. Even Bäumer's critics concede that she "looked for signs of feminism in the Nazi women's organization" and that her "apparent readiness to cooperate with the National Socialist Women's Leadership . . . suggests something more than prudence. Her priority was to try to keep the spirit and activity of the old Women's Movement alive at all costs, in however small a way, and to try and infiltrate some of its ideas into Frau Scholtz-Klink's organization." This policy "was little understood and less welcomed by those women who had formerly admired and supported her and who started from the premise that National Socialism was inherently evil, and that any kind of compromise with it was out of the question." Stephenson, *Women*, 193–194.

205. Ibid., 104–106; Schaser, *Lange und Bäumer*, 287, n.26, 300, n.96.

206. Beckmann, ed., *Band*, 135.

207. Ibid., 135–136, 166–178, 212.

208. Ibid., 144–148.

209. Ibid., 33–45.

210. Ibid., 194–215; See folder marked "*Zu den in der Zeitschrift 'Die Frau' beanstandeten Beiträge*": NL Bäumer, BAK: N 1076, #5; Schaser " 'Innere Emigration," 16–25.

211. Huber, *Bäumer*, 364–377.

212. "Moreover, in the case of some of these ideas – notably Social Darwinism – it is often hard to disentangle the genuinely liberal from the potentially totalitarian. Also, even if the German women's movement had largely succumbed to the protofascist ideas by

1914, this did not make it inevitable that it would support the advent of genuine fascism in 1930–33 . . . Finally, it should be borne in mind that feminist movements in other countries were also turning to the right at the same time, and that elsewhere too there was a general retreat from liberalism in the 1920s. These developments, then, were not confined to Germany, even if the form they took there was rather different from – ultimately much more violent and destructive than – the form they took in other countries." Evans, *Movement*, 273–275; also see Repp, *Reformers*, 300–312; Huber, *Bäumer*, 364.

213. Beckmann, ed., *Band*, 96–100, 150; Lauterer, " 'Fürchte Dich nicht,' " 91–98.
214. See Bäumer's notes, 12.17.46, in NL Bäumer, BAK: N 1076, #1.

Chapter Four: Hitler's War?

1. For earlier work that emphasizes the primacy of foreign policy, see Andreas Hillgruber, *Der Zweite Weltkrieg, 1939–1945: Kriegsziele und Strategie der großen Mächte*, Stuttgart: Kohlhammer, 1982; Klaus Hildebrand, *Deutsche Außenpolitik 1933–1945*, Stuttgart: Kohlhammer, 1990; Jost Dülffer, *Nazi Germany 1933–1945: Faith and Annihilation*, London: St Martin's Press, 1996.
2. See Rainer Behring, *Demokratische Aussenpolitik für Deutschland*, Düsseldorf: Droste, 1999; Stefan Vogt, *Nationaler Sozialismus und Soziale Demokratie: Die sozialdemokratische Junge Rechte 1918–1945*, Bonn: J.H.W. Dietz, 2006.
3. Evans, *Power*, 670–712; Omer Bartov, *Hitler's Army: Soldiers, Nazis, and War in the Third Reich*, Oxford: Oxford, 1991, 179–186; also see General Ludwig Beck letters, 5.05.38, 5.29.38, in NL Beck, BAF: N 1028, #3.
4. See A.J.P. Taylor, *Origins of the Second World War*, New York: Simon & Schuster, 1996; Fischer, *Griff*.
5. See Eberhalb Kolb, *Gustav Stresemann*, München: C.H. Beck, 2003; Wright, *Gustav Stresemann*; Felix Hirsch, *Gustav Stresemann: Patriot und Europäer*, Göttingen: Musterschmidt, 1964; Hans W. Gatzke, *Stresemann and the Rearmament of Germany*, New York: W.W. Norton, 1969; Anneliese Thimme, *Gustav Stresemann*, Hannover: Goedel, 1957; Christian Baechler, *Gustave Stresemann*, Strasbourg: Strasbourg University Press, 1996; Henry Ashby Turner, *Stresemann and the Politics of the Weimar Republic*, Princeton: Princeton University Press, 1963; Manfred J. Enssle, *Stresemann's Territorial Revisionism: Germany, Belgium, and the Eupen-Malmedy Question, 1919–1929*, Wiesbaden: Steiner, 1980. Also see Hess, "*Deutschland*"; Jones, *Liberalism*; Frye, *Democrats*; Kurlander, *Price*; Scholtyseck, *Bosch*; Sassin, *Liberale*; Neumann, *Tantzen*.
6. Scholtyseck, *Bosch*, 547–548; Tooze, *Ökonomie*, 21–37; also see Taylor, *Origins*; Fischer, *Griff*; Timothy Mason, "Some Origins of the Second World War," in Caplan, ed., *Nazism*, 33–52; Andreas Hillgruber, *Deutschlands Rolle in der Vorgeschichte der beiden Weltkriege*, Göttingen: Vandenhoeck & Ruprecht, 1967; Hillgruber, *Kontinuität und Diskontinuität in der deutschen Außenpolitik von Bismarck bis Hitler*, Düsseldorf: Droste, 1969.
7. Kurlander, *Price*, 5–11.
8. Ibid., 347–353.
9. Lothar Albertin, "Das Friedensthema bei den Linksliberalen vor 1914: Die Schwäche ihrer Argumente und Aktivitäten," in Karl Holl and Günther List, eds, *Liberalismus und imperialistischer Staat*, Göttingen: Vandenhoeck & Ruprecht, 89–108; Wildenthal, *German Women*, 54–202; Kurlander, *Price*, 22–41.
10. See Sheehan, *German Liberalism*, 246–264; Heuss, *Naumann*, 31–35, 126–127, 144–145.
11. See Kurlander, *Price*, 21–116; Sell, *Die Tragödie*, 286–298, 361–362; Sheehan, *German Liberalism*, 258–283; Langewiesche, *Liberalism*, 7–11; Frye, *Democrats*, 6–20, 88–101;

Repp, *Reformers*, 104–138, 300–312; Wolfgang Mommsen, "Wandlungen der liberalen Idee im Zeitalter des Liberalismus," and Lothar Gall, "'Sündenfall' des liberalen Denkens oder Krise der bürgerlichen–liberalen Bewegung?" in Karl Holl and Günther List, eds, *Liberalismus und imperialistischer Staat*, Göttingen: Vandenhoeck & Ruprecht, 109–148.

12. See Jones, *German Liberalism*, 12–40; Albertin, *Liberalismus und Demokratie*, 64–67, 143–145, 321–323; Frye, *Democrats*, 48–57, 101–117; Albertin, "Friedensthema," in Holl and List, eds, *Liberalismus*, 89–108; Hess, *"Deutschland*, 317–369; Wildenthal, *German Women*, 54–202.

13. See Rogers Brubaker, *Citizenship and Nationhood in France and Germany*, Cambridge, Mass.: Harvard University Press, 1998; Eugenio F. Biagini, ed., *Citizenship and Community: Liberals, Radicals and Collective Identities in the British Isles, 1865–1931*, Cambridge: Cambridge University Press, 2002; Ian Fletcher, *Women's Suffrage in the British Empire: Citizenship, Nation and Race*, New York: Routledge, 2000; Rieko Karatani, *Defining British Citizenship: Empire, Commonwealth and Modern Britain*, New York: Routledge, 2002.

14. See Peter Theiner, "Sozialer Liberalismus und deutsche Weltpolitik," in P. Theiner, ed., *Friedrich Naumann im Wilhelminischen Deutschland*, 9–10; Evans, *Movement*, 274. Also see Vogt, *Nationaler Sozialismus*; Lars Fischer, *Response*; Roger Fletcher, *Socialist Imperialism in Germany, 1897–1914*, London: Allen & Unwin, 1984; Nina Witoszek and Lars Tragardh, eds, *Culture and Crisis: The Case of Germany and Sweden*, New York: Berghahn, 2002.

15. Hess, *Deutschland*, 187–277; also see Thomas Goethel, *Demokratie und Volkstum: Die Politik gegenüber den nationalen Minderheiten in der Weimarer Republik*, Cologne: SH-Verlag, 2002.

16. Faßbender, "Briefwechsel," 150–156; also see Kurlander, *Price*, 251–260, 347–353; Frye, *Democrats*, 88–117, 131–132, 164–194; Albertin und Wegener, eds, *Linksliberalismus*, 464–471, 576–591.

17. Harry Graf Kessler, *Walther Rathenau: Sein Leben und sein Werk*, Berlin: Hermann Klemm, 1928, 185–187; Henry Cord Meyer, *Mitteleuropa in German Thought and Action, 1815–1945*, The Hague: Nijhoff, 1955, 18–95, 139–140, 194–217.

18. Jürgen Froelich, "Friedrich Naumanns 'Mitteleuropa'. Ein Buch, seine Umstände und seine Folgen," in Bruch, ed., *Friedrich Naumann*, 245–268; Steffen Höhne, "Mitteleuropa. Zur konzeptuellen Karriere eines kulturpolitischen Begriffs," *Bohemia*, 41 (2000), 279–294.

19. Naumann, *Mitteleuropa*, Berlin: G. Reimer, 1915, 6–32; Meyer, *Mitteleuropa*, 194–205.

20. Cord Meyer, *Mitteleuropa*, 84–95, 220–236, 278–295; Paul Rohrbach, ed., *Chauvinismus und Weltkrieg*, Berlin: Engelmann, 1919.

21. Naumann, *Mitteleuropa*, 1–18, 58–70; Cord Meyer, *Mitteleuropa*, 209–214.

22. Naumann, *Mitteleuropa*, 70–102.

23. Froelich, "'Mitteleuropa,'" 252–259; Jens Boysen, "Hesitant Hegemon: Germany and EU enlargement," *Central Europe Review*, 2, no. 18 (May 2000); August Weber, *Erinnerungen*, 64–65; also see Naumann, *Mitteleuropa*, 102–133, 229–262; Cord Meyer, *Mitteleuropa*, 200–203, 329–331.

24. Cord Meyer, *Mitteleuropa*, 291–345; Froelich, "'Mitteleuropa,'" 253; Heinrich Kessler, *Wilhelm Stapel: Als Politischer Publizist*, Nürnberg: Lorenz Spindler, 1967, 15; Adam Tooze, *Ökonomie der Zerstörung: Die Geschichte der Wirtschaft im Nationalsozialismus*, München: Siedler, 2007, 14–16; also see Reginald Horsman, *Race and Manifest Destiny: The Origins of American Racial Anglo-Saxonism*, Cambridge, Mass.: Harvard University Press, 1981.

25. Wright, *Stresemann*, 25–81, 111–125; Thimme, *Stresemann*, 11–33; August Weber, *Erinnerungen*, 107–109: also see Thomas Wagner, *"Krieg oder Frieden. Unser Platz an der Sonne." Gustav Stresemann und die Aussenpolitik des Kaiserreichs*, Paderborn: Schöningh, 2007.

26. Wright, *Stresemann*, 138–157, Thimme, *Stresemann*, 34–54.
27. Wright, *Stresemann*, 177–253; Thimme, *Stresemann*, 61–98.
28. Gatzke, *Stresemann*, 11–65; Peter Berglar, *Walther Rathenau: Sein Zeit, sein Werk, sein Persönlichkeit*, Bremen: Scünemann, 1970, 260–263, 288–293; David Felix, *Walther Rathenau and the Weimar Republic*, Baltimore: Johns Hopkins, 1971, 126–147. Eugen Fischer-Baling, *Walther Rathenau: Ein Experiment Gottes*, Berlin: Weiss, 1952, 16–18; Kessler, *Rathenau*, 332–335; also see Wolfgang Brenner, *Walther Rathenau. Deutscher und Jude*, München: Piper, 2005; Christian Schölzel, *Walther Rathenau. Eine Biographie*, Paderborn: Schöningh, 2006.
29. Stanley Suval, *The Anschluß Question in the Weimar Era: A Study of Nationalism in Germany and Austria, 1918–1932*, London: Johns Hopkins, 1974, 55–56, 128–130.
30. Wright, *Stresemann*, 260–294, 310–387; Gatzke, *Stresemann*, 89–116.
31. For more on this debate, see Jost Dülffer, "Der Weichensteller," *Damals*, 39, nr. 4 (2007), 28–33; Thimme, *Stresemann*, 124–125; Andreas Körber, *Gustav Stresemann als Europäer, Patriot, Wegbereiter und potentieller Verhinderer Hitlers*, Hamburg: Krämer, 1999; Taylor, *Origins*; Manfred Berg, *Gustav Stresemann und die Vereinigten Staaten von Amerika*, Baden-Baden: Nomos, 1990; Wright, *Stresemann*; Kolb, *Stresemann*, Hirsch, *Stresemann*; Gatzke, *Stresemann*; Baechler, *Stresemann*; Enssle, *Revisionism*.
32. Sassin, *Liberale*, 257–258, 268.
33. See Seger to Quidde, 7.14.34, in NL Quidde, BAK: N 1212, #28.
34. Jost Dülffer, Review of Evans, Richard J., *The Third Reich in Power 1933–1939*, London 2005. H-Soz-u-Kult, 24.11.2005, http://hsozkult.geschichte.hu-berlin.de/rezensionen/2005-4-118; see again Behring, *Demokratische Aussenpolitik*; Vogt, *Nationaler Sozialismus*.
35. Quidde to Seger, 9.26.34, in NL Quidde, BAK: N 1212, #28; Holl, *Quidde*, 517–526.
36. Gerlach to Quidde, 11.22.34, in NL Quidde, BAK: N 1212, #28.
37. Ibid.
38. Falk to Quidde, 10.03.34, in NL Quidde, BAK: N 1212, #28.
39. Correspondence between Quidde and Garrison, 6.14.33, 9.14.33, 10.17.33, in NL Quidde, BAK: N 1212, #80; Holl, *Quidde*, 511–516, 527–551.
40. Suval, *Anschluss*, 81; Susanne Heyn, "Der kolonialkritische Diskurs der Weimarer Friedensbewegung zwischen Antikolonialismus und Kulturmission," *Wiener Zeitschrift für kritische Afrikastudien*, 9(2005), 37–65.
41. Scholtyseck, *Bosch*, 127–131, 177–178.
42. Demm, ed., Alfred Weber, *Politische Theorie*, 207–208.
43. Sassin, *Liberale*, 64–65; Neumann, *Tantzen*, 424; Külz's essay "Der deutsche Reichsgedanke und das deutsche Staatswesen"; Külz to Interior Minister Frick, 3.14.34, in NL Külz, BAK: N 1042, #20.
44. Heuss, *Hitlers Weg*, 99; Cord Meyer, *Mitteleuropa*, 84–95, 221–230.
45. Tooze, *Ökonomie*, 107–126, 145–147; Eksteins, *Heuss*, 123–124; Müller, "Theodor Heuss," 210–211; Burger, *Heuss*, 340–344; Lauterer, *Parlamentarierinnen*, 212–215; also see handwritten list entitled "Hitler's Reden"; Lüders to Isay, 10.11.29, NL Lüders, BAK: N 115, #s 236, 250.
46. Ibid. Bund der Freunde der Reichsüniversiät to Gerland, 9.27.35, 4.27.43, in NL Gerland, BAK: N 1010, #35.
47. See letters, articles, and minutes in NL Bronner-Höpfner, BAK: N 1026, #s 9, 17, 18, 29. Frye, *Democrats*, 127–131.
48. Lauterer, *Parlamentarierinnen*, 207–215; Dietrich to von Richthoffen, 12.28.33, in NL Dietrich, BAK: N 1004, #154; Dorothee van Velsen, "Frauen, Volk und Staat"; Else Ulrich-Beil, "Die Eingliederung der Jugend in die Volksgemeinschaft"; Luise Scheffen-Döring, "Einige Gedanken zur Aussenpolitik," *DF*, 3/33.
49. Sassin, *Liberale*, 47.
50. Heuss, *Naumann*, 132–133.

51. Ibid., 141–142, 536–537.
52. Bäumer, folder marked *Vorträge z. T. unvollständig* [1947–48], in BAK: N 1076, #5.
53. Letter from Heuss to Bäumer, 2.03.34, in NL Heuss, BAK: N 1221, #77. Also see Bäumer, "Zum Bruch mit dem Völkerbund," *DF*, 11/ 33.
54. P. Rohrbach, *Handschrift*, Vorwort, 7, 232–233; P. Rohrbach, *Deutsches Volkstum als Minderheit*, Berlin: Englemann, 1926; P. Rohrbach, *Deutschtum in Not! Die Schicksale der Deutschen in Europa ausserhalb des Reiches*, Berlin: Andermann, 1926.
55. Cord Meyer, *Mitteleuropa*, 88–108.
56. Heuss to Erkelenz, 3.01.34, NL Heuss, BAK: N 1221, #396; Kurlander, *Price*, 111.
57. See 1934 article "Russland und Europa," in NL Gothein, BAK: N 1006, #68a.
58. See Gothein, "Das Weltproblem des 20. Jahrhunderts" [1935], in NL Gothein, BAK: N 1006, #68a.
59. Ibid. Gothein, *A World Coalition against Japan*, London: Hamilton, 1934, 471–478.
60. Gatzke, *Stresemann*, 72–111.
61. Burger, *Heuss*, 341–343; Lauterer, *Parlamentarierinnen*, 215–216; Dietz to Gerland, 8.29.36; Gerland to Dietz, 9.17.36, in NL Gerland, BAK: N 1010, #11.
62. Kershaw, *Hitler: Nemesis*, xxxv–xxxvi; Evans, *Power*, 634–637.
63. Sassin, *Liberale*, 275–276.
64. See marginal comments in 1935 article, "Deutsche Sängerschaft," in Külz, BAK: N 1042, #137. Also see memoirs in Hergard Robel, ed., *Wilhelm Külz: Ein Liberaler zwischen Ost und West. Aufzeichnungen 1947–1948*, Munich: Oldenbourg, 1989, 7–24, 43–46; Scholtyseck, *Bosch*, 176–182.
65. Bäumer, "Der Sinn der Erde," *DF*, 12/36.
66. Sassin, *Liberale*, 45–46; Rohrbach, *Handschrift*, 393–394; Suval, *Anschluß*, 94–104, 185–196.
67. Gatzke, *Stresemann*, 90–111; Willinger to Gothein, 2.10.36. NL Gothein: BAK: N 1006, #34; Burger, *Heuss*, 342–344; Lauterer, *Parlamentarierinnen*, 216–219.
68. Sassin, *Liberale*, 63; Burger, *Heuss*, 343–344.
69. Horst Bieber, *Paul Rohrbach: Ein konservativer Publizist und Kritiker der Weimarer Republik*, Munich: Dokumentation, 1972, 9–10.
70. Rohrbach, *German World Politics*, New York: Macmillan, 1914. Also see Walter Mogk, *Paul Rohrbach und das groessere Deutschland*, München: Wilhelm Goldmann, 1972, 4–7, 214–215, 220, 228–229; Cord Meyer, *Mitteleuropa*, 88–108, 221–222; Burger, *Heuss*, 51–52; Schmokel, *Dreams*, 1–14; Wildenthal, *German Women*, 131–202; also see Russell Berman, *Enlightenment or Empire: Colonial Discourse in German Culture*, Lincoln: University of Nebraska Press, 2007.
71. Mogk, *Rohrbach*, 38–41; Cord Meyer, *Mitteleuropa*, 234–236; for more on liberal imperialism in a wider European context, see Berman, *Discourse*; David Thomas Murphy, *The Heroic Earth: Geopolitical Thought in Weimar Germany, 1918–1933*, Kent, Ohio: Kent State University Press, 1997; Schmokel, *Dream of Empire*.
72. Bieber, *Rohrbach*, 35–36; Rohrbach, *Handschrift*, 237.
73. Bieber, *Rohrbach*, 42–64, 97–103; Rohrbach, *Handschrift*, 345.
74. Mogk, *Rohrbach*, 165.
75. Bieber, *Rohrbach*, 75–76, 102–103.
76. Ibid., 113, 201–202; also see Rohrbach's articles in *Leitartikel Korrespondenz*, 3.02.33, "Ungarns Feldzug gegen sein Deutschtums," 3.08.33; "Woher die antideutsche Front in Genf?" regarding a new round of disarmament talks, 3.29.33; "Italiens europäischer Weg," 4.05.33; "Die revidierte Friedensdiktate," 4.11.33; "Der Marsch der Revision und die Zukunft des Völkerbundes," 4.27.33; "Nationaler Wille und nationale Ideologie," 6.01.33; "Der Welt-Unsicherheits-Faktor Amerika," 1.11.34, in NL Rohrbach, BAK: N 1408, #44, in NL Rohrbach, BAK: N 1408, #43–44. Also see Bieber, *Rohrbach*, 104, 203; Kessler, *Wilhelm Stapel*, 183.
77. Rohrbach, "Ein Ranke-Wort zur Rheinland-Frage," 3.11.36, in NL Rohrbach, BAK: N 1408, #46.

78. See Rohrbach's articles "Die Organisation des europäischen Friedens," 3.27.35; "Der Ruf zur Mässigung!" 7.12.35; "Von Malta bis Arabien!" 8.22.35; "Weltfriede und Kolonialbesitz," 9.12.35, in NL Rohrbach, BAK: N 1408, #45.

79. Rohrbach, *Handschrift*, 393, 410–411; See Rohrbach's articles "Die zwei Seelen der englischen Wehrvorlage," 2.12.36, "Das labile Kräftedreieck in Frankreich," 6.11.36, in NL Rohrbach, BAK: N 1408, #46.

80. On the tenuous relationship between Nazi imperialism and antebellic German colonialism, see Robert Gerwarth and Stephen Malinowski, "Der Holocaust als kolonialer Genozid? Europäische Kolonialgewalt und nationalsozialistischer Vernichtungskrieg," *Geschichte und Gesellschaft*, 33, nr. 3 (2007), 439–466. Birthe Kundrus, "From the Herero to the Holocaust?" *Afrika Spectrum*, 40 (2005), 299–308; Kundrus, "Kontinuitäten, Parallelen, Rezeptionen: Überlegungen zur 'Kolonialisierung' des Nationalsozialismus," *Werkstattgeschichte*, 43 (2006), 45–62; Schmokel, *Dream of Empire*, 121–125; H.W. Bauer, *Kolonien oder nicht: Die Einstellung von Partei und Staat zum kolonialen Gedanken*, Leipzig: Richard Bauer, 1935, 3, 31, 41–51; Cord Meyer, *Mitteleuropa*, 98–105, 220–230; Klaus Hildebrand, *Vom Reich zum Weltreich: Hitler, NSDAP und koloniale Frage 1919–1945*, Munich: W. Fink, 1969.

81. Bieber, *Rohrbach*, 201–202; Rohrbach, *Deutschlands koloniale Forderung*, Hamburg: Hanseatische, 1935.

82. Ibid. Rohrbach, *Handschrift*, 393; Rohrbach, *Deutsch-Afrika: Ende oder Anfang? Briefe an einen Jungen Deutschen*, Potsdam: Volk & Heimat, 1935.

83. On the complex relationship between German colonialism, racism, and genocide, see Sara Friedrichsmeyer, Sara Lennox, and Susanne Zantop, eds, *The Imperialist Imagination: German Colonialism and its Legacy*, Ann Arbor: Michigan University Press, 1998; Birthe Kundrus, ed., *Phantasiereiche: Zur Kulturgeschichte des deutschen Kolonialismus*, Frankfurt: Campus Verlag, 2003; Richard King and Dan Stone, eds, *Hannah Arendt and the Uses of History: Imperialism, Nation, Race, and Genocide*, New York: Berghahn, 2007; A. Dirk Moses and Dan Stone, eds, *Colonialism and Genocide*, London: Routledge, 2007.

84. Bieber, *Rohrbach*, 110–112; see Rohrbach's articles "Die deutsche koloniale Forderung," in *Der Getreue Eckart*; "Skizzen aus Frankreich. Freudlose Sicherheit," in *Königsberger Abend-Zeitung*, in NL Paul Rohrbach, BAK: 1408, #103; Rohrbach's contribution to *Handwörterbuch des Grenz u. Auslandsdeutschtum Bd. 1* (1933), "Angola"; article in *Deutsche Zukunft*, 12.10.33, "Die Bewegung in Ostasien und Indien," in NL Rohrbach, BAK: N 1408, #43; Bieber, *Rohrbach*, 103–109.

85. See Rohrbach's articles "Lord Lugar und die Kolonialdebatte," 2.14.36; "Koloniale Fragend und Antworten," 5.06.36, in *Berliner Börsen-Zeitung*; "Der kolonialwirtschaftliche Einzelbetrieb und die deutsche Bedarfsdeckung" [1936], in NL Rohrbach, BAK: N 1408, #102.

86. "Magna Charta der Sklaverei," 1.01.37; "Léon Blums 'Bumerang,' " 2.24.37; "Die Balfour-Erklärung Wird Liquidiert," 7.08.37; "Die Mongolei und die Mongolen," 10.26.37, in NL Rohrbach, BAK: N 1408, #47; Paul Rohrbach and Ludwig Preiss, *Palestine and Transjordania*, New York: Macmillan, 1926. Also see Keith L. Nelson, "The 'Black Horror on the Rhine': Race as a Factor in Post-World War I Diplomacy," *Journal of Modern History*, 42, no. 4 (Dec. 1970), 606–627; Raffael Scheck, *Hitler's African Victims: The German Army Massacres of Black French Soldiers in 1940*, Cambridge: Cambridge University Press, 2006.

87. See Chapter Seven, "Hypothek des Todes," in Rohrbach, *Deutschland: Tod oder Leben?* Munich: Bruckmann, 1930; also see Bieber, *Rohrbach*, 85–86.

88. See Rohrbach's articles "Die 'gelbe' und die 'schwarze' Gefahr," 1.18.34; 1.25.34, "Der österreichische Knoten," 1.25.34; 5.17.34, "Die japanische Gefahr," 5.17.34; "Das Fragezeichen im Fernen Osten," 8.29.34; "Vom Geiste Japans," 9.06.34; in NL Rohrbach, BAK: N 1408, #44; Rohrbach, *Afrika: Beiträge zu einer praktischen Kolonialkunde*, Berlin: Werner, 1943, 6–14.

89. See Rohrbach's articles in *Der getreue Eckart* (Wien), 1933/1934, "Das Deutschtum in Chile," obviously praising the Germans in Chile; Rohrbach's contribution to *Handwörterbuch des Grenz u. Auslandsdeutschtum Bd. 1* (1933), "Angola" [1934]. "Völkerethik und nationale Politik," in NL Rohrbach, BAK: N 1408, #102.

90. See for example Schacht's preface in H.W. Bauer's *Kolonien oder nicht*, 3, 31, 41–51; Hjalmar Schacht, *New Colonial Policy*, Berlin: Drückerei der Reichsbank, 1929; Ernst Jäckh, *Im türkischen Kriegslager durch Albanien: Bekenntnisse zur deutsch-türkischen Freundschaft*, Heilbronn: Salzer, 1911; E. Jäckh, *The New Germany*, London: Oxford, 1927; E. Jäckh, *Der goldene Pflug: Lebensernte eines Weltbürgers*, Stuttgart: Deutsche Verlags-Anstalt, 1954; Cord Meyer, *Mitteleuropa*, 98–105, 220–230.

91. See Rohrbach's articles in *Der getreue Eckart* (1933/1934); *Deutsche Zukunft*, 12.10.33, "Die Bewegung in Ostasien und Indien," in NL Rohrbach, BAK: N 1408, #102.

92. "Die Sudetendeutschen" [Nov. 1938], "Südslavien", 12.19.39; "In mazedonischem Gebiet," 11.28.39; "Oestliche der Adria," 12.24.39; Der Palast Diokletians" [December 1939]; "Eindruck in Finland" [1939], in NL Rohrbach, BAK: N 1408, #103.

93. Paul und Justus Rohrbach, *Afrika Heute und Morgen*, Berlin: Reimar Hobbing, 1939, 3–15, 107–145.

94. The Nazi obsession with race goes a long way toward explaining Hitler's, Himmler's, and Rosenberg's relative lack of interest in restoring the German colonies. Kiesten to Gerland, 10.30.35, NL Gerland, BAK: N 1010, #12. See Klaus Hildebrand, *Foreign Policy of the Third Reich*, Berkeley: University of California Press, 1973, 75–90; Evans, *Power*, 527–529; Kershaw, *Hubris*, 506–507, 571–573.

95. Bieber, *Rohrbach*, 109–110; Rohrbach, *Handschrift*, 417.

96. Rohrbach, *Handschrift*, 493.

97. Heuss report, 12.17.47, in NL Heuss, BAK: N 1221, #94.

98. Schulze-Gävernitz, "Durch die Jahrtausende" (1939), in NL Schulze-Gävernitz, BAF: N 1523, #30; Dietrich, *Auf der Suche nach Deutschland*, Hamburg: von Hugo, 1946, 5–7.

99. August Weber, *Erinnerungen*, 202–203.

100. See article "Danzig und Deutschlands Genf=Austritt, Rheinbaben und Rauschning über neue Ostpolitik," 11.28.33, in NL Rheinbaben, BAK: N 1237, #9; Werner von Rheinbaben, *Viermal Deutschland: Aus dem Erleben eines Seemanns, Diplomaten, Politkers 1895–1954*, Berlin: Argon, 1954, 272–273, 333–339.

101. Williger to Gothein, 11.25.33, 2.19.37, 8.07.37, 9.24.37, in NL Gothein, BAK: N 1006, #334.

102. Williger to Gothein, 10.08.36, 02.10.37, 02.10.36, in NL Gothein, BAK: N 1006, #334.

103. A view also shared by the military leaders who tried to engineer Hitler's downfall. See Stülpnagel to Beck, 12.30.36, in NL Beck, BAF: N 1028, #2.

104. See Catalogue of Hitler's speeches on various questions, 1923 to 1940, followed by "Parteiparolen" and "Kalendarsprüche"; Lüders to Veltchen, 3.29.33, in NL Lüders, BAK: N 1151, #326: Lauterer, *Parlamentarierinnen*, 212–215.

105. Lüders to Neurath, 10.08.36; Lüders to Blomberg, 5.04.37, in NL Lüders, BAK: N 1151, #326; Lüders to General Wilhelm Groener 2.14.35, 3.03.35, in NL Groener, BAF: N 1046, #29; Lauterer, *Parlamentarierinnen*, 215–219.

106. Scholtyseck, *Bosch*, 188–190, 222–227; Fischer, *Schacht*, 175–214.

107. Tooze, *Ökonomie*, 248–259, 334–338.

108. Sassin, *Liberale*, 173.

109. Taylor, *Origins*, 131–150; Kershaw, *Hitler: Hubris*, 64–86.

110. Taylor, *Origins*, 151–186; Kershaw, *Hitler: Hubris*, 114–125.

111. Otto Gessler, *Das deutsche Volk in die europäische Ordnung*, München: Deutsche-Österreichische Arbeitsgemeinschaft, 1937, 3–16; see *Bericht über die Schlussversammlung am 27. Mai 1938*, 5.31.38, in NL Gerland, BAK: N 1010, #11.

112. "Now the path to Austria is again free. That is a development that one can greet only with great enthusiasm." Gerland to Hellpach, 9.06.36, Branca (Deutsch-Oesterreichische Arbeitsgemeinschaft) to Gerland, 7.05.37, in NL Gerland, BAK: N 1010, #11.

113. See Hess, *"Deutschland"*; 317–369; Suval, *Anschluß*, 54–95, 182–196; Cord Meyer, *Mitteleuropa*, 278–295, 318–320; Burger, *Heuss*, 345–348; Heuss to Landesmuseum Treppau, 5.27.39, in NL Heuss, BAK: N 1221, #101; Schiffer to Gerland, 1.07.29; Gerland to Schiffer, 4.09.36, in NL Gerland, BAK: N 1010, #21.
114. The "attitude of the western powers, England in particular . . . is utterly incomprehensible. It is inconceivable how it is possible that the most primitive and brutal series of developments are not better understood." Robinsohn, *Denkschrift* [1938], as quoted in Sassin, *Liberale*, 303; Burger, *Heuss*, 347.
115. Rohrbach, *Handschrift*, 449.
116. Von Rheinbaben, *Viermal Deutschland*, 348.
117. Lüders, *Fürchte Dich Nicht*, 132–145.
118. Ibid.
119. Mary Fulbrook, *The People's State: East German Society from Hitler to Honecker*, New Haven Conn.: Yale University Press, 2005; also see Martin Broszat, *Bayern in der NS-Zeit*, v. I–IV, Oldenbourg, 1977–1983; Gellately, *Gestapo and German Society*.
120. Sassin, *Liberale*, 51–54; Burger, *Heuss*, 345–348.
121. See Robinsohn, *Denkschrift* [3/39], as quoted in Sassin, *Liberale*, 324–326.
122. Ibid., 319; Bäumer to Allied authorities [1946], "Zu März 1939. 'Internationale Frauenbewegung an der Wende,'" NL Bäumer, BAK: N 1076, #5.
123. Robinsohn in Sassin, *Liberale*, 322.
124. Ibid., 323–326.
125. Taylor, *Origins*, 248–278; Kershaw, *Hitler: Hubris*, 155–205.
126. Burleigh, *Third Reich*, 268–276; Overy, "Germany," in Leitz, ed., *Third Reich*, 97–128.
127. See Mason, "Internal Crisis," in Caplan, ed., *Nazism*, 104–130; Aly, *Hitlers Volksstaat*, 346–362; Tooze, *Ökonomie*, 325–427, 745–765.
128. See 1939 Gothein article, "Bewirtschatung von Finanzen, Sachgütern u. Menschen für den Kriegsfall," in NL Gothein, BAK: N 1006, #65.
129. Ibid.
130. Robinsohn, *Denkschrift* [5/39], as quoted in Sassin, *Liberale*, 336–342.
131. Neumann, *Tantzen*, 168–169.
132. Rheinbaben, *Viermal Deutschland*, 318.
133. Scholtyseck, *Bosch*, 218–221.
134. Quidde to Gothein, 2.16.39; Schacht to Gothein, 5.03.35, in NL Gothein, BAK: N 1006, #28, #29; Also see Scholtyseck, *Bosch*, 185.
135. See Rohrbach articles, "Kreuz und Quer in der englischen Palästina – Politik," 5.04.39, "Marschal Pilsudski und Deutschland," 8.10.39; "Polen, völkisch und staatlich gesehen," 8.31.39, in NL Rohrbach, BAK: N 1408, #49.
136. Bäumer to Beckmann in Beckmann, ed., *Band*, 117.
137. Heuss, *Naumann*, 393.
138. Riegler to Heuss, 9.09.39, in NL Heuss, BAK: N 1221, #93.
139. Haar, *Historiker*, 361–362.
140. Sassin, *Liberale*, 197.
141. See Rohrbach's articles "Der russisch-polnische Grenze im Lauf des Jahrhunderts," 9.07.39; "Der ost-mitteleuropäische Raum," 9.21.39; "Pierre Valmigère's 'Und morgen?'" 9.13.39, in NL Rohrbach, BAK: N 1408, #49.
142. See Rohrbach's articles "Grossdeutschland und Südosteuropa," 9.29.39; "Die 'Repatriierung' der baltischen Deutschen," 10.11.39; "Fahrt ins Baltikum," 10.31.39, in NL Rohrbach, BAK: N 1408, #49; also see Rohrbach, *Die Deutsche Stadt Danzig*, Königsten: Langewiesche, 1930.
143. Bieber, *Rohrbach*, 114–117; Rohrbach, *Osteuropa. Historisch-politisch gesehen*, Potsdam: Rütten & Loenig, 1942.
144. See Rohrbach's articles "Die englischen Dominien," 2.09.40; "Früh-Germanisches aus Kopenhagen II," 4.19.40; Wie Engländer urteilen konnten," 6.07.40, in NL Rohrbach, BAK: N 1408, #50.

145. Ibid. Also see series of Rohrbach articles from April 1941 in NL Rohrbach, BAK: N 1408, #51.
146. Rohrbach's articles "Eine deutsch-amerikanische Kontrollfahrt," 3.14.41, "Japans Weg in die Weltpolitik," 3.26.41, in NL Rohrbach, BAK: N 1408, #50.
147. Bäumer to Marianne Weber, 10.02.39, 12.27.39, in Beckmann, ed., *Band*, 125–134.
148. Bäumer to Beckmann, 5.15.41, ibid., 146–147.
149. Sassin, *Liberale*, 208–209.
150. Huch to Baum, 4.06.41, in Baum, ed., *Briefe*, 344.
151. Scholtyseck, *Bosch*, 285.
152. See folder *Auf den Krieg bezugliche Aufsätze* in NL Bäumer, BAK: N 1076, #5; Bäumer to Weber, 5.10.40, in Beckmann, ed. *Band*, 135.
153. Waldemar Dietrich to Hermann Dietrich, 9.22.41; Hermann Dietrich to Waldemar Dietrich, 10.29.40, in NL Dietrich, BAK: N 1004, #171.
154. Koch to Dietrich, 1.01.41, in NL Dietrich, BAK: N 1004, #149.
155. Ibid.; Sassin, *Liberale*, 205–209; Scholtyseck, *Bosch*, 289–295.
156. See Christian Gerlach, *Krieg, Ernährung, Volkermord: Deutsche Vernichtungspolitik im Zweiten Weltkrieg*, Zürich: Pendo, 2001; Omar Bartov, "Soldiers, Nazis and War in the Third Reich," in Leitz, ed., *Third Reich*, 133, 150; Christopher Browning, *Ordinary Men*; Ulrich Herbert, ed., *National Socialist Extermination Policies: Contemporary Perspectives and Controversies*, vol. II, New York and Oxford: Berghahn, 2000; Jan Gross, *Neighbors: The Destruction of the Jewish Community in Jedwabne, Poland*, Princeton, N. J.: Princeton University Press, 2001.
157. Mason, "Internal Crisis," in Caplan, ed., *Nazism*, 104–130; Aly, *Hitlers Volksstaat*, 181–206; Tooze, *Ökonomie*, 551–553, 576–598.
158. See for example Josef Winschuh, "Der Aufgabenrahmen des Unternehmers in der sttaatlichen Wirtschaftslenkung," *Stahl und Eisen*, 58, nr. 24 (1938), 650–652; Winschuh speech, 12.19.41, "Formen der neuen wirtschaftlichen Denkart," in NL Winschuh, BAK: N 1223, #71; Haar, *Historiker*, 362–366; Frye, *Democrats*, 130–131.
159. See again Schulze and Oexle, eds, *Deutsche Historiker im Nationalsozialismus*; Haar, *Historiker*, 11–26, 68–71, 362–373; Fahlbusch, *Wissenschaft*, 20–30.
160. Hermann Freymark, *Die Oder – der Lebensnerv des deutschen Ostens 1934*, Breslau: H. Marcus, 1934, 331–332; also see Freymark, "Das Werden der Wirtschaft Breslaus nach den Befreiungskrieg," in *Beiträge zur Geschichte der Stadt Breslaui*, vol. XI, Breslau: Priebatsch, 1940.
161. Erich Obst, *Schlesien, das deutsche Tor nach dem Osten, Vortrag, gehalten am 25. November 1941 vor der Bezirksgruppe Breslau der WVV*, Berlin: Otto Elsner, 1942, 3–12.
162. Obst, Erich and Hermann Freymark, *Die Grundlagen der Verkehrsentwicklung Schlesiens und die Entstehung des Schlesischen Eisenbahnnetzes*, Breslau: Wilh. Gott. Korn, 1942, 5–12.
163. Obst and Freymark, *Grundlagen*, 32.
164. Winschuh, *Wirtschaft*, 17–40, 89, 142–146, 240–241; Winschuh, "Schwerpunkt Ost," *Deutsche Tageszeitung*, 11.16.1941.
165. Winschuh, *Das neue wirtschaftliche Weltbild*, Berlin: Albert Limbach, 1941, 38–47.
166. Burger, *Heuss*, 346–349; see also Fischer, *Griff*, 170–175.
167. See Bäumer, "Ursprung und Sinn des Arbeitsdienstes in Deutschland," in NL Bäumer, BAK: N 1076, #5.
168. See Heile letter regarding article from *De Telegraaf*, 1.11.40, in NL Heile, BAK: N 1132, #1.
169. Robinsohn, as quoted in Sassin, *Liberale*, 350–351.
170. Josef Winschuh, *Gerüstete Wirtschaft*, 1939, 89; Obst, *Schlesien*, Angelika Ebbinghaus and Karl Heinz Roth, "Vorläufer des 'Generalplans Ost'. Eine Dokumentation über Theodor Schieders Polendenkschrift vom 7. Oktober 1939," *Zeitschrift für Sozialgeschichte des 20. und 21. Jahrhunderts*, 7 (1992), S. 62–94.

171. Obst and Freymark, *Grundlagen*, 32–33; Ruth Andreas-Friedrich, *Der Schattenmann. Schauplatz Berlin. Tagebuchaufzeichnungen 1938–1948*, Frankfurt: Suhrkamp, 2000, 98–110; Generaldirektion der staatlichen Archive Bayerns, eds, *Wege in die Vernichtung. Die Deportation der Juden aus Mainfranken 1941–1943*, Munich: Staatlichen Archive Bayerns, 2003.

172. Baum, *Rückblick*, 302–304.

173. See Rohrbach's articles "Der Bolschewismus in Osteuropa," 6.26.41; "Bolschewisten-Bankerott," 7.02.41, in NL Rohrbach, BAK: N 1408, #50.

174. See Rohrbach's articles "Sowjet-Metamorphose," 3.11.44; "Man erschrickt in Frankreich," 3.22.44, in BAK: N 1408, #52.

175. John Lewis Gaddis, *Strategies of Containment: A Critical Appraisal of American National Security Policy during the Cold War*, Oxford: Oxford University Press, 2005; Gabriel Kolko, *The Politics of War: The World and United States Foreign Policy 1943–1945*, New York: Pantheon, 1990; Fraser J. Harbutt, *The Iron Curtain: Churchill, America, and the Origins of the Cold War*, New York: Oxford University Press, 1986.

176. Bäumer, "Die falsche Emanzipation: Zur Stellung der Frau in der Sowjet-Union," *DF*, 10–11/41.

177. Ibid.

178. Ibid.

179. See article "Verratene Europe" [1944], in NL Bäumer, BAK: N 1076, #5.

180. Bäumer to Graefe, 12.28.43, in Beckmann, ed., *Band*, 217.

181. Winschuh, "Schwerpunkt Ost," *Deutsche Tageszeitung*, 11.16.1941; Burger, *Heuss*, 345–349.

182. Andreas Hillgruber, *Zweierlei Untergang*, Berlin: Siedler, 1986. Ernst Nolte, *Der europäische Bürgerkrieg 1917–1945. Nationalsozialismus und Bolschewismus*, Berlin: Propyläen, 1987.

183. Jürgen Habermas, "Eine Art Schadensabwicklung. Die apologetischen Tendenzen in der deutschen Geschichtsschreibung (*Die Zeit* vom 11.7.1986)," in *Die Dokumentation der Kontroverse um die Einzigartigkeit der nationalsozialistischen Judenvernichtung*, München: Piper, 1987, 62–76.

184. Robinsohn to Elchner, 3.08.47, in NL Robinsohn, BAK: N 1296, #3.

185. See Rohrbach's articles 8.11.41, "Der Polyp USA," 8.11.41 and "Die USA im Stillen Ozean," 12.11.41, in NL Rohrbach, BAK: N 1408, #51; See transcripts from Bäumer's 1946 interrogation, *Zu den in der Zeitschrift 'Die Frau' beanstandeten Beiträge'*: NL Bäumer, BAK: N 1076, #5.

186. Henry Morgenthau, *Germany is Our Problem*, New York: Harper, 1945; Richard Overy, *Why the Allies Won*, New York: Norton, 1996, 311–321; Burleigh, *Third Reich*, 795–796.

187. Ibid., 347–349, 353–354.

188. Sassin, *Liberale*, 49.

189. Bäumer to Ritter, 12.25.41, Graefe, 1.13.42, Beckmann, 2.10.42, in Beckmann, ed., *Band*, 165–181.

190. Andrea Wagner, "Ein Human Development Index für Deutschland: Die Entwicklung des Lebensstandards von 1920 bis 1960," in *Jahrbuch für Wirtschaftsgeschichte*, 2 (2003) 171–199; Richard Overy, *War and Economy in the Third Reich*, Oxford: Oxford University Press, 1995, 205–232, 259–314.

191. Sassin, *Liberale*, 230.

192. *Denkschrift Hans Robinsohns* [Nov./Dez. 1941] in Sassin, *Liberale*, 345–346.

193. See Rohrbach article "Nordafrika und der Invasion," 12.03.42, in BAK: N 1408, #51.

194. See Huch letters, 1.03.43, 4.22.43, 6.01.43, 10.10.43, 12.25.43, in Baum, ed., *Briefe*, 306–382.

195. See Bäumer letters to Beckmann, 3.06.43, 3.19.43, 7.11.43; Bäumer to Marianne Weber, 5.14.43; Bäumer to Hübner, 5.04.43, in Beckmann, ed., *Band*, 175–193.

196. See Maier letter, 3.25.43, in Reinhold Maier, *Ende und Wende: Das Schwäbische Schicksal 1944–1946, Briefe und Tagebuchaufzeichnungen von Reinhold Maier*, Tübingen: R. Wunderlich, 1948.
197. Baum, *Rückblick*, 304.
198. Schaser, *Lange und Bäumer*, 325–327.
199. Bäumer to Weber, 7.28.43; Bäumer to Heuss, 9.07.43, in Beckmann, ed., *Band*, 194–197.
200. Bäumer to Usinger, 2.03.44; Bäumer to van Velsen, 3.10.44; Bäumer to Graefe, 5.05.44; Bäumer to Wagner, 6.29.44, in Beckmann, ed., *Band*, 205–229.
201. Heile to Ostermann, 6.21.44, in BAK: N 1132, #48.
202. See Maier diary entries, 3.25.44, 5.08.44, 5.14.44, 12.26.44, in Maier, *Ende und Wende*.
203. Heuss to Beck, 6.13.44, in NL Heuss, BAK: N 1221, #73.
204. See Rohrbach's articles "An der Atlantikfront," 5.03.43; "Musée de l'homme!" 8.26.43; "Völkische Regeneration," 12.21.43; in NL Rohrbach, BAK: N 1408, #52; Bäumer, "Verratene Europe" [1944], in NL Bäumer, BAK: N 1076, # 5; Robinsohn to Abatz, 7.29.48, in NL Robinsohn, BAK: N 1296, #2.
205. See Rohrbach's article "Der europäische Gedanke," 3.14.44. "Peoples are just as diverse as individual personalities; in both cases there is an interplay of materialistic and idealistic characteristics . . . German ideals should strive to become conceptions of social cosmopolitanism." See "Gedanken der Völker," 12.18.44. Also see Rohrbach, "Die Schrift an der Wand," 1.10.45, in BAK: N 1408, #52.
206. Bieber, *Rohrbach*, 115–119.
207. See Maier entries, 3.05.45, 4.13.45, in Maier, *Ende und Wende*.
208. Hansen, *Bernstorff*, 235–277.
209. Schiffer to Gerland, 11.26.40, in BAK: N 1010, #21; Huch to Baum, 12.02.44, in Baum, ed. *Briefe*, 391; see entries, 10.16.44, 4.02.45, 4.04–07.45, in Maier, *Ende und Wende*; Stig Dagerman, *German Autumn*, London: Quartet, 1988, 5–49; Alfred Weber, *Abschied von der bisherigen Geshichte*, Hamburg: Classen & Goverts, 1946, 1–24, 206–228; Baum, *Rückblick*, 302–304.
210. See again, Kurlander, *Price*; Heß, "*Deutschland*"; Bruendel, *Volksgemeinschaft*; Wildt, *Volksgemeinschaft*; Fritzsche, *Life and Death*.

Chapter Five: "Neither Jews nor Anti-Semites"

1. Pulzer, "The Beginning of the End," in Arnold Paucker and Barbara Suchy, eds, *The Jews in Nazi Germany, 1933–1943*, Tübingen: Möhr, 1986, 22; for more on the Jewish (liberal) perspective, see Avraham Barkai, *"Wehr Dich!" Der Centralverein deutscher Staatsbürger jüdischen Glaubens (C.V), 1893–1938*, Munich: C.H. Beck, 2002; Arnold Paucker, *Der jüdische Abwehrkampf gegen Antisemitismus und Nationalsozialismus in den letzten Jahren der Weimarer Republik*, Hamburg: Hans Christians, 1969.
2. Ibid. Also see Andreas Gotzmann, Rainer Liedtke, and Till van Rahden, eds, *Juden, Bürger, Deutscher: Zur Geschichte von Vielfalt und Differenz 1800–1933*, Tübingen, Mohr Siebeck, 2001; Wolfgang Benz, "Einleitung," Anthony Kauders, "Legally Citizens: Jewish Exclusion from the Weimar Polity," and Peter Pulzer, "Between Hope and Fear: Jews and the Weimar Republic," in Wolfgang Benz, Arnold Paucker, and Peter Pulzer, eds, *Judisches Leben in der Weimares Republik*, Tübingen: Mohr Siebeck, 1997, 1–6, 159–172, 271–279; also see Cornelia Hecht, *Deutsche Juden und Antisemitismus in der Weimarer Republik*, Bonn: Dietz, 2003; Thomas Pegelow, " 'German Jews,' 'National Jews,' 'Jewish Volk' or 'Racial Jews'? The Constitution and Contestation of 'Jewishness' in Newspapers of Nazi Germany, 1933–1938," *CEH*, 35 (2002), 195–221.
3. See Kurlander, *Price*, 78–85; also see Peter Pulzer, "Jewish Participation in Wilhelmine Politics," in David Bronsen, ed., *Jews and Germans from 1860 to 1933*,

Heidelberg: Carl Winter, 1979, 78–99; Jan Palmowski, "Between Dependence and Influence: Jews and Liberalism in Frankfurt am Main, 1864–1933," in Henning Tewes and Jonathan Wright, eds, *Liberalism, Anti-Semitism, and Democracy*, Oxford: Oxford University Press, 2001, 76–101; J. Wright, "Liberalism and Anti-Semitism in the Weimar Republic: The Case of Gustav Stresemann," in Tewes and Wright, eds, *Liberalism*, 102–126.

4. See Hans Mommsen, *From Weimar to Auschwitz*, Princeton: Princeton, 1992; C. Browning, *The Path to Genocide: Essays on Launching the Final Solution*, Cambridge : Cambridge, 1998; Kershaw, *Popular Opinion*; Aly, *Hitlers Volksstaat*; Tooze, *Ökonomie*. Also see Dan Stone, *Constructing the Holocaust: A Study in Historiography*, London: Vallentine Mitchell, 2003.

5. Ibid. David Bankier, *The Germans and the Final Solution: Public Opinion in the Third Reich*, Oxford: Blackwell, 1992; Michael Wildt, "Violence against the Jews in Germany, 1933–1939"; Otto Kulka, "The German Population and the Jews: State of Research and New Perspectives"; Alf Lüdtke, "German Work and German Workers: The Impact of Symbols on the Exclusion of Jews in Nazi Germany," in David Bankier, ed., *Probing the Depths of German Antisemitism: German Society and the Persecution of the Jews, 1933–1941*, New York: Berghahn, 2000, 181–212, 271–281, 296–311; Gellately, *Backing Hitler*; Jeffrey Herf, *The Jewish Enemy: Nazi Propaganda during World War II*, Cambridge, Mass.: Belknap, 2006; Peter Longerich, *"Davon haben wir nicht gewusst": Die Deutschen und die Judenverfolgung, 1933–1945*, Berlin: Siedler, 2006.

6. Paul Lawrence Rose, *Revolutionary Antisemitism in Germany from Kant to Wagner*, Princeton, N.J.: Princeton University Press, 1992; Goldhagen, *Willing Executioners*; Wildt, *Volksgemeinschaft*; Fritzsche, *Life and Death*; according to Lars Fischer, even the Socialists possessed an essentialist and potentially eliminationist anti-Semitic impulse. See Fischer, *The Socialist Response*.

7. See Noel Cary, "Antisemitism, Everyday Life, and the Devastation of Public Morals in Germany," *CEH*, 35, nr. 4 (2002), 551–589.

8. See Heinrich von Treitschke, "Unsere Aussichten", in *Preussischer Jahrbücher*, vol. 44 (1879), 559–576; Karsten Krieger, *Der Berliner Antisemitismusstreit 1879–1881: Eine Kontroverse um die Zugehörigkeit der deutschen Juden zur Nation*, Munich: K. G. Saur, 2003, 699–753.

9. See Pulzer, "Jewish Participation," in Bronsen, ed., *Jews and Germans*, 78–99; Palmowski, "Between Dependence and Influence," in Tewes and Wright, eds, *Liberalism*, 6–101; folder, *A.S.V. Reste vom Abwehrverein*, 101–104, in NL Gothein, BAK: N 1006, #54.

10. Fischer, *Response*, 6–36; van Rahden, *Juden und andere Breslauer: Die Beziehungen zwischen Juden, Protestanten und Katholiken in einer deutschen Großstadt von 1860 bis 1925*, Göttingen: Vandenhoeck & Ruprecht, 2000.

11. Kurlander, *Price*, 32–33, 51–65, 78–93, 192–203; for more on the nature of political anti-Semitism before the First World War, see again Fritz Stern, *Illiberalism*; Stern, *The Politics of Cultural Despair*; Mosse, *The Crisis of German Ideology*; Gellately, *The Politics of Economic Despair*; Shulamit Volkov, *The Rise of Popular Antimodernism in Germany: The Urban Master Artisans, 1873–1896*, Princeton, N.J.: Princeton University Press, 1978.

12. Pulzer, "Jewish Participation," in Bronsen, ed., *Jews and Germans*, 78–99; Palmowski, "Between Dependence and Influence," in Tewes and Wright, eds, *Liberalism, Anti-Semitism, and Democracy*, 76–101.

13. Ibid.; also see letter from Dr Levy to Nathan, 8.12.20, in NL Nathan, BAB: N 2207, #18; Martin Liepach, "Zwischen Abwehrkampf und Wählermobilisierung: Juden und die Landtagswahl in Baden 1929," and Anthony Kauders, "Legally Citizens: Jewish Exclusion from the Weimar Polity," in Benz et al., eds, *Jewish Life*, 9–24, 159–172.

14. Pulzer, "Jewish Participation," in Bronsen, ed., *Jews and Germans*, 78–99; Jones, *German Liberalism*, 104; German Democratic Party (DDP) minutes, 1.07.19, in

BAK: R 45 III, #15,13–25, 40–53; Gothein to Nathan, 10.20.20, in NL Nathan, BAB: N 2207, # 5; also see speeches by Gothein and Landsberg opposing anti-Semitism, 11.16.19, in NL Gerland, BAK: N 1010, #27. "Der Antisemitismus der Alldeutschen", *Der Volksstaat*, 9.19.19; Ingemar Helmrich, *Geschichte der Juden in Liegnitz*, Liegnitz: Selbstverlag, 1938, 90–92; *Breslauer Zeitung*, 7.25.32, 7.28.32; reports on speeches by Neumann in Trebnitz and Bayer in Prausnitz, 11.02.32, Minutes of the German Peoples' Party (DVP) in BAB: R 45 II, #53129.

15. See Kurlander, *Price*, 249–271; Palmowski, "Between Dependence and Influence," in Tewes and Wright, eds, *Liberalism, Anti-Semitism, and Democracy*, 76–101.
16. See *Berichte*, Robinsohn [1934] in Sassin, *Liberale*, 257–258.
17. Mitschke to Schütt, 2.11.33, NL Dietrich, BAK N 1004, #150; Anthony Kauders, "Legally Citizens," in Benz et al., eds, *Jewish Life*, 159–172.
18. Walter Schnell to Dingeldey, 5.15.33, in NL Dingeldey, BAK: N 1002, #63. Even Heuss's *Die Hilfe* included articles criticizing the unhealthy influence of "Ghetto Jews." Froelich, "*Die Hilfe* im Nationalsozialismus," in Studt, ed., "*Diener des Staates*", 122.
19. Heuss to Mück, 5.07.33, in NL Heuss, BAK: N 1221, #648.
20. See B. Mayer-Pantenius to Dietrich, 6.16.33, in NL Dietrich, BAK: N 1004, # 150.
21. Chinua Achebe, "An Image of Africa: Racism in Conrad's *Heart of Darkness*," in C. Achebe, ed., *Hopes and Impediments. Selected Essays*, New York: Anchor, 1990, 13.
22. Goetz in Franz Weidenreich, ed., *Rasse und Geist*, Leipzig: Johann Ambrosius Barth, 7–12, 77–78.
23. Lüders, "*Fürchte Dich Nicht*," 128–143.
24. Remy, *Myth*, 18–19.
25. Dahrendorff, *Heuss*, 241.
26. Heuss to Democratic colleagues, and Dietrich's response 11.09.33, in NL Heuss, BAK: N 1221, # 146. 12.28.33; Dietrich to Koch, 5.02.34, 9.10.38, 9.12.38, 9.29.38; Koch to Dietrich, 2.28.35,1.10.38, 9.18.38, 9.20.38 1.01.41, in NL Dietrich, BAK: N 1004, #149.
27. Schiffer to Gerland, 10.31.40, in NL Gerland, BAK: N 1010, #21; Neumann, *Tantzen*, 198–199.
28. Hockenos, *A Church Divided*, 20–21; 185; Steigmann-Gall, *Reich*, 185.
29. Lindsay, *Solidarity*, 249–251.
30. Scholtyseck, *Bosch*, 268.
31. See folder *Reichstagwahl* [July 1933], in letter from CVDJG to Külz, 3.02.33; Külz to Central Association of Germans of Jewish Confession (CVDJG), 3.03.33; Streicher article in *Der Stürmer*, in NL Külz, BAK: N 1042, #19.
32. Lauterer, *Parlamentarierinnen*, 215–216.
33. See *A.S.V. Reste vom Abwehrverein*, 106–109, in NL Gothein, BAK: N 1006, 54.
34. Williger to Gothein, 6.21.33, 11.14.33, 2.12.35, 5.17.35; Motsei to Gothein, 10.19.33; in NL Gothein, BAK: N 1006, #34.
35. Remy, *Myth*, 23–30; Reinhard Höhn, *Rechtsgemeinschaft und Volksgemeinschaft*, Hamburg: Hanseatische Verlagsanstalt, 1935; R. Höhn, *Reich, Großraum, Großmacht*, Darmstadt: Wittich, 1942; Rudolf Diels, *Lucifer ante Portas: Von Severing bis Heydrich*, Stuttgart: Deutsche Verlagsanstalt, 1950.
36. Stolper to Amonn, 9.02.33, in NL Stolper, BAK: N 1186, #49.
37. Winschuh, *Männer, Traditionen, Signale*, 228–235; Weber, *Erinnerungen*, 152–153; Kempter, *Jellineks*, 476–495; G. Edward White, *Oliver Wendell Holmes: Law and the Inner Self*, Oxford: Oxford University Press, 2001, 405–408.
38. Meurer, *Marianne Weber*, 26–29.
39. Greven-Aschoff, *Frauenbewegung*, 186.
40. See assorted articles by Dorothee van Velsen, "Frauen, Volk und Staat"; Else Ulrich-Beil, "Familie, Volk, und Staat"; Luise Scheffen-Döring, "Einige Gedanken zur Aussenpolitik," *DF*, 3/33, in NL Bäumer, BAK: N 1076, #13; Greven-Aschoff, *Frauenbewegung*, 186.

41. See articles by Bäumer and Baum, in *DF*, 7/34; Lauterer, *Parlamentarierinnen*, 204–207.
42. See Bäumer article, "Die seelischen Erbwerte," *DF*, 1/36.
43. Lauterer, *Parlamentarierinnen*, 213–216.
44. Camilla Jellinek, "Martyrium einer Deutschen, die nicht mehr Deutsche sein durfte," *DF*, 3/35; Jellinek to Lüders, 2.14.33, in NL Lüders, BAK: N 1151, #245; Kempter, *Jellineks*, 497–501.
45. Kershaw, *Hitler: Hubris*, 487–490.
46. Evans, *Power*, 20–41.
47. Ibid., 536–547; Karl Schleunes, *The Twisted Road to Auschwitz*, Champaign: University of Illinois Press, 1971.
48. Kershaw, *Hitler: Hubris*, 575–589; Evans, *Power*, 543–546.
49. Bryan Rigg, *Hitler's Jewish Soldiers*, Lawrence: University of Kansas Press, 2002, 76–115; Evans, *Power*, 548–551.
50. Hans Robinsohn, *Justiz als politische Verfolgung: Die Rechtsprechung in "Rassenschandefällen" beim Landgericht Hamburg, 1936–1943*, Stuttgart: Deutsche Verlags-Anstalt, 1977, 10–11. Indeed, as Claudia Koonz reminds us, similar laws against miscegenation and racial equality persisted across the American South in the interwar period, in some cases providing inspiration for Nazi bureaucrats. See Koonz, *The Nazi Conscience*, Cambridge, Mass.: Harvard University Press, 2003, 172–176.
51. Williger to Gothein, 11.22.35, 12.09.35, 12.23.35, 1.06.36, 10.08.36, in NL Gothein, BAK: N 1006, #34.
52. See Emmy Beckmann, "Das Ringen um das Geist–Seele-Problem," *DF*, 8/37.
53. Marie Baum, *Leuchtende Spur*, 340–345; Burger, *Heuss*, 313–315; Froelich, "*Die Hilfe im Nationalsozialismus*," in Studt, ed., "*Diener des Staates*," 122–123.
54. See *Berichte*, Robinsohn [1936], in Sassin, *Liberale*, 275–279; Koch-Weser, *Hitler and Beyond*, 104–108.
55. *Berichte*, Robinsohn [1936], in Sassin, *Liberale*, 287–288.
56. As late as 1937 one could find examples where "the Hamburg court had . . . taken note of the exceptional circumstances of incarceration in the Third Reich in favor of the accused [Jews]." Robinsohn, *Justiz*, 24.
57. "Were it otherwise," Robinsohn continued, "many of the measures against the Jews should have been unnecessary – then the people themselves would have made certain that there would be no more Jews in Germany." *Berichte*, Robinsohn [1936], in Sassin, *Liberale*, 287–289; also see Frank Bajohr, *"Aryanisation" in Hamburg*, New York: Berghahn, 2002.
58. Bankier, *Final Solution*, 117–145; Longerich, "*Davon haben wir nicht gewusst*," 216–240; Herbert Obenaus, "The Germans: 'An Antisemitic People': The Press Campaign after 9 November 1938," in Bankier, ed. *Probing*, 147–180; Neumann, *Tantzen*, 173–174, 181–186, 203; Remy, *Myth*, 17–18.
59. Bäumer, *Der neue Weg*, 10–12.
60. Koch-Weser, *Hitler*, 105–107. Schmid, ed., *Fritz Elsas*; Avraham Barkai, *From Boycott to Annihilation: The Economic Struggle of German Jews, 1933–1943*, Hanover: Brandeis, 1989; Brian Amkraut, *Between Home and Homeland: Youth Aliyah from Nazi Germany*, Tuscaloosa: University of Alabama Press, 2006.
61. David Cesarani, *Becoming Eichmann: Rethinking the Life, Crimes, and Trial of a "Desk Murderer,"* New York: Da Capo, 2007, 48–56.
62. Bäumer to Heuss, 4.24.37, in Beckmann, ed., *Band*, 103–104.
63. Williger to Gothein, 12.23.35; Gothein to Williger, 9.12.37. NL Gothein, BAK: N 1006, #34; Marie Baum, *Leuchtende Spur*, 380–393; Lüders, *Fürchte Dich Nicht*, 135–145.
64. Hjalmar Schacht. *Abrechnung mit Hitler*, Westport: Greenwood, 1956, 1–17; Artikel von Stolper über Schacht," in NL Stolper, BAK: N 1186, #29; Frye, *Democrats*, 48–57, 101–117.

65. Albert Fischer, "The Minister of Economics and the Expulsion of the Jews from the German economy," in Bankier, ed., *Probing*, 213–225; Fischer, *Schacht*; Tooze, *Ökonomie*, 329–330. For a slightly more positive appraisal, see Evans, *Power*, 383–394.
66. Fischer, "The Minister of Economics," in Bankier, ed., *Probing*, 215; Fischer, *Schacht*, 104–125; Stolper to Schacht, 7.02.33, NL Stolper, BAK: N 1186, #29.
67. Schacht to Kardorff, 1.27.60; Kardorff to Schacht, 2.09.60, NL K. von Kardorff, BAK: N 1039, #65.
68. Fischer, *Schacht*, 126–191, 216–218. Also see Mosse, *Jews in the German Economy*.
69. Fischer, "The Minister of Economics," in Bankier, ed., *Probing*, 215–219.
70. Fischer, "Expulsion," in Bankier, ed., *Probing*, 221–222.
71. Ibid., 223–224; Tooze, *Wages*, 107–173, 260–334.
72. Tooze, *Wages*, 192–223; John Weitz, *Hitler's Banker*, Boston: Little, Brown, 1997, 186–88; Evans, *Power*, 343–358.
73. See Schacht, *Rede des Reichsbankpräsidenten*; Schacht, *Confessions*, 284–285, 318–322; Evans, *Power*, 381–394.
74. Sassin, *Liberale*, 127–128, 162–166; Bajohr, "*Aryanisation*," 45–47.
75. See August Weber, *Erinnerungen*, in BAK: KLE 384, 135–137.
76. Albert Fischer, "The Minister of Economics," in Bankier, ed., *Probing*, 225.
77. Luckemeyer, *Rebell*, 111–114; Evans, *Power*, 360–363; Schacht, *Confessions*, 284–285, 318–322, 446–455.
78. See Robinsohn *Denkschrift* [February 1939] in Sassin, *Liberale*, 306.
79. Schacht, *Abrechnung mit Hitler*, 12–17.
80. Dietrich writes to a Jewish colleague, 9.29.33, in NL Dietrich, BAK: N 1004, #148.
81. Schiftan to Dietrich, 7.26.39, 8.10.35, 8.12.35, 8.29.35, in NL Dietrich, BAK: N 1004, #155.
82. Dietrich to Bihler, 12.12.33; Birk to Dietrich, 7.06.33, 2.14.34, in NL Dietrich, BAK: N 1004, #143; Steiner to Dietrich, 11.29.34, in NL Dietrich, BAK: N 1004, #155.
83. Dietrich to Nuschke, 1.12.34, in NL Dietrich, BAK: N 1004, #152.
84. Alexander Weinstein to Dietrich, 11.21.36, in NL Dietrich, BAK: N 1004, #157.
85. Dietrich to Berlin Treasury Department, 3.30.42, Treasury to Dietrich [April 1942], in NL Dietrich, BAK: N 1004, #365.
86. See folders in NL Dietrich, BAK: N 1004, # 370, 384–386, 406.
87. Ernst Mayer to Heuss, 11.02.35; Heuss to Dietrich, 11.04.35; Mayer to Dietrich, 1.12.36, 3.17.36, 5.28.36; 4.23.36; Dietrich to Mundhenke, 1.13.36; Dietrich to Mayer, 1.04.36, 5.11.36, 5.15.36, 5.22.36, 11.09.36, in NL Dietrich, BAK: N 1004, #150.
88. Koch to Dietrich, 9.01.33, in NL Dietrich, BAK: N 1004, #149.
89. Scholtyseck, *Bosch*, 271; Bajohr, "*Aryanisation*," 20–22, 41–47, 104–108, 142–143, 222–226.
90. Dietrich to Sander family, 11.22.37, 3.08.37, 3.15.37, 3.18.37, 12.13.38; Kaufmann to Dietrich, 11.19.38; also see folders marked *411–421 Anwaltsakten betr. Wilhelm Lieberg u. Co. GMBH*, in NL Dietrich, BAK: N 1004, #155, #s 411–421; Dietrich to Berg, 3.02.36, in NL Dietrich, BAK: N 1004, #143.
91. Dietrich to Zolki, 6.10.37, in NL Dietrich, BAK: N 1004, #364.
92. Dietrich to Nationalsozialistische Rechtswahrerbund (NSRB), 7.01.40; Dietrich to Bein, 6.01.40, in NL Dietrich, BAK: N 1004, #s 364, 143.
93. Troeltsch to Zolki, 7.30.41; Rita Troeltsch to Zolki, 9.07.41; Zolki to Troeltsch, 9.11.41, 9.17.41, in NL Dietrich, BAK: N 1004, #172.
94. Dietrich to Heinemann, 6.28.38, in NL Dietrich, BAK: N 1004, #146; Becker to Dietrich, 12.03.35, 6.06.37, 1.09.38; Dietrich to Becker, 6.08.37, NL Dietrich, BAK: N 1004, #143.
95. Gothein to Dietrich, 11.27.38; Dietrich to Gothein, 11.28.38, NL Dietrich, BAK: N 1004, #145; also see Holocaust claims proceedings, http://www.crtii.org/_awards/_apdfs/Waldstein_Felix_and_Gertrud.pdf.

96. See August Weber, *Erinnerungen*, in BAK: KLE 384, 151–161; Froelich, "He Served the German People Well," 634–636.

97. Paul Sauer, ed., *Reinhold Maier: Briefwechsel mit seiner Familie 1930–1946*, Stuttgart: Kohlhammer, 1989, 5–168.

98. Leo Baeck, as quoted in Bott, ed., *Begegnungen*, 418–421.

99. Heuss, *Hitlers Weg*, 32–35, 41–46.

100. Toni Stolper, as quoted in Bott, ed., *Begegnungen*, 445–448.

101. Heuss to RVDP, 6.15.34, in NL Heuss, BAK: N 1221, #92; Hermann Beck, "Between the Dictates of Conscience and Political Expediency: Hitler's Conservative Alliance Partner and Antisemitism during the Nazi Seizure of Power," *Journal of Contemporary History*, 41, no. 4 (2006), 611–640; 615–616.

102. Heuss to Schnee, 6.21.35, 5.30.47; Schnee to Heuss, 7.15.35, in NL Heuss, BAK: N 1221, #96; Werner Schiefel, *Bernhard Dernburg 1865–1937. Kolonialpolitiker und Bankier im wilhelminischen Deutschland*, Zürich: Atlantis-Verlag, 1974.

103. Stephan to Heuss, 2.16.37, in NL Heuss, BAK: N 1221, #99.

104. Heuss, *Naumann*, 106.

105. Ibid., 107–108.

106. See letters to Wolfgang Jaenicke, 12.15.26, 1.25.28, in NL Jaenicke, BAK: N 1135, #13.

107. Kardorff to Weizmann, 7.22.55, in NL K. von Kardorff, BAK: N 1039, #60; Letter to Kardorff, 2.04.38, in NL K. von Kardorff, BAK: N 1039, #15.

108. For an elaboration of this argument in the British and American context, see Tony Kushner, *The Holocaust and the Liberal Imagination: A Social and Cultural History*, Oxford: Blackwell, 1994.

109. Kershaw, *Hitler: Nemesis*, 115–136, 321–324, 463–505; Burleigh, *Third Reich*, 567–601.

110. Schacht, *Abrechnung mit Hitler*, 16–17.

111. Behrendt, *Külz*, 157–162.

112. August Weber, *Erinnerungen*, 202–203.

113. Koch, *Hitler*, 102–103.

114. Scholtyseck, *Bosch*, 231–232.

115. Ibid., 265–267.

116. Ibid., 271–273, 274–276.

117. Peter Hoffmann, "German Resistance to Hitler," in Bankier, ed., *Probing*, 466–467.

118. Ibid., 467–469.

119. Scholtyseck, *Bosch*, 276–277.

120. Konrad Kwiet, "Resistance and Opposition: The Example of the German Jews," in Bankier, ed., *Probing*, 65–69.

121. Scholtyseck, *Bosch*, 277–279.

122. Schmid in Schmid, ed., *Fritz Elsas*, 43.

123. See *Berichte*, Robinsohn [Nov./Dez. 1941], in Sassin, *Liberale*, 369.

124. Hoffmann, "Resistance to Hitler," in Bankier, ed., *Probing*, 466.

125. Ibid., 466–467.

126. Ibid., 467–472.

127. Scholtyseck, *Bosch*, 279–281.

128. Hans Mommsen, *Alternatives to Hitler: German Resistance under the Third Reich*, Princeton: Princeton, 2003, 253–275.

129. Hoffmann, "Resistance to Hitler," in Bankier, ed., *Probing*, 475–477.

130. Baum, *Rückblick*, 291.

131. See *Berichte*, Robinsohn [Nov./Dez. 1941], in Sassin, *Liberale*, 346.

132. See quote from liberal general Paul Freiherr von Schoenaich in Sassin and Erkins, eds, *Dokumente*, 324; Baum, ed., *Briefe*, 418; Kardorff to Israeli minister, 7.22.55, in NL K. von Kardorff, BAK: N 1039, #60; Bankier, *Final Solution*, 101–115; Longerich, "*Davon haben wir nicht gewusst*," 240–308; also see Browning, *The Path to Genocide*; Omer Bartov, *Germany's War and the Holocaust: Disputed Histories*, Ithaca, NY: Cornell,

     2003. For an excellent new study exploring the relationship between resettlement and genocide, see Wendy Lower, *Nazi Empire Building and the Holocaust in Ukraine*, Chapel Hill, N.C.: University of North Carolina Press, 2007.

133. Fahlbusch, *Wissenschaft*, 11–12, 28–30, 796–797; Haar, *Historiker*, 11–15, 200–201, 308; Remy, *Myth*, 24–28; Also see Ingo Haar, "German Ostfordschung and Anti-Semitism," in Fahlbusch and Haar, eds, *German Scholars and Ethnic Cleansing*, New York: Berghahn, 2004, 1–27; Johannes Hürter and Hans Woller, eds, *Hans Rothfels und die deutsche Zeitgeschichte*, Munich: Oldenbourg, 2005.

134. See Daniel Fraenkel, "Jewish Self-Defense under the Constraints of National Socialism: The Final Years of the Centralverein", in Bankier, ed, *Probing*, 346–351; Koch, *Hitler*, 106–107.

135. Arnold Paucker, *Deutsche Juden im Widerstand 1933–1945. Tatsachen und Probleme*, Berlin: Gedenkstätte Deutscher Widerstand, 1999; Arnold Paucker, "Resistance of German and Austrian Jews to the Nazi Regime," in *Leo Baeck Institute Year Book XL*, London 1995, 3–20; Konrad Kwiet and Helmut Eschwege, *Selbstbehauptung und Widerstand. Deutsche Juden im Kampf um Existenz und Menschenwürde, 1933–1945*, Hamburg: Hans Christians, 1984.

136. See Hannah Arendt, *Eichmann in Jerusalem*, New York: Penguin, 1994, 112–150; Peterson, *The Berlin Liberal Press in Exile*, Tübingen: M. Niemeyer, 1987, 122–132.

137. Pulzer, "Beginning of the End," in Paucker and Suchy, eds, *Jews in Nazi Germany*, 23–25.

138. Frye, *Democrats*, 192.

139. Wolff was on the unofficial Nazi "death list" as early as 1923 and Bernhard's publications were among the first to be burned after the Nazi seizure of power. Settling in Paris, the two longtime rivals collaborated in founding the *Pariser Tageblatt*, an émigré liberal counterpoise to the "coordinated" German press. Its influence in Germany was minimal. Peterson, *The Berlin Liberal Press*, 4–13, 51–62; Frye, *Democrats*, 192.

140. Molt, "Der Beitrag Alfred Webers," in Demm, ed., *Geist und Politik*, 237–238.

141. Remy, *Myth*, 16–20, 80.

142. Toni Stolper, *Gustav Stolper*, 311–319.

143. Ibid., 312–322, 326.

144. Ibid.

145. Stolper to Schacht, 7.02.33, in NL Stolper, BAK: N 1186, #29.

146. Peterson, *The Berlin Liberal Press*, 32–40, 186–190; Frye, *Democrats*, 122–181.

147. Frye, *Democrats*, 171–193; Gerhard Papke, *Der liberale Politiker Erich Koch-Weser in der Weimarer Republik*, Baden-Baden: Nomos, 1989, 167–191; Dietrich to Koch, 12.28.33, 9.12.38, 9.29.38; Zolki to Dietrich, 5.02.34; Koch to Heuss, 2.28.35, in NL Dietrich, BAK: N 1004, # 149; Koch-Weser to Lörner, 12.22.37; Lörner to Koch-Weser, 12.23.37; Koch-Weser to Dietrich, 1.10.38; in NL Dietrich, BAK: N 1004, # 400.

148. Koch, *Hitler*, 104–106.

149. Ibid.

150. Nuschke to Liebig, 5.06.34, in NL Dietrich, BAK: N 1004, #152.

151. John L. Harvey, "Were Chicago and Providence really so far from Königsberg and Tübingen? The Rothfelsstreit in an American Key", 2003, http://hsozkult.geschichte .hu-berlin.de/forum/id=300&type=diskussionen; Jan Eckel, *Hans Rothfels: Ein intellektuelle Biographie im 20. Jahrhundert*, Göttingen: Wallstein, 1995, 166–167; see Rothfels's praise for Heuss, Naumann, and liberal national traditions, in Bott, ed., *Begenungen*, 386–387.

152. Haar, *Historiker*, 199–203.

153. See *Berichte*, Robinsohn [Oct. 1937], in Sassin, *Liberale*, 286–287.

154. Bertha Kahn to Dietrich, 9.22.33, in NL Dietrich, BAK: N 1004, #148.

155. Welkow to Dingeldey, 11.16.33, in NL Dingeldey, BAK: N 1002, #103.

156. As quoted in Hayes, *Industry and Ideology*, 381–382.

157. Paucker, *Juden im Widerstand 1933–1945*, 10–15.

158. Pulzer, "Beginning of the End," in Paucker and Suchy, eds, *Jews in Nazi Germany*, 25.
159. Fraenkel, "Jewish Self-Defense," in Bankier, ed., *Probing*, 339–341, 346–348, 356–357. Also see Paucker, *Die Juden im nationalsozialistischen Deutschland*, Tübingen: Möhr, 1986.
160. See Hilger, *Rechtsstaatsbegriffe*.
161. Robinsohn to Leo Baeck Institute, 12.10.58; Robinsohn to Bauer, 10.15.63, in NL Robinsohn, BAK: N 1296, #2.
162. Sassin, *Liberale*, 66–67, 162–166.
163. Sassin and Erkins, eds, *Dokumente*, 316–320; Petersen, *Tageblatt*, 76–82, 89–96.
164. Sassin, *Liberale*, 19–21, 35, 47, 92, 162–167, 249.
165. See *Berichte*, Robinsohn [February 1939], in Sassin, *Liberale*, 306.
166. Neumann, *Tantzen*, 190.
167. Sassin, *Liberale*, 208–209.
168. Gothein to Dernburg, 11.11.35, 3.31.36; Dernburg to Gothein, 4.15.36, in NL Gothein, BAK: N 1006, #18; Klaus Kempter, "Camilla Jellinek und die Frauenbewegung in Heidelberg," in Meurer, *Marianne Weber*, 111, 125–126.
169. Schmid, ed., *Fritz Elsas: Demokrat*, 11–12, 17–18.
170. Ibid., 31; Jörg Thierfelder, "Fritz Elsas," in Joachim Helhausen, ed., *Zeugen des Widerstands*, Tübingen: J.C.B. Mohr, 1996, 96–99.
171. Sassin, *Liberale*, 50, 76, 116; Schmid, ed., *Fritz Elsas: Demokrat*, 18, 34.
172. Schmid, ed., *Fritz Elsas: Demokrat*, 37–38; Thierfelder, "Fritz Elsas," in Helhausen, ed., *Zeugen*, 102–103; also see Viktor Klemperer, *"I Will Bear Witness": A Diary of the Nazi Years, 1933–1941*, New York: Random House, 1999.
173. Ibid.; Elsas to Robinsohn, 1.24.39, 1.31.39, 4.09.40, 6.03.40; Robinsohn to Elsas, 4.29.40, 5.26.40, 8.25.40, in NL Robinsohn, BAK: N 1296, #28.
174. Schmid, ed., *Fritz Elsas: Demokrat*, 40–42; Thierfelder, "Fritz Elsas," in Helhausen, ed., *Zeugen*, 104–107.
175. Sassin, *Liberale*, 78; Schmid, ed., *Fritz Elsas: Demokrat*, 7–8.
176. Ibid.; Schmid, ed., *Fritz Elsas: Demokrat*, 40–43; Thierfelder, "Fritz Elsas," in Helhausen, ed., *Zeugen*, 108–110.
177. Jürgen Froelich, " 'Die Excellenz' als 'liberaler Demokrat von Jugend auf'? Eugen Schiffer und die liberalen Parteien in Deutschland," in Ramm, ed., *Eugen Schiffer*, 95–131.
178. Ibid.
179. Kurlander, *Price*, 88–116.
180. Schiffer, *Stürm über Deutschland*, Berlin: Otto Libermann, 1932, 49–60, 208–210; Frye, *Democrats*, 71–73, 78–79; Neumann, *Tantzen*, 197–198; Joachim Ramm, *Eugen Schiffer und die Reform der deutschen Justiz*, 11–64, 168–169; Thilo Ramm, "Jurist und Politiker," in Ramm, ed., *Eugen Schiffer*, 131–176; Jürgen Froelich, " 'Die Excellenz' als 'liberaler Demokrat von Jugend auf'?, in Ramm, ed., *Eugen Schiffer*, 95–116.
181. Gerland to Schiffer, 4.09.36, 4.28.36, 1.08.37; Schiffer to Gerland, 12.31.35, 10.31.40, in NL Gerland, BAK: N 1010, #21.
182. Dietrich Goldschmidt, *Erinnerungen an das Leben von Eugen und Marie Schiffer nach dem 30. Januar 1933 – Berlin in Geschichte und Gegenwart*, 117–118; Thilo Ramm, "Jurist und Politiker," in Ramm, ed., *Eugen Schiffer*, 180–187; J. Ramm, *Eugen Schiffer und die Reform der deutschen Justiz*, 67–171.
183. Ibid.
184. Schiffer to Gerland, 12.31.35, in NL Gerland, BAK: N 1010, #21.
185. Schiffer to Gerland, 6.16.39, in NL Gerland, BAK: N 1010, #21; Goldschmidt, *Erinnerungen*, 117–118.
186. Schiffer to Gerland, 1.03.40, 10.31.40; 11.26.40; 3.27.41, in NL Gerland, BAK: N 1010, #21.
187. Schiffer to Gerland, 12.24.41, in NL Gerland, BAK: N 1010, #21.
188. Neumann, *Tantzen*, 197.

189. Heuss to Schiffer, 4.18.36, in NL Heuss, BAK: N 1221, #95.
190. Gerland to Schiffer, 4.09.36, 4.28.36, 1.08.37; Schiffer to Gerland, 6.16.39, 10.31.40, in NL Gerland, BAK: N 1010, #21.
191. Goldschmidt, *Erinnerungen*, 117–118; Neumann, *Tantzen*, 198–199.
192. Goldschmidt, *Erinnerungen*, 120–123; also see Dagmar Hartung von Doetinchem and Rolf Winau, eds, *Zerstörte Fortschritte: das Jüdische Krankenhaus in Berlin, 1756, 1861, 1914, 1989*, Berlin: Hentrich, 1989; Daniel Silver, *Refuge in Hell: How Berlin's Jewish Hospital Outlasted the Nazis*, Boston: Houghton Mifflin, 2003.
193. Moldenhauer to Kardorff, 3.31.43, in NL S. von Kardorff, BAK: N 1040, #11. Moldenhauer peppered his unpublished memoirs with anti-Semitic diatribes against German Jews as well as against Jewish colleagues, including Stresemann's independent-minded wife Käthe, whom anti-Semites in the party despised. Moldenhauer, *Memoiren*, in NL Moldenhauer, BAK: N 1019, #19, 4–5, 87–93, 119, 206.
194. Schiffer to Kardorff, 8.21.46, 3.01.50, in NL K. von Kardorff, BAK: 1039, #65; Goldschmidt, *Erinnerungen*, 124.
195. Goldschmidt, *Erinnerungen*, 123; Kurlander, *Price*, 108.
196. See Schiffer to Kardorff, 8.21.46, 3.01.50, "Nachlass Kardorff." 1039, #65; Lauterer, "Liebe Marquise von O'," *JzLF*, 16 (2004), 273–283; Goldschmidt, *Erinnerungen*, 124.
197. Heide-Marie Lauterer, "Marie Baum und der Heidelberger Freundeskreis," in Meurer, *Marianne Weber*, 91–107.
198. Baum, *Rückblick*, 276–279, 281–286; Lauterer, *Parlamentarierinnen*, 221–222.
199. Thilo Ramm, "Jurist und Politiker," in Ramm, ed., *Eugen Schiffer*, 181–187; Ramm, ed., *Eugen Schiffer*, 167–171.
200. See Till van Rahden, "Mingling, Marrying and Distancing: Jewish Integration in Wilhelminian Breslau and its Erosion in Early Weimar Germany," in Benz et al. eds, *Jews in the Weimar Republic*, 193–217.
201. Baum, *Rückblick*, 282–286; Lauterer, *Parlamentarierinnen*, 223–225.
202. Ibid., 280–282, 286–288.
203. Baum, *Rückblick*, 285–286.
204. For details on this crucial turining point in Nazi Jewish policy, see Peter Longerich, *Die Wannsee-Konferenz vom 20. Januar 1942. Planung und Beginn des Genozids an den europäischen Juden*, Berlin: Hentrich, 1998; Mark Roseman, *The Wannsee Conference and the Final Solution: A Reconsideration*, New York: Picador, 2003.
205. Baum, *Rückblick*, 287–288; Also see Lauterer, "Marie Baum und der Heidelberger Freundeskreis," in Meurer, ed., *Marianne Weber*, 107–108; Julius Schätzle, *Stationen zur Hölle. Konzentrationslager in Baden und Württemberg 1933–1945*, Frankfurt: Röderberg, 1980.
206. Baum, *Rückblick*, 288–291.
207. See Marie Baum, "Introduction," in *Das Tagebuch der Anne Frank (14, Juni 1942–1, August 1944). Mit einer Einführung von Marie Baum*, Heidelberg: Schneider, 1950.
208. Goldschmidt, *Erinnerungen*, 122; Jürgen Froelich, "Ein Nationalliberaler unter 'Demokraten'. Eugen Schiffer und der organisierte Liberalismus vom Kaiserreich bis nach dem Zweiten Weltkrieg," *JzLF*, 18 (2006), 173–174; Schiffer to Heuss, 2.20.40, in NL Heuss, BAK: N 1221, #95.
209. http://www.writing.upenn.edu/~afilreis/Holocaust/wansee-transcript.html.
210. Lauterer, *Parlamentarierinnen*, 226–227.
211. Neumann, *Tantzen*, 176.
212. Ibid., 356.
213. On Heuss's tireless effort to repair German–Jewish relations, see Jay Geller, *Jews in Post-Holocaust Germany, 1945–1953*, Cambridge: Cambridge University Press, 2005, 190–196, 264–265.
214. Margit Gottert in Meurer, ed., *Marianne Weber*, 150.
215. Cary, "Antisemitism," 551–589.

216. Baum, *Rückblick*, 291–292; Bankier, *Final Solution*, 140–152.

217. August Weber, *Erinnerungen*, 180–192.

218. See Nathan Stoltzfus, *Resistance of the Heart: Intermarriage and the Rosenstrasse Protest in Nazi Germany*, New York: Norton, 1996.

219. Baum, *Rückblick*, 309–310; Lauterer, *Parlamentarierinnen*, 226.

220. Kardorff to Weizmann, 5.03.55, 7.22.55, 9.10.48, 5.07.56, in NL K. von Kardorff, BAK: N 1039, #60, 67.

221. Koch-Weser, *Hitler*, 105–106.

222. Karl Jaspers, *The Question of German Guilt*, New York: Dial, 1947.

223. Baum, *Rückblick*, 297.

224. "In Britain the limitations of the liberal imagination made it hard for most to accept the reality of irrational facts such as the planned extermination of the Jews." Kushner, *Liberal Imagination*, 137.

Conclusion

1. Frye, *Democrats*, 186–190; Bertsch, *Die FDP und der Deutsche Liberalismus*, 146–149.

2. See Rütten, *Der deutsche Liberalismus 1945 bis 1955*, 36–37; Christof Brauers, *Liberale Deutschlandpolitik, 1949–1969: Positionen der F.D.P. zwischen nationaler und europäischer Orientierung*, Münster: LIT-Verlag, 1993.

3. Rütten, *Liberalismus*, 30; Brauers, *Liberale Deutschlandpolitik*, 5–7; J.M. Gutscher, *Die Entwicklung der FDP von ihren Anfängen bis 1961*, Meisenheim: Anton Hain, 1967.

4. Schacht to Kardorff, 9.19.47, 10.28.47, 12.22.47; Kardorff to Schacht, 10.28.47, in NL K. von Kardorff, BAK: N 1039, #65; Schacht, *Schlusswort, 9.06.50*, in NL Traub, BAK: N 1059, #67; Schacht, *Abrechnung mit Hitler*, 12–17.

5. Reinhold Maier, *Wir suchen Deutschland*, Gerlingen: Bleicher, 1989, 10–20; Bertsch, *Die FDP*, 223–224.

6. Rütten, *Liberalismus*, 48–49, 57–58. Behrendt, *Külz*, 170–76; Brauers, *Liberale Deutschlandpolitik*, 28–37; Bertsch, *Die FDP*, 195–201.

7. Goldschmidt, *Erinnerungen*, 124.

8. Schiffer to Gerland, 11.26.40, in NL Gerland, BAK: N 1010, #21; Schiffer to Kardorff, 8.21.46, 3.01.50; Kardorff to Schiffer, 7.04.50, in NL K. von Kardorff, BAK: N 1039, #65.

9. Luckemeyer, *Heile*, 129; Frye, *Democrats*, 191–194.

10. Heile to Heuss, 2.11.46; Adenauer to Heile, 2.14.46; Heile to Tantzen, 3.12.46, in NL Heile, BAK: N 1132, #39; Luckemeyer, *Rebell*, 129; Rütten, *Liberalismus*, 36–37; Bertsch, *Die FDP*, 191–192.

11. Rütten, *Liberalismus*, 38–41; Luckemeyer, *Rebell*, 128–129.

12. Official prosecutor to Dietrich, 12.31.46, 8.06.48; Dietrich to prosecutor, 2.05.47; Schacht to Dietrich,12.29.49, in NL Dietrich, BAK: N 1004, #458, #200.

13. Dietrich to Lüders, 9.04.46, 9.08.46, 10.15.46, 4.24.47; Lüders to Dietrich, 10.10.46, 7.26.47; in NL Dietrich, BAK: N 1004, #578; Lauterer, *Parlamentarinnen*, 288.

14. Dietrich, *Auf der Suche nach Deutschland*, 1946.

15. Lauterer, *Parlamentarinnen*, 295–297.

16. See folder including 103. Sitzung d. Btag "Erklärung der Bundesregierung über die antisemitischen Vorfälle," 2.18.60; notes on *Diary of Anne Frank*; article by Hans Lenz, "Demokratie und Nationalbewußtsein," [#13/60 Das Freie Wort]; and Richard Roth, "Deutschland wird die Juden verlieren," *Die Kultur*, 14–15 in NL Lüders, BAK: N 115, #85. Heide-Marie Lauterer, *Lebenswege, politisches Selbstverständnis und Handeln von Parlamentarierinnen in Deutschland 1918–1953*, Heidelberg publisher 2001; Heide-Marie Lauterer, " 'Fürchte Dich nicht' – Marie-Elisabeth Lüders' Stellung zu den beiden deutschen Diktaturen," in *Jahrbuch zur Liberalismusforschung*, 17 (2005).

17. Bäumer to Beckmann, 11.29.47; Bäumer to Graefe, 1.16.48; Bäumer to Heuss, 6.23.48; in Beckmann, ed., *Band*, 344–352. See series of Bäumer notes/articles in NL Bäumer, BAK: N 1076, #9.

18. Bäumer to König, 11.13.45; Bäumer to Baum, 7.19.46; in Beckmann, ed., *Band*, 304–306, 321–322.

19. See Bäumer folder 7/8.1945: "1. Hoffnungen/2. Tatsachen" [pp. 1–10], in BAK: N 1076, #19; Bäumer to Yella Leppmann, 12.17.46; Bäumer to König, 11.13.45; Bäumer to Graefe, 1.16.48; Bäumer to Heuss [1945], in Beckmann, ed., *Band*, 304–308, 348.

20. See Bäumer, *Der neue Weg*, 19–23, 46–47; Stephenson, *Women*, 194.

21. See Heuss articles 4.27.46, 11.11.46, 3.27.46, in NL Heuss, BAK: N 1221, #48; Heuss to Traub, 12.22.46, 12.22.48, in NL Traub, BAK: N 1059, #61.

22. See again Heuss articles: 12.31.46,1.25.47, 1.04.47, 2.13.47, 7.24.47, in NL Heuss, BAK: N 1221, #48.

23. Sassin, *Liberale*, 250–253.

24. Rütten, *Liberalismus*, 28; Ernst Lemmer, *Berlin at the Crossroads of Europe, at the Crossroads of the World*; Frank Spieker, *Hermann Höpker Aschoff – Vater der Finanzverfassung*, Berlin: Duncker & Humboldt, 2004.

25. Maier, *Wir suchen Deutschland*, 11–12; Brauers, *Liberale Deutschlandpolitik*, 53–73; Bertsch, *Die FDP*, 256–277; August Weber, *Erinnerungen*, 296–305; Abatz to Robinsohn, 7.22.48; Robinsohn to Abatz, 7.29.48, in NL Robinsohn, BAK: N 1296, #2; Kardorff to Schacht, 10.28.47, in NL K. von Kardorff, BAK: N 1039, #65; Remy, *Myth*, 245–246. Also see Norbert Frei, *Vergangenheitspolitik. Die Anfänge der Bundesrepublik und die NS-Vergangenheit*, München: C.H. Beck, 1997; Ulrich Herbert, *Best. Biographische Studien über Radikalismus, Weltanschauung und Vernunft 1903–1989*, Bonn: Dietz, 1996.

26. Bäumer to König, 11.13.45, in Beckmann, ed., *Band*, 304–305; Robinsohn to Willy Brandt, 5.13.59, 1.19.61, 2.17.61, 9.16.61, 12.02.61; Brandt to Robinsohn, 1.17.61, 10.22.61; Robinsohn to Dehler, 12.02.56, in NL Robinsohn, BAK: N 1296, #2; Alexander Mitscherlich und Alfred Weber, *Freier Sozialismus*, Heidelberg: Lambert Schneider, 1946; Adenauer to Heuss, 12.19.52, in Hans Peter Mensing and Rudolf Morsey, eds, *Adenauer – Heuss: Unter vier Augen: Gespräche aus den Gründerjahren: 1949–1959*, Berlin: Siedler, 31; Lauterer, *Parlamentarinnen*, 304–305.

27. Lauterer, *Parlamentarinnen*, 305–307; also see Petra Schaffrodt, *Marie Baum: Ein Leben in sozialer Verantwortung*, Heidelberg: Ubstadt-Weiher, 2001.

28. Weber, *Freie Sozialismus*; Remy, *Myth*, 245; Martin Dehli, *Leben als Konflikt. Zur Biographie Alexander Mitscherlich*, Göttingen: Wallstein, 2007, 135–144.

29. Lauterer, *Parlamentarinnen*, 297–301; Kardorff to Külz, 12.07.46; Kardorff to Bähnisch, 1.31.47, in NL K. von Kardorff, BAK: N 1039, #68.

30. Sassin, *Liberale*, 253–254.

31. Dahrendorf, *Society*, 3–45, 397–426; Baum, *Rückblick*, 290–292.

32. Rainer Koch, "Einleitung," in Friedrich Sell, *Die Tragödie*, xxvi–xxix; also see Geoff Eley, "Nazism could only be defeated militarily . . . But the wartime groundwork of democratic renewal was being relaid by socialists, Communists, radical liberals, and Christian democrats, as they came together in a broadening category of the Left." Eley, *Forging Democracy*, Oxford: Oxford University Press, 2002, 492.

33. In postwar Germany, "Liberalism is not just the business of one single party. It makes just as much sense to talk about a 'liberal society' or a 'liberal state.' " Ralf Dahrendorff, as quoted in Dirk Rumberg, "Book Review: Ralf Dahrendorf, *Fragmente eines neuen Liberalismus* (Fragments of a New Liberalism) (Stuttgart: Deutsche Verlags-Anstalt, 1987, 272 pp., DM 24.00)," *Millennium Journal of International Studies*, 16 (1987), 538.

34. See for example Francis Fukuyama, *The End of History and the Last Man*, New York: Penguin, 1992; Timothy Garton Ash, *Free World: Why a Crisis of the West Reveals the Opportunity of Our Time*, New York: Penguin, 2005.

35. Steigmann-Gall, *Reich*, 266–267.

Bibliography

Archive Collections
Bundesarchiv Berlin (BAB)
R 45 I, *Bestandsgruppe R 45 – Liberale Parteien. Nationalliberale Partei*
R 45 II, *Bestandsgruppe R 45 – Liberale Parteien. Deutsche Volkspartei*
R 45 III, *Bestandsgruppe R 45 – Liberale Parteien. Deutsche Demokratische Partei – Deutsche Staatspartei* (microfilm)
NL Barth, Theodor, N 2010
NL Bernhard, Georg, N 2020
NL Nathan, Paul, N 2207
NL Naumann, Friedrich, N 3001
NL Preuss, Hugo, N 2230

Bundesarchiv Freiburg (BAF)
NL Beck, Ludwig, N 1028
NL Groener, Wilhelm, N 1046
NL Halder, Franz, N 1220
NL Hindenburg, Paul von, N 1429
NL Schulze-Gävernitz, Gerhard, N 1523
NL Seeckt, Hans von, N 1247
NL Schleicher, Kurt von, N 1042

Bundesarchiv Koblenz (BAK)
R 45 I, *Bestandsgruppe R 45 – Liberale Parteien. Nationalliberale Partei*
R 45 II, *Bestandsgruppe R 45 – Liberale Parteien. Deutsche Volkspartei*
R 45 III, *Bestandsgruppe R 45 – Liberale Parteien. Deutsche Demokratische Partei – Deutsche Staatspartei*
KLE 325 Naumann, Friedrich
KLE 384 Weber, August
NL Bäumer, Gertrud, N 1076
NL Brönner-Hoepfner, Elisabeth, N 1026
NL Curtius, Julius, N 1065

NL Dernburg, Bernhard, N 1130
NL Dietrich, Hermann, N 1004
NL Dingeldey, Eduard, N 1002
NL Erkelenz, Anton, N 1072
NL Frick, Wilhelm, N 1241
NL Gerland, Heinrich, N 1010
NL Geßler, Otto, N 1032
NL Gothein, Georg, N 1006
NL Heuss, Theodor, N 1221
NL Höpker-Aschoff, Hermann, N 1129
NL Jaenicke, Wolfgang, N 1135
NL Jarres, Karl, N 1099
NL Kardorff-Oheimb, Katharina von, N 1039
NL Kardorff, Siegfried von, N 1040
NL Koch-Weser, Erich, N 1012
NL Külz, Wilhelm, N 1042
NL Lüders, Marie-Elisabeth, N 1151
NL Moldenhauer, Paul, N 1019
NL Quidde, Ludwig, N 1212
NL Rathenau, Walter, N 1048
NL Rheinbaben, Werner von, N 1237
NL Richthofen, Hartmann Frh. v., N 1164
NL Robinsohn, Hans, N 1296
NL Rohrbach, Paul, N 1408
NL Schacht, Hjalmar, N 1294
NL Schiffer, Eugen, N 1191
NL Schücking, Walter, N 1051
NL Stolper, Gustav, N 1186
NL Stresemann, Gustav FC 426 P – FC 506 P (microfilm)
NL Traub, Gottfried, N 1059
NL Weber, Alfred N 1197
NL Wolff, Theodor, N 1207
NL Zapf, Albert, N 1227

Leo Baeck Institute (LBI)

NL Heilberg, Adolf, MF 32

Newspapers and Periodicals

Berliner Tageblatt
Berliner Volkszeitung
Breslauer Morgen-Zeitung
Breslauer Zeitung
Der Demokrat
Deutsche Allegemeine Zeitung
Frankfurter Zeitung
Die Frau (DF)
Hamburger Correspondent
Hamburger Fremdenblatt
Die Hilfe
Kieler Zeitung
Kölnische Zeitung

Schleswiger Nachrichten
Das Schwarze Korps
Der Stürmer
Stuttgarter Neue Tageblatt
Völkischer Beobachter
Volksstaat: Wochenschrift für die Interessen der Deutschen Demokratischen Partei in Schlesien
Volkswacht
Vossische Zeitung

Published Works (Primary)

Aichel, Otto. "Die Rassenforschung. Bemerkungen zu dem gleichnamigen Aufsatz von Walter Goetz," *Archiv für Kulturforschung*, 22, 1932, 372.

Andreas-Friedrich, Ruth. *Der Schattenmann. Schauplatz Berlin. Tagebuchaufzeichnungen 1938–1948*. Frankfurt: Suhrkamp, 2000.

Anschütz, Gerhard. *Die Verfassung des deutschen Reichs vom 11. August 1919*. Berlin: Stilke, 1921.

Barth, Karl. *The German Church Conflict*. London: Lutterworth, 1965.

Bauer, H.W. *Kolonien oder nicht: Die Einstellung von Partei und Staat zum kolonialen Gedanken*. Leipzig: Richard Bauer, 1935.

Baum, Marie. *Anna von Gierke. Ein Lebensbild*. Weinheim: J. Beitz, 1954.

——, ed. *Briefe an Freunde*. Zürich: Manesse, 1986

——. *Leuchtende Spur. Das Leben Ricarda Huch*. Tübingen: R. Wunderlich, 1950.

——. *Rückblick auf meinem Leben*. Heidelberg: f. H. Kerle, 1950.

Bäumer, Gertrud, ed. *Die deutsche Frau in der sozialen Kriegsfürsorge*. Gotha: Perthes, 1916.

——. *Die Frau im deutschen Staat*. Berlin: Junker & Dünnhaupt, 1932.

——. *Die Frau in der Kulturbewegung der Gegenwart*. Wiesbaden: J.F. Bergmann, 1904.

——. *Die Frau im neuen Lebensraum*. Berlin: Herbig.

——. *Gestalt und Wandel: Frauenbildnisse*. Berlin: Herbig, 1939.

——. *Grundlagen demokratischer Politik*. Karlsruhe: G. Braun, 1928.

——. *Im Licht der Erinnerung*. Tübingen: R. Wunderlich, 1953.

——. *Lebenswege durch eine Zeitenwende*. Tübingen: R. Wunderlich, 1934.

——. *Der neue Weg der deutsche Frau*. Stuttgart: Deutsche Verlags-Anstalt, 1946.

——. *Ricarda Huch*. Tübingen: R. Wunderlich, 1949.

——. *Die seelische Krisis*. Berlin: Herbig, 1924.

——. *Die soziale Idee in den Weltanschauungen des 19. Jhr.* Heilbronn: E. Salzer, 1910.

——. *Studien über Frauen*. Berlin: Herbig, 1928.

——. *Die Entwicklung der höheren Mädchenbildung in Deutschland von 1870–1914*. Berlin: Herbig, 1936.

Beckmann, Emmy, ed. *Das Leben wie der liebe Band*. Tübingen: R. Wunderlich, 1956.

Bernhard, Georg. *Die deutsche Trägodie: Der Selbstmord einer Republik*. Prague: Orbis, 1933.

——. *Meister und Dilettanten am Kapitalismus im Reiche der Hohenzollern*. Amsterdam: Lange, 1936.

Bernstorff, Graf Johann-Heinrich von. *Erinnerungen und Briefe*. Zürich: Ploygraphischer, 1936.

Bott, Hans, ed. *Begegnungen mit Theodor Heuss*. Tübingen: R. Wunderlich, 1954.

Boveri, Margaret. *Wir lügen alle: Eine Hauptstadtzeitung unter Hitler*. Olten: Walter, 1965.

Brammer, Karl. *So lebten sie: 700 Milliarden Hitlerschuld*. Berlin: Union-Verlag, 1946.

Brönner-Hoepfner, Elisabeth. *Die Leiden des Memelgebiets*. Berlin: Memelland, 1927.

——. *Das Memelland*. Berlin: Reichsverband der Heimattreuen, 1929.

Brüning, Heinrich. *Briefe, 1946–1960*. Stuttgart: Deutsche Verlags-Anstalt, 1974.

Conze, Werner. *Agrarverfassung und Bevölkerung in Litauen und Weissrussland*. Leipzig: Hirzel, 1940.

——. *Die Geschichte der 291. Infanterie-Division, 1940–1945*. Bad Nauheim: Podzun, 1953.

Curtius, Julius. *Bemühung um Österreich: Das Scheitern des Zollunionsplans von 1931*. Heidelberg: Winter, 1947.

——. *Sechs Jahre Minister der Deutschen Republik*. Heidelberg: Winter, 1948.

Dagerman, Stig. *German Autumn*. London: Quartet, 1988.

Dehler, Thomas. *Begegnungen, Gedanken, Entscheidungen*. Bonn: Liberal, 1978.

Diels, Rudolfs. *Lucifer Ante Portas: von Severing bis Heydrich*. Stuttgart: Deutsche Verlagsanstalt, 1950.

Dietrich, Hermann. *Auf der Suche nach Deutschland*. Hamburg: von Hugo, 1946.

——. *Wir brauchen zwei millionen Kleinhäuser*. Stuttgart: Mittelbach, 1950.

Dingeldey, Eduard. *Botschaft an das nationale Deutschland*. Berlin: Deutsche Erneuerung, 1932.

Eckardt, Hans von. *Ivan the Terrible*. New York: Knopf, 1949.

Erkelenz, Anton und Fritz Mittelmann. *Carl Schurz: Der Deutsche und der Amerikaner*. Berlin: Sieben-Stäbe, 1929.

Frank, Anne. *Das Tagebuch der Anne Frank (14, Juni 1942–1, August 1944). Mit einer Einführung von Marie Baum*. Heidelberg: Schneider, 1950.

Freymark, Hermann. *Die Oder – der Lebensnerv des deutschen Ostens 1934*. Breslau: H. Marcus, 1934.

——. *Das Werden der Wirtschaft Breslaus nach den Befreiungskrieg*, Beiträge zur Geschichte der Stadt Breslau, vol. XI. Breslau: Priebatsch, 1940.

Gerlach, Hellmut von. *Ein Demokrat kommentiert Weimar*. Bremen: Schünemann, 1973.

——. *Du große Zeit der Lüge*. Charlottenburg: Weltbühne, 1926.

——. *Von rechts nach links*. Zürich: Europa-Verlag, 1937.

Gessler, Otto. *Das deutsche Volk in die europäische Ordnung*. Munich: Deutsche-Österreichische Arbeitsgemeinschaft, 1937.

——. *Reichswehrpolitik in der Weimarer Zeit*. Stuttgart: Deutsche Verlags-Anstalt, 1958.

Goebbels, Josef. *Tagebücher*. Teil. 1–2, Munich: Saur, 1998–2000.

Goetz, Walter. *Geschichte der deutschen Dante-Gesellschaft und der deutschen Dante-Forschung*. Weimar: Bohlau, 1940.

——. *Historiker in meiner Zeit*. Cologne: Böhlau, 1957.

——. *Intuition in der Geschichtswissenschaft*. Munich: C.H. Beck, 1935.

——. *Die Rassenforschung*, in *Archiv für Kulturforschung* 22 (1932), 1.

Gothein, Georg. *A World Coalition against Japan*. London: Hamilton, 1934.

Groener, Wilhelm. *Lebenserinnerungen: Jugend–Generalstab–Weltkrieg*. Göttingen: Vandenhoeck & Ruprecht, 1957.

Haffner, Sebastian. *Defying Hitler: A Memoir*. London: Weidenfeld & Nicolson, 2002.

Hellpach, Willy. *Hellpach-Memoiren, 1925–1945*. Cologne: Böhlau, 1987.

Helmrich, Ingemar. *Geschichte der Juden in Liegnitz*. Liegnitz: Selbstverlag, 1938.

Heuss, Theodor, *An und über Juden: Aus Schriften und Reden (1906–1963)*. Düsseldorf: Econ, 1964.

——. *Anton Dohrn in Neapel*. Berlin: Atlantis, 1940.

——. *Bekenntnis und Verpflichtung: Reden und Aufsätze zur zehnjährigen Widerkehr der 20. Juli 1944*. Stuttgart: Vorwerk, 1955.

——. *Die deutsche Nationalidee im Wandel der Geschichte*. Stuttgart: F. Mittelbach, 1946.

——. *Erinnerungen, 1905–1933*. Tübingen: R. Wunderlich, 1963.

——. *Friedrich Naumann: Der Mann, das Werk, die Zeit*. Munich: Siebenstern, 1968.

——. *Hans Poelzig: Das Lebensbild eines deutschen Baumeisters*. Tübingen: Ernst Wasmuth, 1948.

——. *Hitlers Weg*. Stuttgart: Union deutsche Verlagsgesellschaft, 1932.

——. *Lieber Dehler! Briefwechsel mit Thomas Dehler*. Munich: Olzog, 1983.

——. *Robert Bosch*. Stuttgart: Deutsche Verlagsanstalt, 1931.

——. *Robert Bosch: Leben und Leistung*. Tübingen: R. Wunderlich, 1946.

——. *Wider den Antisemitismus*. Berlin: Congress for Cultural Freedom, 1953.

Heuss-Knapp, Elly. *Ausblick vom Münsterturm: Erlebtes aus dem Elsaß und dem Reich.* Berlin, 1934.

Höhn, Reinhard. *Rechtsgemeinschaft und Volksgemeinschaft.* Hamburg: Hanseatische Verlagsanstalt, 1935.

———. *Reich, Großraum, Großmacht.* Darmstadt: Wittich, 1942.

Höpker-Aschoff, Hermann. *Geld und Gold.* Jena: G. Fischer, 1939.

———. *Unser Weg durch die Zeit.* Berlin: Hans Bott, 1936.

Holborn, Hajo. *The Political Collapse of Europe.* New York: Knopf, 1951.

Jäckh, Ernst. *Der goldene Pflug: Lebensernte eines Weltbürgers.* Stuttgart: Deutsche Verlags-Anstalt, 1954.

———. *Im türkischen Kriegslager durch Albanien: Bekenntnisse zur deutsch–türkischen Freundschaft.* Heilbronn: Salzer, 1911.

———. *The New Germany.* London: Oxford University Press, 1927.

———. *Weltsaat. Erlebtes und Erstrebtes.* Stuttgart: Deutsche Verlags-Anstalt, 1960.

Kardoff, Siegfried von. *Bismarck: Vier Vorträge.* Berlin: E. Rowohlt, 1929.

———. *Bismarck im Kampf um sein Werk.* Berlin: E.S. Mittler & Sohn, 1943.

———. *Wilhelm von Kardorff, ein nationaler Parlamentarier im Zeitalter Bismarcks und Wilhelms II, 1828–1907.* Berlin: E.S. Mittler & Sohn, 1936.

Kardorff-Oheimb, Katharina. *Politik und Lebensbeichte.* Tübingen: Hopfer, 1965.

Kessler, Harry Graf. *Walther Rathenau: Sein Leben und sein Werk.* Berlin: Hermann Klemm, 1928.

Klemperer, Viktor. *I Shall Bear Witness: The Diaries of Viktor Klemperer, 1933–1941.* London: Weidenfeld & Nicolson, 1998.

Külz, Wilhelm. *Ein liberaler zwischen Ost und West.* Munich: Oldenbourg, 1989.

———. *Schriften Der LDPD: Wilhelm Külz aus Reden und Aufsätzen.* Berlin: Der Morgen, 1984.

Lange, Helene und Gertrud Bäumer, eds. *Die Handbuch der Frauenbewegung.* Berlin: W. Moeser, 1901.

Lemmer, Ernst. *Berlin at the Crossroads of Europe, at the Crossroads of the World.* Berlin: 1960.

———. *Manches war doch anders. Erinnerungen eines deutschen. Demokraten.* Munich: Herbig, 1996.

Lohmann, Gertrud. *Friedrich Naumanns Deutscher Sozialismus.* Berlin: J. Särchen, 1935.

Lüders, Marie Elisabeth. *Die Entwicklung der gewerblichen Frauenarbeit im Krieg.* Munich: Duncker, 1920.

———. *Frauen Sichern Stalins Sieg.* Berlin: Berliner Frauenbund, 1952.

———. *Fürchte Dich Nicht: Persönliches und Politisches aus mehr als 80 Jahres.* Cologne: Westdeutscher, 1963.

———. *Das unbekannte Heer. Frauen kaempfen fuer Deutschland.* Berlin: E.S. Mittler, 1936.

Maier, Reinhold. *Bedrängte Familie.* Tübingen: R. Wunderlich, 1962.

———. *Ende und Wende: Das Schwäbische Schicksal, Briefe und Tagebuchaufzeichnungen von Reinhold Maier, 1944–1946.* Wuppertal: S. Fingscheidt, 2004.

———. *Ein Grundstein wird gelegt. Die Jahre 1945–1947.* Tübingen: R Wunderlich, 1964.

———. *Die Reden.* Stuttgart: Reinhold Maier-Stiftung, 1984.

———. *Wir suchen Deutschland.* Gerlingen: Bleicher, 1989.

Meinecke, Friedrich. *Ausgewählter Briefwechsel.* Stuttgart: Koehler, 1962.

———. *The German Catastrophe: Reflections and Recollections.* Cambridge, Mass.: Harvard University Press, 1950.

Mitscherlich, Alexander und Alfred Weber, *Freier Sozialismus.* Heidelberg: Lambert Schneider, 1946.

Morgenthau, Henry. *Germany is Our Problem.* New York: Harper, 1945.

Namier, Lewis. *Facing East.* New York: Harper, 1948.

———. *The Jews.* London: Macmillan, 1942.

———. *The Revolution of the Intellectuals.* London: Cumberlege, 1944.

Naumann, Friedrich. *Mitteleuropa.* Berlin: G. Reimer, 1915.

——. *Die politische Parteien.* Berlin: Die Hilfe, 1910.

——. *Der Weg zum Volksstaat.* Berlin: Arbeitsgemeinschaft für staatsbürgerliche und wirtschaftliche Bildung, 1918.

Nuschke, Otto. *Reden und Aufsätze, 1919–1950.* Berlin: Union-Verlag, 1957.

Obst, Erich. *Schlesien, das deutsche Tor nach dem Osten, Vortrag, gehalten am 25. November 1941 vor der Bezirksgruppe Breslau der WVV.* Berlin: Otto Elsner, 1942.

Obst, Erich and Hermann Freymark. *Die Grundlagen Der Verkehrsentwicklung Schlesiens und die Entstehung des Schlesischen Eisenbahnnetzes.* Breslau: Wilh. Gott. Korn, 1942.

Preuss, Hugo. *Deutschlands republikanische Reichsverfassung.* Berlin: Neuer Staat, 1923.

Raumer, Kurt von and Theodor Schieder, eds. *Stufen und Wandlungen der deutschen Einheit.* Stuttgart: Deutsche Verlags-Anstalt, 1943.

Rheinbaben, Rochus von. *Stresemann: The Man and the Statesman.* New York, 1929.

Rheinbaben, Werner. Freiherr von. *Kaiser, Kanzler, Präsidenten: Erinnerungen.* Mainz, 1968.

——. *Um ein neues Europa, Tatsachen und Probleme.* Berlin, 1939.

——. *Viermal Deutschland: Aus dem Erleben eines Seemanns, Diplomaten, Politkers 1895–1954.* Berlin: Argon, 1954.

Rohrbach, Paul. *Afrika: Beiträge zu einer praktischen Kolonialkunde.* Berlin: Werner, 1943.

——. *Amerika und Wir: Reisebetrachtungen.* Berlin: Buchenau, 1926.

——. *Das Baltenbuch: Die baltischen Provinzen und ihren deutsche Kultur.* Dachau: Blumtritt, 1916.

——, ed. *Chauvinismus und Weltkrieg.* Berlin: Engelmann, 1919.

——. *Deutsch-Afrika: Ende oder Anfang? Briefe an einen Jungen Deutschen.* Potsdam: Volk & Heimat, 1935.

——. *Der deutsche Gedanke in der Welt.* Leipzig: Langewiesche, 1920.

——. *Die Deutsche Stadt Danzig.* Königsten: Langewiesche, 1930.

——. *Deutsches Volkstum als Minderheit.* Berlin: Englemann, 1926.

——. *Deutschland: Tod oder Leben?* Munich: Bruckmann, 1930.

——. *Deutschlands koloniale Forderung.* Hamburg: Hanseatische, 1935.

——. *Deutschtum in Not! Die Schicksale der Deutschen in Europa ausserhalb des Reiches.* Berlin: Andermann, 1926.

——. *German World Politics.* New York: Macmillan, 1914.

——. *Der Gottesgedanke in der Welt. Eine Antwort auf die Frage: ist die Menschheit Lebensfähig?* Berlin: Hans Bott, 1937.

——. *Koloniale Siedlung und Wirtschaft der führenden Kolonialvölker.* Cologne: Schaffstein, 1934.

——. *Osteuropa. Historisch-politisch gesehen.* Potsdam: Rütten & Loenig, 1942.

——. *Um des Teufels Handschrift: Zwei Menschenalter erlebter Weltgeschichte.* Hamburg: H. Dulk, 1953.

——. *Unser Weg: Betrachtungen zum letzten Jahrhundert deutscher Geschichte.* Cologne: Schaffstein, 1949.

——. *Weltkunde für den Deutschen.* Cologne: Schaffstein, 1939.

Rohrbach, Paul and Ludwig Preiss. *Palestine and Transjordania.* New York: Macmillan, 1926.

Rohrbach, Paul und Justus Rohrbach, *Afrika Heute und Morgen.* Berlin: Reimar Hobbing, 1939.

Sauer, Paul, ed. *Reinhold Maier: Briefwechstel mit seiner Familie 1930–1946.* Stuttgart: Kohlhammer, 1989.

Schacht, Hjalmar. *Abrechnung mit Hitler.* Westport, Conn.: Greenwood Press, 1956.

——. *"Finanzwunder" und "Neuer Plan". Vortrag vor dem Wirtschaftsrat der Deutschen Akademie.* Berlin: Drückerei der Reichsbank, 1938.

——. *New Colonial Policy.* Berlin: Drückerei der Reichsbank, 1929.

——. *1933. Wie eine Demokratie Stirbt.* Düsseldorf: publishers 1968.

——. *Rede des Reichbankpräsidenten und beauftragten Reichswirtschaftsminister Hjalmar Schacht auf der Deutschen Ostmesse. Königsberg, am 18. August 1935.* Berlin: Drückerei der Reichsbank, 1935.

——. *76 Jahre meines Lebens.* London, 1955.

Schellenberg, Walter. *Hitler's Secret Service.* New York: Harper, 1974.

Schiffer, Eugen. *Ein Leben für den Liberalismus.* Berlin: F.A. Herbig, 1951.

——. *Stürm über Deutschland.* Berlin: Otto Libermann, 1932.

Schulze-Gävernitz, Gerhard. *Zur Wiedergeburt des Abendlandes.* Berlin: Runge, 1934.

Sombart, Werner, Friedrich Naumann, und Matthias Erzberger, eds. *Judentaufen.* Munich: G. Müller, 1912.

Speer, Albert. *Inside the Third Reich: Memoirs.* New York: Macmillan, 1970.

Stephan, Werner. *Acht Jahrzehnte erlebtes Deutschland.* Düsseldorf: Droste, 1983.

Stolper, Gustav. *Deutscheösterreich als Sozial- und Wirtschaftsproblem.* Munich: Drei Masken, 1921.

——. *German Economy, 1870–1940: Issues and Trends.* New York: Reynal & Hitchcock, 1940.

——. *German Realities.* New York: Reynal & Hitchcock, 1948.

——. *Das mitteleuropäische Wirtschaftsproblem.* Vienna: Deuticke, 1917.

Stolper, Toni. *Ein Leben in Brennpunkten unserer Zeit: Gustav Stolper 1888–1947.* Tübingen: R. Wunderlich, 1954.

Traub, Gottfried. *Erinnerungen: Wie Ich das "Zweite Reich" erlebte. Tagebuchnotizen aus der Hitlerzeit.* Stuttgart: E. Traub, 1998.

Treitschke, Heinrich von. "Unsere Aussichten." In *Preussischer Jahrbücher*, vol. 44 (1879), 559–576.

Valentin, Veit. *The German People: Their History and Civilization from the Holy Roman Empire to the Third Reich.* New York: Knopf, 1946.

Weber, Alfred. *Abschied von der bisherigen Geschichte.* Hamburg: Classen & Goverts, 1946.

——. *Kulturgeschichte als Kultursoziologie.* Leiden: A.W. Sijthoff, 1935.

——. *Das Tragische und die Geschichte.* Hamburg: H. Govert, 1943.

——. *Werner Sombart.* Berlin: Neue Rundschau, 1941.

Weber, Marianne. *Lebenserinnerungen.* Bremen: Johannes Storm, 1948.

Winschuh, Josef. "Der Aufgabenrahmen des Unternehmers in der staatlichen Wirtschaftslenkung," *Stahl und Eisen*, 58 nr. 24 (1938), 650–652.

——. *Gerüstete Wirtschaft.* Berlin: Frundsberg, 1939.

——. *Männer, Traditionen, Signale.* Berlin: Friedrich Osmer, 1940.

——. *Das neue wirtschaftliche Weltbild.* Berlin: Albert Limbach, 1941.

——. *Sinn und Unsinn der Wirtschaftsdemokratie.* Heidelberg: Vita, 1952.

Wolff, Theodor. *Die Juden: Ein Dokument aus dem Exil 1942/1943.* Königstein: Athenäum, 1984.

——. *Tagebucher 1914–1919: der Erste Weltkrieg und die Entstehung der Weimarer Republik in Tagebuchern, Leitartikeln und Briefen des Chefredakteurs am "Berliner Tageblatt" und Mitbegrunders der Deutschen Demokratischen Partei.* Boppard: Harald Boldt, 1984.

Published Works (Secondary)

Abelshauer, Werner. *The Dynamic of German Industry: The German Road towards the New Economy and the American Challenge.* New York: Berghahn, 2005.

Abraham, David. *The Collapse of the Weimar Republic: Political Economy and Crisis.* New York: Holmes & Meier, 1986.

Achebe, Chinua. "An Image of Africa: Racism in Conrad's *Heart of Darkness.*" In Achebe, ed. *Hopes and Impediments. Selected Essays.* New York: Anchor, 1990.

Albertin, Lothar. "Die Auflösung der bürgerlichen Mitte und die Krise des parlamentarischen Systems von Weimar." In Kolb and Mülhausen, eds. *Demokratie in der Krise*, 59–111.

——. "Das Friedensthema bei den Linksliberalen vor 1914: Die Schwäche ihrer Argumente und Aktivitäten." In Karl Holl and Günther List, eds. *Liberalismus und imperialistischer Staat.* Göttingen: Vandenhoeck & Ruprecht, 89–108.

——. *Liberalismus und Demokratie am Anfang der Weimarer Republik: eine vergleichende Analyse der Deutschen Demokratischen Partei und der Deutschen Volkspartei.* Düsseldorf: Droste, 1972.

——, ed. *Politischer Liberalismus in der Bundesrepublik.* Göttingen: Vandenhoeck & Ruprecht, 1980.

Albertin, Lothar and Lothar Gall, eds. *Liberalismus und imperialischer Staat: Der Imperialismus als Problem liberaler Parteien in Deutschland 1890–1914.* Düsseldorf: Droste, 1980.

Albertin, Lothar and Konstanze Wegner, eds. *Linksliberalismus in der Weimarer Republik: Die Führungsgremien der Deutschen Demokratischen Partei und der Deutschen Staatspartei 1918–1933.* Düsseldorf: Droste, 1980.

Allen, Ann Taylor. *Feminism and Motherhood in Germany.* New Brunswick: Rutgers, 1991.

——. *Feminism and Motherhood in Western Europe, 1890–1970.* New York: Palgrave, 2005.

Allen, William Sheridan. *The Nazi Seizure of Power: The Experience of a Single German Town. 1922–1945.* New York: F. Watts, 1973.

Aly, Götz. *Hitlers Volksstaat: Raub, Rassenkrieg, und Nationalsozialismus.* Frankfurt: Fischer, 2005.

Aly, Götz and Susanne Heim. *Architects of Annihilation: Auschwitz and the Logic of Destruction.* Princeton, N.J.: Princeton University Press, 2003.

Amkraut, Brian. *Between Home and Homeland: Youth Aliyah from Nazi Germany.* Tuscaloosa: Alabama University Press, 2006.

Anderson, Margaret Lavinia. *Practicing Democracy: Elections and Political Culture in Imperial Germany.* Princeton, N.J.: Princeton University Press, 2000.

Applegate, Celia, ed. *Music & German National Identity.* Chicago: Chicago, 2002.

——. *A Nation of Provincials: The German Idea of Heimat.* Berkeley: University of California Press, 1990.

Arendt, Hannah. *Eichmann in Jerusalem.* New York: Penguin, 1994.

Ash, Timothy Garton. *Free World: Why a Crisis of the West Reveals the Opportunity of Our Time.* New York: Penguin, 2005.

Ayçoberry, Pierre. *The Nazi Question: An Essay on the Interpretation of National Socialism (1922–1975).* London: Routledge, 1981.

Bach, Marie Luise. *Gertrud Bäumer: Biographische Daten und Texte zu einem Persönlichkeitsbild.* Weinheim: Deutsche Studien Verlag, 1989.

Baechler, Christian. *Gustave Stresemann,* Strasbourg: Strasbourg, 1996.

Bajohr, Frank. *"Aryanisation" in Hamburg.* New York: Berghahn, 2002.

——. *"Unser Hotel ist Judenfrei." Bäder-Antisemitismus im 19. und 20. Jahrhundert.* Frankfurt: Fischer, 2003.

Bankier, David. *The Germans and the Final Solution: Public Opinion in the Third Reich.* Oxford: Blackwell, 1992.

——, ed. *Probing the Depths of German Antisemitism: German Society and the Persecution of the Jews, 1933–1941.* New York: Berghahn, 2000.

Baranowski, Shelley. *The Confessing Church, Conservative Elites and the Nazi State.* Lewiston: 1986.

——. *Strength through Joy: Consumerism and Mass Tourism in the Third Reich.* Cambridge: Cambridge University Press, 2007.

Barbian, Jan-Pieter. *Literaturpolitik im "Dritten Reich": Institutionen, Kompetenzen, Betätigungsfelder.* Frankfurt: Buchhändler, 1993.

Barkai, Avraham. *From Boycott to Annihilation: The Economic Struggle of German Jews, 1933–1943.* Hanover: Brandeis University Press, 1989.

——. *Nazi Economics: Ideology, Theory, and Policy.* Oxford: Oxford University Press, 1990.

——. *"Wehr Dich!" Der Centralverein deutscher Staatsbürger jüdischen Glaubens (C.V), 1893–1938.* Munich: C.H. Beck, 2002.

Bartov, Omer. *Germany's War and the Holocaust: Disputed Histories*, Ithaca, NY: Cornell University Press, 2003.

——. *Hitler's Army: Soldiers, Nazis, and War in the Third Reich*, Oxford: Oxford, 1991.

——. "Soldiers, Nazis and War in the Third Reich". In Leitz, ed. *Third Reich*, 133–150.

Beck, Hermann. "Between the Dictates of Conscience and Political Expediency: Hitler's Conservative Alliance Partner and Antisemitism during the Nazi Seizure of Power," *Journal of Contemporary History*, 41 no. 4 (2006), 611–640.

Becker, Ernst Wolfgang. "Ein Haus voller Briefe für die deutsche Geschichte des 20. Jahrhunderts. Zum Stand der Edition 'Theodor Heuss. Stuttgarter Ausgabe,' " *JzLF*, v. 17 (2005), 215–234.

Becker, Werner. "Demokratie des sozialen Rechts: Die Politische Haltung der Frankfurter Zeitung, der Vossischen Zeitung und des Berliner Tageblatts, 1918–1924" (Munich, diss.), 1965.

Behrendt, Armin. *Wilhelm Külz: Aus dem Leben eines Suchenden*. Berlin: Der Morgen, 1985.

Behring, Rainer. *Demokratische Aussenpolitik für Deutschland*. Düsseldorf: Droste, 1999.

Bennecke, Heinrich. *Wirtschaftliche Depression und politischer Radikalismus 1918–1938*. Munich: Olzog, 1970.

Benz, Wolfgang, ed. *Die Juden in Deutschland, 1933–1945: Leben unter nationalsozialistischer Herrschaft*. Munich: Beck, 1993.

Benz, Wolfgang, Arnold Paucker and Peter Pulzer, eds. *Judisches Leben in der Weimarer Republik/Jews in the Weimar Republic*. Tübingen: Möhr Siebeck, 1997.

Berg, Manfred. *Gustav Stresemann und die Vereinigten Staaten von Amerika*. Baden-Baden: Nomos, 1990.

Bergen, Doris. *Twisted Cross: The German Christian Movement in the Third Reich*. Chapel Hill, N.C.: University of North Carolina Press, 1996.

Berghahn, V.R. *Modern Germany: Society, Economy and Politics in the Twentieth Century*. Cambridge: Cambridge University Press, 1998.

Berglar, Peter. *Walther Rathenau: Sein Zeit, sein Werk, sein Persönlichkeit*. Bremen: Schünemann, 1970.

Bertsch, Herbert. *Die FDP und der Deutsche Liberalismus*. Berlin: Deutscher, 1965.

Besier, Gerhard, ed. *Die Mittwochs-Gesellschaft im Kaiserreich: Protokolle aus dem geistigen Deutschland, 1863–1919*. Berlin: Siedler, 1990.

Bessel, Richard, ed. *Fascist Italy and Nazi Germany: Comparisons and Contrasts*. New York: Cambridge University Press, 1996.

——. *Germany after the First World War*. Oxford: Oxford University Press, 1993.

——, ed. *Life in the Third Reich*. Oxford: Oxford University Press, 1987.

Biagini, Eugenio F., ed. *Citizenship and Community: Liberals, Radicals and Collective Identities in the British Isles, 1865–1931*. Cambridge: Cambridge University Press, 2002.

Bieber, Horst. *Paul Rohrbach: Ein konservativer Publizist und Kritiker der Weimarer Republik*. Munich: Dokumentation, 1972.

Binder, Gerhart. *Irrtum und Widerstand: Die deutschen Katholiken in der Auseinandersetzung mit dem Nationalsozialismus*. Munich: Pfeiffer, 1968.

Blackbourn, David. *Class, Religion and Local Politics in Wilhelmine Germany*. New Haven and London: Yale University Press, 1980.

——. *Marpingen: Apparitions of the Virgin Mary in a Nineteenth-Century German Village*. New York: Knopf, 1993.

——. *Populists and Patricians*. Boston: Allen & Unwin, 1987.

Blackbourn, David and Geoff Eley. *The Peculiarities of German History: Bourgeois Society and Politics in Nineteenth-Century Germany*. New York: Oxford University Press, 1984.

Blaich, Fritz. *Staat und Verbände in Deutschland zwischen 1871 und 1945*. Wiesbaden: Steiner, 1975.

Blomert, Reinhard. *Intellektuelle im Aufbruch: Karl Mannheim, Alfred Weber, Norbert Elias und die Heidelberger Sozialwissenschaften der Zwischenkriegszeit*. Munich: Hanser, 1999.

264 Bibliography

Bock, Gisela. *Zwangssterilisation im Nationalsozialismus: Studien zur Rassenpolitik und Frauenpolitik.* Opladen: Westdeutscher, 1986.

Boroth, Ilse and Barbara Serloth, eds. *Gebrochene Kontinuitäten? Zur Rolle und Bedeutung der Geschlechtsverhältnisse in der Entwicklung des Nationalsozialismus.* Innsbruck: Studienverlag, 2000.

Bösch, Frank. *Das Konservative Milieu: Vereinskultur und lokale Sammlungspolitik in ost- und westdeutschen Regionen (1900–1960).* Göttingen: Vandenhoeck & Ruprecht, 2002.

Botz, Gerhard. *Nationalsozialismus in Wien: Machtübernahme und Herrschaftssicherung.* Buchloe: DVO, 1988.

Boysen, Jens. "Hesitant Hegemon: Germany and EU Enlargement," *Central Europe Review,* 2, no. 189 (May 2000), http://www.ce-review.org/00/18/boysen18.html.

Bracher, Karl Dietrich. *The German Dictatorship: The Origins, Structure, and Effects of National Socialism.* New York: Penguin, 1991.

——. *Theodor Heuß und die Wiederbegründung der Demokratie in Deutschland.* Tübingen: Rainer Wunderlich, 1965.

Bracher, Karl Dietrich, Manfred Funke, and Hans-Adolf Jacobsen, eds. *Nationalsozialistische Diktatur, 1933–1945: eine Bilanz.* Düsseldorf: Droste, 1983.

Brauers, Christof. *Liberale Deutschlandpolitik, 1949–1969: Positionen der F.D.P. zwischen nationaler und europäischer Orientierung,* Münster: LIT-Verlag, 1993.

Brechtken, Magnus. "Die Existenz der Journalisten unter den Bedingungen der Diktatur 1933–1945." In Studt, ed., *"Diener des Staates",* 75–98.

Brenner, Wolfgang. *Walther Rathenau. Deutscher und Jude.* Munich: Piper, 2005.

Bridenthal, Renate, Atina Grossman, and Marion Kaplan, eds. *When Biology was Destiny,* New York: Monthly Review, 1984.

Bridenthal, Renate and Claudia Koonz, "Beyond *Kinder, Küche, Kirche*: Weimar Women in Politics and Work." In Bridenthal et al., eds., *When Biology was Destiny.*

Broszat, Martin, *Hitler and the Collapse of Weimar Germany.* New York: Berg, 1987.

Broszat, Martin, Elke Fröhlich, and Anton Grossmann, eds. *Bayern in der NS-Zeit. Soziale Lage und politisches Verhalten der Bevölkerung im Spiegel vertraulicher Berichte.* Munich: Oldenbourg, vols I–IV, 1977–1983.

Browning, Christopher. *The Origins of the Final Solution: The Evolution of Nazi Jewish Policy, September 1939–March 1942.* Lincoln, Nebraska: 2004.

——. *The Path to Genocide: Essays on Launching the Final Solution.* Cambridge: Cambridge University Press, 1998.

Brubaker, Rogers. *Citizenship and Nationhood in France and Germany.* Cambridge, Mass.: Harvard University Press, 1998.

Bruch, Rüdiger von. *Friedrich Naumann in seiner Zeit.* New York: de Gruyter, 2000.

Brück, Carlheinz von. *Bürger gegen Hitler: Demokraten im antifaschistischen Widerstand.* Berlin: Der Morgen, 1986.

Bruendel, Steffen. *Volksgemeinschaft oder Volksstaat: Die "Ideen von 1914" und die Neuordnung Deutschlands im Ersten Weltkrieg.* Berlin: Akademie Verlag, 2003.

Brysac, Sharon Blair. *Resisting Hitler: Mildred Harnack and the Red Orchestra.* New York: Oxford University Press, 2002.

Burger, Reiner. *Theodor Heuss als Journalist.* Hamburg: LIT, 1998.

Burleigh, Michael. *Germany Turns Eastwards: A Study of Ostforschung in the Third Reich.* Cambridge: Cambridge University Press, 1988.

——. *The Third Reich: A New History.* New York: Hill & Wang, 2000.

Canning, Kathleen. *Gender History in Practice.* Ithaca, N.Y.: Cornell University Press, 2006.

——. *Languages and Labor of Gender.* Ann Arbor: Michigan, 2002.

Caplan, Jane. *Government without Administration: State and Civil Service in Weimar and Nazi Germany.* Oxford: Oxford University Press, 1988.

Caplan, Jane, ed. *Nazism, Fascism and the Working Class: Essays by Tim Mason.* Cambridge: Cambridge University Press, 1995.

Cary, Noel. "Antisemitism, Everyday Life, and the Devastation of Public Morals in Germany," *CEH*, 35 nr. 4 (2002), 551–589.

Carsten, F.L. *The German Workers and the Nazis*. Brookfield: Ashgate, 1995.

——, ed. *The German Resistance to Hitler*. Berkeley: University of California Press, 1970.

Cavaillé, Marie-Dominique. *Rudolf Breitscheid et la France 1919–1933*. Frankfurt: P. Lang, 1995.

Cesarani, David. *Becoming Eichmann: Rethinking the Life, Crimes, and Trial of a "Desk Murderer."* New York: Da Capo, 2007.

Chapman, Mark. *Ernst Troeltsch and Liberal Theology: Religion and Cultural Synthesis in Wilhelmine Germany*. Oxford: Oxford University Press, 2001.

——. *Imperial Germany and a World without War. The Peace Movement and German Society, 1892–1914*. Princeton, N.J.: Princeton University Press, 1975.

Chickering, Roger. "A Voice of Moderation in Imperial Germany. The 'Verband für Internationale Verständigung.'" *Journal of Contemporary History*, 8, nr. 1 (1973), 147–164.

——. *We Men Who Feel Most German: A Cultural Study of the Pan-German League, 1886–1914*. Boston: Allen & Unwin, 1984.

Childers, Thomas. *The Nazi Voter: The Social Foundations of Fascism in Germany 1919–1933*. Chapel Hill, N.C.: University of North Carolina Press, 1983.

Childers, Thomas and Jane Caplan, eds. *Reevaluating the Third Reich*. New York: Holmes & Meier, 1993.

Conway, John. *The Nazi Persecution of the Churches, 1933–1945*. London: Weidenfeld & Nicolson, 1968.

Corneissen, Christopher. "Die wiedererstandene Historismus–Nationalgeschichte in der Bundesrepublik der funfziger Jahre." In Konrad Jarausch and Martin Sabrow, eds. *Die historische Meisterzählung*.

Craig, Gordon. *Germany 1866–1945*. Oxford: Clarendon, 1999.

Crane, Cynthia. *Divided Lives: The Untold Stories of Jewish-Christian Women in Nazi Germany*. New York: St Martin's Press, 2000.

Crew, David F. *Germans on Welfare: From Weimar to Hitler*. New York: Oxford University Press, 1998.

Crew, David F., ed. *Nazism and German Society, 1933–1945*. London: Routledge, 1994.

Dahrendorf, Ralf. *Fragmente eines neuen Liberalismus*. Stuttgart: DVA, 1987.

——. *Society and Democracy in Germany*. New York: Doubleday, 1967.

——. *T. Heuss: Zur geistigen Gestalt des Politikers und Publizisten*. Tübingen: R. Wunderlich, 1984.

Davies, Norman and Roger Moorhouse. *Microcosm: Portrait of a Central European City*. London: Jonathan Cape, 2002.

Deak, Istvan. *Weimar Germany's Left-Wing Intellectuals: A Political History of the Weltbühne and its Circle*. Berkeley: University of California Press, 1968.

Dehli, Martin. *Leben als Konflikt. Zur Biographie Alexander Mitscherlich*. Göttingen: Wallstein, 2007.

Demm, Eberhard. *Ein Liberaler in Kaiserreich und Republik. Der politische Weg Alfred Webers bis 1920*. Boppard: Harald Boldt, 1990.

——, ed. *Alfred Weber als Politiker und Gelehrter*. Stuttgart: Steiner, 1983.

——, ed. *Alfred Weber, Politische Theorie und Tagespolitik (1903–1933)*. Marburg: Metropolis, 1999.

——, ed. *Geist und Politik im 20. Jahrhundert: Gesammelte Aufsätze zu Alfred Weber*. Frankfurt: P. Lang, 2000.

——, ed. *Soziologie, Politik und Kultur: Von Alfred zur Frankfurtschule*. Frankfurt: P. Lang, 2003.

——. *Von der Weimarer Republik zur Bundesrepublik: Der Politische Weg Alfred Webers, 1920–1958*. Düsseldorf: Droste, 1999.

Dickinson, Edward Ross. "Biopolitics, Fascism, Democracy: Some Reflections on Our Discourse about Modernity." *CEH*, 37 (2004), 1–46.

——. *The Politics of German Child Welfare from the Empire to the Federal Republic*. Cambridge, Mass: Harvard University Press, 1996.

Diehl, James M. *Paramilitary Politics in Weimar Germany.* Bloomington: Indiana, 1977.

Dörner, Bernward. *"Heimtücke": Das Gesetz als Waffe: Kontrolle, Abschreckung, und Verfolgung in Deutschland, 1933–1945.* Paderborn: Schöningh, 1998.

Doetinchem, Dagmar Hartung von and Rolf Winau, eds. *Zerstörte Fortschritte: das Jüdische Krankenhaus in Berlin, 1756, 1861, 1914, 1989.* Berlin: Hentrich, 1989.

Dotti, Luca. *L'utopia eugenetica del welfare state svedese, 1934–1975: il programma social-democratico di sterilizzazione, aborto e castrazione.* Soverio: Rubbettino, 2004.

Drewniak, Boguslaw. *Das Theater im NS-Staat: Szenarium deutscher Zeitgeschichte, 1933–1945.* Düsseldorf: Droste, 1983.

Dülffer, Jost. *Nazi Germany 1933–1945: Faith and Annihilation.* London: St Martin's Press, 1996.

——. "Der Weichensteller," *Damals*, 39, nr. 4 (2007), 28–33.

——. *Weimar, Hitler und die Marine: Reichspolitik und Flottenbau, 1920–1939.* Düsseldorf: Droste, 1973.

Duhnke, Horst. *Die KPD von 1933 bis 1945.* Cologne: Kiepenheuer & Witsch, 1972.

Ebbingshaus, Angelika, ed. *Opfer und Täterinnen: Frauenbiographien des Nationalsozialismus.* Nordlingen: Greno, 1987.

Eberle, Josef, ed. *Abschied von Theodor Heuss.* Tübingen: R. Wunderlich, 1964.

Ebersbach, Volker. *Heinrich Mann: Leben, Werk, Wirken.* Leipzig: P. Reclam, 1978.

Eckel, Jan. *Hans Rothfels: Ein intellektuelle Biographie im 20. Jahrhundert.* Göttingen: Wallstein, 1995.

Eckhardt, Katja. *Die Auseinandersetzung zwischen Marianne Weber und Georg Simmel über die "Frauenfrage."* Stuttgart: Ibidem, 2000.

Eksteins, Modris. *The Limits of Reason: The German Democratic Press and the Collapse of Weimar Democracy.* London: Oxford University Press, 1975.

——. *Theodor Heuβ und die Weimarer Republik.* Stuttgart: Klett, 1969.

Eley, Geoff. *Forging Democracy.* Oxford: Oxford University Press, 2002.

——. *Reshaping the German Right: Radical Nationalism and Political Change after Bismarck.* Ann Arbor: University of Michigan Press, 1990.

——, ed. *Society, Culture, and the State in Germany, 1870–1930.* Ann Arbor: University of Michigan Press, 1996.

Eley, Geoff and James Retallack, eds. *Wilhelminism and its Legacies: German Modernities, Imperialism, and the Meanings of Reform, 1890–1930. Essays for Hartmann Pogge van Straudmann.* New York: Berghahn, 2003.

Elm, Ludwig. *Zwischen Fortschritt und Reaktion: Geschichte der Parteien der liberalen Bourgeoisie in Deutschland, 1893–1918.* Berlin: Akademie, 1968.

Enssle, Manfred J. *Stresemann's Territorial Revisionism: Germany, Belgium, and the Eupen-Malmedy Question, 1919–1929.* Wiesbaden: Steiner, 1980.

Erker, Paul. *Industrieeliten in der NS-Zeit: Anpassungsbereitschaft und Eigeninteresse von Unternehmen in der Rüstungs- und Kriegswirtschaft, 1936–1945.* Passau: Wissenschaftsverlag Rothe, 1994.

——. *The Coming of the Third Reich.* New York: Penguin, 2004.

Evans, Richard J. *The Feminist Movement in Germany 1894–1933.* London: Sage, 1976.

——. *Rereading German History: From Unification to Reunification, 1800–1996.* New York: Routledge, 1997.

——. *Third Reich in Power, 1933–1939.* New York: Penguin, 2005.

Fahlbusch, Michael. *Wissenschaft im Dienst der nationalsozialistischen Politik? Die "Volksdeutschen Forschungsgemeinschaften" von 1931–1945.* Baden-Baden: Nomos, 1999.

Fahlbusch, Michael and Ingo Haar, eds. *German Scholars and Ethnic Cleansing.* New York: Berghahn, 2004.

——. eds. *Handbuch der völkischen Wissenschaften.* Munich: Saur, 2008.

Fairbairn, Brett. *Democracy in the Undemocratic State.* Toronto: Toronto University Press, 1997.

Falter, Jürgen. *Hitlers Wähler.* München: C.H. Beck, 1991.

———. "Wählerwanderungen vom Liberalismus zu (rechts-)extremen Parteien. Ein Forschungsbericht am Beispiel des NSDAP-Aufstiegs 1928–1933 und der NPD-Erfolge 1966–1970." In Albertin, ed. *Politischer Liberalismus*, 92–124.

Faßbender, Monika. "Zum Briefwechsel zwischen Anton Erkelenz und Gertrud Bäumer, 1933," *JzLF*, 2 (1990), 150–156.

Feldman, Gerald. *Allianz and the German Insurance Business, 1933–1945*. Cambridge: Cambridge, 2001.

———. *The Great Disorder: Politics, Economy and Society in the German Inflation, 1914–1924*. Oxford: Oxford University Press, 1997.

Felix, David. *Walther Rathenau and the Weimar Republic*. Baltimore: Johns Hopkins, 1971.

Ferguson, Niall. *Paper and Iron: Hamburg Business and German Politics in the Era of Inflation 1897–1927*. Cambridge: Cambridge University Press, 1995.

Fest, Joachim. *Plotting Hitler's Death*. London: Weidenfeld & Nicolson, 1996.

Fischer, Albert. *Hjalmar Schacht und Deutschlands "Judenfrage": Der "Wirtschaftsdiktator" und die Vertreibung der Juden aus der deutschen Wirtschaft*. Cologne: Böhlau, 1995.

———. "The Minister of Economics and the Expulsion of the Jews from the German Economy." In Bankier, ed. *Probing the Depths*.

Fischer, Fritz. *Griff nach der Weltmacht*. Düsseldorf: Droste, 1967.

Fischer, Lars. *The Socialist Response to Anti-Semitism*. Cambridge: Cambridge University Press, 2007.

Fischer-Baling, Eugen. *Walther Rathenau: Ein Experiment Gottes*. Berlin: Weiss, 1952.

Fitzpatrick, Matthew. *Liberal Imperialism in Germany: Expansion and Nationalism 1848–1884*. New York: Berghahn, 2008.

Fletcher, Ian. *Women's Suffrage in the British Empire: Citizenship, Nation and Race*. New York: Routledge, 2000.

Fletcher, Roger. *Socialist Imperialism in Germany, 1897–1914*. London: Allen & Unwin, 1984.

Fraenkel, Daniel. "Jewish Self-Defense under the Constraints of National Socialism: The Final Years of the Centralverein." In Bankier, ed. *Probing the Depths*, 339–357.

Freedman, Estelle B. *No Turning Back: The History of Feminism and the Future of Women*. London: Ballantine, 2003.

Frei, Norbert. *Vergangenheitspolitik. Die Anfänge der Bundesrepublik und die NS-Vergangenheit*. Munich: C.H. Beck, 1997.

———, ed. *Martin Broszat, der "Staat Hitlers" und die Historisierung des Nationalsozialismus*. Göttingen: Wallstein, 2007.

Frevert, Ute. *Women in German History: From Bourgeois Emancipation to Sexual Liberation*. Oxford: Berg, 1990.

Fricke, Dieter. *Die bürgerlichen Parteien in Deutschland*, vol. I. Leipzig: Bibliographisches Institut, 1968.

———, ed. *Deutsche Demokraten. Die nichtproletarischen demokratischen Kräfte in Deutschland 1830–1945*. Cologne: Pahl Rügenstein, 1981.

Friedrichsmeyer, Sara, Sara Lennox, and Susanne Zantop, eds. *The Imperialist Imagination: German Colonialism and its Legacy*. Ann Arbor: Michigan, 1998.

Fritzsche, Peter. *Germans into Nazis*. Cambridge: Cambridge University Press, 1998.

———. *Life and Death in the Third Reich*. Cambridge, Mass.: Harvard University Press, 2008.

———. *Rehearsals for Fascism: Populism and Political Mobilization in Weimar Germany*. New York: Oxford University Press, 1990.

Froelich, Jürgen. " 'Die Excellenz' als 'liberaler Demokrat von Jugend auf'? Eugen Schiffer und die liberalen Parteien in Deutschland." In Ramm, ed. *Eugen Schiffer*, 95–131.

———. " 'He Served the German People Well' ". Der politische Weg Hermann Dietrichs vom badischen Nationalliberalen zum baden-württembergischen Freidemokraten," *Zeitschrift für die Geschichte des Oberrheins*, 153 (2005), 619–640.

———. "Nur Versagt? Das liberale Bürgertum und der Nationalsozialismus," *Mut*, 446 (Oktober 2004), 66.

——. "'Die Umformung des deutschen Seins erlaubt keine passive Resignation'. Die Zeitschrift *Die Hilfe* im Nationalsozialismus." In Studt, ed. *"Diener des Staates,"* 115–129.

Frye, Bruce. "The German Democratic Party and the Jewish Problem in the Weimar Republic." In *Year Book of the Leo Baeck Institute* 21 (1976), 249–280.

——. *Liberal Democrats in the Weimar Republic: The History of the German Democratic Party and the German State Party*. Carbondale: University of Southern Illinois Press, 1985.

Fukuyama, Francis. *The End of History and the Last Man*. New York: Penguin, 1992.

Fulbrook, Mary. *The People's State: East German Society from Hitler to Honecker*. New Haven and London: Yale University Press, 2005.

Gaddis, John Lewis. *Strategies of Containment: A Critical Appraisal of American National Security Policy during the Cold War*. Oxford: Oxford University Press, 2005.

Gall, Lothar, ed. *Liberalismus*. Köln: Kiepenheuer & Witsch, 1976.

——. "Liberalismus und 'bürgerliche Gesellschaft.' Zu Charakter und Entwicklung der liberalen Bewegung in Deutschland," *Historische Zeitschrift*, 220 (1975), 324–352.

Gall, Lothar and Dieter Langewiesche. *Liberalismus und Region*. Munich: Oldenbourg, 1995.

Gatzke, Hans W. *Stresemann and the Rearmament of Germany*. New York: W.W. Norton, 1969.

Gay, Peter. *Freud, Jews and Other Germans: Masters and Victims in Modernist Culture*. New York, 1978.

——. *Weimar Culture: The Outsider as Insider*. New York: Harper & Row, 1968.

Gellately, Robert. *Backing Hitler: Consent and Coercion in Nazi Germany*. Oxford: Oxford University Press, 2001.

——. *The Gestapo and German Society: Enforcing Racial Policy 1933–1945*. Oxford: Clarendon, 1990.

Gellately, Robert and Nathan Stolztfus, eds. *Social Outsiders in the Third Reich*. Princeton, N.J.: Princeton University Press, 2001.

Geller, Jay. *Jews in Post-Holocaust Germany, 1945–1953*. Cambridge: Cambridge University Press, 2005.

Generaldirektion der staatlichen Archive Bayerns, eds. *Wege in die Vernichtung. Die Deportation der Juden aus Mainfranken 1941–1943*. Munich: Staatlichen Archive Bayerns, 2003.

Gerlach, Christian. *Krieg, Ernährung, Volkermord: Deutsche Vernichtungspolitik im Zweiten Weltkrieg*. Zürich: Pendo, 2001.

Gerwarth, Robert and Stephen Malinowski. "Der Holocaust als kolonialer Genozid? Europäische Kolonialgewalt und nationalsozialistischer Vernichtungskrieg," *Geschichte und Gesellschaft*, 33, nr. 3 (2007), 439–466.

Geyer, Michael. *Deutsche Rüstungspolitik 1860–1980*. Frankfurt: Suhrkamp, 1984.

Geyer, Michael and John Boyer, eds. *Resistance against the Third Reich, 1933–1990*. Chicago: Chicago University Press, 1994.

Gies, Horst and Gustavo Corni. *Brot, Butter, Kanonen: die Ernährungswirtschaft in Deutschland unter der Diktatur Hitlers*. Berlin: Akademie, 1997.

Gilbert, Martin. *Kristallnacht: Prelude to Destruction*. London: Harper, 2006.

——. *Second World War*. London: Fontana, 1990.

Gilbert, Ursula Susanna. *Hellmut von Gerlach (1866–1935): Stationen eines deutschen Liberalen vom Kaiserreich zum "Dritten Reich"*. Frankfurt: P. Lang, 1984.

Giles, Geoffrey. *Students and National Socialism in Germany*. Princeton, N.J.: Princeton University Press, 1985.

Gillessen, Günther. *Auf verlorenem Posten: Die Frankfurter Zeitung im Dritten Reich*. Berlin: Siedler, 1986.

Gilmore, Stephanie. *Historical Perspectives on Second-Wave Feminism in the United States*. Champaign: Illinois, 2008.

Goethel, Thomas. *Demokratie und Volkstum: Die Politik gegenüber den nationalen Minderheiten in der Weimarer Republik*. Cologne: SH-Verlag, 2002.

Göttert, Margit. *Macht und Eros. Frauenbeziehungen und weibliche Kultur um 1900. Eine neue Perspektive auf Helene Lange und Gertrud Bäumer.* Königstein: Ulrike Helmer, 2000.

Goldhagen, Daniel. *A Moral Reckoning: The Role of the Catholic Church in the Holocaust and its Unfulfilled Duty of Repair.* New York: Vintage, 2003.

———. *Hitler's Willing Executioners.* New York: Knopf, 1996.

Goldschmidt, Dietrich. *Eugen Schiffer: Ein Leben für liberale Politik und volksnahes Recht.* Cologne: Heymanns, 1996.

Goldschmidt, Dietrich. "Erinnerungen an das Leben von Eugen und Marie Schiffer nach dem 30. Januar 1933," *Berlin in Geschichte und Gegenwart. Jahrbuch des Landesarchivs Berlin,* 10 (1991), 117–146.

Gotzmann, Andreas, R. Liedtke, and Till van Rahden, eds. *Juden, Bürger, Deutscher: Zur Geschichte von Vielfalt und Differenz 1800–1933.* Tübingen: Möhr Siebeck, 2001.

Graml, Hermann. *Antisemitism in the Third Reich.* Oxford: Blackwell, 1992.

———. *Widerstand im Dritten Reich: Probleme, Ereignisse, Gestalten.* Frankfurt: Fischer, 1984.

Grau, Günter, ed. *Hidden Holocaust? Gay and Lesbian Persecution in Germany 1933–45.* London: Cassell, 1995.

Gregor, Neil, ed. *Nazism, War and Genocide: Essays in Honour of Jeremy Noakes.* Exeter: Exeter University Press, 2005.

Greven-Aschoff, Barbara. *Die bürgerliche Frauenbewegung in Deutschland 1894–1933.* Göttingen: Vandenhoeck & Ruprecht, 1981.

Gross, Jan. *Neighbors: The Destruction of the Jewish Community in Jedwabne, Poland.* Princeton, N.J.: Princeton University Press, 2001.

Grossmann, Attina. "Feminist Debates about Women and National Socialism," *Gender & History,* 3 (Autumn 1991), 350–358.

Gruchmann, Lothar. *Justiz im Dritten Reich, 1933–1940: Anpassung und Unterwerfung in der Ära Gürtner.* Munich: Oldenbourg, 2001.

Gunther, Irene. *Nazi Chic: Fashioning Women in the Third Reich.* New York: Berg, 2004.

Gutscher, J.M. *Die Entwicklung der FDP von ihren Anfängen bis 1961.* Meisenheim: Anton Hain, 1967.

Haar, Ingo. *Historiker im Nationalsozialismus. Deutsche Geschichtswissenschaft und der "Volkstumskampf" im Osten.* Göttingen: Vandenhoeck & Ruprecht, 2000.

Habermas, Jürgen. "Eine Art Schadensabwicklung. Die apologetischen Tendenzen in der deutschen Geschichtsschreibung (*Die Zeit* vom 11.7.1986)." In *Die Dokumentation der Kontroverse um die Einzigartigkeit der nationalsozialistischen Judenvernichtung.* Munich: Piper, 1987, 62–76.

Hagemann, Karen and Stefanie Schüler-Springorum, eds. *Heimat-Front. Militär und Geschlechtsverhältnisse im Zeitalter der Weltkriege.* Frankfurt: Campus, 2002.

Hagen, William W. *Before the "Final Solution": Toward a Comparative Analysis of Political Anti-Semitism in Interwar Germany [and] Poland.* Berkeley: University of California Press, 1993.

Hamerow, Theodore S. *On the Road to the Wolf's Lair.* Cambridge, Mass.: Belknap, 1997.

Hamilton, Richard S. *Who Voted for Hitler?* Princeton, NJ: Princeton University Press, 1982.

Hamm-Brücher, Hildegard. "Anmerkungen zum Versagen des politischen Liberalismus vor und nach 1933 und zu seinen Folgewirkungen nach 1945," *Liberal,* 25, nr. 1, (1983), 171–180.

Hammerstein, Notker. *Antisemitismus und die deutsche Universitäten, 1871–1933.* Frankfurt: Campus, 1995.

Hansen, Knut. *Albrecht Graf von Bernstorff.* Frankfurt: Peter Lang, 1996.

Harbutt, Fraser J. *The Iron Curtain: Churchill, America, and the Origins of the Cold War.* New York: Oxford University Press, 1986.

Hayes, Peter. *From Cooperation to Complicity: Degussa in the Third Reich.* New York: Cambridge University Press, 2004.

———. *Industry and Ideology: IG Farben in the Nazi Era.* Cambridge: Cambridge University Press, 1987.

Heberle, Rudolf. *From Democracy to Nazism: A Regional Case Study on Political Parties in Germany*. New York: Howard Fertig, 1970.

Hecht, Cornelia. *Deutsche Juden und Antisemitismus in der Weimarer Republik*, Bonn: Dietz 2003.

Heilbronner, Oded. *Catholicism, Political Culture and the Countryside. A Social History of the Nazi Party in South Germany*. Ann Arbor: University of Michigan Press, 1998.

——. *"Freiheit, Gleichheit, Brüderlichkeit und Dynamik." Populäre Kultur, populärer Liberalismus und Bürgertum im ländlichen Süddeutschland 1850 bis 1930*. Munich: Martin Meidenbauer, 2007.

Heineman, Elizabeth. *What Difference Does a Husband Make? Women and Marital Status in Nazi and Postwar Germany*. Berkeley: University of California Press, 1999.

Heinsohn, Kirsten, Barbara Vogel, and Ulrike Weckel, eds. *Zwischen Karriere und Verfolgung. Handlungsräume von Frauen im nationalsozialistischen Deutschland*. Frankfurt: Campus, 1997.

Heinze-Hense, Karl. "Die Liberalen und der Nationalsozialismus," *Liberal*, 34, nr. 1, (1992), 101–110.

Helhausen, Joachim, ed. *Zeugen des Widerstands*. Tübingen: J.C.B. Mohr, 1996.

Herbert, Ulrich. *Best: Biographische Studien über Radikalismus, Weltanschauung und Vernunft, 1903–1989*. Bonn: Dietz, 1996.

——, ed. *National Socialist Extermination Policies: Contemporary Perspectives and Controversies*, vol. II. New York: Berghahn, 2000.

Herf, Jeffrey. *The Jewish Enemy: Nazi Propaganda during World War II*. Cambridge, Mass.: Belknap, 2006.

——. *Reactionary Modernism: Technology, Culture and Politics in Weimar and the Third Reich*. Cambridge: Cambridge University Press, 1984.

Hermelink, Heinrich. *Kirche im Kampf: Dokumente des Widerstands und des Aufbaus in der evangelischen Kirche Deutschlands von 1933 bis 1945*. Tübingen: R. Wunderlich, 1950.

Hertfedler, Thomas and Christiane Ketterle, eds. *Theodor Heuss: Publizist–Politiker–Präsident*. Stuttgart: Klett, 2003.

Herzog, Dagmar. *Sex after Fascism: Memory and Morality in Twentieth-Century Germany*. Princeton, N.J.: Princeton University Press, 2005.

Heβ, Jürgen C. " 'Die deutsche Lage ist ungeheuer ernst geworden': Theodor Heuss vor der Herausforderungen des Jahres 1933," *JzLF*, 6 (1994), 65–136.

——. *Das ganze Deutschland soll es sein: Demokratischer Nationalismus in der Weimarer Republik am Beispiel der Deutsche Demokratische Partei*. Stuttgart: Klett-Cotta, 1978.

——. " 'Die Nazis haben gewuβt, daβ wir ihre Feinde gewesen und geblieben sind': Theodor Heuss und der Widerstand gegen den Nationalsozialismus," *JzLF*, 14 (2002), 143–210.

——. *Theodor Heuss vor 1933*. Stuttgart: Ernst Klett, 1973.

Hettling, Manfred. *Politische Bürgerlichkeit der Burger zwischen Individualität und Vergesellschaftung in Deutschland und der Schweiz von 1860 bis 1918*. Göttingen: Vandenhoeck & Ruprecht, 1999.

Heyn, Susanne. "Der kolonialkritische Diskurs der Weimarer Friedensbewegung zwischen Antikolonialismus und Kulturmission," *Wiener Zeitschrift für kritische Afrikastudien*, 9 (2005), 37–65.

Hildebrand, Klaus. *Deutsche Außenpolitik 1933–1945*. Stuttgart: Kohlhammer, 1990.

——. *Foreign Policy of the Third Reich*. Berkeley: University of California Press, 1973.

——. *Vom Reich zum Weltreich: Hitler, NSDAP und koloniale Frage 1919–1945*. Munich: W. Fink, 1969.

Hilger, Christian. *Rechtsstaatsbegriffe im Dritten Reich. Eine Strukturanalyse*. Tübingen: Möhr Siebeck, 2003.

Hill, Leonidas. "Towards a New History of the German Resistance to Hitler," *CEH*, 14 (1981).

Hillgruber, Andreas. *Deutschlands Rolle in der Vorgeschichte der beiden Weltkriege*. Göttingen: Vandenhoeck & Ruprecht, 1967.

———. *Kontinuität und Diskontinuität in der deutschen Außenpolitik von Bismarck bis Hitler.* Düsseldorf: Droste, 1969.

———. *Zweierlei Untergang.* Berlin: Siedler, 1986.

———. *Der Zweite Weltkrieg, 1939–1945: Kriegsziele und Strategie der großen Mächte.* Stuttgart: Kohlhammer, 1982.

Hirsch, Felix. *Gustav Stresemann: Patriot und Europäer.* Göttingen: Musterschmidt, 1964.

Hobsbawm, Eric and Terence Ranger. *Invented Traditions: Reflections on the Origin and Spread of Nationalism.* New York: 1992.

Hockenos, Matthias D. *A Church Divided: German Protestants Confront the Nazi Past.* Bloomington: Indiana, 2004.

Höhne, Heinz. *Order of the Death's Head.* New York: Penguin, 2001.

Höhne, Steffen. "Mitteleuropa. Zur konzeptuellen Karriere eines kulturpolitischen Begriffs," *Bohemia,* 41 (2000), 279–294.

Hörster-Phillips, Ulrike. *Joseph Wirth, 1879–1956: Eine politische Biographie.* Paderborn: Ferdinand Schöningh, 1998.

Hoffmann, Peter. *German Resistance to Hitler.* Cambridge, Mass.: Harvard University Press, 1985.

———. *The History of the German Resistance.* Cambridge, Mass: MIT Press, 1977.

Hohmann, Joachim. *Geschichte der Zigeunerverfolgung in Deutschland.* Frankfurt: Campus, 1988.

———, ed. *Keiner Zeit für gute Freunde: Homosexuelle in Deutschland 1933–1969.* Berlin: Foerster, 1982.

Holl, Karl. *Ludwig Quidde (1858–1941): Eine Biographie.* Düsseldorf: Droste, 2007.

Holl, Karl and Adolf Wild, eds. *Ein Demokrat Kommentiert Weimar: Die Berichte Hellmut von Gerlachs an die Carnegie–Friedensstiftung in New York 1922–1930.* Bremen: 1973.

Hopf, Caroline. *Frauenbewegung und Pädagogik: Gertrud Bäumer zum Beispiel.* Bad Heilbrunn: Julius Klinkhardt, 1997.

Horch, Hans Otto. *Judentum, Antisemitismus und europäische Kultur.* Tübingen: Niemeyer, 1988.

Horsman, Reginald. *Race and Manifest Destiny: The Origins of American Racial Anglo-Saxonism.* Cambridge, Mass.: Harvard University Press, 1981.

Hornung, Klaus. *Hans Rothfels und die Nationalitätfragen in Ostmitteleuropa, 1926–1934.* Bonn: Kulturstiftung der deutschen Vertriebene, 2001.

Huber, Heinrich, *Dokumente einer christlichen Widerstands-Bewegung: Gegen die Entfernung der Kruzifixe aus den Schulen.* Munich: Schnell & Steiner, 1948.

Huber, Werner. "Gertrud Bäumer, Eine politische Biographie" (Ausgburg diss.), 1970.

Hübinger, Gangolf. *Kulturprotestantismus und Politik: zum Verhaltnis von Liberalismus und Protestantismus im wilhelminischen Deutschland.* Tübingen: Möhr Siebeck, 1994.

Huener, Jonathan and Francis R. Nicosia, eds. *The Arts in Nazi Germany: Continuity, Conformity, Change.* Oxford: Berghahn, 2006.

Huerkamp, Claudia. *Bildungsbürgerinnen. Frauen im Studium und in akdaemischen Berufen 1900–1945.* Göttingen: Vandenhoeck & Ruprecht, 1996.

Hürter, Johannes and Hans Woller, eds. *Hans Rothfels und die deutsche Zeitgeschichte.* Munich: Oldenbourg, 2005.

Hummerich, Helga. *Wahrheit zwischen den Zeilen: Erinnerungen an Benno Reifenberg und die Frankfurter Zeitung.* Freiburg: Herder, 1984.

Hung, Young-Sun. "Gender, Citizenship, and the Welfare State: Social Work and the Politics of Femininity in the Weimar Republic," *Central European History,* 30 (1997), 1–24.

———. *Welfare, Modernity, and the Weimar State, 1919–1933.* Princeton, N.J.: Princeton University Press, 1998.

Hunt, James Clark. *The People's Party in Württemberg and Southern Germany, 1890–1914.* Stuttgart: Klett, 1975.

Jacobsen, Hans-Adolf. *Nationalsozialistische Aussenpolitik, 1933–1938.* Frankfurt: Metzner, 1968.

——. ed. *20. Juli 1944: Die deutsche Opposition gegen Hitler im Urteil der ausländischen Geschichtsschreibung.* Bonn: FRG Press and Information Office, 1969.

Jahnke, Karl-Heinze. *Weiße Rose contra Hakenkreuz. Studenten im Widerstand 1942/43.* Rostock: Koch, 2003.

James, Harold. *The Nazi Dictatorship and the Deutsche Bank.* Cambridge: Cambridge, 2004.

Jarausch, Konrad. *Students, Society, and Politics in Imperial Germany: The Rise of Academic Illiberalism.* Princeton, N.J.: Princeton University Press, 1982.

——. *The Unfree Professions: German Lawyers, Teachers, and Engineers 1900–1950.* New York: Oxford University Press, 1990.

Jarausch, Konrad und Rüdiger Hohls, eds. *Versäumte Fragen: deutsche Historiker im Schatten der Nationalsozialismus.* Stuttgart: 2000.

Jarausch, Konrad and Larry Eugene Jones. "German Liberalism Reconsidered: Inevitable Decline, Bourgeois Hegemony, or Partial Achievement?" In Jarausch and Jones, eds, *In Search of a Liberal Germany,* New York: Berg, 1999.

Jarausch, Konrad and Martin Sabrow, eds. *Die historische Meisterzählung – Deutungslinien deutscher Nationalgeschichte nach 1945.* Göttingen: Vandenhoeck & Ruprecht, 2003.

Jenkins, Jennifer. *Provincial Modernity: Local Culture and Liberal Politics in fin–de–siècle Hamburg.* Ithaca, NY: Cornell University Press, 2003.

Johnson, Eric A. *Nazi Terror: The Gestapo, Jews and Ordinary Germans.* New York: Basic Books, 1999.

Jones, Larry. *German Liberalism and the Dissolution of the Weimar Party System.* North Carolina: Chapel Hill, 1988.

Jones, Larry and James Retallack, eds. *Elections, Mass Politics and Social Change in Germany.* Washington, D.C., 1992.

Judson, Pieter. *Exclusive Revolutionaries: Liberal Politics, Social Experience, and National Identity in the Austrian Empire, 1848–1914.* Ann Arbor: University of Michigan Press 1996.

Kaes, Anton, Martin Jay and Edward Dimendberg. *The Weimar Republic Sourcebook.* Berkeley: University of California Press, 1994.

Karatani, Rieko. *Defining British Citizenship: Empire, Commonwealth and Modern Britain.* New York: Routledge, 2002.

Kater, Michael. *Doctors under Hitler.* Chapel Hill: North Carolina, 1989.

——. *The Twisted Muse. Musicians and their Music in the Third Reich.* Oxford: Oxford University Press, 1997.

Kauders, Anthony. "Legally Citizens: Jewish Exclusion from the Weimar Polity." In Benz et al. eds, *Jews in the Weimar Republic,* 159–172.

Kempter, Klaus. *Die Jellineks, 1820–1955: Eine familienbiographische Studie zum deutsch-jüdischen Bildungsbürgertum.* Düsseldorf: 1998.

Kennedy, Paul. *Nationalist and Racialist Movements in Britain and Germany before 1914.* London: 1981.

Kershaw, Ian. *Hitler: Hubris, 1889–1936.* New York: Norton, 1999.

——. *Hitler Myth: Image and Reality.* Oxford: Oxford University Press, 1987.

——. *Hitler: Nemesis, 1936–1945.* New York: Norton, 2000.

——. *Popular Opinion and Political Dissent in the Third Reich.* Oxford: Clarendon Press, 2002.

Kettenacker, Lothar. *Nationalsozialische Volkstumpolitik im Elsaß.* Stuttgart: Klett, 1973.

——, ed. *The "Other Germany" in the Second World War.* Stuttgart: Klett, 1977.

King, Richard and Dan Stone, eds. *Hannah Arendt and the Uses of History: Imperialism, Nation, Race, and Genocide.* New York: Berghahn, 2007.

Klein, Burton H. *Germany's Economic Preparations for War.* Cambridge, Mass.: Harvard University Press, 1959.

Klemperer, Klemens von. *Der einsame Zeuge: Einzelkämpfer im Widerstand.* Passau: Richard Rothe, 1990.

——. *German Resistance against Hitler: The Search for Allies Abroad, 1938–1945.* Oxford: Clarendon Press, 1992.

Knütter, Hans-Helmuth. *Die Juden und die deutsche Linke in der Weimarer Republik 1918–1933.* Düsseldorf: Droste, 1971.

Kocka, Jürgen. *White-Collar Workers in America, 1890–1940: A Social–Political History in International Perspective.* London: Sage, 1980.

Körber, Andreas. *Gustav Stresemann als Europäer, Patriot, Wegbereiter und potentieller Verhinderer Hitlers.* Hamburg: Krämer, 1999.

Kolb, Eberhard. *Gustav Stresemann.* Munich: C.H. Beck, 2003.

——. *The Weimar Republic.* New York: Routledge, 2005.

Kolb, Eberhard und Walter Muhlhausen, eds. *Demokratie in der Krise: Parteien im Verfassungssystem der Weimarer Republik.* Munich: Oldenbourg, 1997.

Kolb, Eberhard and Ludwig Richter, eds. *Nationalliberalismus in der Weimarer Republik: die Führungsgremien der Deutschen Volkspartei, Quellen zur Geschichte des Parlamentarismus 1918–1933.* Düsseldorf: Droste, 1999.

Kolko, Gabriel. *The Politics of War: The World and United States Foreign Policy 1943–1945.* New York: Pantheon, 1990.

Koonz, Claudia. *Mothers in the Fatherland: Women, the Family and Nazi Politics.* New York: St Martin's Press, 1987.

——. *The Nazi Conscience.* Cambridge, Mass.: Harvard University Press, 2003.

Korenblatt, Steven D. "A School for the Republic: Cosmopolitans and their Enemies at the Deutsche Hochschule für Politik, 1920–1933," *CEH*, 39 (2006), 394–430.

Koselleck, Reinhart. *Preussen zwischen Reform und Revolution.* Stuttgart: 1967.

Krey, Ursula. "Der Naumann-Kreis: Charisma und politische Emanzipation." In Bruch, ed., *Friedrich Naumann.*

Krey, Ursula and Thomas Trump. *Findbücher zu Bestandsgruppe R 45–Liberale Parteien–I. Nationalliberale Partei II. Deutsche Volkspartei III. Deutsche Demokratische Partei–Deutsche Staatspartei.* Koblenz: Bundesarchiv, 1985.

Krieger, Karsten. *Der Berliner Antisemitismusstreit 1879–1881: Eine Kontroverse um die Zugehörigkeit der deutschen Juden zur Nation*, Munich: K. G. Saur, 2003.

Krüger, Christa. *Max und Marianne Weber: Tag- und Nachtgeschichten einer Ehe.* Zürich: Pendo, 2001.

Kübler, Thomas. "Wilhelm Külz als Kommunalpolitiker," *JzLF*, 18 (2006).

Kühne, Thomas. *Handbuch der Wählen zum preussischen Abgeordnetenhaus 1867–1918: Wahlergebnisse, Wahlbündnisse und Wahlkandidaten.* Düsseldorf: Droste, 1994.

Kundrus, Birthe ed. *Phantasiereiche: Zur Kulturgeschichte des deutschen Kolonialismus.* Frankfurt: Campus, 2003.

Kurlander, Eric. "Negotiating National Socialism: Liberal Non-Conformity and Accommodation in the Period of *Gleichschaltung*," *JzLF*, 17 (2005), 59–76.

——. "New Approaches to Bourgeois Resistance in Germany and Austria," *History Compass*, 4 (2006), 1–18.

——. *The Price of Exclusion: Ethnicity, National Identity and the Decline of German Liberalism, 1898–1933.* New York: Berghahn, 2006.

Kushner, Tony. *The Holocaust and the Liberal Imagination: A Social and Cultural History.* Oxford: Blackwell, 1994.

Kwiet, Konrad and Helmut Eschwege. *Selbstbehauptung und Widerstand. Deutsche Juden im Kampf um Existenz und Menschenwürde, 1933–1945.* Hamburg: Hans Christians, 1984.

Langbein, Hermann. *People in Auschwitz.* Chapel Hill: North Carolina, 2004.

Langewiesche, Dieter. *Liberalism in Germany.* Princeton: Princeton, 1999.

——. *Liberalismus im 19. Jahrhundert: Deutschland im europäischen Vergleich* Göttingen: 1988.

——. *Republik und Republikaner.* Essen: Klartext, 1993.

Large, David Clay, ed. *Contending with Hitler: Varieties of German Resistance in the Third Reich.* Cambridge: Cambridge, 1991.

Lauterer, Heide-Marie. "Liebe Marquise von O.: Von den gesellschaftlichen Problemen liberaler Parlamentierinnen in der Weimarer Republik. Kommentar und Edition eines Briefes von Marie Elisabeth Lüders an Katharina v. Oheimb vom 26. Sept. 1924," *JzLF*, 16 (2004), 273–283.

———. *Liebestätigkeit für die Volksgemeinschaft*. Göttingen: Vandenhoeck & Ruprecht, 1994.

———. "Marie Baum und der Heidelberger Freundeskreis." In Meurer, ed., *Marianne Weber*, 91–107.

———. *Parlamentarierinnen in Deutschland 1918/19–1949*. Königstein: Ulrike Helmer, 2002.

Lehmann, Hans-Georg. *Nationalsozialistische und akademische Ausburgerung im Exil: Warum Rudolf Breitscheid der Doktortitel aberkannt wurde*. Marburg: Pressestelle d. Phillips-Universität, 1985.

Lehmann, Hartmut, ed. *Elections, Mass Politics, and Social Change in Modern Germany*. Cambridge: Cambridge University Press, 1992.

Leitz, Christian, ed. *The Third Reich: The Essential Readings*. Oxford: Blackwell, 1999.

Levy, Richard S. *The Downfall of the Antisemitic Parties in Imperial Germany*. New Haven and London: Yale University Press, 1975.

Lewy, Günther. *The Catholic Church and Nazi Germany*. New York: McGraw-Hill, 1964.

———. *The Nazi Persecution of the Gypsies*. Oxford: Oxford University Press, 2000.

Ley, Astrid. *Zwangssterilisation und Ärzteschaft: Hintergrunde und Ziele ärztlichen Handelns 1934–1945*. Frankfurt: Campus, 2004.

Liepach, Martin. "Zwischen Abwehrkampf und Wählermobilisierung: Juden und die Landtagswahl in Baden 1929." In Benz et al., eds, *Jews in the Weimar Republic*, 9–24.

Lindsay, Mark. *Covenanted Solidarity: The Theological Basis of Karl Barth's Opposition to Nazi Antisemitism and the Holocaust*. New York: Peter Lang, 2000.

Löwenthal, Richard und Patrick von der Mühlen, eds. *Widerstand und Verweigerung in Deutschland, 1933 bis 1945*. Berlin: Dietz, 1984.

Longerich, Peter. *"Davon haben wir nicht gewusst." Die Deutschen und die Judenverfolgung, 1933–1945*. Berlin: Siedler, 2006.

Lower, Wendy. *Nazi Empire Building and the Holocaust in Ukraine*. Chapel Hill, N.C.: University of North Carolina Press, 2007.

Luckemeyer, Ludwig. *Föderativer liberaler Rebell in DDP und FDP und erster liberaler Vorkämpfer Europas in Deutschland*. Korbach: W. Bing, 1981.

———. *Kasseler Liberale in zwei Jahrhundere*. Kassel: Alfred Schmidt, 1979.

Lüdtke, Alf, ed. *Alltagsgeschichte: Zur Rekonstruktion historischer Erfahrungen und Lebensweisen*. Frankfurt: Campus, 1989.

———. "The Appeal of Exterminating 'Others': Workers and the Limits of Resistance." In Leitz, ed., *The Third Reich*, 155–177.

McIntyre, Jill. "Women and the Professions in Germany 1930–1940." In Matthias and Nicholls, eds, *German Democracy and the Triumph of Hitler*, 175–213.

Maier, Charles S. *Recasting Bourgeois Europe: Stabilization in France, Germany, and Italy in the Decade after World War I*. Princeton, NJ: Princeton University Press, 1988.

Malinowski, Stephen. "Der Holocaust als kolonialer Genozid? Europäische Kolonialgewalt und nationalsozialistischer Vernichtungskrieg," *Geschichte und Gesellschaft*, 33 (2007), 439–466.

Mann, Reinhard. *Protest und Kontrolle im Dritten Reich: Nationalsozialistische Herrschaft im Alltag einer rheinischen Großstadt*. Frankfurt: Campus, 1987.

Mason, Timothy. "The Containment of the Working Classes in Germany." In Caplan, ed., *Nazism*, 231–273.

———. "Internal Crisis and War of Aggression, 1938–1939." In Caplan, ed., *Nazism*, 104–130.

———. "Some Origins of the Second World War." In Caplan, ed., *Nazism*, 33–52.

———. *Sozialpolitik im Dritten Reich*. Opladen: Westdeutscher, 1978.

———. "Women in Nazi Germany, 1925–1940. Family, Welfare, and Work." In Caplan, ed., *Nazism*, 131–211.

Matthias, Erich and Rudolf Morsey, eds. *Das Ende der Parteien*. Düsseldorf: Droste, 1979.

Matthias, Erich and Anthony Nicholls, eds. *German Democracy and the Triumph of Hitler*. London: Allen & Unwin, 1971.

Matz, Klaus-Jürgen. *Reinhold Maier: Eine politische Biographie.* Düsseldorf: Droste, 1983.

Mayer, Arno. *Why Did the Heavens Not Darken? The "Final Solution" in History.* New York: Pantheon, 1990.

Mazon, Patricia. *Gender and the Modern Research University, 1865–1914.* Stanford, CA: Stanford University Press, 2003.

Medick, Hans. " 'Missionare im Ruderboot'? Ethnologische Erkenntnisweisen als Herausforderung an die Sozialgeschichte," *Geschichte und Gesellschaft,* 10 (1984), 296–319.

Medick, Hans and David Sabean, eds. *Interests and Emotion: Essays in the Study of Family and Kinship.* Cambridge: Cambridge University Press, 1984.

Merson, Allan. *Communist Resistance in Nazi Germany.* London: Lawrence & Wishart, 1986.

Meurer, Bärbel, ed. *Marianne Weber: Beiträge zu Werk und Person.* Tübingen: Möhr Siebeck, 2004.

Meyer, Henry Cord. *Mitteleuropa in German Thought and Action, 1815–1945.* The Hague: Nijhoff, 1955.

Milward, Alan S. *War, Economy, and Society, 1939–1945.* Berkeley: University of California Press, 1977.

Moeller, Robert G. *Protecting Motherhood: Women and the Family in Postwar Germany.* Berkeley: University of California Press, 1993.

Moller, Horst. *Parlamentarismus in Preußen 1919–1932.* Düsseldorf: Droste, 1985.

Molt, Peter. "Der Beitrag Alfred Webers zur Begründung der Politikwissenschaft in Deutschland." In Demm, ed., *Geist und Politik im 20. Jahrhundert.*

Mommsen, Hans. *Alternatives to Hitler: German Resistance under the Third Reich.* London: I.B. Tauris, 2003.

——. *From Weimar to Auschwitz.* Princeton: Princeton, 1992.

——. "Resistance". In Leitz, ed., *The Third Reich.*

——. *The Rise and Fall of Weimar Democracy.* Chapel Hill, NC: University of North Carolina Press, 1996.

——. "Die Widerstand gegen Hitler und die deutsche Gesellschaft." In Schmädeke and Steinbach, eds, *Widerstand.*

Mommsen, Wolfgang J. *Grossmachtstellung und Weltpolitik: Die Aussenpolitik des Deutschen Reiches 1870 bis 1914.* Frankfurt am Main: 1993.

——. *Imperial Germany 1867–1918.* London: 1995.

——. *Max Weber und die deutsche Politik, 1890–1920.* Chicago: Chicago University Press, 1984.

——. "Wandlungen der liberalen Idee im Zeitalter des Liberalismus" and Lothar Gall, " 'Sündenfall' des liberalen Denkens oder Krise der bürgerlichen-liberalen Bewegung?" In Karl Holl and Günther List, eds, *Liberalismus und imperialistischer Staat,* Göttingen: Vandenhoeck & Ruprecht, 109–148.

Moses, A. Dirk and Dan Stone, eds. *Colonialism and Genocide.* London: Routledge, 2007.

Moses, Fritz. *Strehlen: Errinerungen an einen schlesische Kleinstadt und ihre jüdischen Bürger.* Bremen: 1995.

Mosse, Georg. *The Crisis of German Ideology: Intellectual Origins of the Third Reich.* New York: Howard Fertig, 1998.

Mosse, Werner E. *Jews in the German Economy: The German–Jewish Economic Elite, 1820–1935.* Oxford: Oxford University Press, 1987.

——. *Juden im Wilhelminischen Deutschland 1890–1914.* Tübingen: Möhr, 1976.

Mühlberger, Detlef. *Hitler's Followers: Studies in the Sociology of the Nazi Movement.* New York: Routledge, 1991.

Müller, Guido. "Theodor Heuss: Deutscher Bildungsbürger und ethischer Liberalismus. Probleme und Aufgaben einer Heuss-Biographie in der Spannung zwischen politischen–gesellschaftlichen Strukturen und selbstverantworteter Individualität (1884–1963)," *JzLF,* 15 (2003), 210–211.

Neebe, Reinhard. *Grossindustrie, Staat und NSDAP 1930–1933: Paul Silverberg und der Reichsverband der Deutschen Industrie in der Krise der Weimarer Republik.* Göttingen: Vandenhoeck & Ruprecht, 1981.

Nelson, Keith L. "The 'Black Horror on the Rhine': Race as a Factor in Post-World War I Diplomacy," *Journal of Modern History,* 42, no. 4 (Dec. 1970), 606–627.

Neugebauer, Wolfgang, Wolfgang Form und Theo Schiller, eds. *NS-Justiz und politische Verfolgung in Österreich 1938–1945: Analysen zu den Verfahren vor dem Volksgerichtshof und dem Oberlandsgericht Wien.* Munich: Saur, 2006.

Neumann, Franz. *Behemoth: The Structure and Practice of National Socialism 1933–1944.* New York: Oxford University Press, 1944.

Neumann, Martina. *Theodor Tantzen: Ein widerspenstiger Liberaler gegen der Nationalsozialismus.* Hanover: Hansche, 1998.

Nicholls, Anthony. *Freedom with Responsibility: The Social Market Economy in Germany, 1918–1963.* Oxford: Clarendon Press, 1994.

——, ed. *Weimar and the Rise of Hitler.* London: Macmillan, 1991.

Nickel, Lutz. *Dehler, Maier, Mende: Parteivorsitzende der FDP.* München: M. Press, 2005.

Nicosia, Francis and Lawrence Stokes, eds, *Germans against Nazism: Nonconformity, Opposition and Resistance in the Third Reich (Essays in Honor of Peter Hoffman).* New York: Berg, 1990.

Nipperdey, Thomas. *Deutsche Geschichte 1866–1918.* Munich: Hanser, 1993.

——. *Die Organisation der deutschen Parteien vor 1918.* Düsseldorf: Droste, 1961.

Noakes, Jeremy and Geoffrey Pridham, eds. *Nazism: The Rise to Power,* vol. I. Exeter: Exeter University Press, 1998.

Nocker, Horst. *Der Preussische Reichstagswähler in Kaiserreich und Republik.* Berlin: 1987.

Nolte, Ernst. *Der europäische Bürgerkrieg 1917–1945. Nationalsozialismus und Bolschewismus.* Berlin: Propyläen, 1987.

Obenaus, Herbert. "The Germans: 'An Antisemitic People.' The Press Campaign after 9 November 1938." In Bankier, ed., *Probing,* 147–180.

Opitz, Reinhard. *Der deutsche Sozialliberalismus, 1917–1933.* Cologne: Pahl-Rugenstein, 1973.

Overy, Richard. "Germany, 'Domestic Crisis' and War in 1939." In Leitz, ed., *Third Reich,* 97–128.

——. *The Nazi Economic Recovery.* Cambridge: Cambridge University Press, 1996.

——. *War and Economy in the Third Reich.* Oxford: Oxford University Press, 1995.

——. *Why the Allies Won.* New York: Norton, 1996.

Palmowski, Jan. "Between Dependence and Influence: Jews and Liberalism in Frankfurt am Mein, 1864–1933." In Henning Tewes and Jonathan Wright, eds, *Liberalism, Anti-Semitism, and Democracy,* Oxford: Oxford University Press, 2001, 76–101.

——. *Urban Liberalism in Imperial Germany: Frankfurt am Main, 1866–1914.* Oxford: Oxford University Press, 1999.

Papke, Gerhard. *Der liberale Politiker Erich Koch-Weser in der Weimarer Republik.* Baden-Baden: Nomos, 1989.

Passmore, Kevin. *Women, Gender and Fascism, 1919–1945.* Manchester: Manchester, 2003.

Paucker, Arnold. *Deutsche Juden im Widerstand 1933–1945. Tatsachen und Probleme.* Berlin: Gedenkstätte Deutscher Widerstand, 1999.

——. *Der jüdische Abwehrkampf gegen Antisemitismus and Nationalsozialismus in den letzten Jahren der Weimarer Republik.* Hamburg: Hans Christians, 1969.

——. "Resistance of German and Austrian Jews to the Nazi Regime." In *Leo Baeck Institute Year Book XL,* London, 1995, 3–20.

Paucker, Arnold and Barbara Suchy, eds. *The Jews in Nazi Germany, 1933–1943.* Tübingen: Möhr, 1986.

Pauwels, Jacques R. *Women, Nazis and Universities: Female Students in the Third Reich 1933–1945.* Westport, Conn.: Greenwood, 1984.

Pegelow, Thomas. " 'German Jews,' 'National Jews,' 'Jewish Volk' or 'Racial Jews'? The Constitution and Contestation of 'Jewishness' in Newspapers of Nazi Germany, 1933–1938," *CEH,* 35 (2002), 195–221.

Pentzlin, Heinz. *Hjalmar Schacht: Leben und Wirken einer umstrittenen Persönlichkeit.* Berlin: Ullstein, 1980.

Petersen, Edward N. *The Limits of Hitler's Power.* Princeton, NJ: Princeton University Press, 1969.

Peterson, Walter F. *The Berlin Liberal Press in Exile.* Tübingen: M. Niemeyer, 1987.

Peukert, Detlev. *Inside the Third Reich.* New Haven and London: Yale University Press, 1987.

———. *Die KPD im Widerstand: Verfolgung und Untergrundarbeit an Rhein und Ruhr 1933 bis 1945.* Wuppertal: Hammer, 1980.

———. *The Weimar Republic: The Crisis of Classical Modernity.* New York: Penguin, 1991.

Pikart, Eberhard, ed. *Theodor Heuss: Der Mann, das Werk, die Zeit: Eine Ausstellung.* Tübingen: Rainer Wunderlich, 1967.

Pistorius, Peter. "Rudolf Breitscheid 1874–1944." (Cologne diss.), 1970.

Planert, Ute. *Antifeminismus im Kaiserreich: Diskurs, soziale Formation und politische Mentalität.* Göttingen: Vandenhoeck & Ruprecht, 1998.

———. ed. *Nation, Politik und Geschlecht. Frauenbewegungen und Nationalismus in der Moderne.* Frankfurt: Campus, 2000.

Plant, Richard. *The Pink Triangle: The Nazi War against Homosexuals.* New York: Holt, 1986.

Plessner, Helmuth. *Die verspätete Nation: Über die politische Verführbarkeit bürgerlichen Geistes.* Stuttgart: Kohlhammer, 1959.

Plumpe, Werner. *Betriebliche Mitbestimming in der Weimarer Republik: Fallstudien zum Ruhrbergbau und zur chemischen Industrie.* Munich: Oldenbourg, 1999.

Pohl, Karl Heinrich. "Der Liberalismus im Kaiserreich." In Bruch, ed., *Friedrich Naumann,* 65–90.

Pühle, Hans-Jürgen. *Agrarische Interessenpolitik und preussischer Konservatismus in Wilhelminischen Reich 1893–1914: Ein Beitrag zur Analyse des Nationalismus in Deutschland am Beispiel des Bundes der Landwirte und der Deutsch-Konservativen Partei.* Bonn: Neue Gesellschaft, 1975.

———. *Staaten, Nationen und Regionen in Europa.* Vienna: Picus, 1995.

Pulzer, Peter. "The Beginning of the End." In Arnold Paucker and Barbara Suchy, eds, *The Jews in Nazi Germany, 1933–1943.* Tübingen: Möhr, 1986.

———. "Jewish Participation in Wilhelmine Politics." In David Bronsen, ed., *Jews and Germans from 1860 to 1933,* Heidelberg: Carl Winter, 1979, 78–99.

———. *The Rise of Political Anti-Semitism in Germany and Austria.* Cambridge: 1988.

Pyta, Wolfram. *Dorfgemeinschaft und Parteipolitik 1918–1933.* Düsseldorf: Droste, 1996.

Rabinbach, Anson. *In the Shadow of Catastrophe: German Intellectuals between Apocalypse and Enlightenment.* Berkeley: University of California Press, 1997.

Rahden, Till van. "Die Grenze vor Ort- Einbürgerung und Ausweisung ausländischer Juden in Breslau." In *Tel Aviver Jahrbuch für deutsche Geschichte,* vol. XXVII, Tel Aviv, 1998.

———. *Juden und andere Breslauer: Die Beziehungen zwischen Juden, Protestanten und Katholiken in einer deutschen Großstadt von 1860 bis 1925.* Göttingen: Vandenhoeck & Ruprecht, 2000.

———. "Mingling, Marrying and Distancing: Jewish Integration in Wilhelminian Breslau and its Erosion in Early Weimar Germany." In Benz et al., eds, *Jews in the Weimar Republic,* 193–217.

Ramm, Joachim. *Eugen Schiffer und die Reform der deutschen Justiz.* Darmstadt: Luchterwand, 1987.

Ramm, Thilo, ed. *Eugen Schiffer: Ein nationalliberaler Jurist und Staatsmann, 1860–1954.* Baden-Baden: Nomos, 2006.

———. "Der Fehltritt der Frauenrechtlerin: Bemerkungen eines Juristen," *JzLF,* 17 (2005), 235–252.

Reich, Karlheinz. *Die liberalen Parteien in Deutschland 1918–1933.* Osnabrück: Jundemokraten-Landesverband Niedersachsen, 1979.

Reif, Hans. *Liberalismus aus kritischer Vernunft: Vermächtis eines freiheitlichen Demokraten und Europäers.* Baden-Baden: Nomos, 1986.

Reif, Hans, Friedrich Henning and Werner Stephan. *Geschichte des deutschen Liberalismus.* Bonn: Liberal-Verlag, 1976.

Remy, Steven. *The Heidelberg Myth: The Nazification and Denazification of a German University.* Cambridge, Mass.: Harvard University Press, 2002.

Repp, Kevin. *Reformers, Critics, and the Paths of German Modernity: Anti-Politics and the Search for Alternatives, 1890–1914.* Cambridge, Mass.: Harvard University Press, 2000.

Retallack, James. *Germany in the Age of Kaiser William II.* New York: St Martin's, 1996.

——. *Notables of the Right: The Conservative Party and Political Mobilization in Germany, 1876–1918.* Boston: Unwin Hyman, 1988.

——. ed. *Saxony in German History: Culture, Society and Politics, 1830–1933.* Ann Arbor: University of Michigan Press, 2000.

Richter, Ludwig. *Die Deutsche Volkspartei, 1918–1933.* Düsseldorf: Droste, 2002.

——. "Nationalliberalismus, Nationalsozialismus und die Krise der Weimarer Republik. Zur innerparteilichen Diskussion in der Deutschen Volkspartei 1929–1933," *JzLF*, 11 (1999), 107–133.

Rigg, Bryan. *Hitler's Jewish Soldiers.* Lawrence: University of Kansas Press, 2002.

Ringer, Fritz. *The Decline of the German Mandarins: The German Academic Community, 1890–1933.* Hanover: Wesleyan University Press, 1969.

——. *Toward a Social History of Knowledge.* New York: Berghahn, 2000.

Ritter, Gerhard. *Carl Goerdeler und die deutsche Widerstandsbewegung.* Stuttgart: Deutsche Verlags-Anstalt, 1954.

Robinsohn, Hans. *Justiz als politische Verfolgung: Die Rechtsprechung in "Rassenschandefällen" beim Landgericht Hamburg, 1936–1943.* Stuttgart: Deutsche Verlags-Anstalt, 1977.

Rohe, Karl. *Wahlen und Wählertraditionen in Deutschland: Kulturelle Grundlagen deutscher Parteien und Parteien Systeme im 19. und 20. Jahrhundert.* Frankfurt: 1992.

——, ed. *Elections, Parties, and Political Traditions: Social Foundations of German Parties and Party Systems 1867–1987.* New York: Berg, 1990.

Roloff, Stefan und Mario Vigl, eds. *Die "Rote Kapelle": Die Widerstandsgruppe im Dritten Reich und die Geschichte Helmut Roloffs.* Munich: Ullstein, 2002.

Roon, Ger van. *German Resistance to Hitler: Count von Moltke and the Kreisau Circle.* London: Van Nostrand Reinhold, 1971.

Rose, Paul Lawrence. *Revolutionary Antisemitism in Germany from Kant to Wagner.* Princeton, NJ: Princeton University Press, 1992.

Roseman, Mark. *A Past in Hiding: Memory and Survival in Nazi Germany.* New York: Picador, 2001.

Rosenberg, Hans. *Bureaucracy, Aristocracy and Autocracy: The Prussian Experience 1660–1815.* Cambridge, Mass.: Harvard University Press, 1966.

Roth, Karl Heinz and Angelika Ebbinghaus, eds. *Rote Kapellen, Kreisauer Kreise, Schwarze Kapellen: Neue Sichtweisen auf den Widerstand gegen die NS-Diktatur 1938–1945.* Hamburg: VSA, 2004.

Rothfels, Hans. *The German Opposition to Hitler.* Chicago: Henry Regnery, 1963.

Rütten, Theo. *Der deutsche Liberalismus 1945 bis 1955.* Baden-Baden: Nomos, 1984.

Saldern, Adheleid von. *The Challenge of Modernity: German Social and Cultural Studies, 1890–1960.* Ann Arbor: University of Michigan Press, 2002.

——. *Hermann Dietrich: Ein Staatsmann der Weimarer Republik.* Boppard: Harald Boldt, 1966.

——. "Victims or Perpetrators? Controversies about the Role of Women in the Nazi State." In Leitz, ed., *Third Reich,* 207–228.

Sassin, Horst. "Ernst Strassmann und der 20. Juli 1944: Anmerkungen zu Klemens von Klemperer und Joachim Scholtyseck," *JzLF*, 13 (2001), 193–199.

——. *Liberale im Widerstand: Die Robinsohn–Strassman Gruppe, 1934–1942.* Hamburg: Hans Christians, 1993.

——, ed. *Widerstand, Verfolgung und Emigration Liberaler 1933–1945.* Bonn: Liberal-Verlag, 1983.

Sassin, Horst and R. Erkens, eds. *Dokumente zur Geschichte des Liberalismus in Deutschland.* St Augustin: COMDOK, 1989.

Schätzle, Julius. *Stationen zur Hölle. Konzentrationslager in Baden und Württemberg 1933–1945.* Frankfurt: Röderberg, 1980.

Schaffrodt, Petra. *Marie Baum: Ein Leben in sozialer Verantwortung.* Heidelberg: Ubstadt-Weiher, 2001.

Schaser, Angelika. "Bürgerliche Frauen auf dem Weg in die linksliberalen Parteien (1908–1933)," *Historische Zeitschrift*, 263 (1996), 641–680.

——. "Erinnerungskartell: Der Nationalsozialismus im Rückblick der deutschen Liberalen." In Schaser, ed., *Erinnerungskartelle: Zur Konstruktion von Autobiographien nach 1945*, Bochum: Winkler, 2003, 49–80.

——. *Helene Lange und Gertrud Bäumer: Eine politische Lebensgemeinschaft.* Cologne: Böhlau, 2000.

——. "Liberalismus-Forschung und Biographie. Ein Beitrag aus geschlechtergeschichtlicher Perspektive," *JzLF*, 15 (2003), 185–198.

Scheck, Raffael. *Hitler's African Victims: The German Army Massacres of Black French Soldiers in 1940.* Cambridge: Cambridge University Press, 2006.

——. *Mothers of the Nation: Right-Wing Women in Weimar Germany.* Oxford: Berg, 2004.

Scheurig, Bodo, ed. *Deutscher Widerstand 1938–1944: Fortschritt oder Reaktion?* Nordlingen: DTV, 1969.

Schieder, Theodor. *Nationalismus und Nationalstaat: Studien zum nationalen Problem im modernen Europa.* Göttingen: Vandenhoeck & Ruprecht, 1991.

Schiefel, Werner. *Bernhard Dernburg 1865–1937. Kolonialpolitiker und Bankier im wilhelminischen Deutschland.* Zürich: Atlantis-Verlag, 1974.

Schivelbusch, Wolfgang. *Entfernte Verwandschaft: Fascismus, Nationalsozialismus, New Deal, 1933–1939.* Munich: Carl Hanser, 2005.

Schlabrendorff, Fabian von. *The Secret War against Hitler.* Boulder: Westview, 1994.

Schlangen, Walter. *Die deutschen Parteien im Überblick: Von den Anfängen bis heute.* Düsseldorf: Droste, 1979.

Schleunes, Karl. *The Twisted Road to Auschwitz.* Champaign: Illinois, 1971.

Schmädeke, Jürgen and Peter Steinbach, eds. *Der Widerstand gegen den Nationalsozialismus: Die deutsche Gesellschaft und der Widerstand gegen Hitler.* Munich: Piper, 1985.

Schmid, Christoph. *Nationalsozialistische Kulturpolitik im Gau Westfalen-Nord: Regionale Strukturen und locale Milieus (1933–1945).* Paderborn: Ferdinand Schöningh, 2006.

Schmid, Manfred, ed. *Fritz Elsas: Ein Demokrat im Widerstand.* Gerlingen: Bleicher, 1999.

Schmitthenner, Walter and Hans Buchheim, eds. *Der deutsche Widerstand gegen Hitler.* Cologne: Kiepenheuer & Witsch, 1966.

Schmokel, Wolfgang. *Dream of Empire: German Colonialism 1919–1945.* New Haven: Yale University Press, 1964.

Schneider, Werner. *Die Deutsche Demokratische Partei in der Weimarer Republik, 1924–1930.* Munich: Wilhelm Fink, 1978.

Schölzel, Christian. *Walther Rathenau. Eine Biographie.* Paderborn: Schöningh, 2006.

Schoenbaum, David. *Hitler's Social Revolution.* New York: Norton, 1997.

Scholder, Klaus, ed. *Die Mittwochs-Gesellschaft: Protokolle aus dem geistigen Deutschland 1932 bis 1944.* Berlin: Severin & Siedler, 1982.

Scholtyseck, Joachim. *Robert Bosch und der liberale Widerstand gegen Hitler 1933 bis 1945.* Munich: C.H. Beck, 1999.

Schulze, Winfried and Otto Gerhard Oexle, eds. *Deutsche Historiker im Nationalsozialismus.* Frankfurt: Fischer, 1999.

Schumacher, Martin. *MdR Die Reichstagabgeordneten der Weimar in Zeit der Nationalsozialismus. Politische Verfolgung.* Düsseldorf: 1993.

Schustereit, Hartmut. *Linksliberalismus und Sozialdemokratie in der Weimarer Republik. Eine vergleichende Betrachtung der Politik von DDP und SPD 1919–1930.* Düsseldorf: Schwann, 1975.

Sell, Friedrich. *Die Tragödie des deutschen Liberalismus*. Baden-Baden: Nomos, 1981.
Sheehan, James. *German History 1770–1866*. Oxford: Oxford University Press, 1989.
——. *German Liberalism in the Nineteenth Century*. Chicago: Chicago University Press, 1978.
——. "What is German History? Reflections on the Role of *Nation* in German History and Historiography," *Journal of Modern History*, 53 (1981), 1–23.
Shirer, William. *The Rise and Fall of the Third Reich*. New York: Simon & Schuster, 1990.
Silver, Daniel. *Refuge in Hell: How Berlin's Jewish Hospital Outlasted the Nazis*. Boston: Houghton Mifflin, 2003.
Silverman, Daniel P. *Hitler's Economy: Nazi Work Creation Programs, 1933–1936*. Cambridge, Mass.: Harvard University Press, 1998.
Skidmore, James. *The Trauma of Defeat: Ricarda Huch's Historiography during the Weimar Republic*. Frankfurt: P. Lang, 2005.
Smith, Helmut Walser. *German Nationalism and Religious Conflict: Culture, Ideology, Politics, 1870–1914*. Princeton, NJ: Princeton University Press, 1995.
Smith, Woodruff. *The Ideological Origins of Nazi Imperialism*. New York: Oxford, 1986.
——. *Politics and the Sciences of Culture in Germany, 1840–1920*. New York: Oxford University Press, 1991.
Sneeringer, Julia. *Winning Women's Votes: Propaganda and Politics in Weimar Germany*. Chapel Hill, NC: University of North Carolina Press, 2002.
Speier, Hans. *German White-Collar Workers and the Rise of Hitler*. New Haven and London: Yale University Press, 1986.
Sperber, Jonathan. *The Kaiser's Voters: Electors and Elections in Imperial Germany*. Cambridge, Mass.: Harvard University Press, 1997.
Spicer, Kevin P. *Resisting the Third Reich: The Catholic Clergy in Hitler's Berlin*. DeKalb: Northern Illinois University Press, 2004.
Spieker, Frank. *Hermann Höpker Aschoff – Vater der Finanzverfassung*. Berlin: Duncker & Humboldt, 2004.
Stachura, Peter. *Nazi Youth in the Weimar Republic*. Santa Barbara: Santa Barbara, 1975.
Stackelberg, Roderick. *Idealism Debased: From Völkisch Ideology to National Socialism*. Kent: Kent, 1981.
Stegmann, Dirk. *Die Erben Bismarcks. Parteien und Verbande in der Spätphase des Wilhelminischen Deutschlands. Sammlungspolitik 1897–1918*. Cologne: Kiepenheuer & Witsch, 1970.
Stehkämper, Hugo. "Protest, Opposition und Widerstand im Umkreis der (untergegangenen) Zentrumspartei." In Schmädeke and Steinbach, eds, *Widerstand*.
Steigman-Gall, Richard. *The Holy Reich: Nazi Conceptions of Christianity, 1919–1945*. Cambridge: Cambridge University Press, 2003.
Steinbach, Peter. *Der einsame Zeuge: Einzelkämpfer im Widerstand*. Passau: R. Rothe, 1990.
Steinbach, Peter und Joannes Tuchel, eds. *Widerstand gegen die nationalsozialistische Diktatur 1933–1945*. Berlin: Lukas, 2004.
Steinweis, Alan. *Art, Ideology, and Economics in Nazi Germany*. Chapel Hill, NC: University of North Carolina Press, 1993.
Stephan, Werner. *Aufstieg und Verfall des Linksliberalismus 1918–1933: Geschichte der demokratische Partei*. Göttingen: Vandenhoeck & Ruprecht, 1973.
——. *Joseph Goebbels: Daemon einer Diktatur*. Stuttgart: Union, 1949.
Stephenson, Jill. *Women in Nazi Germany*. New York: Longman, 2001.
Stern, Fritz. *The Failure of Illiberalism*. New York: Columbia University Press, 1992.
——. *The Politics of Cultural Despair: A Study in the Rise of the Germanic Ideology*. Berkeley: University of California Press, 1974.
Stolleis, Michael. *The Law under the Swastika: Studies on Legal History in Nazi Germany*. Chicago: Chicago University Press, 1998.
Stoltenberg, Gerhard. *Politische Strömungen im schleswig-holsteinischen Landvolk 1918–1933*. Düsseldorf: Droste, 1962.

Stoltzfus, Nathan. *Resistance of the Heart: Intermarriage and the Rosenstrasse Protest in Nazi Germany.* New York: Norton, 1996.

Stone, Dan. *Constructing the Holocaust: A Study in Historiography.* London: Vallentine Mitchell, 2003.

Struve, Walter. *Elites against Democracy: Leadership Ideals in Bourgeois Political Thought in Germany, 1890–1933.* Princeton, NJ: Princeton University Press, 1973.

Studt, Christoph, ed. *"Diener des Staates" oder "Widerstand zwischen den Zeilen." Die Rolle der Presse im "Dritten Reich."* Berlin: LIT, 2007.

Stürmer, Michael. *Kaiserliche Deutschland: Politik und Gesellschaft 1870–1918.* Düsseldorf: Droste, 1970.

Süchting-Hänger, Andrea. *Das "Gewissen der Nation." Nationales Engagement und politisches Handeln konservativer Frauenorganisationen 1900–1937.* Düsseldorf: Droste, 2002.

Suval, Stanley. *The Anschluβ Question in the Weimar Era: A Study of Nationalism in Germany and Austria, 1918–1932.* Baltimore, Md.: Johns Hopkins University Press, 1974.

——. *Electoral Politics in Wilhelmine Germany.* Chapel Hill, NC: University of North Carolina Press, 1985.

Tamir, Yael. *Liberal Nationalism.* Princeton, NJ: Princeton University Press, 1995.

Taylor, A.J.P. *Origins of the Second World War.* New York: Simon & Schuster, 1996.

Thadden, Rudolf von. *Der Krise von Liberalismus zwischen den Weltkriegen.* Göttingen: Vandenhoeck & Ruprecht, 1978.

Theiner, Peter. *Sozialer Liberalismus und deutsche Weltpolitik: Friedrich Naumann im Wilhelminische Deutschland (1860–1919).* Baden-Baden: Nomos, 1983.

Theodor, Gertrud. *Friedrich Naumann.* Berlin: Rütten & Loerning, 1957.

Thimme, Anneliese. *Gustav Stresemann.* Hanover: Goedel, 1957.

Thompson, Alastair. *Left Liberals, the State, and Popular Politics in Wilhelmine Germany.* Oxford: Oxford University Press, 2000.

Tilton, Timothy. *Nazism, Neo-Nazism, and the Peasantry.* Bloomington: Indiana, 1975.

Tober, Holger J. *Deutscher Liberalismus und Sozialpolitik in der Ära des Wilhelminimus: Anschauungen der liberalen Parteien im parlamentarischen Entscheidungsprozess und öffentlichen Diskussion.* Husum: Matthiesen, 1999.

Tooley, T. Hunt. *National Identity and Weimar Germany: Upper Silesia and the Eastern Border 1918–1922.* Lincoln: Nebraska, 1997.

Tooze, Adam, *Ökonomie der Zerstörung: Die Geschichte der Wirtschaft im Nationalsozialismus.* Munich: Siedler, 2007. English version: *The Wages of Destruction: The Making and Breaking of the Nazi Economy.* London: Allen Lane, 2006.

Turner, Henry A. *German Big Business and the Rise of Hitler.* New Haven and London: Yale University Press, 1984.

——. *Stresemann and the Politics of the Weimar Republic.* Princeton, NJ: Princeton University Press, 1979.

Verhey, Jeffrey. *The Spirit of 1914: Militarism, Myth and Mobilization.* Cambridge: Cambridge University Press, 2000.

Voelter, Hans. *Friedrich Naumann und der deutsche Sozialismus.* Heilbronn: E. Salzer, 1950.

Vogt, Stefan. *Nationaler Sozialismus und Soziale Demokratie: Die sozialdemokratische Junge Rechte 1918–1945.* Bonn: J.H.W. Dietz, 2006.

Volkov, Shulamit. *The Rise of Popular Antimodernism in Germany: The Urban Master Artisans, 1873–1896.* Princeton, NJ: Princeton University Press, 1978.

Wachsmann, Nikolaus. *Hitler's Prisons: Legal Terror in Nazi Germany.* New Haven and London: Yale University Press, 2004.

Wagner, Andrea. "Ein Human Development Index für Deutschland: Die Entwicklung des Lebensstandards von 1920 bis 1960." In *Jahrbuch für Wirtschaftsgeschichte*, 2 (2003), 171–199.

Wagner, Thomas. *"Krieg oder Frieden. Unser Platz an der Sonne." Gustav Stresemann und die Aussenpolitik des Kaiserreichs.* Paderborn: Schöningh, 2007.

Wallraff, Charles R. *Karl Jaspers: An Introduction to his Philosophy*. Princeton, NJ: Princeton University Press, 1970.
Walter, Dirk. *Antisemitische Kriminalitaet und Gewalt. Judenfeindschaft in der Weimarer Republik*. Bonn: Dietz, 1999.
Wehler, Hans-Ulrich. *Deutsche Gesellschaftsgeschichte*, vol. IV. Munich: C.H. Beck, 2003.
——. *The German Empire 1871–1918*. Providence, RI: Berg, 1993.
Weigand, Wolf Volker. *Walter Wilhelm Goetz*. Boppard: Harald Boldt, 1992.
Weinberg, Gerhard L. *Hitler's Foreign Policy: The Road to World War II*. New York: Enigma, 2004.
Weindling, Paul. *Health, Race and German Politics between National Unification and Nazism, 1870–1945*. Cambridge: Cambridge University Press, 1989.
Weitz, Eric. *A Century of Genocide: Utopias of Race and Nation*. Princeton: Princeton, 2003.
Weitz, John. *Hitler's Banker*. Boston: Little, Brown, 1997.
Welchert, Hans Heinrich. *Theodor Heuss. Ein Lebensbild*. Bonn: Athenäum, 1959.
Wheeler-Bennett, John. *The Nemesis of Power: The German Arm in Politics, 1918–1945*. New York: Palgrave, 2005.
White, Dan S. *The Splintered Party: National Liberalism in Hessen and the Reich 1867–1918*. Cambridge: Cambridge University Press, 1976.
White, G. Edward. *Oliver Wendell Holmes: Law and the Inner Self*. Oxford: Oxford University Press, 2001.
Wildenthal, Lora. *German Women for Empire, 1884–1945*. Durham, N.C: Duke University Press, 2001.
Wildt, Michael. *Generation of the Unbound: The Leadership Corps of the Reich Security Main Office*. Jerusalem: Yad Vashem, 2002.
——. *Volksgemeinschaft als Selbstermächtigung: Gewalt gegen Juden in der deutschen Provinz 1919 bis 1939*. Hamburg: Hamburger, 2007.
Winkler, Heinrich August. *Mittelstand, Demokratie und Nationalsozialismus: Die politische Entwicklung von Handwerk und Kleinhandel in der Weimarer Republik*. Köln: Kiepenheuer & Witsch, 1972.
Wirsching Andreas and Jürgen Eder, eds. *Vernunft republikanismus in der Weimarer Republik: Politik, Literatur, Wissenschaft*. Stuttgart: Franz Sterner, 2008.
——. *Weimar 1918–1933: Die Geschichte der ersten deutschen Demokratie*. München: 1993.
Wirthle, Werner. *Frankfurter Zeitung und Frankfurter Societäts-Druckerei GMBH: Die wirtschaftlichen Verhältnisse, 1927–1939*. Frankfurt: Societäts-Verlag, 1976.
Witoszek, Nina and Lars Tragardh, eds. *Culture and Crisis: The Case of Germany and Sweden*. New York: Berghahn, 2002.
Witte, Barthold C. "Liberaler in schwierigen Zeiten – Werner Stephan (15 August 1895–4 Juli 1984)," *JzLF*, 18 (2006), 241–251.
Wolf, Ernst. *Die evangelischen Kirchen und der Staat im Dritten Reich*. Zürich: EVZ, 1963.
Wolf, Rodolf, ed. *Heinrich Mann: Werk und Wirkung*. Bonn: Bouvier, 1984.
Wolfes, Matthias. "Die Demokratiefähigkeit liberaler Theologen: Ein Beitrag zum Verhältnis des Protestantismus zur Weimarer Republik." In Bruch, ed., *Friedrich Naumann*.
Wright, Jonathan. *"Above Parties": The Political Attitudes of the German Protestant Church Leadership*. New York: Oxford University Press, 1974.
——. *Gustav Stresemann: Weimar's Greatest Statesman*. Oxford: Oxford University Press, 2002.
——. "Liberalism and Anti-Semitism in the Weimar Republic: The Case of Gustav Stresemann." In Henning Tewes and Jonathan Wright, eds, *Liberalism, Anti-Semitism, and Democracy*. Oxford, 2001, 102–126.
Wulf, Peter. "Antisemitismus in bürgerlichen und bäuerlichen Parteien und Verbände in Schleswig-Holstein (1918–1924)." In *Jahrbuch für Antisemitismusforschung*, 11 (2002), 52–75.
Wurtzbacher-Rundholz, Ingrid, ed. *Theodor Heuss über Staat und Kirche 1933 bis 1946 – mit Materialenanhang über Konkordatsfragen 1927*. Frankfurt: P. Lang, 1986.

Zeller, Eberhard. *The Flame of Freedom: The German Struggle against Hitler*. London: Oswald Wolff, 1967.

Zimmermann, Clemens. *Medien im Nationalsozialismus: Deutschland, Italien und Spanien in den 1930er und 1940er Jahren*. Vienna: Böhlau, 2007.

Index